HOW TO
BUY A HOUSE
IN CALIFORNIA

4th Edition

BY

RALPH WARNER

IRA SERKES

GEORGE DEVINE

EDITED BY MARCIA STEWART & ROBIN LEONARD

ILLUSTRATED BY LINDA ALLISON

APPENDIX 1 BY TIM DEVANEY

NOLO PRESS BERKELEY

Your Responsibility When Using a Self-Help Law Book

We've done our best to give you useful and accurate information in this book. But laws and procedures change frequently and are subject to differing interpretations. If you want legal advice backed by a guarantee, see a lawyer. If you use this book, it's your responsibility to make sure that the facts and general advice contained in it are applicable to your situation.

Keeping Up-to-Date

To keep its books up to date, Nolo Press issues new printings and new editions periodically. New printings reflect minor legal changes and technical corrections. New editions contain major legal changes, major text additions or major reorganizations. To find out if a later printing or edition of any Nolo book is available, call Nolo Press at 510-549-1976 or check the catalog in the *Nolo News*, our quarterly publication.

To stay current, follow the "Update" service in the *Nolo News*. You can get a free two-year subscription by sending us the registration card in the back of the book. In another effort to help you use Nolo's latest materials, we offer a 25% discount off the purchase of the new edition of your Nolo book if you turn in the cover of an earlier edition. (See the "Recycle Offer" in the back of this book.) This book was last revised in: September 1996.

Fourth Edition	SEPTEMBER 1996
Editors	MARCIA STEWART AND ROBIN LEONARD
Book Design	TERRI HEARSH
Cover Design	TONI IHARA
Production	STEPHANIE HAROLDE
Proofing	ELY NEWMAN
Index	SAYRE VAN YOUNG
Printing	BERTELSMAN INDUSTRIES

```
Warner, Ralph E.
   How to buy a house in California   / by Ralph Warner, Ira Serkes,
George Devine. -- 4th California ed.
     p.   cm.
   Includes index.
   ISBN 0-87337-356-1
   1. House buying--California.  2. Real property--California.
3. Mortgages--California.  4. Housing--California--Finance.  5. Real
estate business--California.     I. Serkes, Ira, 1949-    .    II. Devine,
George, 1941-    .   III. Title.
HD266.C2W37  1996
643'.12'09794--dc20                                    96-9764
                                                       CIP
```

Acknowledgments

Collecting and organizing the material for this book turned out to be a daunting task, one that might have defeated us had it had not been for the enthusiastic help of Nolo Press legal editors Robin Leonard and Marcia Stewart. Not only did they help gather and organize material, but they also contributed many creative ideas.

Special thanks to Michael Cohen, Berkeley-based loan broker with Schnell Investment Company, who was extremely generous with his time and knowledge on the financial aspects of buying a house.

Tim Devaney also played a central figure in developing this work. A fine geographer and writer, he contributed much of the original research and writing in Appendix 1, Welcome to California.

A number of real estate professionals contributed their good ideas and constructive criticisms. Recognizing that they don't necessarily agree with some of our conclusions or points of emphasis, many thanks to John Murphy, branch manager of AccuBanc/Medallion Mortgage Company in Benicia, California; John Pinto, J.P. and Associates, San Jose; Terry Moerler, RE/MAX Realtor, Thousand Oakes; Rob Bader, Santa Rosa loan broker; Judy Cranston, Realtor; Shel Givens, Realtor; Elizabeth Hughes, Realtor; Donald Pearman, author of *The Termite Report*; Martin Reutinger, residential designer and consultant in San Francisco's East Bay; Temmy Walker, President, James R. Gary & Co. Ltd., East, Studio City; and Judy Rydell, real estate broker with Zephyr Realty in San Francisco.

Special thanks to all those house buyers who shared their house purchase experiences with us. Many of their stories appear in the personal boxes scattered throughout the book, though sometimes slightly edited and with fictional names. Contributors (and general reviewers) include Mike and Carmella Boschetti, Valerie Brown, David Cole, Steve Elias, Jo and Don Gallo, Mary Glaeser, Rose Green, Barry Gustin, Ann Heron, Barbara Hodovan, Helen and Roger Humphrey, Wendy Lewis, Jackie and Tony Mancuso, Ed and Maria Martinek, Mary Randolph, Barbara Kate Repa, Ed Shelton and Leya Steiber.

Thanks, too, to San Francisco Supervisor Barbara Kaufman, founder of KCBS's "Call for Action," for her help with Chapter 7, New Houses; the California Association of Realtors, for information on regional median house prices; Sue Giesberg of the California Attorney General's Office; David Meyers, Real Estate Editor of the *Los Angeles Times* who helped us find a Southern California reviewer; Susan Tubbesing, Executive Director of the Earthquake Engineering Research Institute in Oakland, California, for her help in updating the earthquake, fire and flood information; and Mike Mansel, Certified Insurance Counselor, local insurance specialist.

Special thanks to Terri Hearsh, whose creative book design, financial savvy, and cheerful nature made a tremendous difference to this book. A number of other Nolo Press people contributed greatly to this project, including our excellent research assistants, Stanley Jacobsen, David Freund and Eric Duong; proofreader Ely Newman; manuscript preparer (and all-purpose kibbitzer par excellence) Stephanie Harolde; cover designer Toni Ihara; writing coach Mary Randolph.

Finally, the work of several prominent real estate writers especially inspired us, including Robert Bruss, Peter G. Miller, Jack Reed and Leigh Robinson.

Dedications

To Carol Serkes, who showed me how to buy a home when I'd only known how to acquire houses;

To Snidely and Gouger, furry felines, who kept me company in the wee hours of the night and helped give birth to the book by sleeping on the manuscript whenever possible;

To those of you willing to open your mind to new ideas, especially when your friends tell you that you're dreaming. At 20, I had my entire life planned; at 40, I have no idea what opportunities lie ahead!

—Ira Serkes

To my wife and Realtor-Associate, Joanne.

—George Devine

Table of Contents

Introduction

1 Describe Your Dream House

2 How Much House Can You Afford?

7 New Houses, Developments and Condominiums

8 Financing Your House: An Overview

9 Fixed Rate Mortgages

10 Adjustable Rate Mortgages

11 Government-Assisted Loans

12 Private Mortgages

13 Obtaining a Mortgage

14 Buying a House When You Already Own One

15 How Much Will You Offer?

16 Putting Your Offer in Writing

17 Presenting Your Offer and Negotiating

18 After the Contract Is Signed: Escrow, Contingencies and Title Insurance

19 Check Out a House's Condition

20 Legal Ownership: How to Take Title

21 If Something Goes Wrong During Escrow

Introduction

Buying a house should be fun. A good house not only provides shelter, warmth and a place to lay your head, but it has the potential to "come to life" and be a true friend to you and your family.

Even though prices in most areas are still well below their peak of the late 1980s, locating an affordable house that suits your needs isn't easy. And even if you find your dream house, that's only the first step to making it yours: You still must bargain with the seller for a favorable price, arrange for a good deal on a mortgage, have the house inspected for physical defects and make decisions regarding dozens of other potentially expensive issues.

Especially if you are a first-time purchaser, you probably must make these important decisions with little experience, under considerable time pressure and on a tight budget. Accomplishing all of this can be a daunting task, especially given that many people in the real estate business who pretend to give you sound advice are more concerned with making a buck at your expense.

This book gives you the information you need to understand how California houses are financed, inspected and, finally, purchased. House purchase lessons learned in other parts of the country are often of only marginal value in this, America's fastest-growing and most ethnically and geographically diverse state.

Whether you're looking for a luxury beach-front home in Southern California, a brown-shingle family house in the San Francisco Bay Area or an affordable tract house in fast-growing Sacramento or Fresno, this book shows you how to buy a house in California.

A. House-Buying Worries

Buying a house can be exciting, but also anxiety-producing. Most people must face and overcome a number of worries, including:

- We can't afford a decent house.
- We can't afford a house in the neighborhood we want.
- Even though I am now doing well financially, my credit history or debts will disqualify me from obtaining a mortgage.
- We'll pay too much.
- I may lose my job or be transferred in the next few years—maybe buying a house is too risky?

- I know people whose houses aren't worth what they paid for them three or five years ago. I'm afraid I'll end up in the same situation.
- As soon as I begin looking for a house, aggressive real estate salespeople will drag me from one wretched place to another, and will try to talk me into buying anything just so they'll earn a commission.
- We'll buy a house loaded with hidden problems that will cost us time, anxiety and a small fortune to fix.
- House prices and interest rates seem to be on a roller-coaster. How can I get a good handle on such a fluctuating market?
- I'll buy a house beset by one or more of modern America's social problems, such as noisy neighbors, drug-infested parks, parking problems, bad schools, a horrible commute or all of the above.
- With so many types of mortgages available, how can I make sure I get the best deal?
- The only mortgage we can afford will be full of fine-print provisions that will cost us an arm and a leg and, if interest rates increase substantially, possibly our house.
- Lenders, loan brokers, title companies, insurers, property inspectors and lawyers will add significant and needless cost and hassle to purchasing a house.

Fortunately, this book gives you sound answers to all these worries.

B. The Basics of Buying a Good House

Before getting into all the details, let's slow down and briefly discuss what is really involved in purchasing a superior house at the best possible price. You must commit yourself to doing three things:

1. **Understand all the important aspects of the purchase process.** That's what this book is all about—giving you a thorough, practical discussion of the steps necessary to find and finance a California house. Once you are armed with this current information, you can make informed decisions on dozens of factors, such as deciding on the optimum size and location of your potential house, choosing a suitable agent, how big a down payment you can afford, the best type of mortgage for your situation and how to arrange for an inspection that will truly reveal hidden problems.

2. **Be patient.** Once you understand all the house-buying basics, you must plan carefully so that at each stage of the

purchase process—and the sale of your old house, if you have one—you will be prepared to take your time. Being relaxed and having time on your side, when others are anxious and hurrying, is often the key to saving a lot of money on your house purchase.

Why is a slow, deliberate approach so important to buying a good house at a good price? Start by understanding that sellers, who have all sorts of personal needs and levels of market sophistication, are sure to price similar houses quite differently. And then realize that most houses are different enough from each other to make comparisons of price and features imprecise. Add to this the fact that the quality of the advice the approximately 500,000 real estate salespeople give buyers and sellers as to whether a house is fairly priced varies widely. The result is that while the majority of houses probably sell for about what one would expect, many buyers pay too much while many others find real bargains.

This is obviously where patience comes into the equation. First, you must do your homework so that you really know what houses in a particular area are worth. Then, follow any one of several good techniques discussed in this book to find an under-priced house. If you do these two things, and are prepared to move quickly, you can often buy a good house for a comparatively low price. Unfortunately, the reverse is also true. If you're less informed and less patient, you are almost sure to pay too much for too little.

3. **Trust yourself, not biased experts.** The traditional approach to buying a house is to trust brokers, agents, mortgage lenders and other "experts" to protect your interests. While many thousands of good, helpful people work in real estate, conflicts of interest between real estate professionals and buyers are a part of the purchase process. For example, an agent who helps you find a house earns more if you bid high than low, for at least two reasons. First, you are more likely to successfully compete with other prospective buyers and buy the house (assuring the agent a commission). Second, the size of the agent's commission is normally a percentage of the purchase price (the more you pay, the more the agent gets). Knowing this, it is obviously just as foolish to rely primarily on an agent's advice on how much you should offer as it is to ask a child how much ice cream she wants.

Because understanding this point can literally save you tens of thousands of dollars, and failing to grasp it can

make you miserable for years, let us repeat it: Never take the unchecked word of people who will profit by your making a purchase—by definition, they won't be objective. To avoid relying on potentially poor advice by self-interested people, you should:

- Look at houses in addition to those suggested by an agent or brokerage office you are working with.
- Never accept an agent's recommendation on price and terms without thoroughly checking them yourself.
- Assess for yourself important factors such as commute time, the quality of schools and neighborhood safety.
- Shop around for a mortgage.
- Choose your own tough inspectors to check out any house you make an offer on and examine their reports with a critical eye. Understand that everyone else in the house purchase transaction, from the seller to your agent, is biased towards your making this purchase and is likely to suggest inspectors who won't find serious problems.

All these, and many other strategies, are discussed in detail later in this book. First, the process of getting all the information necessary to deal with them may seem like an almost impossible task. Not so. Once you know the areas in which your interests and those of real estate professionals diverge, you are in an excellent position to take steps to get objective help.

ADOBE

C. A Place to Live for Almost Everyone

California media repeatedly emphasize how hard it is to afford a house, any house. And many prospective purchasers do have a hard time raising a down payment. Nevertheless, the media have exaggerated the affordability problem. Because of the large size and population of the Golden State, few places on earth have as much quality housing available across such a wide price range. In short, most Californians can, with enough determination and creativity, afford to buy a house—perhaps not their dream house, but a decent, livable one.

The Starter House. The first time out, few people can afford the house they'd ultimately like to live in. But even in California's most expensive urban areas, including greater Los Angeles and the San Francisco Bay Area, a surprising amount of housing is available within the financial reach of the average buyer. And in areas where undeveloped land still exists, such as the Central Valley, new houses are an excellent affordable housing choice.

 CONDOS OFTEN MAKE POOR STARTER HOUSES
Especially in high-priced cities, first-timers buyers often look at and buy condominiums. Think twice. Condos—especially those in areas with plenty of open space—usually don't make good starter houses because they aren't likely to go up in value as fast as stand-alone houses are. As soon as one condo fills up, more will be built. In cities where land is scarce, it can be harder to build new condos, but if condo prices appreciate significantly, landlords will find a way to convert existing rental units to condos and builders to shoehorn more in.

The Middle-Market House. It's often possible to save as much as 20% on a middle-price house, an amount which can be the difference between affording to buy or not. In Chapter 3, we discuss a number of overlooked strategies for getting more house for your money than you might otherwise think possible.

REALIZE THAT FEW CALIFORNIA HOUSES HAVE GONE UP IN VALUE DURING THE 1990s
From the 1950s to the late 1980s, it didn't make much difference how much you paid for a house—a few years later, it was almost always worth more. But during the 1990s, when prices have stagnated or dropped, a sloppy approach to buying a house has proved fatal to the economic dreams of many families. In other words, people who have paid even close to top dollar for their houses (often on the recommendation of real estate professionals) have found that a few years later that they can't resell them for enough to even cover what is owed on their mortgages.

The Luxury House. If you're buying a house worth more than $500,000, consumer savvy is particularly necessary. Far more money can be saved in this price range than at the low end of the market. Sure, some of this difference merely reflects the bigger dollars involved, but there's more. Because fewer higher-priced houses are on the market at any one time, and they tend to be less like one another, price comparisons are far more difficult. When you add to this a much smaller pool of prospective buyers, the result is that if you're in the right place at the right time, with your financing lined up in advance, you may occasionally get a real bargain. If you doubt this, consider that in the early and mid-1990s, when prices in many California communities dropped precipitously, savvy buyers picked up many luxury houses for hundreds of thousands of dollars less than the sellers had paid for them just a few years before.

The New House. Some buyers pay significantly more than others for the same, or sometimes even a lesser quality, new house. To buy a good new house at a good price, it's important to select the best developer (not necessarily the most exciting house), understand what new house sellers are trying to accomplish and position yourself to profit from this knowledge. Especially in areas with a surplus of new houses, sellers will occasionally mark down or auction good houses at very affordable prices.

The Rural House. If you plan to buy country land, complete with a dwelling, you'll need to think about a host of issues including access to good-quality water, road access and maintenance, septic tank regulations, easements, zoning laws and many more issues we don't cover in depth. And if you plan to buy empty land and build your own place later, all of these concerns will be even more pressing. The best one-stop source of information on these subjects is *Finding & Buying Your Place in the Country,* by Scher and Scher (Dearborn Financial Publishing).

D. How to Use This Book

Please read all relevant sections of the book before beginning the house purchase process. Yes, it will take a few hours to get a good overview of the whole task, but doing so really can also save you a bundle. To take but one of many examples, before you spend much time searching for a house (discussed in Chapter 6), it's an excellent idea to prequalify for a mortgage (Chapter 2) so that when you make an offer, you are in a position to close the deal quickly. This can be the key to getting a bargain if you find a good house whose seller is willing to cut the asking price to make a fast sale.

This doesn't mean you need to read every word that follows. Obviously, you should concentrate on material that applies to your financial and practical situation. The detailed Table of Contents should make it easy for you to focus on this material.

Readers who are new to California, or are moving from one part of the state to another, will particularly want to read Appendix 1, Welcome to California, for an overview of the state's unique environment, including its geography, weather, air, water, traffic, public schools, public services and natural hazards such as earthquakes.

Look for these icons to alert you to certain kinds of information.

FAST TRACK

This icon suggests that you pause and consider whether to skip or skim a section that may not apply to your situation.

WARNING

This icon alerts you to special pitfalls you may encounter when buying a house in California's unique real estate market.

TIP

This icon alerts you to a practical tip or good idea.

RESOURCES

This icon highlights lists of books and other resources you may want to consult on the particular issue or topic discussed in the text.

CONTACT AN EXPERT

This icon gives practical suggestions for getting technical or legal advice on a particular topic.

PERSONAL STORIES ABOUT BUYING A HOUSE.

This icon tells you that these are real life stories and anecdotes of house buyers. ■

Describe Your Dream House

A. You Know the House You Want to Buy

This book is full of practical, up-to-date information about the financial realities, legal rules and real estate industry customs you must understand to successfully purchase a California house. Two crucial things, however, no book can tell you—the location and type of house you want to live in. No matter how many experts you consult or how many opinions you get, you and only you are qualified to describe your dream house and ideal neighborhood.

Given your family's needs, tastes and finances, you probably already have a good idea of the type of house you want to buy. Indeed, if you sit quietly for a few moments, shut your eyes and let your imagination do the walking, you can probably conjure up an image of the house or, perhaps if you're a flexible sort, several houses that you would dearly love to call home.

Because this is true, we skip the typical first chapter in many homebuyers' books, in which the author compares such things as the joys of living on a dusty road in outer suburbia, to the convenience of living in a townhouse in a major city. If you aren't focused enough to make these broad choices on your own, no book will help you much.

COLONIAL FANTASY

TIPS ON WHERE TO LOCATE

Perhaps you've heard it said that choosing a house's location wisely is as important as picking a good house. In a state the size of California, it's a vast understatement to say you have a lot of locations to choose from. To help you think about specific California areas, we include Appendix 1, Welcome to California.

Despite the title, Welcome to California isn't meant only for newcomers to the state. Whether you're a San Franciscan moving closer to a San Ramon job, a San Diego family moving to Sacramento, New Yorkers (or Taiwanese) relocating to Los Angeles or simply unfamiliar with certain California areas, you'll find a wealth of information. From climate and air quality to earthquakes and schools, Appendix 1 presents valuable information to help you decide where to live. You can also get valuable information from the numerous online real estate sites described in Chapter 6. In addition, in Chapter 5 we discuss working with a local real estate agent to get essential information on neighborhoods.

But keep this in mind: no matter how much help you get from secondary sources, there's no substitute for your own legwork. Ask your friends and colleagues, walk and drive around neighborhoods, talk to local residents, read local newspapers, check the library's community resources files, visit the local planning department and do whatever else will help you get a better sense of a neighborhood or city.

➡️ If you've already found the house you want to purchase and are mainly interested in the ins and outs of financing, skip the rest of this chapter and move on to Chapter 2, How Much House Can You Afford?

B. Don't Be Talked Into Buying the Wrong House

Although we skip the conventional discussion on the types of houses available in California, this doesn't mean we have nothing to say about the mechanics of buying a house you'll be happy with. You need an organized house-buying method to translate your dream into reality. This is particularly true in today's high-priced market, in which most buyers face an affordability gap between the house they'd like to buy and the one they can afford. Without an organized approach, there is a good chance you'll be talked into compromising on the wrong house by friends, relatives, a real estate agent or even yourself.

"Not me, I know my own mind," you say. "Nonsense," we reply. In today's market, almost everyone must trim their desires to fit their pocketbook, and it's easy to buy the wrong house in the wrong location. So easy, in fact, that every day many confident and knowledgeable people become so anxious and disoriented in the process of searching for a house in California's confusing real estate market that they purchase one they later come to regret buying, sometimes bitterly.

In outline, here is our method to all but insure that you buy a house you'll enjoy living in, even if it's substantially more modest than your dream house:

- Firmly establish your priorities before you look at a house.
- Insist that any house you offer to buy meets at least your most important priorities.
- Do this even if, in buying a house which meets your priorities, you must compromise in other areas and purchase a house less desirable than you really want.

The reason this method works well should be obvious. If your priorities are clearly set in advance, you're likely to compromise on less important features. If they aren't, you may become so disoriented by the house purchase process that you buy a house without the basic features that motivated you to buy in the first place.

C. Create a House Priorities Worksheet

In this section, we provide an efficient method to help you consider a range of house features and then establish your priorities. In Section D, below, we present an approach to making compromises which is far superior to making important decisions late on a Sunday afternoon, pressured by a real estate agent and/or your spouse, significant other, kids or parents.

Our method is based on your creating a worksheet identifying the features most important to you. Your finished worksheet will allow you to systematically evaluate and record information about each house you see. More importantly, it

will help you make compromises should affordability problems result in your lowering your sights and considering houses that don't have all the features you'd like.

On the pages that follow are copies of our "House Profile Checklist" and "House Priorities Worksheet." A tear-out copy of the worksheet is in Appendix 4. Before entering information, make several photocopies to allow for mistakes or the eventual scaling back of your priority list if it turns out you can't afford all the features you would like. Here is the method we suggest.

Step 1: Skim the House Profile Checklist to familiarize yourself with our approach. If you're buying with another person, review the list together. Note that the left column contains broad categories of features and the right contains examples to get your mind turning over. Then take a quick look at the House Priorities Worksheet (it follows the checklist). On it, you'll be noting your mandatory (must have) and secondary (it would be nice) priorities and your absolute "no ways."

Step 2: Once you're familiar with the overall system, re-read the checklist carefully and complete the worksheet. Try to limit your mandatory priorities to those features any house must have, such as, "within ten minutes of my job," "in a town with a very low crime rate," "three bedrooms," "near Balboa Park in San Diego" or "in an excellent school district."

Step 3: Once you have listed your mandatory priorities, list your secondary priority items—things you'd really like, but that won't make or break your decision.

Step 4: Then list your "no ways" (you simply won't buy a house which has any of these features), such as property on landfill near a major earthquake fault. Take time with this. Avoiding things you hate can be even more important than finding a house which contains all your mandatory priorities.

Step 5: Finally, we include a space for other comments, such as "potential undeveloped lot next door" or "neighbors seem very friendly." Take the time to make notes such as these. If you look at a lot of houses, you'll surely forget important information if you don't make notes.

Be as general or as specific as you want in completing your worksheet. We have found that it's best to focus on essentials and to not list features that you'd like but aren't crucial to your decision of whether or not to buy.

HOUSE PROFILE CHECKLIST

Price Range & Special Financing Needs	Most people will have an upper limit on the house they can afford. Unless you already know your price range, read Chapter 2, How Much House Can You Afford? Also, if you have any special financing needs, such as qualifying for VA or FHA financing or having the seller take back a second mortgage (these financing terms are defined in Chapters 8 and 11), list these as priorities.
Types of Community and Location	If you know specifically what town(s) or neighborhood(s) you want to live in, list them. If you want to live within a half-hour of a great hiking area, wind-surfing site or ski slope, note that here. At the very least, specify urban/city, suburban, rural, mixed urban and suburban or mixed suburban and rural.
Property Ownership	Mostly owners, mostly renters or mixed owners and renters.
School Needs	• Within a particular school district. (Information on California school districts is in Appendix 1, Welcome to California.) • Walking distance from a top-rated public junior high school. • Near a pre-school/day care center. Pay close attention to this category if you have, or plan to have, school-age children. Buying a great house at a great price in a lousy school district may mean years of paying for private schools. By contrast, paying a little more for a good house in an excellent school district may be a bargain in the long run.
Weather & Air Quality	Hot and dry, sunny, foggy, little smog, cool, near snow, etc.
Political or Social Makeup	Liberal, conservative, mixed, bohemian, etc.
Traffic & Noise Level	Need extreme quiet, don't want to be near major streets or a freeway off ramp.
Zoning Restrictions	To add rooms later, you'll need to be sure zoning rules allow it. By contrast, if you want a view and don't want your neighbors to later add a room that will block it, you'll want strict zoning laws.
Community Services	Certain distance from, and/or certain quality of, police, fire station, hospital, library or other community services.
Neighborhood Features	Think about this one carefully; it covers a lot. Things that may concern you include: crime rates, near a specific church/synagogue, walking access to a park or bookstore, the presence or absence of a neighborhood association, restrictions on how the property can be used in a new house development or condominium, a limited access community or a community that allows only folks over 55.
Work Commute	Maximum times and distances you're willing to travel to and from work by car and/or public transit. If you want to walk or bike to work, note that here. When checking out a house, never take anyone else's word (especially the seller's or agent's) on how long it takes. You won't know for sure until you make the trip at the times you'll normally have to go. An easy half-hour drive on a Sunday afternoon can turn into a stress-filled hour nightmare on Friday afternoon.
Public Transit	Near a bus line or the train into the city.
Other Transit Needs	Near an airport, specific freeway or Amtrak station.
Site or Slope	The house's site on the street (interior, corner, cul-de-sac). Your options will differ depending on whether you look in a city, suburb or rural area. If you want to face a certain direction (north, east, west or south), list it. Also, if you want to live on a hillside, list any essentials about the degree and direction of the slope.
View	Should reflect the general area you plan to live in. For example, if you must have a panoramic ocean view, but you're looking in Bakersfield, you'll have a long search.
Privacy Needs	Distance between houses, wanting a house with the bedrooms in the back or not wanting neighbors or passers-by to see into your windows or yard.

HOUSE PROFILE CHECKLIST (continued)

Move-In Condition	Top-notch (you can happily move in as is), needs some work, needs lots of work or is a major league fixer-upper.
Style, Age & Levels	Two-story, under 50 years old, etc. Specific house types include: Bungalow, Cape Cod, Colonial, Contemporary, Cottage, Ranch, Spanish, Split Level, Victorian, Tudor and many more. If you're looking at condos, specify any preference for two-unit, six- to ten-unit or larger building.
Exterior	Aluminum siding, brick or stone, concrete, shingles, stucco, wood or vinyl siding, to mention just a few.
Roof	You may have strong feelings about style (flat, peaked, A-frame) or composition (shingle, slate, tar and gravel, tile or wood shake.) You'll have to do some mixing and matching if you have strong feelings about both style and composition.
Yard	Size (particularly if you have a large dog or want room for kids to play), garden (and specific requirements, such as soil composition), setback (privacy in front and on the sides), room for a pool or deck; also think about convenience (no lawn, little maintenance).
Parking	Two car carport, easy on-street parking or restricted (such as a parking sticker) on-street parking. This is a *major* issue for condominium buyers.
Miscellaneous Exterior Features	Deck, patio, fenced-in yard, pool, hot tub or sauna. If you buy in an area with zoning laws that allow it, you can add most of these items later. If you're looking at condos, you may have concerns about the building security. Note that.
Size	You can approach this by considering square feet (e.g., minimum 1/2 acre), house size (minimum 1,500 square feet) or room size (large living room for entertaining). Most people are more concerned with the number and size of rooms than the overall size of the house.
Number of Rooms	How many bedrooms, bathrooms, or other rooms do you need? Don't be concerned with the specific rooms or specific features of a room; they're described below.
Desired Rooms	Master bedroom with bath, family room, den, finished basement, eat-in kitchen or formal dining room, separate quarters for live-in au pair.
Ceilings	Type of ceiling (beams, cathedral) in a certain room or rooms.
Floors	Type of floor (hardwood, wall-to-wall carpeting, tile) in a certain room.
Storage Needs	Attic, unfinished basement, storage for bicycles, tool shed, or a minimum (specify) number of closets.
Laundry	Are washer and dryer hookups, or a separate laundry room, essential?
Bathrooms	Tub, separate shower, storage space, type of sinks.
Kitchen	Gas or electric stove and oven, dishwasher or garbage disposal. Some of these items can be added or changed after you buy the house, so list only what's truly essential. If a modern kitchen with lots of counter space and good light is important to you, however, be sure to list it.
Other Interior Needs	House must be wheelchair accessible, have an in-law unit, get constant sun light during the day, have a living room fireplace, be highly energy efficient or have a certain layout.
Air Conditioning System	Central air, window unit or a heat pump.
Heating System	Gas forced air, gas wall furnace or gas floor furnace; electric baseboard, electric wall or electric radiant; or oil/steam radiant or floor.
Radio, TV, Cable Reception	ESPN (you're a sports reporter for a newspaper), Disney Channel for your kids, proximity to public radio or excellent radio reception.
Other Utilities	Septics versus city sewage, well water versus city pumped, bringing in bottled gas versus a gas line, solar heating versus gas or electric, high voltage for a potter's kiln.

ELLEN: HOW NOT TO BUY A HOUSE

I was a first-time purchaser on a relatively tight budget when I set out to buy an older, attached row house in San Francisco. I wanted two bedrooms, no (or a very small) yard, proximity to a downtown bus route and walking access to a neighborhood market and bookstore. I looked for many months at houses that were completely unsuitable, far too expensive or, with depressing regularity, both. So I broadened my search by reading the classifieds in the Sunday paper. When I saw that prices were more reasonable in the suburbs, I spent a sunny Sunday afternoon browsing in Contra Costa County.

At the first open house I visited, I met an energetic real estate agent who spun a wonderful word picture of the joys of suburban life—lots of sun, room for a tomato garden and friendly neighbors. She showed me a split-level house with an apple tree in full bloom in my price range. Almost before I realized what I was doing, I signed on the bottom line.

That was the fun part. Soon I was getting up at 6:00 a.m., driving to the train station and standing for the 40-minute ride to San Francisco. My fantasy about the joy of suburban life was just that. It's hard to believe now, but I seemed to have temporarily overlooked the fact that I'm allergic to direct sun, detest tomatoes and moved out of the suburbs to get away from overly involved neighbors.

Fortunately, I sold the house six months later, at a small profit. I went in with a friend and together we bought a house in San Francisco that meets my needs perfectly.

STARTER HOME

D. How to Use Your House Priorities Worksheet

Now let's look at how your house priorities worksheet can help you buy a house you both like and can afford.

1. Buy a House You Like

You should seriously consider only those houses with all of your mandatory priorities and with none of your no ways. Be strict about this. If you visit a nice, reasonably priced house which doesn't come close to matching your list and can't be easily changed to do so, say no. Take the time to find a more suitable house; you'll be glad you did.

Spelling out your priorities is particularly valuable for couples or others buying a home together. In completing the worksheet, be sure that each person's strong likes and dislikes are respected. Otherwise, your living arrangement is bound to have problems. For example, you might care most about a modern kitchen, at least three bedrooms and a space large enough to do woodworking. If so, you'll surely be miserable if you allow your mate to talk you into buying a two-bedroom cottage with its original 1928 kitchen, because it has a rose garden and a great view.

2. Buy a House You Can Afford

A common result of completing the House Priorities Worksheet is to become depressed. If you're typical, you'll wonder how you'll ever afford a house with the features you've listed. Don't despair—at least not until you understand the strategies (discussed in Chapter 3) to help you buy an affordable house. For now, perhaps you'll cheer up when you consider that your worksheet provides a logical basis to trim your wish list to better fit your wallet in a way that lets you hold on to the maximum number of features you consider essential. For example, if your priority list includes a sunny exposure for your beloved garden, a big yard for your even more beloved dog, and a dining room, but you don't entertain as often as you garden, consider eliminating the dining room.

Also, consider whether any of your priority items can be added after you move in. This will be possible for some, and totally impossible for others.

If you're not sure how much you'll have to compromise on cost, prepare two scaled-back House Priorities Worksheets—

HOUSE PRIORITIES WORKSHEET

Address : _____

_____

Date: _____

Price: $ _____

Contact: _____

Phone Number: _____

Mandatory Priorities:

☐ _____
☐ _____
☐ _____
☐ _____
☐ _____
☐ _____
☐ _____
☐ _____

Secondary Priorities:

☐ _____
☐ _____
☐ _____
☐ _____
☐ _____
☐ _____
☐ _____
☐ _____

Absolute No Ways:

☐ _____
☐ _____
☐ _____
☐ _____
☐ _____
☐ _____

Comments About the Particular House:

_____

_____

_____

one an "if I can afford it" list, and the other a "true miser's" list. Doing this will force you to further come to grips with and define your most basic needs.

Once you complete the left column of your worksheet, you're ready to use it when looking at houses (Chapter 6 contains more information on how to make your search). Specifically:

1. Make many copies of the worksheet.

2. Enter the address, asking price, contact person (listing agent or seller, if it's a for sale by owner) and his phone number, and the date you saw the house.

3. As you walk around the house and talk to the owner or agent, enter a check if the house contains the desired (or undesirable "no way") features listed. You may need to do some additional research to see if the house meets your priorities—for example, if you want to find out about city zoning restrictions on second story additions.

4. Makes notes next to a particular feature that can be changed to meet your needs.

5. Staple the completed House Priorities Worksheet to other information on the property, such as a property description sheet from the open house. (See househunting tips in Chapter 6, Section A.) ■

How Much House Can You Afford?

Most prospective California home buyers—even those with a comfortable income—face an affordability problem when it comes to buying the house they'd really like to live in. This is still true, even though most house prices are more affordable than they were a few years ago and mortgage interest rates are (as of late 1996) fairly low.

It's essential to determine how much you can afford to pay before you look for a house. Sounds basic, but apparently it isn't, as many people never take the time to understand how institutional lenders (banks, savings and loans, credit unions) calculate a buyer's personal affordability amount until they make an offer on a house and apply for financing. Then reality hits. Often they can't qualify for the necessary loan. The result is wasted money (in loan application fees) and a lot of wasted time.

Even worse, if you're on the borderline of qualifying for a mortgage (the money you borrow to pay for a house), waiting too long to consider your affordability may actually doom your mortgage application. Why? Because you'll be under intense time pressure to get a loan and it will be too late to take creative steps towards improving your financial profile.

 If money is no object or you already know how much house you can afford, skip this chapter.

Most readers, though, will find this chapter useful in two ways:

- to help you determine your price range—before you go house hunting, and
- to explain some of the techniques experienced agents and real estate loan brokers (who specialize in helping house buyers arrange for financing) use to help financially marginal candidates qualify for a loan from a bank, savings and loan or other lender.

A. The Basics of Determining Housing Affordability

As a broad generalization, most people can afford to purchase a house worth about three times their total (gross) annual income, assuming a 20% down payment and a moderate amount of other long-term debts. With no other debts, they can afford a house worth up to four or five times their annual income.

A much more accurate way to determine how much house you can afford is to compare your monthly carrying costs plus your monthly payments on other long-term debts to your gross (total) monthly income. Carrying costs are the money needed to make a monthly payment (both principal and interest) plus one-twelfth of the yearly bill for property taxes and homeowner's insurance. In real estate industry jargon, monthly carrying costs are often referred to as PITI (pronounced "pity"), which simply stands for principal, interest, taxes and insurance.

Lenders normally want you to make all monthly payments with 28%-38% of your monthly income. This is called the "debt-to-income ratio." You'll find that you can qualify near the bottom or the top of this range depending on the amount of your down payment, the interest rate on the type of mortgage you want, your credit history, the level of your other long-term debts, your employment stability and prospects, the lender's philosophy and the money supply in the general economy.

Generally, the greater your other debts, the lower the percentage of your income lenders will assume you have available to spend each month on housing. Conversely, if you have no long-term debts, a great credit history and will make a larger than normal down payment, a lender may approve carrying costs that exceed 38% of your monthly income—sometimes as high as 40% or 42%. In either case, these rules aren't absolute. For example, some lenders will accept a higher debt-to-income ratio if you'll take a less attractive loan, such as one with a higher than market interest rate or higher than usual points. (Points, an up-front loan fee figured as a percentage of the loan, are discussed in Chapter 8, Section F.)

DEBT-TO-INCOME RATIO

Down Payment	Carrying Costs Only	Carrying Costs & Other Debts	Credit Rating
10%	28%	33%-34%	Excellent
20%	28%-33%	36%-38%	Good to Very Good
30% or more	33%-40%	40%	Excellent

These figures are for loans resold on the secondary market—that is, backed by Fannie Mae or Freddie Mac—which do not exceed $207,000, the limit as of late 1996. Other lenders generally follow these standards, but sometimes have more flexibility.

Lenders have taken years to arrive at these monthly debt-to-income ratios. The ratios are conservative because lenders have learned that the more income a borrower uses for housing expenses, the higher the risk of default (missing payments). Also, many lenders must adhere to these ratios to comply with the fairly inflexible rules of the Federal National Mortgage Association (FNMA—Fannie Mae) or the Federal Home Loan Mortgage Corporation (FHLMC—Freddie Mac), the two largest mortgage loan purchasers. (See Chapter 8, Section C, for more information on the secondary mortgage market, including Fannie Mae and Freddie Mac.) Selling a loan lets the lender pocket a chunk of the profit while freeing up capital to make more loans.

Fortunately, many California lenders aren't bound by Fannie Mae or Freddie Mac. Some keep the loans for themselves, making their profit from the points and fees you pay and the interest spread between what you pay them and what they pay their depositors. These "portfolio" lenders tend to be slightly more flexible in judging debt-to-income ratios, how much house you can afford and down payment requirements. So if you have a great credit rating, a lot of savings and a great earning potential (for example, you just graduated from medical school), and borrow from a portfolio lender, you may qualify at a higher ratio. Some lenders offer low down payment loans that accept higher monthly carrying costs for qualified buyers. (See Chapter 4, Section B, for more on low down payment plans.) Also, as discussed in Chapter 11, loans insured by government agencies allow for more flexible qualification rules.

Given all these variables, determining in advance the percentage of your income you'll need to make monthly costs on a mortgage of a particular amount is key. This chapter shows you how to approach the problem as a lender would. There's work involved, but it's well worth the trouble; when you're done, you'll fairly accurately know how much house you can afford.

What do we mean by "afford"? Because most houses are purchased with a down payment of only 10%-25%, affordability usually comes down to how much you can borrow from a lender to cover the balance. This is where ratios between monthly mortgage payments and monthly income (and between income and the value of the house) come into play.

B. Prepare a Family Financial Statement

The first step to determine the purchase price you can afford is to thoroughly prepare a family financial statement, which includes:

- your monthly income
- your monthly expenses, and
- your net worth (your assets minus your liabilities).

We use the word "family" as shorthand for the economic unit that will buy a house. For our purposes, an unmarried couple or a single person is just as much a family as is a married couple with ten kids.

Preparing a family financial statement begins the process of learning how much house you can afford—in terms of both the down payment and monthly mortgage payments. It also gives real estate people and potential lenders a sense of your general financial situation. And if you haven't prequalified for a mortgage loan (see Section G, below) when you make a purchase offer, a financial statement can be extremely useful in convincing the seller that you're a serious bidder. This may be crucial, especially if there's more than one prospective buyer. The person who can convince the seller that she's financially able to swing the deal often prevails, even if her offer isn't the highest.

Below are instructions for completing a family financial statement. A tear-out copy of the statement itself is in Appendix 4. Make several photocopies (and fill out the form in pencil) so you'll have a clean copy if you make errors or your financial status changes. If you need more space when filling out any section, include an attachment. Do this work carefully. It will be very useful when you complete the mortgage loan application. (See Chapter 13, Section E.) By having this information available early on, you'll speed up the loan approval process and impress the loan officer.

BACK TO THE FUTURE

Things to Remember When Completing Your Family Financial Statement

Don't list incorrect or incomplete information. You'll be showing your financial statement to sellers, lenders and real estate professionals, and referring to it to fill out other loan forms. A lender will surely check with credit reporting agencies, and usually with employers and banks to verify your information.

Although you may want to purchase a more expensive house than you can afford, don't unrealistically maximize income and minimize expenses, unless it is the only way to buy a starter house. If you have enough money to comfortably afford a good house, but attempt to throw every last cent at a more luxurious one, however, you'll probably do more harm than good in the long run. Even if a lender lets you overextend yourself (and most won't), you'll have little money for emergencies and other important things, like straightening the kids' teeth, replacing the car's transmission and going on vacations.

Check your credit rating, and, if necessary, clean up a bad credit file. Lenders evaluate your credit history and outstanding debts in reviewing your mortgage application. You, too, have the legal right to the information credit reporting agencies have gathered about you; check your file early and take steps to correct or deal with problems (see Section F6, below).

Directions for Completing Family Financial Statement

Top. Indicate the name(s), address(es), home phone number(s), employer's name(s) and address(es) and work phone number(s) for yourself and any co-borrower. A co-borrower includes a spouse, lover, friend or non-spouse relative with whom you are purchasing the house.

Worksheet 1: Income and Expenses

This worksheet shows you how much disposable income you have each month, a key fact in determining how big a mortgage you can qualify for. In columns 1 and 2, you and any co-borrower each list your monthly income and expenses. Total them in column 3.

IA. Monthly gross income. List your gross monthly income from all sources. Gross income means total income before amounts such as taxes, Social Security or workers' compensation are withheld.

1. **Employment.** This is your base salary or wages plus any bonuses, tips, commissions or overtime you regularly receive. If your income is irregular, take the average of the past 24 months. If you have more than one job, include your combined total.

2. **Public benefits.** Include income from Social Security, Disability, Aid for Families with Dependent Children (AFDC), Supplemental Security Income (SSI) and other public programs.

3. **Dividends.** Include all dividends from stocks, bonds and similar investments.

4. **Royalties.** If you have continuing income from the sale (licensing) of books, music, software, inventions or the like, list it here.

5. **Interest and other investment income.** Include interest received on savings or money market accounts, or as payments on rental property. If the source of the income has costs associated with it (such as the costs of owning rental property), include the net monthly profit received.

6. **Other.** Include payments from pensions, child or spousal support or separate private maintenance income. Specify the source.

IB. Total monthly gross income. Total items 1-6. This is the figure which lenders use to qualify you for mortgages.

IIA. Monthly non-housing expenses. List what you spend each month on items such as child care and clothing. These won't interest the lender as much as they are important to you in evaluating how much house you can afford. Here are some notes clarifying specific items

3. **Food.** Include eating at restaurants, as well as at home.

6. **Personal.** Include costs for both personal care (hair cuts, shoe repairs and toiletries) and personal fun (attending movies; buying CDs and lottery tickets; subscribing to newspapers).

7. **Education.** Do not include the repayment of education loans here. Instead, include educational payments, such as your child's private school tuition.

FAMILY FINANCIAL STATEMENT

	Borrower	**Co-Borrower**
Name		
Address		
Home phone number		
Employer's name and address		
Work phone number		

WORKSHEET 1: INCOME AND EXPENSES

I. INCOME

	Borrower ($)	Co-Borrower ($)	Total ($)
A. Monthly gross income			
1. Employment			
2. Public benefits			
3. Dividends			
4. Royalties			
5. Interest & other investment income			
6. Other (specify):			
B. Total monthly gross income			

II. MONTHLY EXPENSES

	Borrower ($)	Co-Borrower ($)	Total ($)
A. Non-housing			
1. Child care			
2. Clothing			
3. Food			
4. Insurance			
a. auto			
b. life			
c. medical & dental			
5. Medical & dental care (not insurance)			
6. Personal			
7. Education			
8. Taxes (non-housing)			
9. Transportation			
10. Other (specify):			
B. Current housing			
1. Mortgage payment			
2. Taxes			
3. Insurance			
4. Utilities			
5. Rent			
C. Total monthly expenses			

9. **Transportation.** Include costs for both motor vehicle (excluding insurance) and public transit. You can include monthly upkeep for a vehicle and a reasonable amount for repairs; if you do, expressly say so.

10. **Other.** Specify such expenses as regular charitable or religious donations and savings deposits, but not regular installment payments such as student loans, automobile loans or credit cards. They are listed on Worksheet 2.

IIB. Current housing expenses. If you currently own a home, list the mortgage and interest, taxes, insurance and utilities, including gas, electricity, water, sewage, garbage, telephone and cable service. If you rent, include your monthly rent and renter's insurance (if any).

IIC. Total monthly expenses. Here, total your non-housing and housing expenses.

Worksheet 2: Assets and Liabilities

I.   Assets. In columns 1 and 2, you and any co-borrower write down the cash or market value of the assets listed. Total them up in column 3.

A. **Cash and cash equivalents.** List your cash and items easily converted into cash. Deposits include checking accounts, savings accounts, money market accounts and certificates of deposit (even if there is a withdrawal penalty).

B. **Marketable securities.** Here you list items like stocks and bonds that are regularly traded and which you can normally turn into cash fairly readily, although not always at the price you'd wish. List the cash surrender value of any life insurance policy. Include items such as a short-term loan you made to a friend under the category "Other."

C. **Total cash and marketable securities.** Add up items A and B.

D. **Non-liquid assets.** These are items not easily converted into cash.

1. **Real estate.** List the market value—the amount the property would sell for.

2. **Retirement funds.** Include public or private pensions and self-directed accounts (IRAs, Keoghs or 401(k) plans). List the amount vested in the plan.

3. **Business.** If you own a business, list your equity in it (market value less the debts on the business). Many small businesses are difficult to sell, and therefore difficult to value, but do your best.

4. **Motor vehicles.** List the current market value of any car, truck, RV motorcycle, even if you're still making payments. Check used car guides at the library for the information.

5. **Other.** Include non-tangible assets such as copyrights, patents and trademarks, the current value of long-term loans you've made to others and any really valuable personal property such as expensive jewelry or electronic gear. Yes, it is hard to value this type of asset, but it can be done, especially if you've been receiving income and it promises to continue. Depending on your field, author, inventor, musician or software writer organizations may be able to help.

E. **Total non-liquid assets.** Total up items D1-5.

F. **Total all assets.** Total up items IC and IE.

IIA. Liabilities—Debts. In column 1, circle whether you, the borrower (B), or your co-borrower (C) is the debtor and the total outstanding or balance remaining. In column 2, enter your monthly payments. In addition, for non-revolving debt, such as a mortgage, a car loan, student loan or personal loan, indicate the number of months remaining on the loan.

Under "Other," don't include monthly insurance payments or medical (non-insurance) payments, as these go on Worksheet 1, Section II.A., Monthly Expenses—Non-housing. Do include stock pledges, lawyer's and accountant's bills and the like.

IIB. Total Liabilities. Total the monthly payments and balances remaining for items 1-7.

III. Net Worth. Total of all assets minus total liabilities

C. How Much Down Payment Will You Make?

Unless you're eligible for a government-subsidized mortgage that has low or—in the case of the Veterans Administration—no down payment, you'll probably need to put down 10%-25% of the cost of the house to qualify for a loan. While a number of lenders offer loans with as little as 3% down—often as the centerpiece of their first-time buyer programs—these are rarely the best choice. (See Chapter 4, Section B, for more on low

WORKSHEET 2: ASSETS AND LIABILITIES

I. ASSETS (Cash or Market Value)	**Borrower ($)**	**Co-Borrower ($)**	**Total ($)**
A. Cash and cash equivalents			
1. Cash	_____	_____	_____
2. Deposits (list):	_____	_____	_____
_____	_____	_____	_____
_____	_____	_____	_____
_____	_____	_____	_____
B. Marketable securities			
1. Stocks & bonds (bid price)	_____	_____	_____
2. Other securities	_____	_____	_____
3. Mutual funds	_____	_____	_____
4. Life insurance	_____	_____	_____
5. Other (specify):	_____	_____	_____
_____	_____	_____	_____
_____	_____	_____	_____
C. Total cash & marketable securities	_____	_____	_____
D. Non-liquid assets			
1. Real estate	_____	_____	_____
2. Retirement funds	_____	_____	_____
3. Business	_____	_____	_____
4. Motor vehicles	_____	_____	_____
5. Other (specify):	_____	_____	_____
_____	_____	_____	_____
_____	_____	_____	_____
_____	_____	_____	_____
E. Total non-liquid assets	_____	_____	_____
F. Total all assets	_____	_____	_____

II. LIABILITIES	**Outstanding Balance ($)**	**Monthly Payment ($)**	**Months Remaining**
A. Debts			
1. Real estate loans	B C _____	_____	_____
2. Student loans	B C _____	_____	_____
3. Motor vehicle loans	B C _____	_____	_____
4. Child or spousal support	B C _____	_____	_____
5. Personal loans	B C _____	_____	_____
6. Credit cards (specify):	B C _____	_____	_____
_____	B C _____	_____	_____
_____	B C _____	_____	_____
_____	B C _____		
7. Other (specify):	B C _____	_____	_____
_____	B C _____	_____	_____
_____	B C _____	_____	_____
B. Total Liabilities	_____	_____	

III. NET WORTH (Total assets minus total liabilities)   _____

down payment plans.) Also, you'll have to pay the closing costs (see Chapter 18), an additional 2%-5% of the cost of the home.

Generally speaking, the larger the percentage of the total price of a house you can put down, the easier it will be for you to qualify for a mortgage. This isn't because lenders like only people who put a major stake in a house—a fair number of people who can make small down payments (10% or so) also qualify for loans.

The main reason a big down payment equals easier qualifying is that larger down payments mean less money due each month to pay off your mortgage. As we discuss below, the monthly mortgage payment (plus taxes and insurance) is the major factor in determining the purchase price of the house you can afford. And with a higher down payment, a lender's financial interests are better protected: If you default on your mortgage, a lender has more room to sell the property and recover its investment.

For now, you need down payment money. How much do you have by way of liquid and non-liquid assets? If you have a house or other property you plan to sell, estimate what you're likely to receive after subtracting costs of sale. If necessary, think about other ways to reasonably raise cash. Can you liquidate other assets or get a gift or loan from a relative or friend? (These and other money-raising techniques are discussed in Chapter 4.)

Total up the amounts and then multiply this number first by five and then by ten. These figures represent the very broad price range of house prices you can likely afford, based on your ability to make a down payment of 10% to 20%. These numbers are a little on the optimistic side, as you will also need cash for closing costs.

EXAMPLE: Brad and William pool all available cash and come up with $30,000. Viewed very broadly, they can afford a house costing between $150,000, (based on a 20% down payment) and $300,000 (based on a 10% down payment). When they add closing costs, normally 2%-5% of the cost of a house, they realize that they need to lower this price range somewhat, unless they raise additional cash before closing.

But, remember, in addition to the down payment, you must be able to afford the monthly mortgage, interest and property tax payments. If your income is relatively low, you'll have to increase your down payment to 25%-30% or even more of the price of a house to bring down the monthly payments. (See Section E, below.) If, however, you have both a good income and enough money set aside for a larger-than-required down payment, you have a choice—you can put more money into the down payment or invest it elsewhere. We discuss your options in Chapter 4.

MISSION REVIVAL

NO MONEY DOWN DEALS

Books about making a million in real estate are full of stories of people who purchased financially-distressed properties, or assumed a seller's existing loan while borrowing the entire balance of the purchase price from the seller or another lender, in order to buy a house for little or no money down. If you're looking for a nice house in a pleasant California neighborhood, you can skip these strategies. In the booming California housing market, where a reasonably large pool of potential buyers will put up real money, few realistic opportunities to buy a good house for no money down exist. By and large, if you find a no down payment house deal, you won't want to live there.

D. Estimate the Mortgage Interest Rate You'll Likely Pay

The next step in arriving at your monthly mortgage is to determine the interest rate you'll need to pay on a mortgage. This is important because over the life of your mortgage, you will pay much more in interest than you will in principal. Thus, a relatively small difference in your interest rate will amount to a big difference in your total debt, and hence the amount of your monthly payments. The table below illustrates the differences by interest rate and mortgage term.

MONTHLY AND TOTAL PAYMENTS ON A $100,000 FIXED RATE MORTGAGE

Interest Rate (%)	15-year period		30-year period	
	Mo. pmt.($)	Total pmts.($)	Mo. pmt.($)	Total pmts.($)
5.0	790.80	142,344	536.83	193,259
5.5	817.09	147,076	567.79	204,404
6.0	843.86	151,895	599.56	215,842
6.5	871.11	156,799	632.07	227,544
7.0	898.83	161,789	665.30	239,509
7.5	927.01	166,862	699.21	251,717
8.0	955.65	172,017	733.76	264,155
8.5	984.74	177,253	768.91	276,809
9.0	1,014.27	182,569	804.62	298,664
9.5	1,044.22	187,960	840.85	302,708
10.0	1,074.61	193,430	877.57	315,926
10.5	1,105.40	198,972	914.74	329,306
11.0	1,136.60	204,588	952.32	342,836
11.5	1,168.19	210,274	990.29	356,505
12.0	1,200.17	216,031	1,028.61	370,301
12.5	1,232.52	221,854	1,067.26	384,214
13.0	1,265.24	227,743	1,106.20	398,232
14.0	1,331.74	239,713	1,184.87	426,554

Because different mortgage types carry different interest rates, start by deciding the mortgage type you want. If you haven't yet decided, read Chapters 8-12 for a thorough review of mortgage options.

⚠ INTEREST RATES CHANGE RAPIDLY

Follow the general principles and guidelines set out in this book and don't expect to find the exact same interest rates as quoted in our examples. For a reading of the market's direction, check the mortgage interest rate round-up published in the real estate sections of many Sunday newspapers. (See Chapter 13, Section A, for more information.)

In general, adjustable rate mortgages (ARMs) have lower initial interest rates and payment requirements than do fixed rate loans, and may therefore be more affordable than fixed rate loans. However, since most lenders do not qualify you based on the start rate of an ARM, choosing one to qualify may not work. Before selecting an ARM, compare interest rates by looking at the ARM's annual percentage rate (APR), not just its introductory rate. (APR is an estimate of the credit cost over the entire life of the loan. APR comparisons can sometimes be deceptive. See Chapter 13 for more on this.)

E. Calculate How Much House You Can Afford

When you have a pretty good idea of the size of your down payment and the interest rate you expect to pay, you can calculate how much house you can afford.

Here are directions for completing the Monthly Carrying Costs Worksheet, with a sample shown below. (There's a tear-out copy in Appendix 4.)

Line 1: Estimate how much money you'll need to spend on a house with the features you listed as your priorities in Chapter 1.

Line 2: Enter the down payment you plan to make.

Line 3: Subtract the down payment (line 2) you want to make from your estimated purchase price (line 1). The result is the amount you'll need to borrow.

Line 4: Estimate the likely mortgage interest rate you'll end up paying. (See Chapters 8 through 12.)

Line 5: List your principal and mortgage interest factor per $1,000 over the length of the loan (30 years is most common) using the amortization chart below.

Line 6: Multiply the factor from the amortization chart (line 5) by the number of thousands you'll need to borrow (line 3). The result is your monthly mortgage (principal and interest) payment.

EXAMPLE: You estimate the house you want to buy will cost $260,000. A 20% down payment of $52,000 leaves you with a $208,000 mortgage loan. You plan to finance with an adjustable rate mortgage (ARM), with a starting interest rate of 6%. The monthly factor per $1,000 for a 30-year loan at 6% rate is 6. So your monthly mortgage payments will begin at (because it's adjustable) 208 x 6, or $1,248.

Line 7: Estimate the cost of homeowner's insurance. Very roughly, homeowner's insurance costs about $400 per $100,000 of house value. On a $260,000 house, expect to pay $1,040 per year or $87 per month. You can get exact quotes in advance from insurance agents. You should also shop around a bit for your insurance. The cost and availability of home insurance policies can vary widely, especially for earthquake coverage. See Chapter 18, Section C. (Also, if you're buying a condo, the building policy may be for the bulk of this insurance. You may need only a supplemental policy for much less.)

Line 8: Estimate property taxes. Property taxes are initially based on the new assessed value (market price) of the house as of the date of transfer of title, according to the following formula:

Market Value	X	1%	=	Annual Tax
(actual price as of		(or slightly higher,		(divide this total
the date of sale)		such as 1.25%, in		by 12 to find
		counties with voter		the monthly
		approved bonds)		tax equivalent)

On a $260,000 house, taxes would be about $3,250 per year or $270.83 per month in a county with a 1.25% tax rate.

Note: The annual tax will actually be a little less than the examples shown here because there is a $1,000 homeowner's exemption for an owner residing in the house.

PUEBLO

AMORTIZATION CHART

Mortgage Principal & Interest Payment Factors (Per $1,000)

Interest rates (%)	15-year mortgage	20-year mortgage	25-year mortgage	30-year mortgage
5.00	7.91	6.60	5.85	5.37
5.25	8.04	6.74	5.99	5.52
5.50	8.17	6.88	6.14	5.68
5.75	8.30	7.02	6.29	5.84
6.00	8.44	7.16	6.44	6.00
6.25	8.57	7.31	6.60	6.16
6.50	8.71	7.46	6.75	6.32
6.75	8.85	7.60	6.91	6.49
7.00	8.99	7.75	7.07	6.65
7.25	9.13	7.90	7.23	6.82
7.50	9.27	8.06	7.39	6.99
7.75	9.41	8.21	7.55	7.16
8.00	9.56	8.36	7.72	7.34
8.25	9.70	8.52	7.88	7.51
8.50	9.85	8.68	8.05	7.69
8.75	9.99	8.84	8.22	7.87
9.00	10.14	9.00	8.39	8.05
9.25	10.29	9.16	8.56	8.23
9.50	10.44	9.32	8.74	8.41
9.75	10.59	9.49	8.91	8.59
10.00	10.75	9.65	9.09	8.78
10.25	10.90	9.82	9.26	8.96
10.50	11.05	9.98	9.44	9.15
10.75	11.21	10.15	9.62	9.33
11.00	11.37	10.32	9.80	9.52
11.25	11.52	10.49	9.98	9.71
11.50	11.68	10.66	10.16	9.90
11.75	11.84	10.84	10.35	10.09
12.00	12.00	11.01	10.53	10.29
12.25	12.16	11.19	10.72	10.48
12.50	12.33	11.36	10.90	10.67
12.75	12.49	11.54	11.09	10.87
13.00	12.65	11.72	11.28	11.06

SAMPLE MONTHLY CARRYING COSTS WORKSHEET

MONTHLY CARRYING COSTS WORKSHEET

1.	Estimated Purchase Price	$	260,000
2.	Down Payment	$	52,000
3.	Loan Amount (line 1 minus line 2)	$	208,000
4.	Interest Rate	6 %	
5.	Mortgage Payment Factor	6.00	
6.	Monthly Mortgage Payment (multiply line 3 by line 5)	$	1,248.00
7.	Homeowner's Insurance (monthly)	$	87.00
8.	Property Taxes (monthly)	$	270.83
9.	Total Monthly Carrying Costs (add lines 6-8)	$	1,605.83
10.	Long-Term Debts (monthly payments)		
	car loan	$	214.88
	student loan	$	179.46
	personal loan	$	55.66
		$	
	Total Long-Term Debts (monthly payments)	$	450.00
11.	Private Mortgage Insurance	$	
12.	Homeowners' Association Fee	$	
13.	Total Monthly Carrying Costs and Long-Term Debts (add lines 9-12)	$	2,055.83
14.	Lender Qualification (between .28 and .38)		38 %
15.	Monthly Income to Qualify (divide line 13 by line 14)	$	5,410.08
16.	Yearly Income to Qualify (mutiply line 15 by 12)	$	64,920.96

LET YOUR COMPUTER OR CALCULATOR DO THE WORK

If you hate making calculations, we recommend purchasing *The Banker's Secret* software, which quickly and easily lets you compute the amount of your monthly payments for mortgages of all rates and lengths. A book is also available with the same title. For price and order information, contact Good Advice Press, P.O. Box 78, Elizaville, N.Y., 12523, phone: (800) 255-0899.

You can also purchase an amortizing calculator, or check out one of the amortization programs available on commercial online networks. (See Chapter 6, Section G.).

Line 9: Now add up your mortgage payment (line 6), insurance (line 7) and taxes (line 8). The total in the our example is $1605.83. This is your monthly carrying costs (also called PITI—principal, interest, taxes, insurance).

As mentioned, a lender normally requires a buyer to be able to pay these costs with about 28%-38% of total monthly income, assuming moderate other long-term debts (ten months or longer), such as child support, car payments and student loans. If you have no other long-term debts, lenders may approve a loan where you'll use up to 36%-38% of your monthly income to pay carrying costs.

Line 10: List and total the monthly payments on your long-term debts. Our example shows total monthly debts of $450.

Line 11: If you're making a down payment of less than 20%, estimate monthly payments for private mortgage insurance. (See Chapter 4, Section C.)

Line 12: If you're looking at a condo or house in a development, you'll probably be paying a monthly home-owners' association fee. Enter it here.

Line 13: Add lines 9-12 for the sum of your total monthly carrying costs and long term debts ($2,055.83 in our example).

Line 14: Estimate the lender qualification which should be a number between .28 and .38, depending on your debt level (the fewer your debts, the higher number you can use). We use 38% in our example.

Line 15: Divide line 13 by line 14 to determine the monthly income needed to qualify, in this case about $5,400.

Line 16: Multiply line 15 by 12 to calculate the yearly income to qualify. In our example, you need an annual income of about $65,000 to qualify for the $260,000 house.

 If you'd rather not make all these calculations, a loan broker can work with you in determining how much house you can afford.

F. Tips on Improving Your Financial Statement

Bringing your carrying costs and long-term debts within the generally acceptable debt-to-income range of 28%-38% should allow you to finance a house. Many people will find, however, that it will require more than 38% of their monthly income to make house payments plus their other long-term debts. If you fit this description, here are some ways to bring yourself within the acceptable range.

1. Pay Off Long-Term Debts

The best way to improve your debt-to-income ratio is to pay off some long-term debts. Not only will this reduce your total monthly payments and thus, in the eyes of lenders, leave more of your income to be used for mortgage payments, it will result in other savings.

First, because the interest rates on consumer debts (such as credit cards) are almost always higher than the interest on mortgage debts, paying off the first type to qualify for more of the second can result in substantial savings. And second, because the interest paid on consumer debts is not tax deductible, while the interest portion of your mortgage is fully tax deductible, you qualify for another substantial savings. For example, if you're in the 28% federal tax bracket and 9.3% state bracket, 34.7% of all interest you pay on your mortgage is subtracted from your tax bill. (This takes into account the fact that state income taxes are a deductible item on your federal tax return. For more on the tax deductibility of mortgage interest, see Chapter 4, Section D.)

Paying off some long-term debts can have a down side, however, if it means you'll be short for the down payment as a result. If that's your situation, consider selling some of your possessions or tapping friends or relatives for help (discussed below).

2. Convert Assets to Cash

If you need a few thousand extra dollars to pay off debts or increase your down payment, look for it in your garage, basement or attic. If you're like most people, you may have many saleable items you don't really need. If you sell them and use the cash to either pay off other debts or increase your down payment, your financial picture can be made to look significantly better. One family we know raised over $5,000 by:

- selling some cameras, home electronics equipment and a seldom-used computer through a local penny-saver newspaper
- holding an enormous garage sale and selling household objects and even old clothing, some of which were donated by relatives and friends who wanted to help
- selling two small collections (guns and coins) through classified ads in a local hobbyists' magazine, and
- selling two late model cars and using the proceeds (after paying off the loans) to purchase two older, but still serviceable, vehicles. This didn't net any cash, but eliminated almost $400 in long-term monthly payments.

Also look at your investments as a source of cash. Consider cashing in whole life insurance policies (if the cash value is significantly high) or withdrawing money from a retirement account or plan.

⚠ Keep records to show "source of funds." Lenders may suspect that any new savings with less than a three- to four-month history is really a loan. (See Section 5, below.)

3. Emphasize Future Income

In rare cases, some lenders will approve an application for a home loan, even if you don't meet the normal income qualification ratios, if there's a high probability that your income will increase soon. In a sense, you're asking the lender to figure monthly carrying costs as a percentage of your future, not current, income.

If you have just successfully completed a job probationary period, for example, and can show that over the next few months that you'll qualify for a large pay increase, some lenders will consider your future earnings probability. Similarly, if you've just graduated from a professional or trade school and have been offered a relatively high-paying job, a lender may waive the common requirement that you have been employed for at least a year before receiving a loan.

If future raises are given at the discretion of your employer, consider discussing your house purchase with your boss. If he believes that your future with the company is bright, he may commit to a pay raise now, or, in some cases, even arrange for your employer to make you a loan at a lower-than-market rate of interest.

4. If You Work for Yourself, Show a Profit or Make a Big Down Payment

Millions of Americans work for themselves, or supplement their income by operating a small business on the side. Few of these businesses show large taxable profits; rather, most owners take advantage of the Internal Revenue Code rules which make it reasonably easy for small business owners to minimize their taxable earnings. Unfortunately, when a small business person wishes to borrow money, the fact that she has done everything legally possible to minimize her income for tax purposes is likely to come back to haunt her.

Typically, a small business person will try to convince a lender that the $28,000 of taxable income reported to the IRS was really closer to $50,000, if deductible business expenses such as transportation, meals, a home work space, depreciation, contributions to an IRA or Keogh plan, self-employment tax, contributions to medical insurance and entertaining are added back in. But this may be difficult to do. Lenders have heard it all before, and although they may privately acknowledge that an applicant's financial situation is likely to be better than reported to the IRS, they won't normally lend money in this situation unless the buyer can make a down payment of 25% or more. With a high down payment (and excellent credit rating), a borrower may qualify to purchase within accepted debt-to-income ratios even though his taxable income is relatively modest.

Normally, however, to qualify for a mortgage if your business shows an artificially low profit, you'll need to report a larger taxable profit. If your business really is quite profitable, this should take only a year or two. Instead of writing off every possible personal expense as a business expense, while paying yourself a low salary, raise your pay and treat more expenses as personal. You'll pay more federal income tax, but once you qualify for a mortgage loan, you can cut it back by deducting your mortgage interest and property tax payments.

5.   Borrow From Friends or Family

We discuss ways to raise money from family and friends in Chapter 12, Private Mortgages. For purposes of bringing your monthly income ratio to within 28%-38% of your income, you'll need an outright gift, or a loan that doesn't need to be paid back for a considerable period of time, and you may need to get it into your bank account a few months prior to loan approval. A lender wants you to *have* the money necessary to qualify, not to create another debt which will compete for repayment with your mortgage.

A gift made at the time you're purchasing a house requires documentation that it is a gift, not a loan. (See Chapter 4, Section F, for more on gifts.)

6.   Check Your Credit Rating and Clean Up Your File

All prospective house buyers should check their credit files kept by credit reporting agencies (also called credit bureaus) before applying for a loan. Unfortunately, credit files often contain out-of-date or just plain wrong information in their files. Sometimes they confuse names, addresses, Social Security numbers or employers. If you have a common name (say John Brown), don't be shocked if you find information in your credit file on other John Browns, or John Brownes or Jon Browns. Obviously, you don't want this incorrect information given to prospective lenders, especially if the person you're being confused with is in worse financial shape than you are.

The three largest credit bureaus, with offices throughout California, are TRW, Equifax and Trans Union. TRW provides an annual free copy of your file; the other bureaus charge $8. To obtain a free report, send your name, recent addresses, telephone number, Social Security number and date and year of birth to TRW Complimentary Report Request, P.O. Box 8030, Layton, UT 84041-8030. For questions, call TRW at (800) 392-1122.

If you find any wrong information, check your files at the other two agencies. Start by calling (800) 851-2674 (Trans Union) and (800) 685-1111 (Equifax). Then take steps to correct the error. You have the right to insist that the credit

bureau verify any wrong, inaccurate or out-of-date information. If it can't be verified, it must be removed.

Typical problems include:
- You're a self-employed carpenter, yet your file says you work as a TV repairperson or, worse, as unemployed.
- You're listed as owing a debt that's been repaid.
- A department store bill you owed eight years ago is still listed as outstanding. Although you legitimately owe the bill, a credit agency cannot keep information on file for more than seven years—with one exception: bankruptcies may be listed for ten years.

If the credit reporting agency insists on retaining inaccurate, wrong or outdated information, or lists a debt you refused to pay because of a legitimate dispute with the creditor, you have the right to place a 100-word statement in your file giving your version of the situation. Do so immediately.

 If the information in your credit file is both accurate and favorable, skip ahead to Section E7.

If the information in your file is accurate, but unfavorable, your best strategy is to clean up your credit before seriously trying to purchase a house. Here are some tips:
- Fully pay off small debts ($500 or less). For larger accounts, contact the creditor and attempt to work out a payment plan so that you're no longer listed as delinquent. Then stay current on the account.

  Some creditors you've owed for a while may accept less than the total amount owed "as payment in full." A creditor who has given up on collecting may jump at a lump sum payment of two-thirds of what's due. If so, make sure the creditor acknowledges in writing that you've satisfied the debt in full. If the creditor has a court judgment, make sure a "satisfaction of judgment" is filed with the court that issued the judgment. Show the satisfaction of judgment to the credit reporting agency. Be aware that a bank creditor that waives $600 or more must report your "saving" to the IRS. The IRS considers it income to you and you may have to pay income taxes on it next April.
- If you owe several creditors varying sums, and need help determining how much to pay whom, consider contacting a Consumer Credit Counseling Service (CCCS) office. CCCS, a nonprofit organization with offices all over California, will help you write a budget and set up a payment plan.

- If you've suffered a major financial set-back in the past few years (repossessed automobile, judgment against you for a large debt, foreclosed home or bankruptcy), you'll need to rebuild your credit, unless a creditworthy person will co-sign your mortgage loan, you have cash or can borrow from friends or family.

It normally takes two to three years to rebuild your credit. Here are four steps to doing so:

1. **Create a budget.** Most of the information you need is in your Family Financial Statement. Compare your monthly income to your total monthly expenses. To live within your means, your total expenses obviously cannot exceed your monthly income. If they do, sit down with your family and decide whether you're serious about buying a house. If the answer is yes, commit to some spending reductions and stick to them.

2. **Get a secured credit card.** Many banks will give you a credit card and a line of credit if you first deposit money into a savings account or certificate of deposit. The line of credit can be up to 150% of the amount you deposit. Use the credit card, and keep absolutely up-to-date on payments. A major drawback with these cards is that the interest rate often nears 20%. To avoid piling up new debts, use the card to cash checks or to charge items which you would have purchased anyway, and pay it off in full each month. After a year or two, banks and other large creditors will likely grant you a higher credit limit and drop the savings account requirement.

3. **Borrow from a bank.** Requesting between $1,500 and $5,000, take out a personal loan. To qualify, you may need a co-signer. Make your monthly payment on time and your credit will improve rapidly.

If you have enough cash to handle more than one loan payment, deposit the loan you received from the first bank in a second bank, again turning in the passbook in exchange for a loan. Now your credit report shows that two banks have extended you loans. Make all loan payments on time.

EASY QUALIFIER LOANS HAVE BEEN CUT BACK

A few years ago, if you had little in the way of long-term debts, and had lots of assets, a good income and credit history and were willing to make a large down payment (or if you met most of these qualifications), you could enjoy "easy qualifier" status with many lenders. This often meant that the lender wouldn't closely scrutinize the income and expense figures on your application and might let you use up to 38%-40% of your monthly income to pay carrying costs.

In today's tighter lending environment, easy qualifier loans are a thing of the past, except for those who qualify for jumbo loans ($207,000 or more). Even so, lenders are more and more requesting financial and tax records to verify income, no matter how big your down payment—so make sure your information is accurate.

---

4. **Obtain a revolving credit card.** Many department stores and gasoline companies will issue credit cards with low lines of credit to almost anyone. Even though you've had a major financial setback, before long you're likely to receive offers for store or gas company credit cards in the mail. Accept one or two, charge small amounts for items you need and pay all bills promptly.

   Note: Strategies 2, 3 and 4 are also useful for someone who has never used credit to build a credit history.

5. **Work with a local creditor.** Purchase an item that you really need (such as furniture or possibly a car) on credit. Even if you have a poor credit history, many local businesses will work with you to set up a payment schedule, but be prepared to make a large deposit (up to 30%), pay a high

CARPENTER GOTHIC

rate of interest or find someone to co-sign your loan. Don't be late or miss a payment. Once you've established a favorable profile with one store, you should be able to get credit elsewhere.

For additional information on credit files and re-building credit after a financial setback, see *Money Troubles: Legal Strategies to Cope With Your Debts*, or *Nolo's Law Form Kit: Rebuild Your Credit*, both written by Robin Leonard and published by Nolo Press. Also, the Federal Reserve has a free IBM-compatible computer diskette for Windows called "Partners," which includes ten suggestions improving your financial condition in order to qualify for a mortgage. Contact the Federal Reserve's Community Affairs office at (415) 974-3314.

7. Get a Co-Signer

If you have enough money for a down payment and monthly payments, but are considered a poor credit risk because you went bankrupt or for some other reason, consider asking a relative or friend to co-sign the loan. Some lenders will require that a co-signer be a blood relative, if not an actual occupant of your home.

While a co-signer doesn't "clean up" your credit rating, he brings his own, which is presumably much better. The co-signer may be able to help with ratios, savings or even credibility.

A drawback with co-signing is that if you default, the co-signer will legally be obligated to pay any difference between what the property fetches in a foreclosure sale and what you owe the lender. If you make a good-sized down payment, this shouldn't be much of a risk. If you default, the house is likely to be sold for enough to pay off the mortgage without obligating the co-signer.

Don't ask anyone to co-sign who doesn't fully understand the risks she's taking, and who isn't financially solvent enough to handle a possible loss. Chapter 12, Section A, discusses the precautions to take against death or disability of the borrower to protect a person who lends a friend or relative money to buy a house. That discussion also applies to co-signers.

G. Get Loan Prequalification or Preapproval

As an important step towards purchasing a good house at a reasonable price, consider getting a loan prequalification letter from a lender or loan broker. Pre-qualifying lets you determine exactly how much you'll be able to borrow, based on your income and credit history, and how much you'll need for a down payment and closing costs. Prequalification says that ultimate loan approval is likely, but stops short of guaranteeing it. The prequalification letter will likely read like this: "John and Andrea Chen qualify for an adjustable rate first mortgage loan from Better-Rate Financial for up to $260,000, at an interest rate of 9% or less."

Get prequalified as soon as you know your general price range and the general location you want to buy in. Sellers who are anxious to sell (the best kind from your perspective) often accept offers from purchasers who can close quickly (that is, have already arranged financing and have a prequalification letter), even if they don't make the highest offer. A seller who has had earlier deals fall through because of a buyer's financing problems is especially likely to accept an offer, even a low one, backed by a loan prequalification.

While loan prequalification is good as a lender's preliminary opinion as to your ability to afford monthly housing costs, a letter of preapproval is stronger. When you have been preapproved for a loan, a lender has actually done a credit check on you and evaluated your financial situation, rather than simply relied on your own statement about your income and debts. Preapproval means that the lender would actually fund the loan, pending an appraisal of the property.

In slow mortgage markets, some lenders may preapprove a loan even before you find a house. Most lenders, however, will hesitate to make an actual loan commitment until you have made an offer on the property and the lender has had a chance to appraise it. (See Chapter 13, Obtaining a Mortgage.) ■

Narrowing the Affordability Gap:
How to Afford Buying a House

➡️ Those few readers with enough money to purchase the house of their dreams and no inclination to bargain hunt can safely skip this chapter. The other 90% should stick around and learn how to overcome the affordability gap. Despite the recent softening of house prices, this will include many families with seemingly comfortable incomes who still can't afford a decent house in an area they want to live in.

A. Why California Houses Are Expensive

The concept of the affordability gap is simple—most potential California house buyers can't afford to buy their ideal house. Some can't afford any house at all. The gap, while particularly acute in urban coastal areas of California, exists all over the state, for three reasons:

- In the past generation, millions of baby boomers have entered their prime house-buying years, creating heavy demand.
- Despite relatively poor economic conditions, more people continue to move to California than leave, underpinning demand.
- Rising construction and lumber costs and, in many areas, restrictive government regulations and taxes, have made it expensive, and sometimes even impossible, to build new housing.

The convergence of these three factors has been sadly predictable: Competition for existing houses has increased, the supply of affordable new houses has failed to keep up with the demand, and prices of houses—although lower than their peak in most areas—remain among the highest in the country.

The affordability gap is particularly bad in established cities with little undeveloped building land and in municipalities where voters have backed "slow growth" planning and zoning measures. Indeed, in cities like Berkeley, Palo Alto, Mill Valley, Santa Monica and Pasadena, there's been little or no new housing in the last two decades, contributing to the enormous rise (up to 500%) in house prices since the 1970s.

The affordability gap is also seriously affected by the level of interest rates, as should be obvious when you consider that most people borrow from 70% to 90% of a house's purchase price. When interest rates are relatively high, purchasers must obligate themselves to a far larger level of debt than when interest rates are low. And because many lenders strictly enforce rules governing how much one can borrow (see Chapter 2, How Much House Can You Afford?), high interest rates automatically result in lower levels of affordability. Fortunately, because interest rates are now substantially lower than they were a few years ago, this component of the affordability gap is much less of a problem.

Let's translate the affordability gap into dollars and cents. In mid-1996, the median sales price of an existing California house was about $180,000, according to the California Association of Realtors. The median price is the middle point of all sales prices, meaning that one-half of all houses sold for more than $180,000 and one-half sold for less. This is different from the average, which is considerably higher (because high-priced luxury homes pull the average up).

In much of the San Francisco Bay Area and Southern California, the median sales price was considerably higher, exceeding $270,000 in some communities. Median prices are often two-thirds these amounts, or less, in small towns or rural areas such as the Central Valley, far Northern California, parts of Riverside County and the Sierra foothills.

Based on the $180,000 figure, the California Association of Real Estate (CAR) estimates that about 38% of Californians can afford to buy a house. But, like house prices, this affordability index varies widely throughout the state. According to the CAR, only 28% of San Francisco Bay Area residents can afford to buy a house, while over 57% of the people living near Sacramento can. (See Appendix 2 for a regional median house price list.)

And these figures represent major gains in the affordability index in the past few years, as a result of overall declining sales prices, combined with low interest rates. In April 1991, for example, the CAR estimated that only 18% of San Francisco Bay Area residents could afford to buy a median-priced home.

ART DECO

Despite the increase to the current level of 38%, obviously hundreds of thousands of Bay Area residents are believed to be unable to afford to buy a house.

LOOKING BEHIND HOUSING AFFORDABILITY FIGURES

Real estate trade groups base their conclusion that only a certain percentage of Californians can buy a house on the assumption that all purchasers put 20% down and get a fixed rate mortgage. In fact, however, many purchasers qualify for down payments of less than 20% and many obtain adjustable rate mortgages (ARMs), which have lower initial monthly payments than fixed rate loans. In addition, in some areas of California, many buyers qualify for FHA-insured or VA-guaranteed loans (see Chapter 11), which require a very low down payment.

Also, published affordability numbers don't consider the many creative ways Californians have found to beat affordability problems—such as using equity in a starter house to finance a more expensive one later, having relatives or friends help with the down payment, buying a low-cost fixer-upper (substituting sweat equity for capital) and getting the seller to finance part of the purchase by taking back a second mortgage. All told, these approaches allow tens of thousands of people to buy a house who would be ineligible under the published assumptions.

B. Don't Buy a House at All— Rent and Invest Elsewhere

Let's start with a view your local Board of Realtors would never approve. It doesn't make sense for everyone to strive to overcome the affordability gap in order to purchase a house. If you're happy renting and think you'll continue to be for years, there's little point in stretching your finances to buy a house. There are many advantages to renting—you don't tie up a lot of money in house equity and improvements, and someone else worries about (and pays) property maintenance, repairs, insurance and taxes. In addition, putting all your savings towards a house leaves you with no financial cushion to fall back on in case of an emergency, something that too many Californians have learned the hard way after their employers down-sized them out of a job.

Commonly, even if you're content to rent, your house-loving friends are likely to pressure you to put down roots. And even if you resist their arguments, a financial planner may claim that, "for tax reasons, you can't afford not to own a house." Bunk. In many areas of California (especially those covered by rent control ordinances), it's possible to rent for a very reasonable amount when compared to the total cost of buying a house.

A principal advantage of renting is that money not tied up in down payments and improvements can be invested in ways that may produce a better long-term return than a house will. Is this likely, you may ask? Haven't California houses appreciated on average faster than most other reasonably sane investments in the last several decades? No. While house prices went up faster than many other types of investments in the 1970s and '80s, the reverse has been true in the 1990s. For example, the California market has cooled so much in the 1990s, you would have done far better by investing in almost anything else.

The major disadvantage of renting is that your entire monthly payment vanishes. With home ownership, part of each mortgage payment goes towards equity in your home. The remainder (interest), along with local property taxes, is deductible from your income taxes. People in higher tax brackets obviously have the most to gain (in terms of the largest tax break) by buying a house versus renting. So, what's the bottom line? Is it better to buy or rent? Too many variables make it impossible to produce a definitive answer. Below are a few other factors to consider which, depending on your circumstances, may tip the balance one way or the other:

- The shorter the time you plan to stay put, the more financially advantageous it is to rent. People who buy and sell often incur transactional costs such as real estate commissions and closing costs not paid by long-term purchasers. Commonly, a buyer must own a house for at least three to five years, and sometimes considerably longer, for its increase in value to just cover these costs.

- It's a lot easier to move from a rental unit than from a house. With a house, you can't just give the landlord notice and pick up and leave. As a renter, even if you have a long-term lease and leave mid-term, there are ways to reduce or eliminate any financial liability, such as helping the landlord find a new tenant. (The flip side of this is that the landlord can also terminate the tenancy on fairly short notice, unless you have a long-term lease or the protection of a local rent control law.)

- Except in rent control areas, renters have no protection against rent increases beyond the term of their rental agreement or lease. If you have a fixed rate mortgage, your loan payments remain constant, and with a capped adjustable rate mortgage, your payment increases are limited by the cap.

- Rent payments are often less than mortgage payments for the same house, and usually a lot less than the total monthly cost of owning a house, even after the tax benefits of owning are factored in. This is true for both less expensive digs and luxury property. Lower cash outlays for housing leaves money available for other investments.

- If you're not good at saving and investing money, buying a house is a good way for you to build up a financial nest egg, especially as compared to renting and spending your excess money.

C. Fix Up the House You Already Own

If you own a house and plan to sell it to purchase a more expensive one in the same area, consider remodeling rather than selling—unless you live in a part of California where underdeveloped land is still relatively cheap and, as a result, new houses are still relatively affordable. In urban coastal California, however, where land is scarce and expensive, you often get more for your money, and possibly a better location, by fixing up and adding on to your existing house than by moving up, especially if your alternative is to buy a nicer house that is many miles from your job, your friends or your children's school. Indeed, land prices are so high in some cities, such as Beverly Hills and Palm Springs, that they dwarf the cost of construction to the point that buyers commonly purchase modest houses on desirable lots, only to tear them down and build afresh.

There are several other economic advantages to staying put and spending a large sum to redo your house. For one, you save the transactional costs of selling your existing house and closing on a new one. And this isn't chicken feed—moving from a $200,000 house to a $350,000 one would cost you close to $30,000, unless you sold your old house without professional help.

It's easy to underestimate remodeling costs. In figuring out how much it would cost to fix up and perhaps add on to your

existing house, don't take short cuts. Make a detailed plan and cost it out carefully. Here's how to think about the cost of remodeling as compared with the cost of moving:

Moving

- Figure out how much cash you would net for your existing house by subtracting what you owe from its likely sales price.

- From this amount, subtract 6%-8% of the sales price for real estate commissions and other sales costs.

- Now add any money you've saved for housing. The total is the amount you have to put down toward the purchase of a new house.

- Now estimate how much you'll need to pay for a suitable new house.

- Add 5% for your share of closing costs and moving expenses.

- Add at least 5% for immediate repainting and remodeling.

Remodeling

- Estimate the cost of hiring an architect experienced in house-remodeling to draw the plans you need.

- Get a hard-eyed contractor's estimate for work you decide on.

- Add 10%-20% to the estimate to cover things you haven't considered and inevitable cost overruns.

- Now, add these costs to what you already owe on your house plus any costs of temporarily moving out and renting another place while remodeling, if that will be necessary.

- Now consider how much you've saved to pay for remodeling or moving. You'll have to borrow any difference between what you have and what you need. If mortgage interest rates have gone down since you bought your house, often the cheapest way to borrow is to get a short-term construction loan and then, when the work is done, refinance the entire loan and your mortgage together. If interest rates have risen, however, keep your original mortgage and take out a second mortgage to finance the new construction.

- Finally, estimate how much the house will be worth in its remodeled condition. Ask local real estate agents and appraisers for their opinions on the house's current value and estimated value after remodeling.

Now ask yourself some big questions. How do the out-of-pocket costs of moving vs. remodeling compare? And when all is said and done, how much will each house be worth? As a general rule, if the cost of fixing your existing house is only 20%-30% of the purchase price of the new house, you're probably better off staying put.

It's not usually financially wise to remodel an existing house if any of the following are true:

- You plan to sell the house in a year or two. Although remodeling will increase the house's value, and you'll get more when you sell it, you're unlikely to get enough more to pay for your investment and trouble. In short, your improvements will benefit the next owner, not you.
- You live in a marginal area and your renovated house will be substantially bigger and nicer than its neighbors. It's always hard to get full value when selling the best house on the block. One big indication that you may want to go ahead is if others in your neighborhood are also improving, and prices are on the rise.
- The work you plan won't substantially increase your house's sales price. Remodeled kitchens, bathrooms and extra bedrooms tend to increase the value of the house by 75%-100% of what the remodeling work costs. A family room or finished basement typically recovers about 50%-75%. Swimming pools and spas often increase the value by only 50%. Improvements to the foundation, roof, wiring or plumbing often result in an even smaller increase in house value as purchasers assume they should be in good shape to begin with.

D. Strategies for Buying an Affordable House

One obvious way to beat the affordability gap is to find a good house at a comparatively reasonable price. But is it possible to find a bargain in today's market, considering that you're competing with hordes of other potential buyers? The answer is clearly yes, if you're willing to:

- learn about the housing market and what you can afford
- make some sensible compromises as to size and amenities, and
- above all, as we emphasized in the Introduction, commit to being patient, both in the purchase of your new house and, if you're already a homeowner, in the sale of your present one.

If you'll sincerely do these three things, you can find good houses, in all price ranges, for less than you might expect. This doesn't mean you'll find an impeccably maintained, four-bedroom house in Pacific Palisades, Laguna Beach or Mill Valley for nothing down and $800 a month. But it does mean that with enough persistence and common sense, you can find a decent house at a price you can afford, even if conventional real estate wisdom says otherwise.

Beating the odds and buying real property on favorable terms is possible because the residential real estate market is a highly imperfect one. A big reason why this is true is that there's no central mechanism, as is the case with a stock exchange or commodity market, to carry out transactions and set published prices. Instead, well over a half-million existing California houses and over 100,000 new ones are sold every year on local real estate markets that commonly do a relatively poor job of comparing the often very different types of houses that are put up for sale.

Not only are the houses offered for sale different, but the sellers and buyers, who often have little prior experience with real estate, have vastly different family situations, tastes and even prejudices. For example, the house at 111 Maple St. may be offered for sale by a retired financial planner determined to get top value, while a similar house at 112 Maple may be offered for fast sale by a divorcing couple or an out-of-town seller who has just inherited it. Although the involvement of real estate professionals, including lenders, agents and appraisers, tends to eliminate the most radical pricing errors, significant pricing imperfections remain. So much so that it's not uncommon for houses to sell for 10%-20% more or less than their inherent value. Think of it this way. If you sell a $200,000 home for $220,000 and buy a $350,000 for $315,000, you've saved $55,000 by beating the market by only 10%. If you do the opposite—that is, undersell and overpay by 10%, you've lost $55,000.

Below are 18 strategies to narrow the affordability gap by 10%-20%. Most are practical in today's market. A few have less merit, but are included because potential home buyers often ask about them. These strategies, which will be discussed in more detail in the remainder of this chapter, aren't mutually exclusive; many buyers successfully combine several.

1. Don't buy until you've saved more money.
2. Move to a more affordable part of the state.
3. Buy a less desirable house than you really want.
   a. Buy a marginal house in a desirable area.
   b. Buy a desirable house in a marginal area.
   c. Buy a marginal house in a marginal area.

4. Buy a fixer-upper cheap.

5. Buy a small house and add on later.

6. Buy a house at a probate sale.

7. Buy a house with a structural problem.

8. Buy a house subject to foreclosure.

9. Make multiple back-up offers.

10. Buy a "shared equity" house with someone you'll live with.

11. Buy a "shared equity" house with only one owner (you) living in the property.

12. Buy with the idea of renting part of the house.

13. Buy a duplex, triplex or house with an in-law unit.

14. Lease a house you can't afford now with an option to buy later.

15. Buy a condominium.

16. Buy a town house.

17. Buy a limited equity house.

18. Buy a house at an auction.

 SOME OF THE 18 STRATEGIES WON'T BE RELEVANT TO YOU

If you're looking for an upscale house in a lovely location, but want to save money (for example, you want to spend $700,000, not $900,000), you won't care that starter houses in marginal areas can often be bought cheap at foreclosure sales. So start by reading the list of the 18 sections carefully, and then turn only to the discussions that apply to your situation.

WHAT YOU CAN AFFORD RELATES TO YOUR FINANCING

The focus of this chapter is on how to purchase a good house for 10%-20% below what many others will pay. A major consideration to being able to do this is how you finance the purchase—including type of mortgage, the interest rate and the amount of the down payment. For details on these topics, see the following chapters:

• Raising Money for Your Down Payment (Chapter 4)

• Financing Your House: An Overview (Chapter 8)

• Fixed Rate Mortgages (Chapter 9)

• Adjustable Rate Mortgages (Chapter 10)

• Government-Assisted Loans (Chapter 11)

• Private Mortgages (Chapter 12)

• Obtaining a Mortgage (Chapter 13).

---

1. Don't Buy Until You've Saved More Money

First time purchasers often ask whether it's better to buy a less than perfect house now or to save like mad for a few years to afford a better one later. Traditionally, the answer has been "buy now." In California, waiting and saving has rarely been smart because house prices have tended to increase faster than savings. In the 1970s and '80s, in particular, buyers who scrimped to purchase a starter house, and then sold at a good profit in a few years, built sufficient equity to make a large enough down payment to purchase a much nicer house. Unfortunately, since about 1990, when house prices have leveled off or dropped, this strategy hasn't worked

A main reason why, in an up market, it's possible to trade up to a better house quickly is that investing in a house gives you a unique chance to make a big gain on a small investment. For example, if you buy a house for $200,000, putting $40,000 down and taking a $160,000 mortgage, and a few years later the house goes up in value 20%, you've doubled your $40,000 investment. Pros call this being "highly leveraged." If you put the same $40,000 into a government bond earning 6%, it would take you nearly 12 years to achieve the same result.

Because we believe that, overall, California house prices will come out of the price decline of the early 1990s and start to rise—especially in areas not directly affected by job reductions in defense industries—we think postponing your purchase instead of scrimping to buy now will likely be the wrong strategy for most purchasers.

EXAMPLE: After assessing her resources and the local market, Wendy concludes that the most she can afford is a $150,000 older house in a fairly run down area. What she covets, however, is a $300,000 house in a nicer setting. If Wendy saves her money for a few years to buy the more expensive house, she may find that it has gone up to $350,000, while the $150,000 house she spurned costs over $190,000. Unless Wendy can accumulate substantial money quickly, waiting is a poor strategy and may even result in her being unable to afford the less desirable house.

Given the fact that prices are going up, Wendy would be smarter to purchase the $150,000 house now and sell it in a few years. Her profit would cover much of the down payment on the ideal house, even if it's now $350,000.

Here's how: If Wendy put 15% down on the $150,000 house, on its sale she'd get that $22,500 back, plus the profit on its sale. To figure out how much she would gain, begin with the $40,000 increase in the value of the house, and subtract $13,500 for sale and closing costs, leaving $26,500. Add it to the $22,500 and Wendy has $49,000 to invest plus anything additional she has saved in the meantime. This should be enough to allow her to purchase the $350,000 house.

This general advice to buy now doesn't apply to everyone. If you expect to receive a good sum of money soon, such as an inheritance, or you have a solid plan to invest your money elsewhere at a very high rate of return, you'll probably come out ahead by delaying purchasing a house. For example, if you plan to start a small business and expect it to flourish, you may want to invest every cent you have in the business and wait a few years for the pay-off before buying a house. Also, if you believe that house prices in the area you are interested in are currently too high as compared to prices generally, you may do better by saving your money and waiting a few years.

 ONE PROBLEM WITH LEVERAGED INVESTMENTS IS THE POSSIBILITY OF A LARGE LOSS, PARTICULARLY IF YOU ONLY PLAN TO STAY IN THE HOUSE A FEW YEARS
In the example above, if the $150,000 house declined in value by 15%, Wendy's entire investment (down payment) would be wiped out, which is exactly what happened to many Californians in the early and mid-1990s. By contrast, even if Wendy put her $22,500 down payment in the stock market and it declined by 15%, she'd still have over $19,000 left.

2. Move to a More Affordable Part of the State

There's no better strategy to buying an affordable house than moving from an area with high housing costs to an area where houses cost far less. A house that would cost $750,000 in a posh suburb of Los Angeles or San Francisco would sell for much less in some communities near San Diego or Sacramento.

Many real estate writers claim that the savings you can attain by buying in a low housing cost area are largely ephemeral because wages are also likely to be low, or jobs unavailable. Not necessarily. For lots of people (such as state and federal workers), wages are the same no matter the location. And many others, for example, commissioned sales representatives and the millions of people who work at home and let their computers and faxes do their walking, have considerable flexibility as to where they live.

Even if you need to live close to work and aren't lucky enough to work for the government or other employer who pays uniformly throughout the state, relocating and taking a lower-paying job can still often make economic sense. The ratio of your earnings to local house prices is what's important to comparing the affordability of housing in different areas. For example, if you can make 60% of your Orange County salary in Merced, but comparable houses cost 35% as much, your ability to buy a nice house has increased greatly.

WHAT'S AHEAD FOR CALIFORNIA HOUSE PRICES?

The median sales price of a California house has dropped nearly 5% in the last few years. The sales prices of more expensive homes have dropped even more dramatically. But in 1996, prices either have been fairly flat or increasing slowly in most parts of the state.

Obviously it's difficult to predict the future. But even if prices of residential real estate in California generally hold steady, prices for starter homes, which are usually bought by young adults, should appreciate. Here's why:

- Because of the affordability problems of the last decade, there is pent-up demand from hundreds of thousands of Californians who haven't yet bought their first homes. Many aging baby boomers are still candidates for affordable starter houses.

- California has the highest immigration rate of any state in the nation. Many of these new Californians come from Asia, Central America or South America. Many are working hard to save money to afford their first home. This keeps the demand high for all types of housing, especially at the low end of the market.

- The size of California families is projected to decline in the next two decades; meaning more houses, especially smaller ones, will be needed to house the same number of people.

- Slow-growth ordinances in many desirable areas may continue to restrict the number of new houses that will be built; the houses that are built in these communities will mostly be above the starter house price range, meaning the supply of low cost housing won't increase significantly except in outer suburbia and semi-rural areas where land is still available.

3. Buy a Less Desirable House Than You Really Want

People caught in an affordability squeeze typically must scale down their new house wish list. While there are many bargain-hunting techniques, a good percentage fall into three broad categories:

a. Buy a marginal house in a desirable area.
b. Buy a desirable house in a marginal area.
c. Or, if you face a severe affordability gap, buy a marginal house in a marginal area.

Which is best? Because your house is not a passive investment (you'll live there), this is as much a personal decision as an economic one. Probably the majority of people prefer a marginal house in a good area, but some favor the more substantial (but relatively cheap) house in the less desirable neighborhood. Only those with no other options choose a marginal house in a less desirable or even semi-ghetto area.

Let's look at each choice in more detail.

a. Buy a Marginal House in a Desirable Area

In older residential areas, where houses were typically built one-by-one or in small groups, house size, construction techniques and lot size often vary significantly. On the same block, house prices can differ by a hundred thousand dollars. So don't be so intimidated by the reputation of an upscale community that you avoid looking there. Indeed, because others on a limited budget may avoid the area, you can occasionally get a better deal on a medium-priced house in a lovely neighborhood than you can on a similar house in a modest-priced community. This doesn't mean that people with modest incomes are apt to find a large supply of charming starter houses in West Los Angeles. It does mean, however, that bargains can and do pop up where you might not expect to find them.

Here are some houses that seem undesirable, but can be greatly improved at modest expense:

- Houses with ugly exteriors but pleasant interiors. You'd be amazed at the number of prospective buyers who won't even get out of the car to enter a truly homely house. The fewer people who look at a house, the smaller the pool of potential buyers and the better your chance of finding a bargain.
- Houses on busy streets that can be "turned around" to focus on a backyard by sprucing up or adding a deck or patio almost always sell for far less than if they were located on quiet streets.
- Houses on busy streets with master bedrooms at the back, where it's quiet. (Kids, who usually aren't as bothered by traffic noise, can sleep in smaller front bedrooms.)
- Houses with run-down interiors that need a lot of elbow grease and creative tinkering. Not only is paint cheap, but replacing wallpaper, linoleum, formica, light fixtures, hollow core doors and even aluminum sash windows can normally be done by the owner at a reasonable cost.
- Houses that can be screened from a busy street or other factor making them undesirable. If there's room (and zoning rules allow you) to build a stout redwood fence or plant a thick tall hedge, you can often block the problem from view. Street noise can often be reduced by walls, fences and certain types of vegetation. (See, for example, Sunset Magazine's *Landscaping for Privacy: Hedges, Fences, Arbors.*) Another possibility is to install a small pump-driven fountain in a backyard to mask offensive sounds with pleasant water sounds.

PROBLEM HOUSES IN GOOD AREAS CAN BE A BARGAIN
Our friend Tim, a savvy real estate professional, recently conducted an experiment. He blindfolded Kim, an experienced agent, and drove her to a house for sale, telling her only that it was located in a particular upscale neighborhood. When Kim entered the house, Tim removed her blindfold and asked her to look around, but not to open the blinds covering the front windows. After ten minutes, Kim was asked how much the house was worth. She replied that if the house didn't have any major structural problems, she'd guess it would sell for about $525,000.

When Tim told her the actual asking price—$410,000—Kim was flabbergasted. She then opened the blinds and saw that the house was on a busy local street. Even so, she continued to maintain that the house was underpriced.

The point should be readily understood—problem houses in nice neighborhoods are often underpriced, even when a reasonable amount is subtracted to compensate for the problem. Here, Kim felt the house was still a bargain, despite the busy street, because it had two large quiet bedrooms in the back, a large private backyard and was located on a steep hillside, so that the front windows looked over, not at, the passing traffic. With the addition of a six-foot fence or a stout hedge, a good bit of additional privacy could be gained at low cost. Kim concluded that given the amenities of the neighborhood, the high quality schools and the proximity to mass transit, the house was underpriced by as much as $50,000.

b. Buy a Desirable House in a Marginal Area

If your goal is to maximize your economic gain over the next few years, your best bet is to buy a good house in a marginal area which will improve quickly after your purchase. In many scruffy-turned-fashionable California residential areas, real estate values made huge gains in the last 10 or 20 years. On the other hand, there are also many areas that have long seemed to have much upside potential, but never realize it.

How do you pick an area where house prices are modest now, but will likely jump soon? That is, how do you spot a trend about to happen? The key isn't finding where values will appreciate over the long term (that's not too hard), but determining where prices will go up fast enough to make a short- or medium-term difference to you.

We don't have a sure-fire technique for spotting a marginal area about to improve. (If we did, this book would cost a lot more than it does!) But we can give you a few useful hints:

- **Avoid slums.** Prices in desperately poor areas with high crime rates may improve eventually, but not as soon as you'd like; in the meantime, you face the day-to-day reality of living in a dangerous environment. One possible exception is undesirable areas where many new immigrants are moving in. (See last bullet point, below.)
- **Avoid marginal areas on the immediate periphery of slums.** As long as the blighted area is there, the marginal area is unlikely to improve much.
- **Look for areas that have been substantially devalued by something no longer, or soon to be no longer, an issue.** For example, house values are likely to be depressed by the proximity of a large, loud and filthy factory, cannery or railroad spurline. If you conclude that the offending feature is so outmoded it's about to close, and the surrounding area is otherwise desirable, you may have found a terrific place to buy.
- **Look for blighted areas where a few hardy middle class pioneers have already settled.** One trick is to spot a warehouse or factory that's been taken over by artists and craftspeople. Once these pioneers begin turning things around, small business people often follow, restaurants and cafes open, and then, seemingly overnight, individuals and developers buy and transform the dilapidated housing stock in the area. Many formerly undesirable neighborhoods have undergone this sort of positive transformation throughout the state. People who spotted this sort of trend and bought early got incredible bargains. If you think you have a good idea about such an area, check with local planning departments. Applications for building permits and plans can tell you a lot about future prospects for a particular area. And drive by on Saturday morning. If you hear lots of hammers and saws, get out your checkbook—an improving trend is already in full swing.
- **Look for lower-priced areas touching on more desirable ones.** Many affluent California cities have one or more poorer cousins nearby. Areas particularly likely to improve are pockets of larger old houses. In cities near the coast, these are often found in downscale flatland areas in the shadow of more expensive hill neighborhoods. Avoid sections dominated by ticky-tacky 1950s style two-story apartments. Unless the multi-unit buildings are torn down, the area is not likely to significantly appreciate in value.
- **Look for affordable areas where transportation, especially public transportation, is good, or will improve soon.** As the 21st century nears, much of California is already experiencing almost terminal traffic gridlock. Despite the certain growth of digital communication technologies making work at home more feasible, the result is that older residential areas convenient to rail or ferry systems are almost sure to increase in value faster than the average residential area.

BACKWOODS EGYPTIAN

• Look for affordable areas within excellent school districts. Because California's large unified school districts often embrace both upscale and poorer cities, it's sometimes possible to find a pocket of affordable housing in an upscale school district. If you do, you surely won't be alone. Because families with children are often desperate to locate in areas with good public schools, chances are prices in the area will be bid up faster than average.

THINK TWICE BEFORE BUYING A NICE HOUSE IN A POOR SCHOOL DISTRICT

Because house prices (and their chances of appreciating comparatively quickly in the future) are always affected by the quality of local schools, even people without children should think twice about buying where schools are poor, unless, of course, they can do so at a commensurably low price.

• **Pay attention to where immigrants are locating.** Property values in many previously depressed areas have jumped substantially as large numbers of hardworking new Americans locate there.

c.   Buy a Marginal House in a Marginal Area

There's not much positive to say about buying a relatively undesirable house in a slum, even though you can do this comparatively cheaply. We purposely de-emphasize this approach, both because of immediate problems (high crime and run-down public and private services), and because property values in desperately poor areas usually appreciate far more slowly than in other neighborhoods. But as with any general rule, there are exceptions. Again, as mentioned, the most obvious is an area where large numbers of immigrants move in and quickly change the neighborhood's character. Another involves areas with an extremely desirable location which the city or private developers have already targeted for improvement. For example, plans to build a new ballpark or convention center in an area is often a tip-off that other major changes for the better are likely to follow.

4.   Buy a Fixer-Upper Cheap

The era when a dilapidated house in a reasonably decent area could be purchased dirt cheap and fixed up at a moderate cost is past. The demand for this type of house has risen steadily for at least the last two decades, resulting in comparatively high prices for remaining fixer-uppers in all but the most undesirable neighborhoods. Part of the reason is that buying distressed houses, fixing them up quickly and reselling at a profit is a profitable business for many small contractors, which means house buyers face professional competition.

While most fixer-uppers are no longer great deals, they still cost less than a comparable house in good shape. Ask your real estate agent about special loans available from Fannie Mae and the Federal Housing Administration for fixer-uppers. (See Chapter 11, Section B.) Also, consider purchasing a foreclosed property, which will often be a fixer-upper. (See Section 8, below.)

When you consider the time, effort and cost of finding and renovating a house, however, a fixer-upper is unlikely to be a bargain. Indeed, many fixer-uppers sell above their fair market value when you take a hard-eyed approach to the real costs of repair. This is especially true for lower-priced houses, where it will be hard to recover the costs of major repairs in a subsequent sale. Fixer-upper bargains are more likely to be found in higher price ranges, where affluent buyers tend to look for houses already in good condition.

But the fact that buying a fixer-upper probably is one of the best strategies to purchase a good house cheap doesn't mean you should always reject this approach. If you are a person who has a relatively small down payment but good construction skills, buying a property cheap that needs lots of work may be a sensible approach to close your personal affordability gap. Still, be cautious and think it through before you saddle yourself with years of repairs. If you can get a second job that will enable you to make the payments on a better house, weigh this approach against spending hundreds of hours trying to fix up a ratty house that you're simultaneously living in.

DON'T OVERLOOK SOLID-LOOKING HOUSES WITH DEFECTS

As we discuss in Section 7, below, buying an obvious fixer-upper is not the only, or often even the best, approach to buying a house with physical problems at a reasonable price. Today's stricter inspection and disclosure rules, discussed in Chapter 19, commonly uncover major hidden structural problems in sound houses. Sometimes these problems scare off potential buyers, and then the only way the seller can move the house is by reducing the price to the point where it becomes a very good deal.

HOW TO JUDGE WHETHER A FIXER-UPPER IS A GOOD DEAL

If you're seriously interested in a particular fixer-upper, hire a reliable remodeling contractor to check it out carefully and give you an estimate of needed renovation costs. Add the contractor's estimate to the purchase price and ask yourself if the house in rehabilitated condition will be worth that amount. If the total cost of the rehabilitated house is 90% or more of the cost of a comparable house in good shape, keep looking. By the time you factor in the trouble you'll go through and the likelihood of cost overruns, you won't save anything.

HOW TO FIND AN UGLY DUCKLING

Bargain hunters who want to find a reasonably-priced ugly duckling and turn it into a swan don't always know where to look. Certainly, no matter how ugly a house is, no one in the hype-happy real estate business will come right out and admit it in a listing or ad. Still, it's not hard to locate such houses. Look for ads or write-ups that say "not a drive-by," "a diamond in the rough," "has potential" or "needs TLC." Roughly translated, these are real estate euphemisms for "Oh no, we'll never sell this one unless we talk the owner into listing it cheap."

---

5. Buy a Small House and Add On Later

Many house hunters focus primarily on the house (number of bedrooms, size of living room, condition of the kitchen, existence of a fireplace), not on the lot or remodeling potential. This creates an opportunity for the canny shopper. If you find a small house on a relatively large lot priced comparable, or only slightly above, similar houses on ordinary-sized lots, you pay little or nothing for the extra land. In addition to the added privacy and room to play and garden, you normally have the space to enlarge the house anytime you can afford to hire a contractor or have the time to do the work yourself.

Even if the lot isn't that large, consider buying a smaller house with remodeling potential, and adding a second story addition. Of course, check first to be sure that local zoning laws allow the changes you want to make.

MONICA AND DAVE: BUILDING ADDITIONS

When Monica and Dave began house hunting, they knew they wanted a three bedroom, two bath house in the Berkeley-Oakland area on the east shore of San Francisco Bay, for a maximum of $250,000. They also dreamed of a large deck for weekend lounging and parties. After 18 months of looking at nearly 200 houses, they began to despair. Nothing even marginally decent was available in their price range. Their agent tried to convince them that neighboring towns a little further from San Francisco offered more for the money, but Monica and Dave, who both worked in Berkeley, were determined not to commute, and knew where they wanted to live. So they took a new approach—they looked at smaller houses with expansion potential.

Within weeks, they found a house in North Berkeley. It had only two bedrooms and one bath (and no deck), but at $240,000, the price was right. Best of all, the backyard was deep enough to leave plenty of room to add onto the back of the house and still have room for a good-sized garden. After checking carefully and assuring themselves it was feasible to add on a bedroom later, they said yes. With their savings and a small no-interest loan from Monica's parents, Monica and Dave added a second bathroom (using a space that had been a closet/hallway) and a large deck. After five years, the house had appreciated considerably. Their new equity allowed them to qualify for a home equity loan to add a second-story master bedroom. They now have a very pleasant house less than a mile from their respective jobs.

6. Buy a House at a Probate Sale

Probate sales occur when a homeowner dies leaving property to be divided among inheritors, or to be sold to pay debts or taxes. The sale is handled by the executor of the homeowner's will (or a court-appointed administrator if there is no will). It is often supervised by the probate court judge, through a bidding process. The highest bidder gets the property. Some probate sales are handled directly by the executor of an estate without going through the court bidding process.

Occasionally it's possible to buy a house at an estate or probate sale for substantially less than the current market rate. We know one man who bought a house for less than $70,000 this way. Sure, the house was small, in a down-scale neighborhood and had many structural problems, but still, it was a steal—especially as the borderline ghetto neighborhood had already begun to show signs of gentrification.

Not all probate sales are bargains. There is always the chance that a house will be bid up too high. But many are, mainly because the time and uncertainty involved in bidding discourages many potential buyers from participating. Less buyer competition can mean a lower-than-market price. Also, the cost of bidding (you will likely be required to include a cashier's check for 10% of the price you're offering) discourages people from making casual bids.

While you may find a bargain through a probate sale, there's also a down side. Probate sales are an exception to the California law requiring sellers to disclose all known problems (Civil Code §1102, discussed in Chapter 19). Although agents must still legally disclose all pertinent facts, many probate-sold houses are sold "as is," and your bid made in court (as opposed to independently administered probate sales with more flexibility) cannot contain financing, inspection or other contingencies (a subject covered in Chapter 16).

If you're considering buying a house at a probate sale, here's some advice for getting the best deal:

- Hook up with a knowledgeable broker or salesperson who knows the ropes of probate sales. There are a few in every community.

AVOID NOVICE REAL ESTATE SALESPEOPLE
Most agents who have been in the business only a few years don't really understand how the probate sale process works. To cover their ignorance, they are prone to discourage potential purchasers from exploring this approach.

- If you plan to bid at a court-supervised probate sale, line up a highly trustworthy and thorough inspector to check out any house before the court confirmation procedure. (See Chapter 19 for details on inspections.)
- Find a house which has been appraised too low. This may be less difficult than you imagine, since a good percentage of houses subject to probate sales are run down. (Chapter 15 discusses how to evaluate sales prices.)
- For court-supervised sales, consider holding off on your bid until the court procedure begins and the first round of bids are in. (See "How a Court-Supervised Probate Sale Works," below.) At some probate sales, many bids are placed by investors hoping to pick up a house very cheaply and quickly resell it for a profit. If you can figure out what professional investors will offer and bid just a little higher, you can sometimes save a bundle. Call the probate court clerk (it's part of your county's superior court) for a list of probate sales on the court calendar. Then check out the property carefully. If it looks like the buyer got a great price, inspect the property, line up your financing, and hope to overbid them at the court confirmation. Contact the attorney handling the estate for the date and time of the confirmation hearing.

Understanding the details of probate sales may seem complicated and not worth the effort. If, however, you've more time than money, will do your homework and, above all, will patiently bid on a number of properties until you get one at a favorable price, a probate sale can work to help close your personal affordability gap. And because probate sales involve houses in all price ranges in all areas of the state, it's a process open to all bargain hunters.

HOW A COURT-SUPERVISED PROBATE SALE WORKS

Here are the basic steps in a court-supervised probate house sale:

- The house is advertised for sale in a newspaper (often a legal or fairly obscure one) published in the county in which the property is located and, if listed with a broker, in a Multiple Listing Service. (See Chapter 5, Section A.)
- An appraisal value is established.
- Bids are accepted by a certain date.
- During the court procedure, higher bids are accepted. A cashier's check may be required with each bid. The first higher bid (called an "overbid") must exceed the original highest bid by at least 10% of the first $10,000, plus 5% of the balance. For example, the first overbid on a $100,000 offer must be $105,500:

10% of $10,000	=	$1,000
5% of $90,000	=	$4,500
		$5,500

- Subsequent overbids are allowed in amounts set by the probate judge. For example, he might require that each new bid exceed the previous one by $1,000.
- The highest bid, if it is at least 90% of the property's court-appraised value, is accepted.
- Purchase of the property is normally financed in the same way as any other purchase.

7. Buy a House With a Structural Problem

California law strictly requires that a seller and her agent disclose all known problems with a house, using a detailed form entitled "Real Estate Transfer Disclosure Statement." (Civil Code § 1102; a copy is in Chapter 19.) In addition (as discussed in Chapter 19), most buyers and lenders insist on careful pre-purchase inspections before the sale. As a result, many California houses are inspected two or three times. This is particularly true in areas where earthquakes are likely. If there's a disagreement as to the extent of structural problems, a house has been on the market for a while or a serious seismic vulnerability is identified, multiple inspections are common.

Recently, fear of lawsuits for failing to disclose house defects has resulted in some inspectors exaggerating flaws and generally emphasizing the negative. This makes some houses far more difficult to sell than was the case ten years ago. If buyer interest dries up (as it often does when a house has a long list of problems), the asking price of a house will almost surely drop, sometimes precipitously. The house is likely to be perceived by local agents as being stale (hard to sell at any price) and thus it will be shown to fewer prospective purchasers. Before long, the price may be lowered again, creating a bargain, despite the physical problems.

Consider, for example, a gracious 65-year old, two-story wood-frame house located on a hillside, near an earthquake fault. The house has settled a little over the years, and cracks in the concrete foundation have been patched several times. Fifteen years ago, one fairly casual inspection report noted that despite the foundation cracks, there was little danger of the house sliding off the hill.

Today, the same house will be inspected more closely. The seller is apt to hire a general contractor to make a routine inspection. This person will likely prepare a report full of disclaimers stating that no matter what problems are discovered in the future, he isn't legally responsible. In addition, he may state that while he hasn't taken soil borings or done stress tests, significant structural work is needed to bring the foundation up to current standards.

A prospective purchaser worried by all these disclaimers may have the house reinspected. The second inspector, too, may worry about a possible lawsuit if she says the house is in okay shape and then it suffers major damage in an earthquake. As a result, her report may say that she isn't sure whether the old foundation will hold up, but to be safe, she'd jack the house up and install a new reinforced foundation for about $75,000.

Reading this, the prospective buyer will probably look elsewhere.

Depending on how long it's on the market and how paranoid the various inspectors are, the pile of negative paper on this otherwise lovely house may grow tall. To unload it, the frustrated seller is likely to lower the asking price. But the house still may not sell because any prospective mortgage lender will discover the negative inspection reports and, as a result, require that at least $50,000 of foundation work be done before approving a loan. Local agents, who will now see the house as hard to finance, will increasingly take their customers elsewhere. Eventually, the frustrated seller is likely to cut the price again, this time significantly. Now the house is a real bargain, especially if a buyer can find a trustworthy contractor who can figure out exactly how much foundation work really needs to be done to make the house safe.

So how can a buyer with limited savings raise the money to buy this house if the seller, who, after all, has already significantly lowered the price, refuses to pay for the foundation work? One possibility is to finance the work with part of the buyer's down payment money, with the seller agreeing to take a second mortgage for the balance.

A second option is to find one of the relatively few lenders who'll allow the price of the house to be raised somewhat to reflect the fact that it will be worth more once the foundation is fixed. The seller would then credit the buyer in escrow with the full dollar amount of the work needed to be done. (Chapter 18 discusses escrow in detail.)

EXAMPLE: Betty and Hannah locate a house with an asking price of $375,000 that's been on the market for five months. The price has been marked down twice from $450,000, principally because the house has settled at one corner and a structural engineer recommends $50,000 of rehabilitation work. Betty and Hannah offer $375,000, contingent upon the seller paying for half of the repairs in the form of an escrow credit. They also find a lender who agrees to loan 85% of $400,000 if the work is done. In effect, the price is marked up to that amount, with a $50,000 escrow credit (half of which is paid by the seller and comes out of the sale price) set aside to pay for the construction. The work is done, meaning Hannah and Betty end up paying $400,000 for a house in excellent shape. And, because the bank was willing to loan on a higher value than the sales price, they didn't need to come up with cash beyond the down payment.

Unfortunately, it is more difficult to get loans that include funds for major repairs or renovations than it used to be. Your best bet is to find a portfolio lender (see Chapter 2) with more flexible policies. To do this, you'll probably need the help of a fairly sophisticated mortgage broker who knows local lending practices well. (See Chapter 13, Section B.)

A third way to swing a deal for a house laden with an inspection report calling for much expensive work is to finance the entire purchase through a relative or friend. No financial institution will require you to immediately perform the rehabilitation work; you can assess what's really needed and do the work at your convenience. If you have the cash in hand, you may be able to buy a distressed house for as much as 25% less than comparable houses. Few other affordability strategies produce savings this big. Financing through friends or relatives isn't possible for everyone. But if someone in your immediate circle may be willing to help you, read Chapter 12, Private Mortgages.

BILL AND EILEEN:
LENDER FLEXIBILITY CAN MEAN GREATER SAVINGS

We bought our home for $300,000, in effect putting only $30,000 (10%) down, but paying for no mortgage insurance or other higher costs normally associated with making a low down payment. We did it like this.

The house had originally been listed at $338,000 but was reduced in two stages to $308,000, in part because an inspection report said that the house needed $40,000 of work, and in part because houses were selling slowly that fall. The seller, who had already moved to Texas and was anxious to unload the house, quickly accepted our $300,000 offer, with 20% down, that required him to credit us with $30,000 to partially compensate for the repairs. Our lender didn't require that the work be done before sale, because the appraisal showed that we didn't overpay, even without the repair work and credit.

The day after the sale closed, we picked up our $30,000 escrow credit check from the title company. This meant we had only $30,000 invested in the house. We used the escrow credit money to remodel the house. In the process, we fixed the serious problems in the inspection report but skipped the non-essential ones, and used the extra money to sand floors, move a wall and reface cabinets. Now, a few years later, our lovely, extensively remodeled house is worth over $400,000.

8. Buy a House Subject to a Foreclosure

If you are considering buying a small starter house or a house in a marginal area or a community with high unemployment, purchasing a house subject to foreclosure may further narrow your affordability gap. For many people it's a great way to buy a house for less than its appraised value. Be aware, however, that financing a foreclosed house may be difficult because many sales require full payment upfront. Also, this technique is less available for upscale houses, since such houses are frequently sold before foreclosure occurs. Finally, if you need to buy quickly, foreclosure sales are not for you because the process may take six months or so from when a homeowner defaults on his mortgage to final sale.

Foreclosure normally begins when a homeowner misses several mortgage payments. Either the original lender (or the financial institution that has purchased the loan) instructs the trustee to file a notice of default. (In California the term "mortgage" is real estate slang for a "deed of trust." With a deed of trust, a trustee—usually a title company—has the power to sell the property if the borrower defaults, without first obtaining court approval.)

During the three months following a notice of default, the homeowner can make the back payments and cure the default. If she does not pay up, the house proceeds to foreclosure. A prospective buyer can purchase the house at various stages during this process.

 In all stages, it's usually best to hook up with a real estate agent who knows the foreclosure ropes.

The three broad approaches to buying a house subject to foreclosure are:

1. Purchase from the owner, during the three-month period before the foreclosure sale. During the three-month period the owner has to make up the back payments, he may want to sell the property to avoid foreclosure and severe damage to his credit rating. To find out who is in default, you'll need to check Notices of Default at the county recorder's office (or look under the heading "Foreclosure" in a local newspaper of general circulation which carries such notices—often a legal newspaper). You can also ask about commercial foreclosure services and special publications that list local foreclosures. The County Recorder's Office or local Board of Realtors should be able to steer you to these publications, which can then be

purchased. Once you locate a property subject to future foreclosure, contact its owner and offer to buy his house in return for a discounted purchase price.

💡 THE CLOSER TO ACTUAL FORECLOSURE, THE MORE LIKELY THE OWNER WILL PROBABLY BE TO UNLOAD THE PROPERTY

If the owner doesn't make the back payments (or sell the house) during the three-month period, the trustee publishes a "notice of sale" in a general circulation paper in the county where it's located. This notice states basic loan information and where and when (at least 21 days later) the sale will be held. At this point, many owners are delighted to sell for little or nothing more than they owe to the lenders, because they've given up hope of keeping the house.

2. **Purchase at the foreclosure sale.** Assuming no one brings the mortgage current or buys the house within the three-month and 21-day periods, the trustee holds a foreclosure sale and sells the house to the highest bidder. Potential buyers (often investors) attend the sale or auction with cash or a cashier's check in hand for a little more than the amount they plan to bid (to allow for a small increase). This upfront cash requirement eliminates casual bidders from foreclosure sales.

The trustee opens the bidding at the amount of the outstanding mortgage being foreclosed. If several people are interested in the house, a "bidding war" may ensue. The highest bidder who can produce the cash gets the property. If the house has a second mortgage on it, the holder of that mortgage will likely be present to make sure that bids are high enough to cover the amount of his mortgage, in addition to the first. If not, he'll likely make the high bid which, like other bids, must be at least enough to cover the first mortgage) to avoid having someone else buy it for the amount of the first mortgage, therefore wiping out his investment.

Check legal newspapers for information on foreclosure auctions.

3. **Purchase after the foreclosure sale if no one bids.** If no one bids at the sale, the foreclosing mortgage holder gets the property back. In recent years, savings and loans and other lenders have ended up with a fair number of houses this way, most of which they want to sell quickly, even if it means taking a loss. (These properties are often called REOs, for "Real Estate-Owned.") Many of these houses have serious pest control or structural problems, or are located in undesirable areas, but there are exceptions.

Some lenders sell the properties themselves (often with favorable prices and low down payments); the better properties, however, are commonly turned over to real estate brokers, who try to sell them as they would any other house. Even so, the fact that the foreclosed house wasn't prepared for sale by an owner, and thus may be in less than perfect shape, often means there are bargains to be had.

Before purchasing a home through a private or government foreclosure sale, ask these questions:

- Is the house worth significantly less than you would have to bid to get it on the open market? If not, don't bother. (See Chapter 15 for how to assess the value of a house.)
- Are there major problems with the house or property? Like probate sales, foreclosure sales are an exception to California Civil Code §1102 requiring sellers to disclose all known problems. Many foreclosed properties are sold "as is," so (if possible) be sure to arrange your own thorough inspection for any structural or pest control problems before you commit to a purchase. (See Chapter 19 for details on inspections.)
- Are you taking clear title? (Title is the history of ownership; see Chapter 18 for more information.) The owner may have had other financial problems and creditors may have placed liens on the house. Normally, these are paid off or wiped out during the

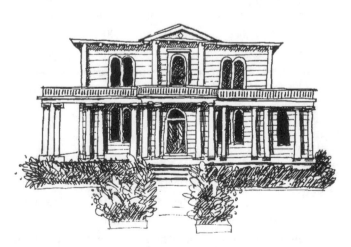

ITALIANATE

foreclosure process, but before agreeing to buy the house, you'll want to be sure all liens really have been removed.

- Are there tenants living in the house? If so, make sure they're gone when you get the house. The last thing you want to do is evict a tenant who doesn't want to leave. If you're buying in a rent control area, however, you may have to buy subject to "tenants' rights." Although as an owner you are entitled to live in your house, you may very well have to assert this right by evicting the existing tenants after you purchase. If so, we suggest the *Landlord's Law Book, Vol. 2: Evictions,* by Attorney David Brown (Nolo Press).

GOVERNMENT FORECLOSURE

If the distressed house had financing guaranteed by the U.S. Department of Veteran Affairs or insured by the Federal Housing Administration (of the U.S. Department of Housing and Urban Development), bidding at a foreclosure sale must follow the agency's rules (typically sealed bids submitted by mail). Buyers frequently must go through a time-consuming and bureaucratic process before the sale is final. But don't let this scare you—government agencies often have good-sized inventories of foreclosed properties and will sometimes offer bargain prices, low down payments and attractive financing deals to move them.

A real estate agent experienced with government foreclosures can help you locate and buy these types of houses. Government foreclosed properties are often advertised in local newspapers. For more information contact the U.S. Department of Veteran Affairs or Department of Housing and Urban Development. (For addresses, see Chapter 11, Government-Assisted Loans.)

RESOURCES ON FORECLOSURES

The Smart Money Guide to Bargain Homes: How to Find and Buy Foreclosures, by James Wiedemer (Dearborn Financial Publishing).

Big Money in Real Estate Foreclosures, by Ted Thomas (John Wiley & Sons).

9.   Make Multiple Back-Up Offers

If you are both patient and flexible, you may be able to buy a good house at a substantial discount by placing low back-up offers on houses for which the seller has already accepted a higher offer. In doing this, you're gambling on two things: that the first offer will fall through, and that the seller will accept your back-up offer, rather than put the house back on the market.

Is it a good gamble? Fair. Our best guess is that between 10%-20% of sales fall through. In some of these situations (perhaps half), a seller is so anxious to get on with his life that he will accept a lower back-up offer rather than start over at the original asking price. Remember, some of the best real estate deals are made when the other person is in a hurry. A seller whose deal has just fallen through, and who needs to get on with his life, is often emphatically in this situation.

EXAMPLE: John, recently widowed, has two young daughters. He lives 200 miles from his parents, who have offered to care for the girls after school if John moves near them. He enters into one contract to sell his existing house and a second contract to buy a house near his parents. The deal to sell his house falls through when the buyer fails to get a loan, putting John in a bind—he needs to sell fast to pay for the house he wants to buy, and he needs immediate help caring for the girls.

John remembers Sue who made a written back-up offer for 12% less than the first offer. John didn't accept Sue's low offer, because he believed he had a much better deal. Now he calls Sue and says he'll sell to her if she raises her offer by $10,000. She offers to raise it by $5,000, and John reluctantly accepts. The house, which once seemed sold for $290,000, goes to Sue for $261,000. When you also consider how much Sue will save in mortgage interest costs—as much as twice this amount over the years—it's easy to see that by being patient, she has made a fantastic deal.

Here are some basic rules to follow in making back-up offers:

- **Take the time to learn the local market.** As you'll probably be making offers on more than one house, you need to know what properties are truly worth. Remember, it's no bargain to buy a house for 10% less than either the asking price or the amount of the first offer if its price was 15%

too high in the first place. (See Chapter 15, How Much Will You Offer?)

- **Adopt a bidding strategy.** Normally, you'll want to bid about 10%-15% lower than a house's fair value (not the asking price). If you bid lower, you probably won't be taken seriously. Many sellers who have received another higher offer won't require a deposit from you because they won't want to open a second escrow. But, if required, be ready to make a small deposit to show you are serious. You'll get it back, of course, if the first deal goes through.

- **Be patient and stick to your plan.** Many people (especially real estate agents who want a commission now) will tell you that you'll never get a house this way. Don't buy this nonsense. If you are patient enough, sooner or later you will find a seller who will say yes.

- **Make all back-up offers contingent on your subsequent right to approve, should the seller accept.** (See Chapter 17, Section D.) Reserving to yourself a right of approval is essential if you make more than one back-up offer; otherwise, if two or more are accepted simultaneously, you may find yourself in a legal mess and may lose any deposit you've made. Even if a seller refuses your back-up offer because he seems confident his first deal will close, stay in touch via an occasional call or card. If the seller's deal falls through, you want him to know you are still interested.

10. Buy a "Shared Equity" House With Someone You'll Live With

Equity sharing is a fancy term for buying a house with someone other than a spouse. The attraction of equity sharing is that two or more people with pooled resources can buy more house than each can alone. For many people, the downside of equity-sharing arrangements is that living with someone else results in a loss of privacy. It goes without saying that if you own and live in a house with others, you'd better be personally compatible. Otherwise, no matter how nice the house, it won't be worth it.

Equity sharing tends to be most popular among unmarried heterosexual and gay and lesbian couples, although it's also reasonably common with friends and relatives not in sexual relationships. Although many equity-sharing couples live lives similar to married couples, their legal property ownership arrangements are bound to be different, since California's marital property laws do not affect them.

Regardless of whether the equity sharers are a couple or not, they should have a written contract. It should spell out the percentage of the house each person owns, who pays how much each month for the mortgage, taxes, insurance and other costs, what happens if the household breaks up or an owner dies, as well as a number of other practical ownership issues. We discuss a few of these issues in Chapter 20, Legal Ownership: How to Take Title, but to draw up an equity-sharing contract, you'll need additional information. (See Resources, below.)

Equity sharing also can make sense when an older relative lives with his family and wants to contribute to the down payment and mortgage payments. In some families, a parent or other relative would rather just give down payment money to the younger relative with whom he plans to live, reasoning that the younger person will inherit the property at his death anyway. We prefer equity sharing, unless the older person is wealthy enough to remain financially independent after giving the house purchase money. (Chapter 4, Section F, discusses financial gifts from relatives.) The reason should be immediately familiar to anyone who has read Shakespeare's *King Lear*. Once an older person gives up all material possessions, she tends to lose her independence and the right to be taken seriously.

As mentioned, equity sharing makes sense for many people other than unmarried couples and extended families. Often, the only way to afford a house is to pool resources and buy a large house (or duplex or triplex). But if you'll want to build walls, doors or install a second kitchen or bathroom, make sure you add these costs in to the price of the house when figuring whether equity sharing is cost-effective.

> **EXAMPLE:** Martha and Robert, married with two children, want to buy a house. So does their good friend Sally, who is single. Neither Sally nor Martha and Robert have saved enough money to swing a purchase on their own. Fortunately, they find a large two-story house with separate flats, one with three bedrooms and the other with two. They conclude that the $350,000 price is at least $100,000 less than the cost of two separate houses with the same space and amenities, so they buy together. Martha and Robert contribute 62% of the down payment and occupy the three-bedroom flat, and Sally puts up 38% for the two-bedroom flat. The mortgage, tax and insurance payments are paid in the same portions. They write a home ownership contract detailing their rights and responsibilities.

RESOURCES FOR WRITING SHARED EQUITY CONTRACTS
Nolo Press publishes or sells the following books to help equity sharers cope with owning property together:

The Living Together Kit, by Ihara and Warner, contains several sample house purchasing contracts for unmarried couples.

A Legal Guide for Lesbian and Gay Couples, by Curry, Clifford and Leonard, contains sample contracts similar to those in *The Living Together Kit,* but adapted to address the special concerns of lesbian and gay couples and groups buying together.

The Deeds Book, by Mary Randolph, discusses the different ways of taking title to and transferring real property in California.

11. Buy a "Shared Equity" House With Only One Owner (You) Living on the Property

Equity sharing between a resident owner and an investor is often touted as a good solution for people with affordability problems. The idea is for a non-resident investor to put up a chunk of the down payment in exchange for a share of profits when the house is sold.

Before the 1986 Tax Reform Act limited the number of housing units on which a person may deduct interest and tax payments, many parents equity shared with their kids—the parents got a tax shelter and the child got a place to live which, hopefully, would go up in value. Today, strict rules limiting the deductibility of interest on more than one house, equity-sharing arrangements like this normally make little sense from a tax point of view. (The Tax Reform Act of 1986 limits mortgage interest deductibility to two personal residences, each costing $1,000,000 or less.)

Equity sharing can make some sense tax-wise, however, if you are the resident owner and pay most or all of the monthly mortgage payments. You can then deduct the mortgage interest because the house is your personal residence. The non-occupant equity sharer could pay most or all of the property taxes, which should be deductible for him whether or not he lives on the property. However, because the IRS requires that the non-resident investor receive fair market rent (which is taxable income) from the resident owner based on the amount invested, a portion of the tax benefits will be canceled out.

Even given the benefits of this kind of tax strategy, on balance, equity sharing is not a good way for one person to help

another buy a house. From the house purchaser's point of view, it's usually better to simply borrow the money and own the entire property. Similarly, equity sharing is often a poor idea for the investor. When a house is viewed as an investment by a lender and as a home by its occupant, the potential conflicts are huge. What if the resident wants to make improvements that will enhance the house's livability but which won't increase its market value? What if the non-resident wants his money back, but the resident doesn't want to sell and can't afford to pay the non-resident his share? Or, even more serious from the investor's point of view, what if the resident owner ceases making payments and refuses to vacate the house? Yes, a written contract can and should deal with these and many other similar questions, but, contract or not, the possibilities for future conflict are considerable.

If, despite these warnings, you want to pursue equity sharing with a non-resident because you've no other way to raise enough money for a down payment, it may make the most sense to buy with someone who is not a relative or friend, so as to establish that it's clearly a business deal. A good real estate agent should be familiar with programs in your area that bring buyers and investors together. Typically, the investor supplies all or most of the down payment while the buyer lives in the house, maintains it and pays all or most of the mortgage, insurance and tax payments. At an agreed-upon date, the home buyer refinances and pays the investor the down payment plus a specified share of the appreciation. A clear, written agreement is necessary to cover the following:

- the use of the home
- the amount of the initial investment and the percentage of ownership
- buy-out provisions
- the amount and type of insurance to carry and allocation of the proceeds should the house be damaged or destroyed (for example, if a fire destroys the home)
- the responsibility for daily costs and capital improvements, and
- the details of any sale or refinance (such as time, price and profit splits).

TAKE TAX RULES SERIOUSLY
It's crucial that the buyer and investor clearly understand tax laws regarding shared equity arrangements. Consult your tax attorney or accountant for advice on your particular situation.

RESOURCES ON EQUITY SHARING

The Complete Guide to Equity Sharing, by Marilyn Sullivan (Venture 2000 Publishers) contains sample contracts, useful tax information and tips on how to make an equity sharing transaction work, for both the investor and the resident owner.

Another good book on equity sharing is *The Equity Sharing Book*, by Bull and St. James (Penguin).

12. Rent Out Part of the House

For some prospective purchasers, the down payment presents less of a problem than do the monthly payments. Take, for example, a single parent with a $48,000 gross annual income and few other debts, who would typically qualify for a house in the $170,000 range, figuring 10% down and a mortgage for the rest, charging interest at a 6% rate. (See Chapter 2, How Much House Can You Afford?) This is enough to buy a decent house in Chico, Ukiah or Merced. Unfortunately, however, in California's coastal urban areas, few good houses suitable for a moderate-sized family are realistically available in this price range.

As it turns out, the lowest priced decent house this single parent can find costs $200,000. She wouldn't qualify for the mortgage even if she was able to put 10% down because her monthly debt-to-income ratio would be above the 28%-38% normally allowed. So how does she increase her income enough to bring her debt-to-income ratio down? One slightly old-fashioned way is to take in a boarder, at least until her income rises enough so that it's no longer necessary. Renting out a room or two should bring in $800 per month or more in many urban areas. That would add $9,600 a year to the $48,000, enough to allow her to afford a house selling for up to $200,000. Renting also offers tax advantages. A homeowner can deduct only property taxes and mortgage interest on her income taxes, while a rental owner can also deduct business expenses, such as repairs and utilities, and take depreciation on the portion of the home that is rented out.

And having a stranger live in your home is not necessarily inconvenient or dangerous. In urban areas with tight rental housing, you've a large pool of potential renters to choose from. A thorough search and careful check of business and personal references, as well as previous landlords, should allow you to find a person with whom you feel compatible. In fact, for many single parents and people who live alone, having someone else in the house can be a safety factor.

If you're seriously considering renting out a room or two as part of your house-financing strategy, you'll need to do some homework. Start by finding out how much rent you can reasonably charge—that is, what local tenants pay for similar space. Rent control ordinances in several California cities limit what landlords can charge for residential property. Renting out one or two rooms in an owner-occupied house, however, is exempt from rent control ordinances, which means you can legally charge whatever you wish. Then check with your financial institution or loan broker to be sure they'll let you count the expected rent as part of your monthly income.

As soon as your offer on a house is accepted, get to work finding a tenant. By starting early, the tenant should be ready to move in when you do, or soon after, thus maximizing your income at a critical time. But because your deal to buy the house could fall through, make any written lease or month-to-month agreement with the prospective tenant contingent upon your actually buying. This way, you'll have no liability to the prospective tenant if you don't get the house.

13. Buy a Duplex, Triplex or House With an In-Law Unit

In the past, families lacking enough income to make monthly payments, or who were trying to sock away money to buy a better house, often bought a duplex or triplex. They lived in one unit and rented out the others, using the rental income to help with the monthly payments. A variant of this approach was to buy a large house with a separate smaller "in-law" unit.

Both of these strategies can still be implemented, but it is not as easy as it once was to use them to significantly close the affordability gap. There's considerable competition for these types of houses, which means prices are often marked up to the point that rental income is entirely eaten up by the extra monthly costs of the larger mortgage.

Still, it may be possible to buy a reasonably-priced house with a second unit. Your goal is to find a house selling for little more than if the second (or third) unit wasn't there. The more unconventional the second unit, the more likely you are to be able to accomplish this. For example, if an "in-law" unit is tucked under a hillside house with access down a driveway and around two trees and a rose bush (as opposed to being attached to your unit, with a door facing the street), the real estate market may undervalue it. If you're near a university or other source of reasonably adventurous tenants, buying this sort of multiple-unit dwelling may be an excellent way to at least partially close your affordability gap.

EXAMPLE: Andrea found a nice old house with a beautiful view and a private, spacious in-law unit. Because the house was somewhat rundown and had several structural problems, its price was very reasonable. Finding a distressed property with an in-law unit was a double bargain for Andrea, whose uncle was happy to lend her the money to fix the foundation. When the repairs were made, the house's value rose substantially above what Andrea paid. The monthly rent of the second unit paid off her uncle's loan in several years, and then Andrea was able to use it to prepay monthly mortgage payments.

MAKE SURE AN EXTRA UNIT IS LEGAL

In some California municipalities, homeowners have been able to convert garages and other spaces into second or third living spaces without ever getting a building permit. The danger, of course, is that a neighbor's complaint or some other event will trigger the city or county to order the unit closed because it doesn't conform to building codes. So, especially if an extra living space looks homemade, demand to see necessary permits. If they don't exist, don't pay any more for the property than you would if the extra unit didn't exist.

DEBORAH, DOUG AND ROSE: THE JOY OF LIVING NEAR GRANDMA

Deborah and Doug have a two-year-old daughter. Both artists, they wanted at least 1,500 square feet to accommodate their family and need for studio space. Here's how they bridged their affordability gap:

"We were determined to stay in our long-time neighborhood, but unfortunately, we couldn't afford even the low-end condos sprouting up. Then we heard about a place right around the corner which sounded great—except that it was more expensive and larger than we needed.

"Deborah's mother Rose provided an unexpected solution. She offered to help us with the down payment and monthly mortgage payments in exchange for living in one of the units. We quickly struck a 2/3–1/3 financial split. Our family took the 3-bedroom unit on the top floor, converted the bottom floor unit into a home for Rose, and the middle unit into a fantastic studio space. We now have our ideal house at a price we can afford while still retaining our privacy. But the best part is the special relationship between our daughter and her grandma. We wouldn't miss it for the world."

AUTHOR IRA SERKES' PURCHASE OF A SMALL BERKELEY MULTI-UNIT BUILDING

When I first got interested in real estate, I couldn't afford a single family home. Instead, I looked for a small apartment building where I could live in one unit and have rental income from the others subsidize the mortgage. I originally looked at triplexes, but ended up buying a fixer-upper seven-plex. My family invested in order to help with the down payment and share the appreciation. For the next five years, I lived in one of the units. With the help of some tenants, I renovated each apartment as it became vacant. As the value of the building went up, I borrowed against it and used the money for a down payment on another small building. My successes inspired a friend of mine to begin investing with me. Now, I own a nice house and a number of investment properties.

14. Lease a House You Can't Afford Now With an Option to Buy Later

A lease option is a contract where an owner leases her house (usually from one to five years) to a tenant for a specific monthly rent (which may be scheduled to increase during the contract term) and gives the tenant the right to buy the house for a price established in advance. The tenant pays some money for the option—a lump sum payment at the start of the contract or periodic payments. Depending on the contract, the potential buyer normally can exercise the option to purchase at any time during the lease period, or at a date specified.

EXAMPLE: Ted and Jane lease Robin's house for $1,700 per month for two years. In addition, they pay Robin $4,000 for the option to purchase the house for $280,000 at any time during the two years. If Ted and Jane decide to buy, the $4,000 will be credited against the purchase price; if not, Robin keeps it.

This example is deliberately made simple to give you the general idea. Most lease option deals are more complicated. For example, the house purchase price might be a fixed dollar amount, plus an amount tied to any increase in the Consumer Price Index. Or, instead of an up-front option fee, the rent might be set at a higher than normal amount, with part, or all, of the extra applied to the purchase price if the option to purchase is ever exercised.

LEASE OPTION CONTRACT (RENTER-BUYER'S PERSPECTIVE)

A lease option contract should address the following:

- When the option can be exercised. You want as long an option period as possible, and much flexibility about when you exercise it. Avoid lease-option contracts that only allow you to exercise your option under very restrictive circumstances—for example, for one week at the end of the second and fourth year.

- The purchase price if you exercise the option. It's far better to have it fixed at the start of the lease period, even if an increase for inflation is built in, not set by an appraisal at the time you exercise the option to purchase.

- How much of the rent or up-front option payment will be applied toward the down payment or purchase price if the option is exercised.

 BUYERS WANT ALL EXTRA PAYMENTS CREDITED TOWARDS THE PURCHASE PRICE

A prospective purchaser who pays a flat fee in exchange for a option to purchase, or agrees to a higher monthly rent to achieve this benefit, only makes a good deal if all money over and above a reasonable rent will be credited towards the purchase price if the option is exercised.

- Exactly how you can exercise the option. Written notice sent by certified mail is a good approach.

- If the seller will help you finance the house by taking back a second mortgage, and if so, the details.

- An inspection of the house. It is best to have the house thoroughly inspected before the lease option is signed to determine what repairs are needed, and, of course, the seller should pay for a portion of any needed work if the option is exercised.

- Assignability. If you choose not to exercise your option, you want to be able to sell that right to someone else, if possible, for cash or a share of the house's equity.

- Any other significant terms of a purchase.

⚠ BEWARE OF TERMINATION CLAUSES

Avoid any clause in a lease-option contract that ends your option if you fail to perform your duties under the rental agreement in a timely manner. Such a clause could let the owner end the option contract if you're late with the rent, even once. Instead, you want a clause that lets you exercise the option to buy if your rent is paid up at the time you choose to exercise the option.

In addition, make sure lease purchase contract is notarized and recorded at the County Recorder's Office. This will insure that your right to purchase will appear on any title search, meaning the owner can't duplicitly sell the house out from under you without your knowledge.

Finally, unless you're experienced in this field, have the contract checked by someone who is. For sample lease option contracts, see Resources, below.

FLOATING HEARTH

A lease option is often a good arrangement for a potential buyer because it lets him move into a house he may buy, without having to come up with a down payment or financing. Even better, it allows him the luxury of waiting to see if the value of the house reaches or surpasses the amount of the option price, before deciding whether to purchase. If the value does increase, the house will be easier to finance, as the buyer will already have equity (the difference between the sales price and the then current market value). If the market value rises significantly, this equity may even cover the down payment. If a portion of the rent is applied toward the down payment, it would become a credit in escrow from the seller to the buyer and could be transferred to the lender as part of the buyer's down payment.

> **EXAMPLE:** Continuing the above example, assume the $280,000 house rises in value to $315,000 in three years, at which point Ted and Jane exercise their option to buy. A lender, seeing that they will have an immediate equity of $39,000 (the $35,000 increase in value plus the $4,000 option fee credited to the purchase), agrees to lend the entire $280,000, meaning that the only cash Ted and Jane ever needed to come up with was the initial $4,000 option price.

Few sellers are willing to offer lease option deals on houses easy to sell. Why should they share their chance at future appreciation with a buyer? Exceptions exist, however, and lease options can often fairly easily be arranged when houses are hard to sell. Here's what to look for:

- An owner having trouble selling her house at the asking price. Instead of reducing the price, she may be willing to lease, giving you an option to purchase at the asking price. The owners hope a little patience will pay off.
- An owner who needs to move now, but who, for tax reasons, doesn't want the profit on the sale to be taxed in the current fiscal year. Often owners about to retire and enter a lower tax bracket fit this description.
- An owner for whom the initial option fee and/or higher-than-normal rent means an excellent short-run return.
- An owner who hopes you won't exercise the option, giving the owner a premium rent (or up-front option fee payment), while keeping the house.
- An owner who thinks you will take better care of the house, and perhaps even improve it, if you think you may buy it.

If you find a good house that hasn't sold for an extended period of time, the seller is probably frustrated—and being pressured to lower the price. If she can survive without immediately selling, don't be shy about proposing a lease option. If you offer an option price near the asking price, and a reasonably generous rent (or one-time option payment), the seller may jump at your offer and allow you to credit a portion of the rent or an up-front option payment against the sales price if you later buy.

RESOURCES ON LEASE-OPTIONS

How Home Buyers, Sellers, Realty Agents and Investors Can Profit from Lease-Options, by Robert Bruss. Available for $4.00 from Tribune Publishing Company, 64 E. Concord Street, Orlando, Fla. 32801.

How to Sell Your House in a Buyer's Market, by Shenkman and Boroson (John Wiley & Sons). Contains an excellent chapter on lease options, including a sample lease option agreement.

For Sale by Owner, by George Devine (Nolo Press). Includes a sample lease-option contract.

15. Buy a Condominium

A condominium (condo) owner owns her unit outright plus an undivided share of common areas (halls, parking areas, roof, plumbing, yard, deck and the like). To maintain these areas, owners usually pay fees to a condominium association, in addition to local property taxes assessed on each unit. Condos include a number of restrictions on how the property can be used, such as the type of landscaping you can do or the number or weight of pets you can own. These restrictions are spelled out in a document called the covenants, conditions and restrictions (CC&Rs).

Condos come in all shapes and sizes, from duplexes to high-rises, and there can be good reasons for buying one. For example, if you've fallen in love with a particular condo and plan to live there a long time—plus it's a bargain—by all means pursue it further. Particularly if you're considering buying in a city or other area where there's limited land on which to build, a condo may be a very good choice. In these situations, you can follow the general principles of buying a house throughout this book. For specific information on condos and CC&Rs, see Chapter 7.

In the rest of this section, we primarily address people who have the common fantasy of buying a relatively inexpensive condo with little or no money down, holding on to it for a few years, selling it at a good profit and using the profit for a down payment on a house. Normally, we don't think this will work. True, many California condos are priced temptingly low when compared to houses. Unfortunately, these prices will probably still be low when you want to sell, thus defeating your strategy of using your condo to build equity.

Most condos—outside of those located in cities or areas with strict limitations on new building—don't usually appreciate in value as fast as many single family houses do. This is because when condos become in short supply in an area, and prices start to appreciate, developers quickly build more, skimming off profits for themselves. The condo oversupply cycle then begins again. By contrast, houses can't be built quickly (if at all) in most parts of California, since very little vacant land remains. As a result, single family homes are much less likely to see their value eroded by an oversupply of new construction.

If you're strapped for down payment money, and are considering a condo, think about buying a town house instead. (See Section C16, immediately below.) On the whole, we believe they make better low-cost starter houses.

16. Buy a Town House

Town houses—usually single family houses with common walls—have surged in popularity in California because they're relatively inexpensive. And well they should be; they save on land because common walls and roofs are cheap to build. With most town houses, you hold legal title to your house and the land it's on. You must pay real estate taxes even though you and your neighbors sit on the same piece of land and share common walls.

Before you get too excited about buying a town house, be aware that townhouses are simply a modern invention for an old concept—the row or attached houses common in some eastern cities at the beginning of the 20th century. The California version, usually built on greenfield sites, is usually an improvement, since architects and builders have learned a few things since the earlier generation of cramped, noisy, dark row houses. Today, many town houses are decent-sized, airy and, thanks to improvements in sound-containing material, reasonably quiet. Even so, sharing roofs and walls with neighbors is rarely conducive to the sort of privacy available with a single family house.

Town houses may be a better investment than condos. One reason for this is that most town houses, unlike most condos, are two-story, which means they physically look somewhat like single family houses; condos, which often contain many units, physically look more like apartment units. Because many people prefer the size and scale of a house (regardless of form of ownership), town houses are a bit more likely than condos to increase in value.

Does this mean that town houses are as a good an investment as small detached starter houses are? On the whole, with exceptions for particularly desirable projects, usually not. Most people prefer living in a house that doesn't share walls with its neighbor. In addition, in areas with undeveloped land, developers are almost sure to overbuild town houses, making short-term price appreciation unlikely. Still, if you can't afford a nice starter house in a decent area, an affordable town house may be a better choice than buying a run-down, detached house in a marginal neighborhood.

Chapter 7 discusses issues relevant to people in the market for a newly-built town house.

HANDMADE HOUSE

17. Buy a Limited Equity House

In many parts of California, limited equity housing is becoming popular. It allows a purchaser to buy a house (often an attached townhouse) at an extremely favorable price with a low down payment. Often, a certain percentage of units are reserved for low and moderate income families on even more favorable terms. Unfortunately, there's a catch. When an owner sells, she gets her down payment back with interest, and little more. If the market value of the unit has gone up, she gets none of this profit. This lets the unit be resold at a very affordable price.

To increase the supply of affordable owner-occupied housing in high cost areas, limited equity housing is a wonderful device. And if your primary goal is to find a decent place to live with a comparatively low upfront and monthly payment, it may be a good choice. But if your goal is to build equity to afford a nicer house later—or to help finance your retirement—look elsewhere.

Limited equity housing is usually built by nonprofit organizations, often with city or county help. To learn if any such projects are in your area, contact city or county building departments.

18. Buy a House at an Auction

In some parts of California where the real estate market has been particularly slow, sellers try to attract buyer interest by auctioning houses. Many auctions are of new houses in situations where developers need to raise quick cash to pay lenders. Foreclosed properties are also sometimes sold at auction. (See Section C8, above.) Which leads naturally to the question, is buying a house at auction a good way to get a bargain?

As a general rule, no. Most people who bid at auctions have little or no experience buying property that way. It should go almost without saying that amateurs (home buyers) rarely beat pros (homesellers familiar with auction procedures and investors who regularly buy at auctions) at their own game. This is especially true when you understand that the seller will take steps to be sure that the house won't sell at a rock bottom price, including:

- setting a floor price—a price below which the house won't be sold
- advertising extensively—to be sure to collect a crowd

- hiring a professional auctioneer skilled at loosening up the crowd and building auction fever, and
- although it's illegal, sometimes planting shills in the audience to bid up the price.

If auctions are held in your area, a better strategy than actually bidding at the auction is to compare the prices for houses sold at auction with those of houses sold in the normal way. (You may need to attend a few auctions to get this information.) Just learning which sellers are motivated to sell is extremely valuable. And if you like what you see at the auction, and the seller has other houses to sell (which is common with developers), stop by on a weekday near the end of the month and offer to buy for slightly less than the auction price. Or, make a list of sellers with similar properties not being auctioned and offer to buy for a little less than the auction price. Auctions for a number of houses can cost up to $200,000 to promote and run; developers who don't sell this way may actually be willing to undercut the auction price.

We don't mean to say it's impossible to get a good deal at an auction—only that your chances of using the other techniques in this chapter to negotiate a good purchase are likely to achieve a better result. If, however, despite this advice you decide to bid at auction, follow these basic rules:

- Research how much comparable houses are selling for in the same area—if you don't know the local market well, you're almost sure to get taken. (See Chapter 15 for how to find out comparable sales prices.)
- Attend several auctions without your checkbook (or paying a bidding fee) to get the hang of how they work.
- Research deposit requirements and financing options before you commit yourself to buying property at an auction.
- Check local newspapers for upcoming auctions and ask for brochures that describe the property. Be sure to read all the fine print.
- Check out the house's physical condition before buying. Real estate auction companies must disclose known structural problems and defects of property (excluding foreclosures). See Chapter 19 for details on state disclosure law and inspections.
- Be sure you're taking clear title to the property. (See Chapter 18 for details.)
- Don't pay more than 10% above the minimum or "floor price" or 70%-75% of the original asking price.
- Get help researching.

- Decide in advance how much you'll pay and don't bid a penny more.
- If there is lots of bidding on a particular house, drop out fast—if you get into a bidding war, you'll surely pay too much.

 ANNE AND FRANK: WE BOUGHT A GREAT HOUSE AT AN AUCTION

We bought a nice house 13 years ago for $200,000. In 1994, we sold it for $450,000. Because we both have fairly good jobs, we had the down payment and the income necessary to move up.

We wanted to live in Marin County and heard that some new luxury houses which had originally been listed at $900,000 had proved unsaleable and were being auctioned with a floor bid requirement of $625,000. We were there for first sale, but didn't bid. The house went for $710,000, which we figured was too high. On the second and third house to be auctioned, we noticed that one person (let's call him Ollie) who bid at the first sale was bidding again, but each time dropped out at the last minute.

We smelled a rat (a shill), but didn't say anything. We wanted the fourth house and bid several times until the price was $650,000. Then, when Ollie bid higher we objected and said we were going to call the District Attorney's Consumer Fraud Unit and the State Real Estate Department and file a complaint. Ollie immediately disappeared and we got a great house at a good price. ∎

Raising Money for Your Down Payment

et's start with the basics. Down payments are always discussed as a percentage of a house's purchase price, not a specific dollar figure. A 20% down payment is 20% of the price you pay for the house, such as $60,000 on a $300,000 house. In addition, lenders often use the real estate industry jargon "loan-to-value ratio" (LTV) in referring to the down payment required. A mortgage with an LTV of 90% requires only 10% down, an LTV of 80% requires 20% down, and so on.

The down payment amount depends on the interplay of many factors, including:

- your savings from all sources
- your monthly income
- the house's purchase price
- the type of mortgage you choose
- your credit history, and
- the size of the mortgage.

We discuss all of these below. For now, the only generalization we can make is that most buyers put down between 10%-25%, unless they qualify for one of the low down payment plans discussed in Sections A and B.

➡️ If you're relatively affluent and will put 25% or more down, you can skip most of this chapter, except for Section D on the pros and cons of making a big down payment.

Most home buyers don't have large cash reserves and will want to make as low a down payment as possible. It's often possible to buy a house—especially a starter house—for a modest down payment.

For houses costing $350,000 and up, most buyers will need to come up with a down payment of 20% or more because on high-priced houses, a chunky down payment is normally needed to reduce the total borrowed to a level lenders will approve. As discussed in Chapter 2, Section A, lenders usually prohibit a homeowner from spending more than 28%-38% of her monthly income on monthly carrying costs. (Carrying costs are the monthly payment for principal, mortgage interest, and taxes and insurance.)

EXAMPLE 1: Brian and Ed want to buy a two-year old townhouse for $160,000. Their combined annual income is $64,000, and they've saved up $23,000. They hope to make a 10% down payment, use $5,000 for closing costs, and get a fixed rate mortgage at 8.25%. If they borrow $144,000 from a lender, their mortgage payments will be $1,082 per month, plus monthly expenses of $160 for taxes, $50 for insurance and $48 for private mortgage insurance. The total carrying costs will be $1,340, or 25% of their income. Brian and Ed should have no problem qualifying for a loan.

EXAMPLE 2: Robert and Katherine, who earn about $114,000 per year, want to buy a $300,000 house making a down payment of 10%. Their monthly mortgage payments would be about $2,172, assuming a 9% fixed rate mortgage on a $270,000 loan. Their monthly expenses would include $312 for taxes, $79 for insurance and $117 for private mortgage insurance, bringing their monthly carrying costs to $2,681. If Robert and Katherine have no other long-term debts, they'd need a monthly income close to $8,500-$9,000 to qualify (based on a 28% debt-to-income ratio). Because their combined monthly income is $9,500, they're in good shape.

EXAMPLE 3: Maeve and Johnny, who earn $100,000 a year, want to buy a $450,000 house, putting 10% down. Lenders will likely turn them down because they would have to use 35% of their monthly income to make their monthly carrying costs. Maeve and Johnny are told that to get a loan approval, they'll need to lower the size of the mortgage by increasing the down payment. Fortunately, they are able to do this through a $45,000 gift from Maeve's mother, raising their down payment to 20%, and reducing their mortgage to $360,000, with $2,732 in carrying costs. The higher down payment lets them spend 33% of their monthly income on carrying costs, and they now qualify for a mortgage loan.

A. Low Down Payment Plans Offered by Government Agencies

The Federal Housing Administration, U.S. Department of Veterans Affairs, California Housing Finance Agency, Cal-Vet program, and a few California municipalities offer either no down payment or low down payment mortgage plans. Because of rules limiting the maximum house price and loan amount, however, these plans are available for only moderately-priced housing. Down payment and eligibility rules for these programs are discussed in Chapter 11, Government-Assisted Loans.

B. Five Percent and Ten Percent Down Payment Mortgages

Many lenders offer mortgages to people who put 10% down, assuming the buyer has enough income to make the monthly payments within lender debt-to-income guidelines. Be aware that it is difficult to get a 10% down loan over $350,000.

If you're really strapped for cash, ask your lender about 5% down payment plans such as FannieNeighbors and the Community Home Buyer's Program. Many California lenders offer these Fannie Mae mortgage plans which feature a 5% down payment (even 3% in some cases) and flexible qualifying guidelines. The maximum loan amount for a 3% or 5% down loan is $207,000 with a 15-, 20- or 30-year fixed rate mortgage. FannieNeighbors is available to buyers of all incomes who purchase a home within designated central cities or eligible census tracts. The Community Home Buyer's Program is available for loans outside of these designated areas, for home buyers whose income is 120% or less of the area median income.

If you take out a very low down payment loan, be ready to pay a slightly higher rate of interest and loan fee (points), and to show that you have an excellent credit history. In addition, be prepared to purchase private mortgage insurance (PMI), discussed below. With most 10% down loans, you will have to buy PMI, but you will probably find loans with interest and points competitive with 20% down loans. Most lenders and mortgage brokers advise buyers to scrimp and save to come up with 10% for the down, rather than put down 5% and pay a bundle more (in interest) for the next 15, 20 or 30 years.

C. Private Mortgage Insurance

Private mortgage insurance (PMI) policies are designed to reimburse a mortgage lender up to a certain amount if you default on your loan and the foreclosure sale price is less than the amount you owe the lender (the mortgage and the costs of sale).

Today, virtually all California lenders require PMI on loans where the borrower makes a down payment of less than 20%. Lenders that don't require PMI often compensate by charging a higher rate of interest. PMI typically protects lenders for 20%-25% of the purchase price of the house, usually more than enough to make good any loss resulting from foreclosure and resale.

EXAMPLE: Ron purchases a house for $175,000, with a down payment of 15% and a loan for the remaining 85% from the XYZ Mortgage Company. In exchange for lending 85%, XYZ requires Ron to buy PMI from Racafrax Insurance that will pay XYZ for any loss if Ron defaults. Ron loses his job and can't make his payments. XYZ forecloses and the house is resold for $150,000, with Racafrax Insurance making up what Ron failed to pay on the mortgage, the loss suffered by XYZ on the resale, as well as costs of sale. As an alternative, Racafrax could pay off the entire loan to XYZ Mortgage, and thus own the house. They'd later resell it and hope to get a better price than the foreclosure brought.

So how much will PMI cost you? It depends. While, fortunately, many lenders allow all but the first few PMI premiums to be paid monthly, there can be quite a difference in the amount of PMI you must pay up front.

Traditionally, PMI policies have been higher the first year (initial policy) and lower in subsequent years (renewal policy). Under this model, the first year's PMI premium for a loan with 10% down will be about .5%-.65% of the loan. The cost will be

VICTORIAN

about .3%-.55% of the loan for the renewal policy. With this type of PMI policy, buyers must come up with a rather large amount of cash at the close of escrow—typically, one year (the initial policy amount), plus two months' payment for the renewal policy.

> **EXAMPLE 1:** An initial policy of .65% on a $200,000 loan is $1,300. Two months of the renewal policy (assuming a .4% renewal policy) adds another $134, for a total of $1,434 a buyer must pay up front for private mortgage insurance.

To make PMI more palatable, many mortgage insurance companies offer an even monthly option, with no difference between the initial PMI and renewal rates—for example, a uniform rate of .48%. This allows for a slightly lower cost at the close of escrow, but is still quite high.

> **EXAMPLE 2:** A monthly payment plan option for PMI on a $200,000 loan requires a buyer to pay .48% of 14 months of the loan, or $1,120 at the close of escrow.

Recently, many mortgage insurance companies have offered a third option, modeled after the even monthly payment plan, but with no upfront deposit of the first year's premium. In this case, the buyer pays only the first two months' payments to close escrow. These policies are usually pegged at .52% of the loan amount.

> **EXAMPLE 3:** A buyer pays two months' PMI payment at the close of escrow, or $174 (two months at .52% of $200,00).

While this third option is somewhat more expensive in the long run, many buyers prefer it because of the savings in closing costs. It's over $1,200 less than the traditional PMI policy (different rates for the initial and subsequent renewal policies), and $946 less than the even monthly option.

Except for California Housing Finance Agency loans (see Chapter 10, Section C), California law allows you to drop PMI once your loan is no more than 75% of either the original purchase price or the current fair market value of the house and you meet the following requirements (Civil Code §2954.7):

- the house was purchased after January 1, 1991
- you own and live in a one- to four-unit residential building

- you pay at least two years of PMI premiums
- you are up-to-date on mortgage payments
- you have not been more than 30-days overdue on any mortgage payment during the previous two years, and
- you make a written request to the lender based on an appraisal you paid for.

Similarly, if your loan is sold to Fannie Mae or Freddie Mac (see Chapter 8, Section C), your lender must agree to drop PMI once your equity reaches 20% and you've made timely payments for at least 12 months.

Some PMI policies are better consumer deals than others. Here's what to look for:

Premium rates. Some lenders charge higher PMI premiums than others. Although you can't choose your own PMI company, you can choose your lender and, if all else is equal, borrow from a lender offering PMI with lower rates.

Impound account. PMI policies also require that you set up an impound account, where you pay each month to the lender (or organization that services the loan), which in turn pays your property taxes and homeowner's insurance. These impound accounts result in your paying for taxes and insurance before you need to, thus losing the interest you'd earn if you kept that money in the bank. Even worse, lenders require that you make up to a years' payments of PMI into the impound account when the house purchase closes, thus increasing your up-front costs. And you still pay an amount monthly. If you're required to set up an impound account, monitor it carefully. Recently, many borrowers have faced significant hassles because the lender forgot to pay the taxes and insurance, with the buyers unfairly receiving a negative credit rating as a result. This should change in the future, however, at least regarding property taxes. New federal regulations require lenders to analyze impound accounts once a year to make sure enough (but not too much) money is in the account to cover your payment. If there's not enough, your monthly payment will increase to cover what's needed. If there's too much, you'll get a refund.

 AVOID IMPOUND ACCOUNTS FOR PROPERTY TAXES AND HOMEOWNER'S INSURANCE BY BORROWING 89.95% OF THE PURCHASE PRICE
Mortgage insurance companies typically require impound accounts for loans of 90% and over. If you can get your loan below 90%, you can save thousands of dollars in advance payment of property taxes and homeowner's insurance.

10% DOWN PAYMENT PLANS WITH NO PMI

To compete on the mortgage market, some lenders offer loans with 10% down payments and no PMI required. Most are fixed, not adjustable, rates, though it's possible to find an adjustable for 10% down and no PMI. These loans are self-insured by the lender who usually charges somewhat higher interest or more points to compensate for the absence of PMI. The good news is interest and points are tax-deductible while PMI premiums aren't. The bad news is that the interest rate on fixed rate mortgages is permanent, while PMI can be dropped eventually.

You should also check out 10% down equity loans (or lines) that don't require private mortgage insurance. A few lenders are offering equity loans for 90% financing without mortgage insurance. There are limitations for first-time buyers. The maximum loan is usually $25,000 (up to $50,000 in some circumstances), and you must have a good credit history. The monthly loan payment is usually 1% of the outstanding balance.

These equity loans are almost always adjustable rate mortgages and they usually have a much higher index than other loans. The margin can be higher and the upper cap can be 18% or more. (These ARM terms are defined in Chapter 10.) Even so, it's usually easier to qualify for a higher loan because there is no private mortgage insurance with 10% down equity loans.

EXAMPLE: Robert and Katherine, who earn about $114,000 per year, want to buy a $300,000 house making a down payment of 10%. With a 9% fixed rate mortgage, their monthly carrying costs (including private mortgage insurance) would be $2,681 and they'd need a monthly income of $8,500-$9,000 to qualify. (For details, see Example 2 at the beginning of this chapter.) With a 10% down equity loan at of 7.25% for the first six months (and 8.5% after that), Robert and Katherine would only pay $2,622 per month ($1,931 principal and interest, $312 taxes, $79 insurance and $300 for the 1% monthly loan payment). With the lower monthly payments of a 10% down equity loan, Robert and Katherine could qualify at a much lower monthly income—$7,200-$7,300 as opposed to $8,500-$9,000. Since this kind of equity loan is part of the purchase transaction, there are some income tax advantages. Also, after it is paid down, the equity line remains on title and the borrower is given a checkbook and credit card to access the funds, which may be used for any purpose. Under present law, this is totally deductible interest. One of the biggest negatives of 10% down equity loans is that the interest rate could conceivably skyrocket to the 18% maximum cap, but this seems somewhat unlikely for the foreseeable future, based on current market conditions of late 1996.

PMI is only one factor to consider in looking for the best mortgage. Prefer a PMI-required loan only if the non-PMI loan comes with a substantially higher rate of interest, more points, negative amortization and uncompetitive loan caps. Negative amortization and loan caps are features of adjustable rate mortgages and are discussed in Chapter 10.

D. How Much Should Your Down Payment Be?

Some buyers, especially those selling an existing house at a good profit, or those who've received a substantial gift or inheritance, have enough money to make a higher than required down payment. Should they? It's impossible to generalize. The best we can do is give you the pros and cons of putting substantial equity into your house and let you decide.

1. Arguments Supporting a Large Down Payment

Consider the following seven factors in support of making a large down payment:

- The larger your down payment, the lower your monthly payments. It feels good to have adequate money each month for other expenditures, while knowing you own a good chunk of your house.

  EXAMPLE: Pedro and Janice, who earn nearly $70,000, plan to start a family. They have several long-term debts and can qualify for monthly house payments of $1,825 (33% of their monthly income). They've saved substantially toward a down payment and first consider putting 10% down and investing the rest in growth securities. But they're concerned about overextending themselves monthly, especially because Janice will reduce her work hours when the kids are born. They decide to make a large down payment, which will mean correspondingly lower monthly payments while the kids are small.

- The larger your down payment, the less it will cost you to borrow. For example, if you put 20% down on a $300,000 house and borrow $240,000 at 10% for 30 years, you'll pay $758,222 in interest over the life of the loan. If, however, you put 40% down and borrow $180,000, you'll pay $568,666 in interest. This is a big difference well worth considering.
- Lenders won't require private mortgage insurance (PMI) if you make a down payment of 20% or more.
- To get the lowest possible interest rate and the lowest number of points on the market, you often need to make a large down payment (and have excellent credit). While there is only a very small difference in the interest rate and

points you qualify for with a 20% down payment as opposed to a 30% or 40%, it's a factor.
- If your credit history is less than perfect, you're between jobs or retired, or you simply want to avoid much loan qualification red tape, a down payment of 25% or more somewhat reduces lender scrutiny, especially for large (jumbo) loans. With a large down payment, the lender knows you're unlikely to default, and even if you do, the house can almost surely be resold for enough to cover the mortgage. While a lender will still check your credit, he may be less aggressive about it and more flexible in applying qualification rules.
- A large down payment is like forced savings. Money tied up in a house can't be spent on frivolous things. But it may be available if you need it in an emergency by refinancing the house or taking a home equity loan.
- A large down payment and a short term mortgage means you are likely to own your house well before you retire (or even before your kids go off to college). Many people sensibly want to pay off their mortgage before they retire (when their income is likely to decrease) or have to pay college tuition.

2. Arguments Supporting a Small Down Payment

So much for the good reasons to invest heavily in your house. There are also reasons not to:

- By making a 10% or 15% down payment, you can buy a more expensive house than if you make a larger down payment (assuming you qualify for the monthly mortgage payments).
- You'll have more cash available for closing costs and loan fees, which can total 2%-5% of the house's cost, and for moving, redecorating and other "new house" expenses.
- The interest portion of your mortgage is tax deductible. Most people have few ways to shelter money from income tax. One method is to deduct the annual interest paid on mortgage loans up to $1,000,000 from your federal and California income tax returns.

  But is this truly an advantage? Yes, if you owe other debts which are nondeductible and you use the money you free up by making a smaller down payment to repay those debts. Otherwise no. While it's nice to deduct the interest if you can afford to do so, it's better not to pay it in the first place. If you own a house free and clear and make no payment, and earn no deduction, you're better off than someone who pays $1,800 a month on mortgage interest and deducts over a third of it.

 KEN AND VICKIE:
LARGE OR SMALL DOWN PAYMENT?

We inherited $150,000 just as we were planning to sell our small two-bedroom house and buy a bigger one. We had about $75,000 worth of equity in the existing house and sold it ourselves, so there were no real estate commissions to pay. The house we chose cost $600,000. To bring our debt-to-income ratio down to the 33% a lender would approve, we needed to make a down payment of $140,000. The question became, "should we put down more?"

We increased our down payment to $200,000, or 33.3%. This left us $25,000 in savings. Several friends counseled us otherwise, saying that while our large down payment qualified us for a mortgage for a slightly better interest rate and fewer points, the difference was fairly small. They suggested that we instead make the minimum allowable down payment and invest our extra money in the stock market or other real estate. This made some sense, and we do plan to invest fairly aggressively in the future, but for now, we wanted to be sure that we had a secure roof over our heads. We're also pleased that we can afford our monthly house payments with no strain.

- You can invest the money you free up by making a small down payment. Whether you'll earn more doing this than it costs you to borrow the money with a large mortgage depends on your rate of investment return. If you make the minimum possible down payment and invest your extra money in a bank or money market account, chances are you will come up short. If you invest in other real estate, or stocks, or a business, however, you could come out ahead if you choose an investment that appreciates significantly. But remember that any investment with the potential to rack up major gains also has a chance of falling in a hurry, especially in times of recession or depression.
- You have money available for other needs. If you tie money up with a big down payment, you'll have to borrow it back on a home equity loan (at a higher interest rate than on a first mortgage) if you want to remodel the house, put your kids through college or whatever else.

And such a loan may be difficult or impossible to get if you become unemployed or ill. In addition, interest paid on a home equity loan is only deductible on your federal income tax for loans up to $100,000. If you need to borrow more, there is no deduction. By contrast, interest on a mortgage used to purchase property in the first place is deductible for loans up to one million dollars.

- If your home goes down in value, you'll limit your financial loss.
- If your house appreciates, you'll receive a higher return on your investment with a lower down payment. For example, if you put 20% down and took out a loan for the balance at 10% interest, if the house appreciated 8%, your return on your original investment would be 40%. If you put 10%, by contrast, your return on that same house would be 80%.

E. Using Equity in an Existing House as a Down Payment on a New One

Trading up is an integral part of the American dream of owning a nice house. You buy a starter house, wait for it to go up in value, and sell it, and use the profit as most or all of the down payment on a nicer house. If the California real estate market is strong in the next decade, it may take two or three sales to get your dream house.

Assuming a rising real estate market, trading up to raise down payment money works better than saving money, or making other investments, because purchasing a house is a highly leveraged transaction—the amount you invest is only a small part of the amount you borrow. In any leveraged transaction, you see big gains not only on your money, but also on money you've borrowed. For example, if you put $20,000 down on a $200,000 house (borrowing $180,000), and the house jumps to $300,000, you've made $100,000 with a $20,000 investment. By contrast, if you deposited the same $20,000 in an unleveraged investment, such as stock or art, and it goes up the same 50%, you'd end up with $30,000.

Leveraged investments also work in the reverse as some Californians who bought at the peak of the market in 1989-90 are learning today. If you put $30,000 down on a $300,000 house, a 10% decline in value wipes out your entire investment.

F.   Using a Gift to Help With the Down Payment

If you're fortunate enough to receive a gift of part or all of the money you need for a down payment, you're in great shape—you get the money and you don't have to pay it back. Your monthly payments will be lower and the amount of house you can afford will be higher than if you borrow for the down payment.

> **EXAMPLE:** Tom and Barbara earn $96,000 a year and have saved $60,000. They have no long-term debts and will qualify for a $350,000 house if they get an adjustable rate mortgage at 6%, use $50,000 to put almost 17% down and allocate $10,000 for closing costs and moving expenses. Then Barbara's aunt gives them another $25,000. They first think this will let them put 15% down on a $500,000 house, but soon realize that their $96,000 income doesn't qualify them for the payments on a $500,000 house, as their debt-to-income ratio would be considerably more than the normally allowed 28% for low down payment loans. But they do put the gift to good use. Because they can now afford a $75,000 down payment, they can probably qualify for a house up to about $400,000.

Receiving a substantial gift of money isn't a possibility for many people. Often, however, parents, grandparents and older friends will help when it comes to buying a house. This is true even if you're reluctant to ask. Unfortunately, some people attach emotional conditions to a gift, making it no gift at all. We can say little to help if you're faced with this situation.

If you stand to inherit substantial dollars in the future, you may be a good candidate for a gift now. If an older member of your family has an estate worth more than $600,000, the amount over $600,000 will be taxed heavily (beginning at 37%) when the owner dies unless it's left to a spouse or charity. For example, a $750,000 estate will net $55,500 ($150,000 x .37) for the government.

One way to lower this tax liability is to give away money or property before death, to the people who would inherit it. While large gifts are taxed by the government at substantially the same rate as estates, gifts up to $10,000 per year per person can be given gift tax free. This means, for example, that every year your mother and father can give you and your spouse $40,000 total without incurring taxes.

> **EXAMPLE:** David and Melanie want to buy a three-bedroom house in a moderately-priced suburb, but are shocked to learn it costs $500,000. Even though they earn $130,000 a year, they need help. Ben and Ellie, Melanie's parents, are financially comfortable and offer to lend them money for the down payment. But this doesn't help, as the monthly repayments to Ben and Ellie make David and Melanie's debt-to-income ratio over the level needed to qualify for a loan. Lenders normally want a buyer's carrying costs (mortgage principal and interest plus insurance and taxes) to be repaid with 28%-38% of the buyer's income.
>
> Ben and Ellie consult their tax accountant, who points out the following:
> - Their net worth is well over $600,000 and growing.
> - They each plan to leave their entire estate to the other, a tax-free transaction.
> - When both have died, a significant portion of their combined estate will go to Melanie.
> - If the survivor dies owning more than $600,000, the excess will be taxed as follows:

UNIFIED FEDERAL ESTATE TAX SCHEDULE

If the estate is in excess of:	But not in excess of:	Taxes are initially:	Plus the excess times:
600,000	750,000	155,800	37%
750,000	1,000,000	248,300	39%
1,000,000	1,250,000	345,800	41%
1,250,000	1,500,000	448,300	43%
1,500,000	2,000,000	555,800	45%
2,000,000	2,500,000	780,800	49%
2,500,000	3,000,000	1,025,800	53%
3,000,000	infinity	1,290,800	55%

> - Ben and Ellie can each give both Melanie and David a $10,000 gift ($40,000 total) tax-free each calendar year, reducing their estate by this much.
>
> Armed with this information, Ben and Ellie decide to each give both Melanie and David $10,000 each in two separate calendar years, for a total of $80,000. Melanie and David combine $70,000 of this money with a $50,000 profit they made selling their starter house, and make a down payment of $120,000. Now they need to borrow

only $380,000 on a fixed rate mortgage at 8%, for which they easily qualify, given their $130,000 income. They use the remaining $10,000 for closing costs.

RESOURCES ON GIVING GIFTS

For detailed information on giving gifts as part of your overall estate plan, see *Plan Your Estate*, by Denis Clifford and Cora Jordan (Nolo Press).

GET A GIFT LETTER

If you don't have all or a part of the gift money in your account before applying for a loan (perhaps because the giver wants to wait until the new tax year begins to give you the balance), be sure to get a gift letter. A sample gift letter is below. The letter should specify the amount of the gift and the type of property for which it will be used. Most importantly, the letter should say that the money need not be repaid. In addition, if money has not yet been transferred, be prepared to document that it's available by providing the name of the savings or securities institution where it's kept, the account number and a signed statement that the mortgage lender has authority to verify that this is true.

SAMPLE GIFT LETTER

To Whom It May Concern:

I/We _____ certify the following:
(names)

I/We have made a GIFT of _____
(amount)

to (recipient(s)) _____

my/our (relationship) _____

to be applied toward the purchase of the property, which is located at: _____

_____
(address)

I/We further certify that there is no repayment expected or implied in this gift, either in the form of cash or by future services, and as such no lien will be filed by me/us against the property.

The SOURCE of this GIFT is: _____

_____

_____
Signature of Donor(s)

_____
Print or type name of Donor(s)

_____
Address of Donor(s), Street, City and State

_____
Telephone Number of Donor(s)

ATTACHMENTS:

1. **Evidence of Donor(s) ability to provide funds**

2. **Evidence of receipt of funds by Borrower**

GREEK REVIVAL

G. Borrowing Down Payment Money From a Relative or Friend

Another way to raise money for a down payment is to borrow it—many people prefer to ask their loved ones for a loan rather than a gift. Unfortunately, borrowing money for a down payment isn't nearly as advantageous as getting a gift. You must repay borrowed money and the loan is simply added to your debt burden and included when the lender determines your debt-to-income ratio. The same holds true if you borrow from yourself by getting a cash advance with your credit card. (See Section L, below.)

But borrowing can help if:

- **You're short for the down payment, but have a relatively high monthly income.** If lenders conclude that you have enough income to pay a first mortgage and another loan, they'll typically let you borrow up to half of the down payment. Most lenders will usually require that at least 5% of the purchase price come from your own funds.

- **The person lending you money for the down payment will accept no, or very low, payments for several years.** If you don't need to make payments, your debt burden won't increase. Understanding this, a relative or friend may forgive payments for a few years. If these loan payments are eliminated or substantially reduced for three to eight years, the house will likely have risen in value; you can then refinance the mortgage and pay off the down payment loan. We discuss this strategy in Chapter 12, Private Mortgages. And make sure you explore company relocation programs if you're a new hire or are being relocated. Your employer may give you a low-interest loan (or gift) for your down payment as an incentive for you to move.

 BEFORE ARRANGING FOR A LOAN FOR THE DOWN PAYMENT, CHECK WITH YOUR LENDER OR LOAN BROKER (Loan brokers are discussed in Chapter 13.) There are many ways to structure down payment loans and you want to be sure that your plan will be approved by the lender. In general, the loan must be at least pegged at "market" interest for a minimum of five years.

H. Is It a Gift or Loan? Sometimes It Pays to Be Vague

Some people are tempted to ask for a loan from a friend or relative, but tell the lender it's a gift when applying for a mortgage. This scenario may be superficially attractive, but it's technically fraud. While it's unlikely you'd be prosecuted, it's nevertheless a poor idea to obtain a loan under false pretenses.

But fortunately, you can legally treat money as a gift, as far as a lender is concerned, while reserving the right to repay your benefactor if necessary. For example, if your parents advance you money, but worry that circumstances might cause them to need it later, your response might be that you'll do your best to help if they run into problems. As long as there's no written loan agreement, and your statement is one of intent (not a promise), the money qualifies as a gift.

Suppose that instead of a vague promise to repay your parents, you orally state you'll return the money when you can, but there's no written loan agreement, no requirement that the money be repaid by a certain date, nor any requirement that you pay interest. This, too, can reasonably be interpreted as a gift. If you do eventually give the money back, it too is a gift.

Common Sense Note: Don't ask a relative on a tight budget or who may be financially strapped in the near future to lend or give you money. You don't want to find yourself in a position in which the person who advanced you the money badly needs it back when you can't return it.

I. Borrowing From Your 401(k) Plan

An excellent source of down payment money is a loan against your 401(k) plan. Check with your employer whether your plan allows for loans. If it does, the maximum loan amount under the law is the lesser of one-half of your interest in the plan or $50,000. Other conditions—including maximum term, the minimum loan amount, the interest rate and applicable loan fees—are set by your employer. Be sure to find out what happens if you leave the company before fully repaying a loan from your 401(k) plan. If the loan would become due immediately upon your departure, income tax penalties may apply to the outstanding balance.

Borrowing against your 401(k) plan has several advantages:

- by borrowing against your own plan you are receiving the interest payments,
- the loan fees are usually lower than a bank, and
- there's less paperwork than is usually required in getting a bank loan.

J. Sharing Equity

One way to enlist the help of family or friends, or even an investor, is to give up a share of the ownership of your house in exchange for a cash contribution. We discuss this approach in Chapter 3, Sections D10 and D11.

K. Substituting a Second Mortgage for a Down Payment

As you should understand by now, a principal function of a down payment is to bridge the gap between what you can borrow and the purchase price of the house. If a lender will lend $250,000 on a $300,000 house, you can make up the balance with a down payment of $50,000. There are other ways as well. One is to get the seller or a private investor to take a second mortgage for some or all of the $50,000.

> **EXAMPLE:** Ralph wants to buy a house but has saved only $12,000 and has no friends or relatives to borrow from. He has an excellent salary with good prospects of earning more, so he looks for a seller who will accept a second mortgage instead of a cash down payment. Ralph finds Mimi, who is anxious to sell her $190,000 house. She still owes $160,000 on her adjustable rate mortgage which can be assumed by a qualified purchaser.
>
> Mimi offers Ralph a six-year second mortgage at 10% interest to cover the $30,000 difference between her $160,000 loan, which he'll assume, and the sale price. Because making payments on this second mortgage would increase Ralph's debt-to-income ratio to a level most lenders won't approve, Mimi agrees to a flexible payment schedule with no payments for three years, and interest only for the three following. At the end of six years, Ralph will owe Mimi the balance in the form of a large balloon payment. If the property has gone up in value, he can refinance the mortgage and pay Mimi her balance.
>
> The lender, who must approve Ralph assuming the mortgage, likes most of the deal. He demands, however, that Ralph put 10% (or $19,000) down; Mimi's second mortgage is reduced to $11,000. To comply, Ralph uses his savings and sells his new car, which fortunately was paid for.

In addition to reducing the down payment, a second mortgage may have other advantages:

> **EXAMPLE:** Ralph puts $19,000 (10%) down on Mimi's $190,000 house. He gets a second mortgage from Mimi for $19,000 (10%) and borrows the remaining $152,000 from a conventional lender. If he had borrowed 90% from the conventional lender, instead of 80%—the scenario, above, known as 80-10-10 financing—the lender would probably require private mortgage insurance (see Section C, above). With 80-10-10 financing, Ralph eliminates the costs of PMI.

You should also consider the downsides of second mortgages.

- Second mortgage interest rates are often higher than first mortgage interest rates.
- Most sellers want cash when they sell a house, not a note from the buyer, especially a note backed by a second mortgage, which is riskier than a first mortgage. Thus, it's not easy to locate a very desirable property that can be financed this way. In short, you face the danger of paying too much for a second-rate house in an effort to reduce your down payment.
- You must have a relatively high income to afford two mortgage payments (even if the second requires only low payments for a few years).
- A short-term second mortgage with low payments may have a lump sum (balloon payment) at the end. If the house is fairly priced, house prices increase and interest rates don't go through the roof, you shouldn't have trouble refinancing the first mortgage to pay the balloon payment. But if refinancing proves impossible, you'll need another way to raise the cash (or face foreclosure) unless your second mortgage lets you either gradually increase payments, or delay the payment date if you can't refinance when it first comes due.

For more on second mortgages and seller financing, see Chapter 12, Section C.

BALLOON PAYMENTS AND SECOND MORTGAGES

A balloon payment is the balance owed at the end of a loan term when the loan is not fully paid off. To help buyers qualify for loans, a loan may be amortized (calculated) as though the buyer had 30 years to pay it off, when in fact, the buyer may have only seven. The payments are kept artificially low, and at the end of the seven years, the buyer can pay off the balance in a balloon payment.

L. Getting a Cash Advance With Your Credit Card

If you have no other way of qualifying for a mortgage, consider getting a cash advance on a credit card and using the money to increase the size of your down payment. In theory, this shouldn't help, because the payments necessary to pay off the credit card advance will be counted as one more long-term debt by the mortgage lender. You can't get around this by borrowing a few thousand dollars at the last minute after the mortgage lender has checked your credit history. If you borrow on your credit card, you'll need to do so a few months before buying a house. This is because lenders typically require a two-to-three month history of savings to be used for a down payment on closing costs.

Obviously, borrowing on your credit card should be a last, not a first, resort, as interest rates are extremely high. ■

Working With Real Estate Professionals

This chapter focuses on the principal ways California home buyers can work with real estate agents and brokers to find a good house. In Section E, it also discusses the pros and cons of buying a house on your own. Assuming you decide you want some professional help, we recommend the following approach:

• Prepare a detailed list of your wants, including location, by completing a House Priorities Worksheet in Chapter 1.

• Understand how housing affordability is determined and decide how much you can afford to pay after reading Chapter 2.

• Estimate what it will cost to buy the type of house you want in the area you want by checking prices of recently sold comparable houses. The information in Chapter 15 will help you do this.

• Decide what legal relationship you want to establish with a real estate professional after reading Sections B, C and D of this chapter.

• Find a good real estate professional. We discuss how to do this in Section F.

A. Pros and Cons of Working With a Real Estate Professional

Before describing the different ways you can choose to work with a real estate professional, here are some of the pluses and minuses to consider.

1. Advantages of Working With a Real Estate Professional

Access to the market through the Realtors' Multiple Listing Service (MLS) Book, and allied computer services. The MLS book and computer services list most homes currently on the market. A salesperson who works under a broker who belongs to the local Board of Realtors (most do) will share this information with buyers. The salesperson can also share information from the Realtors' Comparable Sales Book (comp book), a price list of recently sold homes. Together, these lists provide a good overview of the housing market. A computer savvy salesperson can use the techniques discussed in Chapter 6, How to Find a House, to quickly identify new listings.

Access to a broker's in-house listings. A salesperson employed by a large or well-connected firm will have access to houses listed for sale with that firm before they appear in the MLS book, or are otherwise widely advertised.

Leg work. An energetic salesperson should do lots of house searching for you. This includes going to open houses held for real estate professionals (and closed to the public), as well as personally checking out all listed houses that seem to meet your criteria. If your salesperson thoroughly knows the market, will listen to and respect your requirements, and won't show you hopeless houses, this work can be quite valuable.

Business experience. An outstanding real estate salesperson will have successfully completed many transactions. His experience may be valuable in helping your house purchase run smoothly. As discussed below, however, be aware that the salesperson you work with only gets paid if a sale goes through, and this may bias his advice.

Knowledge of related professionals. A good salesperson will be one source of referrals to pest, asbestos and general contractor inspectors, title and escrow companies, loan brokers, lenders and government assistance programs that are best for you.

No cost to the buyer. Under the typical contractual arrangement, the seller pays the commission, and the services of the real estate salesperson are free to the buyer.

2. Disadvantages of Working With a Real Estate Professional

Most real estate professionals are conscientious, honest and understand that they'll do better in the long run through word of mouth of satisfied customers, not by making a quick profit selling you the wrong property at an inflated price. But real estate has its share of people who are incompetent or only care about their own self-interest. Because it's a relatively easy field to enter and one where minimally trained newcomers can have tremendous financial impact on buyers and sellers, it definitely makes sense to watch out for the bad apples.

Unfortunately, some other agents are lazy, working in the profession to "augment" their already very high family income. These agents are often late for meetings, take several days to return your phone calls and make you wonder why they're in the profession at all. You're better off finding someone else then using an agent who considers the biggest purchase in your life to be an afternoon hobby.

REAL ESTATE PEOPLE DEFINED

Before getting help from someone in the California real estate business, it helps to know who the players are.

Agent or Salesperson

She is one of the foot soldiers of the real estate business who shows houses, holds open houses and does most of the other nitty-gritty tasks inherent in selling real estate. An agent or salesperson (the terms are synonymous) must have a license from the state and must be supervised by a licensed real estate broker. Most are completely dependent on commission income; they receive no other compensation from the broker they work for.

Broker

He may legally represent either the seller or buyer in the sale or purchase of real property. While brokers (except buyer's brokers) almost always receive compensation from sellers, they owe the highest legal duty (fiduciary duty) to whomever they have agreed in writing to represent (seller and/or buyer). A fiduciary duty is one of utmost care, integrity, honesty and loyalty, like that of a doctor to a patient. A broker can legally supervise one or more agents, and must have two years of full-time experience as a real estate agent or salesperson, pass a state licensing exam and complete a continuing education requirement every four years.

Buyer's Agent

She helps the buyer find a house and owes a legal duty of trust to the buyer, but is paid a commission by the seller.

Buyer's Broker

He's hired and paid by the buyer to help find and purchase a house. He owes allegiance to the buyer, and has no legal relationship with the seller.

Dual Agent

A dual agent is paid by the seller but, at least in legal theory, represents both buyer and seller. This legal arrangement must be confirmed in writing by the buyer, seller and agent.

Listing Agent

She is simply a broker (or salesperson who works for a broker) who lists the seller's house for sale and markets it for the seller. Unless she signs a Dual Agency Agreement, she represents the seller.

Real Estate Professional

A term we occasionally use to include both a real estate broker and a real estate salesperson or agent.

Realtor

He is a real estate broker who belongs to the National Association of Realtors, a private trade group. An agent or salesperson may also belong as a Realtor-Associate. There are corresponding state associations (California Association of Realtors) and local Boards of Realtors; the latter usually operate Multiple Listing Services (MLS).

Seller's Agent

He helps a buyer find a house, but is paid by (and owes a legal duty to represent) the seller. This legal relationship must be confirmed in writing by the buyer, seller and real estate professional.

Selling Agent

This is a general term for an agent who locates a buyer. Depending on the written agreement the parties sign, she can be either the buyer's legal agent, the seller's legal agent or a dual agent.

Sub-Agent (or Co-Operating Agent)

This is another general term for the broker or salesperson who helps a buyer find a house. Unless all parties agree in writing that he exclusively represents the buyer, or is a dual agent, he is legally a sub-agent of the seller's broker (the person the seller retains to list the house), and owes a legal duty of trust to the seller, not the buyer. He is paid a commission by the seller. Put slightly differently, although a sub-agent may work with the buyer and never even meet the seller, his legal duty as the seller's sub-agent is to the seller who pays his commission, not to the buyer.

Even though your salesperson has a legal duty to fairly represent your interests (unless she represents the seller exclusively as a "seller's agent"), she has a more basic conflict of interest. Unless you've agreed to pay her by the hour, she won't get paid until you buy a home, and the amount she gets paid depends on the price of the house you buy.

HOW CALIFORNIA REAL ESTATE BROKERS AND AGENTS ARE PAID

Understanding how brokers and agents are paid will give you a better idea of why there's so much pressure to sell.

Most listing brokers get sellers to pay a commission of 6%-8% of the sale's price (except in probate sales, where commissions are set by the court, and for more expensive homes over $400,000, where sellers sometimes negotiate a lower sliding scale for commissions). An occasional "discount" broker charges 4%-5%, but they're unusual. A 6%-8% commission on a $200,000 home is $12,000 to $16,000; on a $500,000 house, it's $30,000-$40,000. Because most real estate transactions involve two brokers—the one producing the buyer and the one helping the seller—the commission is divided, usually 50-50 between the two brokerage offices. That's $6,000-$8,000 per office on the $200,000 house.

Within each office, the salesperson who handled the transaction gets a share, usually 50%. Thus, on a $200,000 sale, the salesperson earns a $3,000-$4,000 commission before expenses, which include wear and tear on a car, gas, phone and the like. She must sell a considerable number of houses in a year to make a decent living and is under relentless pressure to "close deals."

Some real estate offices often try to sell a house to their own buyers before offering it to the public through the MLS. If they succeed, they keep the entire 6-8% commission. This practice is controversial, even within the real estate business, as it raises the possibility of conflict of interest. When houses are not offered widely to the public, few buyers bid, decreasing competition.

Here are some ways the agent's self-interest (desire to be paid) can manifest itself to your disadvantage:

1. The salesperson may try to convince you that a house is worth more than it really is because:
   - If you bid high, you're more likely to get the house and the salesperson will get the commission. If you bid low, your offer is more apt to be rejected, in which case the salesperson gets nothing.
   - The salesperson's commission is a percentage of the sales price; the more you pay, the higher the commission.
   - If the salesperson owes a legal duty of trust (fiduciary duty) to the seller, he is legally obligated to protect the seller's interest by maximizing the price. This is true if the salesperson is legally a seller's agent rather than a buyer's agent or a dual agent.

2. The salesperson may downplay the shortcomings of a particular home or neighborhood, be it size ("you can convert the closet into a study"), commute time ("at that hour, it's a piece of cake"), quality of local schools ("every kid is above average") or weather ("sure it's foggy and raining over the hill, but this spot is sunny"), in an effort to get you to say yes and hence earn the salesperson a commission.

3. The salesperson may show you a long list of unsuitable houses. If a salesperson doesn't know of any houses that meet your specifications at a price you can afford, rather than admit it, some (especially inexperienced ones) will drag you over half the county muttering something like: "I know this isn't your cup of tea, but I want you to get a feel for the market." Don't believe it. He's hoping that if he wears you out, you'll eventually purchase one of the houses he shows you.

A salesperson's self interest or lack of competence may not be the only reason she fails to show you suitable houses. Given the likely affordability gap between the house you can afford and the one you want, a failure to produce a wonderful house in your price range is often understandable. Showing you one sad sack house after another is not the way to solve this problem, however. A savvy agent should help you face your affordability gap problem and suggest a strategy such as those discussed in Chapter 3 to deal with it. Unfortunately, because of inexperience and a lack of creative energy, some salespeople will do little more than drive you from one listed house to the next.

4. The agent may lack the experience or ethics to best represent the buyer's interest. In unusual situations, he may even try to pressure you into buying by misrepresenting the facts (for example, implying that you need to offer the full asking price because of competition which doesn't exist), or withholding material information (not telling you the roof leaks or there have been drug problems in the neighborhood). Sometimes these tactics are subtle, such as "This place is such a bargain; I'd buy it myself if I could." Again, it's foolish to rely solely on the opinion of a person with a financial stake in a transaction. You must do your homework.

We're not saying that salespeople as a group are dishonest, or that they violate the law requiring disclosure of defects. We are emphasizing that when you evaluate the suitability of a house, don't rely principally on the advice of a person with a major financial stake in your buying it.

HANDYMAN'S DREAM

Take the responsibility to make your own informed choices; among other things, be knowledgeable about the house buying process, your ideal affordable house and neighborhood, your financing needs and options, and your legal rights, and know how to evaluate comparable prices. As long as you do this, and you're strong-minded about your desires, you should be able to get valuable help from a salesperson familiar with the houses offered for sale in the area where you want to buy without compromising your interests in the process.

BARBARA KATE AND RAY: TOURING WITH TRACI

Tired of paying too much rent for too little space in our San Francisco apartment, we began to ponder buying. When we became more serious, we met with Traci, an agent at a large real estate firm. Traci led us to a plush conference room, then through an elaborate list of considerations designed to elicit a Wish List for Our Ideal Home.

"Naive," proclaimed Traci, scanning our list: two bedrooms, good sunlight, lots of closet space, perhaps a little room for a garden, under a half million dollars. "But I'll see what I can find—in this price range." She added a final admonition: "I only work with people I really, really like."

Apparently, Traci really, really liked us—she phoned at 7 the next morning with three houses for us to see that very evening. The space in all three was mostly taken up by the kitchen—the one room we confirmed restaurant-goers hadn't even thought of including on the Wish List. None of them had a second bedroom—our number one priority.

Two nights later, an excited Traci phoned at 11:50 with an exclusive news flash. A nearby two-bedroom owned by her co-worker was going on sale the next day. "I've got the keys. I can tour you through right now, before any one else sees it. I have already prepared the paperwork. I think we can close on this one," whispered Traci. We declined the offer of the midnight ride; the house was still for sale six months later.

A week later, Traci had pegged Barbara Kate as the softer sell and suggested that "just the girls" go look at houses. She tracked Barbara Kate down at home, where she was in bed with double pneumonia, unwilling and unable to make any girlish outing. But Traci was undaunted. She phoned back that afternoon with a weather report promising a warming of five degrees and "a blanket for you in the trunk."

Two weeks later, Traci called, having found our "dream house:" two bedrooms, good sunlight, good neighborhood. She never mentioned it had only one small closet—in the pantry. Outside, post-tour, Traci became adamant. "What can I do to get you to buy that place?" she asked, with a Rumpelstiltskin-like stomp for punctuation.

It was our sixth tour with Traci. It was our last. We're still paying too much rent for too little space. But it beats the alternative.

B. Work With a Real Estate Professional Paid by the Seller

Normally, the seller pays the commission of the real estate salesperson who helps the buyer locate the seller's house. Even though the salesperson you work with is typically paid out of the seller's brokerage commission, that doesn't necessarily mean she legally represents the seller. Recognizing potential conflicts, California law requires salespeople who help buyers find houses to alert them in writing that they have three different options:

1. Buyer's agent—the salesperson you work with legally represents you exclusively.
2. Dual agent—the salesperson you work with legally represents both you and the seller.
3. Seller's agent—the salesperson you work with legally represents the seller exclusively.

These three choices are outlined in the two forms you'll be asked to sign as soon as you start working with an agent. The forms—"Disclosure Regarding Real Estate Agency Relationships" and "Confirmation, Real Estate Agency Relationships"— are shown below in a combined form.

1. Buyer's Agent (your best choice)

This is your best choice. A buyer's agent has "a fiduciary duty of the utmost care, integrity, honesty, and loyalty" to you. By selecting this option, your real estate professional rejects any legal duty of care to the seller (called "sub-agency" in real estate speak) and represents you exclusively. Can you legally insist that a real estate professional be a buyer's agent? Unfortunately, no. You can ask, but the seller and real estate professional must agree. Practically speaking, however, if you're insistent, you should be able to get all concerned to agree to the buyer's agent option, or at the very least, to the dual agent

option. After all, you have considerable clout as the one who proposes to buy the house.

2. Dual Agent (your second choice)

Here the real estate professional is paid by the seller, but represents both the buyer and seller in a house sale, and owes the same legal duty of fair conduct to each. Are you in a good legal situation under dual agency? In theory, yes: A dual agent can not disclose to the seller (without your written permission) that you are willing to pay more than the offering price; conversely, a dual agent can not tell you if the seller is willing to accept less than the asking price.

A dual agency situation can arise if you've entered into an agency relationship with a real estate agent, and subsequently look at a house listed with that agent's company—even if the listing agent is not your agent and works in a different branch office of the company. Your agent should disclose immediately if a property you're interested in is listed by his or her company. Dual agency should only be entered into under a written agreement signed by both buyer and seller.

It's still better, however, to work with a real estate professional as a buyer's agent than a dual agent (often preferred by large brokerage companies which want to sell houses buyers have listed with them and to do so can't solely represent the buyer), because dual agency can mean divided loyalties.

3. Seller's Agent (a poor choice)

Run, don't walk, from this agency relationship where the seller pays "your" salesperson's commission, and "your" salesperson legally represents the seller. This is the way it was in the old days (and still is in most states), and some real estate offices still push it. Why is this such a poor choice? Because "your" real estate professional is legally the sub-agent of the seller and owes a fiduciary duty of honesty, integrity and loyalty to the seller, not to you. Specifically, if you make a low offer but the agent knows you will go higher or will pay for repair work, she should tell the seller.

The only time you might have to accept the seller's agent option is if you're buying a new home in a development, where all transactions are handled by the seller directly or by a broker who represents the seller.

DISCLOSURE REGARDING
REAL ESTATE AGENCY RELATIONSHIPS
(As required by the Civil Code)
CALIFORNIA ASSOCIATION OF REALTORS® (C.A.R.) STANDARD FORM

When you enter into a discussion with a real estate agent regarding a real estate transaction, you should from the outset understand what type of agency relationship or representation you wish to have with the agent in the transaction.

SELLER'S AGENT

A Seller's agent under a listing agreement with the Seller acts as the agent for the Seller only. A Seller's agent or a subagent of that agent has the following affirmative obligations:
To the Seller:
A Fiduciary duty of utmost care, integrity, honesty, and loyalty in dealings with the Seller.
To the Buyer and the Seller:
   (a) Diligent exercise of reasonable skill and care in performance of the agent's duties.
   (b) A duty of honest and fair dealing and good faith.
   (c) A duty to disclose all facts known to the agent materially affecting the value or desirability of the property that are not known to, or within the diligent attention and observation of, the parties.

An agent is not obligated to reveal to either party any confidential information obtained from the other party that does not involve the affirmative duties set forth above.

BUYER'S AGENT

A selling agent can, with a Buyer's consent, agree to act as agent for the Buyer only. In these situations, the agent is not the Seller's agent, even if by agreement the agent may receive compensation for services rendered, either in full or in part from the Seller. An agent acting only for a Buyer has the following affirmative obligations:
To the Buyer:
A fiduciary duty of utmost care, integrity, honesty, and loyalty in dealings with the Buyer.
To the Buyer and the Seller:
   (a) Diligent exercise of reasonable skill and care in performance of the agent's duties.
   (b) A duty of honest and fair dealing and good faith.
   (c) A duty to disclose all facts known to the agent materially affecting the value or desirability of the property that are not known to, or within the diligent attention and observation of, the parties.

An agent is not obligated to reveal to either party any confidential information obtained from the other party that does not involve the affirmative duties set forth above.

AGENT REPRESENTING BOTH SELLER & BUYER

A real estate agent, either acting directly or through one or more associate licensees, can legally be the agent of both the Seller and the Buyer in a transaction, but only with the knowledge and consent of both the Seller and the Buyer.

In a dual agency situation, the agent has the following affirmative obligations to both the Seller and the Buyer:
   (a) A fiduciary duty of utmost care, integrity, honesty and loyalty in the dealings with either Seller or the Buyer.
   (b) Other duties to the Seller and the Buyer as stated above in their respective sections.

In representing both Seller and Buyer, the agent may not, without the express permission of the respective party, disclose to the other party that the Seller will accept a price less than the listing price or that the Buyer will pay a price greater than the price offered.

The above duties of the agent in a real estate transaction do not relieve a Seller or Buyer from the responsibility to protect his or her own interests. You should carefully read all agreements to assure that they adequately express your understanding of the transaction. A real estate agent is a person qualified to advise about real estate. If legal or tax advice is desired, consult a competent professional.

Throughout your real property transaction you may receive more than one disclosure form, depending upon the number of agents assisting in the transaction. The law requires each agent with whom you have more than a casual relationship to present you with this disclosure form. You should read its contents each time it is presented to you, considering the relationship between you and the real estate agent in your specific transaction.

This disclosure form includes the provisions of Sections 2079.13 to 2079.24, inclusive, of the Civil Code set forth on the reverse hereof. Read it carefully.

I/WE ACKNOWLEDGE RECEIPT OF A COPY OF THIS DISCLOSURE.

BUYER/SELLER _____ Date _____ Time _____ AM/PM

BUYER/SELLER _____ Date _____ Time _____ AM/PM

AGENT _____ By _____ Date_____
    (Please Print)   (Associate Licensee or Broker-Signature)

This Disclosure form must be provided in a listing, sale, exchange, installment land contract, or lease over one year, if the transaction involves one-to-four dwelling residential property, including a mobile home, as follows:
   (a) From a Listing Agent to a Seller: Prior to entering into the listing.
   (b) From an Agent selling a property he/she has listed to a Buyer: Prior to the Buyer's execution of the offer.
   (c) From a Selling Agent to a Buyer: Prior to the Buyer's execution of the offer.
   (d) From a Selling Agent (in a cooperating real estate firm) to a Seller: Prior to presentation of the offer to the Seller.

It is not necessary or required to confirm an agency relationship using a separate Confirmation form if the agency confirmation portion of the Real Estate Purchase Contract is properly completed in full. However, it is still necessary to use this Disclosure form..

OFFICE USE ONLY
Reviewed by Broker or Designee _____
Date _____

FORM AD-14

UFLS-APR 96

EXAMPLE: Connie lists her home using Acme Real Estate Associates. Troy works with a salesperson from Basic Realty, which represents sellers exclusively. Basic Realty locates Connie's house for Troy. Even though the Basic salesperson has been showing Troy houses for months and has never met Connie, the Basic salesperson is the legal sub-agent of Connie. This means that while he must act fairly and with good faith toward Troy, he owes the highest duty of trust to Connie. If he knows that Connie needs to sell her house in a hurry and that she'd accept a lower offer than Troy makes, he can't tell Troy this, even though he's been working with Troy for months. Conversely, if he knows Troy will pay more than his first offer, or accept the house "as is," even though it needs $25,000 worth of pest control work, he can, and should, tell Connie.

C. Hire a Buyer's Broker and Pay the Commission

More and more brokers are marketing their services directly to buyers. They call themselves "buyer's brokers." Like a buyer's agent, they owe a fiduciary duty to the buyer, not the seller. They are paid a commission from the buyer, usually a percentage of the purchase price. The buyer's broker agrees to refuse any commission from the seller or seller's agent. The arrangement between the buyer and the buyer's broker is often laid out in a written agreement entitled a "Buyer's Listing Agreement" or "Exclusive Authorization to Locate Property (Buyer-Broker Agreement)."

EXAMPLE: Bart hires Joy Broker. Alice of Joy's office is assigned to work with Bart. Bart and Joy complete the agency forms required by law and sign a contract under which Bart agrees to pay Joy's firm a 3% commission on any house located by Alice that Bart buys. Alice finds a house owned by Ollie. Neither Joy nor Alice owe any legal duty to Ollie. When Bart purchases Ollie's house, Ollie pays his broker a commission, but pays nothing to Joy, who is paid by Bart under their contract.

Before California law was changed in the late 1980s to allow buyer's agents, salespeople who helped buyers find houses were almost always the legal representatives (sub-agents) of the seller. This led to the types of conflicts of interest discussed in Section B3 above. It also led to some buyers preferring to hire and pay for a buyer's broker. Today, the law has been changed and there is much less reason for a buyer to agree to pay her own broker.

One reason to hire a buyer's broker, however, is that creative payment arrangements are possible. For example, a few buyer's brokers in California charge a $500 retainer "loyalty fee" to begin house searching for a buyer. If the buyer purchases a house using that broker, the retainer (and sometimes more) is returned when the buyer's broker receives his share of the house sale commission from the seller's broker.

The best reason to hire a buyer's broker is the fact that a buyer's broker is motivated to show you all homes which meet your criteria, including those which:

- are sold by owner (FSBO or For Sale by Owner)
- offer a reduced commission to the buyer's agent, or
- are not even on the market yet.

Traditional agents often hesitate to show FSBOs because they fear that the buyer will go directly to the seller and they will lose a commission. A buyer's broker doesn't have this concern because she will be paid by the buyer per the terms of their contract.

There are four primary disadvantages of hiring a buyer's broker.

First, you typically pay a commission to a buyer's broker and therefore must come up with 3%-4% of the purchase price, above the down payment. From a practical standpoint, however, the fee that you agree to pay your buyer's broker is offset by the amount that the seller agrees to pay to the broker who brings in the buyer. In most cases, the buyer's broker accepts this commission as payment in full for his or her services. The entire buyer's broker fee can usually be financed as part of the purchase price.

The commission a seller must pay if you hire a buyer's broker (and the seller's broker therefore need not share her commission) depends on the seller's contract with his broker and the broker's attitude. Many contracts let a seller's broker keep the entire 6%-8% commission if she doesn't have to split it with a buyer's agent. But, in practice, if a buyer pays his own broker, most seller's brokers will voluntarily give up a portion of their commission. This is especially likely if the seller's broker realizes that a sale may not go through if she doesn't reduce her commission to let the seller pass the savings on to the buyer.

If the house is a "For Sale By Owner," a reduction may be easier to arrange, as the seller owes no commission at all. If you

were working with a buyer's agent, but the seller was selling on his own, your broker would ask the seller to "cooperate" by paying her a 3%-4% commission if you buy the house. If the seller says no, the broker's agent won't show you the house. Thus, many for-sale-by-owner sellers agree to cooperate, knowing that paying half (or sometimes slightly less) of the standard 6%-8% commission is still a good deal. So if a for-sale-by-owner seller would pay up to half of a traditional brokerage commission, but you hired a buyer's broker, ask that the price of the house be correspondingly lowered.

Even if a seller and a listing agent agree to this, a buyer's broker deal still has a major disadvantage: A buyer's broker must be paid in real money. If the seller lowers the purchase price, most of the savings will be reflected in a smaller mortgage, not in your down payment.

Another disadvantage of hiring a buyer's broker is that in many contracts, the broker gets a commission on any house you purchase during the term of the contract, whether he finds it or not. If you consider a buyer's broker, ask that this condition be eliminated, especially if you plan to look in two different geographical areas—one with the help of a buyer's broker and the other on your own.

The third disadvantage is that you and the broker have a conflict of interest. As with all agents, he buyer's broker doesn't get paid unless you buy a house, but under many buyer's broker contracts, the broker's commission rises as the price of the house you buy rises. To slightly reduce this conflict, ask that the contract provide that the commission be based on a mutually agreed upon price at the low end of your range.

ENGLISH VILLA

EXAMPLE: Anne and Roger hire Frank, a buyer's broker, to help them locate a house, for which they expect to pay between $275,000 and $350,000. They agree to pay Frank 3% of the purchase price of any house Frank locates up to $275,000. If they buy a house for more than $275,000, Frank still only gets 3% of $275,000. If they buy one that Frank has nothing to do with, they owe no commission.

While putting a limit on the buyer's broker's commission eliminates one potential conflict of interest, it doesn't eliminate the key one: The broker doesn't get paid until you buy, and therefore wants you to buy quickly. You, of course, want to buy the best possible house at the best possible price, and don't want to be hurried into making a poor choice.

A final disadvantage is that you might be stuck with an agent who you really don't want to work with. If you enter a buyer's broker agreement, negotiate a release clause that lets either of you cancel the agreement with 48 hours' notice as long as you have not made an offer or signed a contract to buy a house.

Is there anything positive to be said about hiring a buyer's broker? Because an agent can now be paid by the seller to represent the buyer, not much. Some brokers who market this service claim that a real estate professional who gets a written commitment from the buyer to pay her commission will work harder. We find this unconvincing in a situation in which the real estate professional gets paid the same amount by the seller if there is no buyer's broker contract.

D. Hire a Broker by the Hour

A few brokers market their services directly to potential buyers at an hourly fee. They commonly charge between $50 and $150 per hour, with a typical house purchaser using between 20 and 50 hours of time.

Most of these arrangements are with licensed real estate brokers. A salesperson (agent) can legally provide advice by the hour, but only with the permission of an employing broker.

1. Advantages of Hiring a Broker by the Hour

The two advantages of hiring a broker by the hour are:
- You get expert help with no built-in conflict of interest. As the broker is paid by the hour, he has no financial stake in whether or not you buy a particular house, or for that matter, any house.
- You get access to nonconfidential information in the Realtors' Multiple Listing Book, Comparable Sales Book, and other services, assuming your broker is a member of the local Board of Realtors (most are). See Chapter 6, How to Find a House, for more information.

2. Disadvantages of Hiring a Broker by the Hour

The primary disadvantages of hiring a broker by the hour are:
- You pay for the hours you use, whether or not you buy a house.
- You must do a lot of leg work yourself; it's normally too expensive to pay a person by the hour to look for a house for you.
- An unscrupulous broker may try to "run up the meter" by selling you more time than you need. While this isn't a major concern, it can happen.
- Brokers who offer this service are usually independent business people not connected with a large brokerage company. This means they do not have access to a big broker's in-house listings before they appear in the MLS book.
- You may have trouble locating an outstanding broker by the hour; few brokers go this route because more money can be made on commission, and they don't want to take on all potential liability for their involvement with the real estate purchase agreement without proportional compensation.

On balance, we believe that hiring a broker by the hour is wise for many buyers. We say many, not most or all, because hiring a broker by the hour is cost-effective only if you're committed to doing most of the grunt work inherent in finding a house, deciding on the offer amount and negotiating with the seller, yourself. The professional is then paid for a very reasonable number of hours primarily to assist with the unfamiliar technical aspects of the purchase, such as preparing the written offer, advising on negotiations and removing contingencies. The following steps outline how the relationship can work.

Step 1: Meet with a broker (or salesperson who works for a broker) who will and can work by the hour. Explain what help you want and don't want, and see if she has the kind of experience you need. Ask the broker how she prefers to work. If you seem compatible, agree on an hourly rate.

Step 2: Sign a contract (a sample is below). Make sure it states that you'll pay no commission and that the broker will accept no commission from the seller.

Step 3: Ask the broker for her assessment of local market conditions. Review your general strategy with her and be prepared to modify it on the basis of constructive give and take. Also, ask the broker to inform you of all likely properties contained in the MLS book. But to save money, go out and look at them on your own.

Step 4: Stay in close touch with the broker. Have her call you once a week or more, if necessary, to alert you to new listings.

Step 5: When you've located a house you want to buy and are ready to make an offer, discuss your strategy with the broker.

Step 6: Decide who'll negotiate with the seller or his agent. (See Chapter 17.) If you're not an experienced negotiator, consider having the broker present and possibly even handling negotiations during the offer and counter-offer conferences. As she gets no commission, you can be pretty confident that she'll give you unbiased advice.

Step 7: While negotiating price with the seller and his agent, point out that your broker needn't be paid half of the commission. Request that the house price be lowered by this amount, usually about 3% of the sales price.

E. Buy a House Yourself With No Professional Help

If you have the time, you can find and purchase a house completely on your own, without a broker. Many people enjoy looking for a house and find that professionals get in the way. The process of bidding and negotiating with the seller isn't nearly as mysterious and intimidating as it at first often appears. The routine offer and acceptance forms, along with details on filling them out, are in this book. Only in rare situations will serious legal problems develop, and then you'll need a lawyer, not a broker.

One small caveat is in order, however: If you're house hunting in a competitive market, where homes move quickly and aren't always advertised in newspapers, there's a lot to be said for having an energetic salesperson hunting for suitable

SAMPLE HOURLY FEE AGREEMENT

This agreement is made between (Buyer) _____
and (Broker) _____
on _____ , 19__, concerning the contemplated purchase by Buyer of real property generally described in the Buyer's House Priorities Worksheet, which is attached. *[You created this Worksheet in Chapter 1. A copy should be marked Attachment A and stapled to this agreement.]*

1. Buyer agrees to retain Broker as a consultant on an hourly fee basis to assist Buyer in his attempt to locate and purchase property described in Buyer's House Priorities Worksheet. The terms of this agreement shall be as follows:

   A. Broker shall mean the licensed real estate broker or agent named above, acting directly as the employing broker of record or through an agent employed under the Broker's license.

   B. Buyer is retaining Broker as an independent contractor and not as an employee.

   C. Broker is a member of a local Multiple Listing Service (MLS); Broker will share with Buyer nonconfidential information from any Multiple Listing Service to which Broker has access as a participating member concerning properties fitting the description in Buyer's House Priorities Worksheet.

   D. Buyer and Broker agree that Broker shall assist Buyer, to the extent requested by Buyer, in completing offer and counter-offer forms, arranging financing, dealing with escrow procedures and completing other paperwork pertaining to the real property purchase. This advice shall not include legal or tax advice.

2. Broker shall charge Buyer for consultation services at the rate of _____ dollars per hour. Broker's services shall not exceed hours for the contemplated purchase unless the parties mutually agree in writing. Buyer shall pay no commission to Broker; Broker will accept no commission from any Seller from whom Buyer buys.

READ, UNDERSTOOD AND AGREED TO BY:

BUYER: _____ DATE: _____ 19 ___
BUYER: _____ DATE: _____ 19 ___
BROKER: _____ DATE: _____ 19 ___

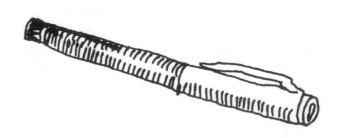

houses for you. In slower markets, or those with a lot of FSBOs (for sale by owners), however, you should do just fine on your own.

F.   Finding a Good Agent

As you read this, a veritable herd of real estate salespeople is trying to find you—the ready, willing and able buyer. About half a million Californians arc licensed real estate salespeople or brokers and most are underemployed. So the problem isn't finding someone to work with, but finding someone you *want* to work with. The best way to do this is through recommendations from people who've purchased a house in the last few years and whose judgment you trust. (Sellers may give you a good steer too, but salespeople who primarily work with sellers have somewhat different skills than those who work with buyers.)

REFERRALS MEAN A LOT

Co-author Ira Serkes, a Berkeley realtor, puts it this way:

"Many real estate agents take a long-term approach. We want our buyers to be satisfied customers, so we try to negotiate the best price possible. If we can save the buyer $5,000 we'll do it, even if that means we earn $150 less in commission. We look upon that $150 as our investment in our future with you. We simply hope that our clients will be so delighted with our service that they will refer friends, family, and neighbors who want to buy or sell a house. For many agents, the long-term value of a referral business is much more important than receiving a few hundred dollars more on one sale."

Another possible source for obtaining recommendations is from local title companies. They usually know who is good. Call two or three title companies to find out who they say the best buyer's salespeople are. As with any recommendation, the tip you get is likely to be as reliable (or unreliable) as the person making it.

After collecting the names of several salespeople, arrange to talk to each before making a decision. While you can always get rid of a salesperson or broker you don't like, it's better to find someone good in the first place. But play fair; if you're considering several salespeople before you make a final decision, disclose this to all candidates.

The person you choose should have (ideally at least) the following six traits:

- integrity
- selling real estate full-time
- business sophistication
- experience in the type of services you need
- knowledge of the area you want to live in, and
- sensitivity to your taste and needs.

While the first trait, integrity, needs little elaboration, here are a few words about the other characteristics you should look for in a real estate agent:

Selling real estate full-time and business sophistication. The exam necessary to get a real estate salesperson's license isn't difficult. Thousands of people qualify each year who have little or no real savvy about real estate. Many try to work in real estate for a few months or years, often part-time, and become discouraged and move on. You don't want to be the guinea pig that one of these neophytes practices on.

Here are some questions to ask an agent:

- How long have you been in real estate?
- Are you a licensed real estate broker or an agent?
- Are you full time? If yes, for how long?
- How many buyers have you personally found houses for in the past year or two?
- Can you give me the names and phone numbers of satisfied customers, or testimonial letters? (Talk to these people for details on the agent's work.)
- Have you completed any nationally-sponsored advanced real estate training programs offering professional designations, such as Graduate Realtors Institute (GRI), Certified Residential Specialist (CRS) or Certified Relocation Professional (CRP)? (While advanced training doesn't guarantee that an agent will do a good job, typically people who invest time and money in these courses take their profession seriously.) For more information or referral to a Residential Specialist, call the Residential Sales Council at (800) 462-8841.
- What systems do you use to make sure all transaction details are completed in a timely manner? (Ask to see sample transaction logs the agent uses to document communications with housebuyers and sellers and checklists of housebuying details.)
- Do you have the MLS online? If yes, how will this help you find the right house for me? Do you use other online services that might be useful in my house purchase? (See

WORKING WITH REAL ESTATE PROFESSIONALS

Chapter 6, Section F, for details on real estate-related online services now available.)

Experience in the type of services you need. A first-time home buyer will probably need more patient guidance, especially with financing issues, than will someone who has owned several houses. If you're looking for a new tract house or a condominium (read Chapter 7 carefully), you may need very different help than your friend who just bought a 50-year-old house in an established residential area.

Knowledge of the area. Be sure the salesperson is extremely knowledgeable about the city, county or, better yet, the neighborhood you want to live in. When it comes to finding a good house at a good price, there's no substitute for knowing the turf.

Sensitivity to your tastes and needs. When it comes to taste, real estate salespeople, like all people, have a wide range of likes, dislikes and aesthetic sensibilities. Some have an excellent eye for quality; others don't. While it's not essential that you and your real estate agent agree on everything (you're not marrying the person, after all), it certainly helps if you and the salesperson have compatible tastes or the salesperson is sensitive to yours.

TWO INSIDER VIEWS

A broker friend of ours in Southern California puts the quality of real estate agents this way: "Of the hundred or so salespeople I work with routinely, a minority (about 10%) are just plain dangerous and shouldn't be in the business. When it comes to the rest, the 80-20 rule applies. That is, the top 20% are really terrific and the rest muddle along but are nothing special."

Co-author and Berkeley realtor Ira Serkes puts it this way: "Marginally competent agents get into the real estate business because the licensing exam test doesn't test for 'real world' knowledge. Unbelievably, new agents don't have to prove they know how to complete a purchase agreement, shop for the best loan or negotiate for their client. It's possible to become a real estate agent with only a few hours of study, and there are minimal course requirements to renew a license. Top agents, however, recognize the value of education, and continually reinvest their time and money learning how to serve their clients better."

FINDING AN AGENT WHEN YOU'RE NEW TO AN AREA

If you're completely unfamiliar with the area you wish to move to and under pressure to relocate quickly (for example, your employer transfers you or you change jobs), you're at a serious disadvantage—and finding a good real estate agent is only part of your problem. Even if you find the best, you still lack the basic knowledge normally considered helpful in locating a good house in a congenial neighborhood at a fair price.

This "new kid in town" disadvantage can be ameliorated if a relative, friend or co-worker at your new job can help orient you. Better yet, rent a furnished house, apartment or condo until you have a feel for the area. Then buy. Sure, this means moving twice, but it's better than overpaying for a house in an uncongenial area that you may have difficulty selling.

If you are determined to buy immediately, however, and want a real estate professional's help, follow our advice in Chapter 6, Section M, on finding a house when you're new to an area.

One way to get an idea about how well a salesperson understands the sort of house you want is to provide him a copy of your House Priorities Worksheet and then ask him to show you a few houses he thinks you'd like. If what you see looks pretty decent (don't expect miracles on the first day), you're probably on the right track. If he immediately and repeatedly shows you houses that you simply wouldn't live in, end the relationship pleasantly but firmly.

While you're checking out real estate salespeople, keep in mind that they'll surely be assessing you. Especially at times and in locations where there are many potential buyers and a comparative shortage of good houses, an experienced salesperson with lots of business possibilities will ask herself if you're worth the time and effort it will take to show you a number of houses. She'll want to know if you:

- are highly motivated to buy, or are just a "Looky-Lou" (real estate slang for a person who makes a hobby out of looking at houses and is, essentially, a waste of time)
- can realistically afford to buy a decent house, and
- are reasonably sensible and considerate. An experienced real estate professional will know how miserable it is to

work with people who are demanding and rude. If you come across in this way, most will back off.

To alleviate an agent's understandable concerns, and show you're really serious about househunting, here are some tips for your first meeting:

- Give the agent a copy of your House Priorities Worksheet (Chapter 1).
- Give the agent an idea of your price range and a copy of your financial statement, or even better, a letter from a lender stating that you pre-qualify for a mortgage up to a designated amount (see Chapter 2).
- Explain why you want to purchase a house in the near future.
- Treat the salesperson in a business-like way. This should allay fears that you're demanding, complaining or neurotic.

WORK WITH ONE AGENT WITHIN AN OFFICE

Many people think that agents within an office share commissions when their office "listings" sell. This is simply not true. For this reason, once you decide to work with a particular agent, don't call someone else in the office and ask them to show you a particular property. (And definitely, don't call the seller's agent or office on this!) It puts you in an awkward situation, because the other agent will want you to buy the house through them. This jeopardizes your representation and makes it difficult for your agent to negotiate the best terms for you.

G. How Not to Find an Agent

Here is some advice on how not to find an agent:

Generally, avoid asking an agent where you live now to make a referral in the new area (unless they actually know an experienced agent in the area). An agent who receives a referral from someone else in the business is expected to compensate the referrer with 20% of his commission. A good agent will want to refer you to someone who will successfully find you a home (and earn them a referral fee). Be warned, though, that some salespeople are overanxious to make referrals and may steer you to someone they met once at a real estate conference or otherwise

know only casually. Other sales people are required to go through their relocation department and can't recommend the best agent for you.

When you do receive a referral, be sure to check that person out.

AMY AND BRUCE: OTHER PEOPLE'S AGENTS

We found our real estate agent, Marsha, through the grapevine of friends and co-workers. We were happy with the choice; she was knowledgeable, efficient and cooperative, never pushy. We felt comfortable knowing she was looking out for our interests.

We came to feel very differently about the seller's agent, Bob. The annoyances were minor at first. He was always late for meetings. The papers he prepared were sloppy and full of mistakes. When we asked him the fourth time for information on the recently-purchased roof, he looked at us like it was the first time we requested the information. He didn't tell our agent that another prospective buyer was making a bid the same day we did, then claimed he'd left a phone message. (Marsha rechecked her tape; he hadn't.) The last straw was when Bob's failure to relay messages about key points to the sellers nearly made the deal fall through.

By this time, the sellers weren't happy with Bob, either, but they didn't fire him, and we couldn't. Luckily, we could go around him. We went to the broker Bob worked for and told her that from then on, we would either speak to the sellers directly or communicate through her, not Bob. From that point on, we got reliable information—and soon we got the house.

Don't choose an agent just because they're with a nationally advertised chain real estate operation unless you receive a strong recommendation for a particular person. The only thing that matters is the quality of the individual agent, not the size of the company or the franchise they belong to. Be sure that your agent has a strong personal track record helping buyers like you.

Most offices of a nationally advertised are individually owned and operated.

Their primary connection with the national organization is the payment of a franchise fee. While the national organization may establish some operational standards and provide a degree of training and support, a local branch is no better than its particular owner and staff. If you're considering an unconventional arrangement—such as hiring a broker by the hour—most offices that are part of franchises will say "no."

Don't pick someone from the Yellow Pages, a newspaper ad or a direct mail flyer, unless and until you thoroughly check them out. As in any business, the best salespeople get plenty of word-of-mouth referrals.

Don't seek referrals from the Better Business Bureau or local Board of Realtors. They either won't make a referral or will simply send you to the next name on their list.

Don't work with someone just because you meet her at an open house, unless and until you thoroughly check the person out. Many real estate salespeople offer to keep houses open for other agents precisely because they're short of business and looking for clients. While you may meet a wonderful salesperson this way, you can usually do better by getting recommendations from people you trust. And if you don't want to be bombarded with phone calls, don't sign the registry sheet when you visit an open house.

Don't work with someone just because he's your first contact when you phone or visit a real estate office. Salespeople take turns handling cold-calls and greeting walk-ins; you'll end up with the person "on the floor" when you call or walk through the door. Many real estate offices have "client protection" policies, meaning that you "belong" to the first salesperson you happened to talk to or who showed you a house. Obviously, the salesperson is the only person protected by this sort of arrangement, so if you're treated like you were the property of someone you don't even know, leave.

QUEEN ANNE

H. Getting Rid of a Broker or Agent You Don't Like

Suppose you realize that your relationship with a real estate person isn't working. Perhaps the salesperson repeatedly shows you houses you hate or doesn't show you enough houses. Or maybe you discover that the salesperson isn't as ethical or careful as you'd like—he dismisses your legitimate concerns about the physical condition of the property or pushes you towards a particular lender even though you suspect there are cheaper alternatives. Even if he simply doesn't return your phone calls promptly, you'll want to work with someone else.

In short, because your home is probably the biggest purchase you'll ever make, you should be very satisfied with your salesperson. If you're not, don't hesitate to switch. Your salesperson is a business colleague, not a personal friend. As warm and cordial as the agent may seem, her first priority is to earn a commission, and yours should be to work with someone with whom you're comfortable.

Here is how to legally end a relationship with a particular broker or salesperson:

- If you're working with a salesperson in a relationship where the seller pays the commission, you need only notify the salesperson that you no longer want to work together. This is true whether you've signed a Confirmation of Real Estate Agency Relationship form or not. That's it.

- If you've hired a broker by the hour, pay for the services you've used and end the relationship. If you pre-committed to a set number of hours and haven't used them, pay only for what you've used. The broker may demand payment for the rest. If so, point out that she has a legal duty to try to earn other income in remaining hours and to subtract that income from what you owe (this is called "mitigating damages"). You may eventually decide to make a small settlement, but don't be in a hurry or pay for time you haven't used.

- If you've hired a buyer's broker, there are three ways to end the relationship:

  1. If you're unhappy with the broker before you locate a house, simply write a letter terminating the relationship and don't look at any other houses the broker shows you. Even if the contract states that you're bound to work with the broker for a longer period, the letter should legally put you in the clear.

  2. If you've found a house you want to buy, with the help of the broker, you're legally (and ethically) bound to

honor the terms of the contract. In short, pay the broker her commission; she's earned it.

3. If you locate a house on your own because your broker isn't serving you well, but it's during the term of the buyer-broker contract which calls for the broker to get a commission on any house you buy, and you haven't written the broker to terminate the contract, you technically owe the broker a fee. Should you grit your teeth and pay it? Should you refuse? Consider the fairness of the situation. If the broker did a lot of work for you, but didn't happen to locate the house you bought, you owe the money and should pay it if that's what the contract says.

But don't pay a large chunk of money to someone who has done nothing to earn it. If you refuse to pay because you received no services, the broker must sue you to collect. This costs time, money and good will. Few brokers want it known publicly that they sued a buyer because the broker didn't do his job. Also, before you're actually sued, you'll probably have a chance to settle the dispute for a smaller amount. If you do, get a release of all claims when you make your payment. (See *Simple Contracts for Personal Use*, by Elias and Stewart (Nolo Press) for forms.)

WHEN YOU'RE REALLY THRILLED WITH YOUR AGENT

In fewer than 10% of all house purchases, buyers adore their agent and become lifelong friends. Buyers often wonder if it's okay to "do something" for their agents. The best thing to do is refer her to your friends, co-workers and relatives. In addition, consider buying her a gift. Some people we know bought their agent the finest bottle of Napa wine they could afford. Another couple we know gave their agent some books on topics of interest to him. Another gave a $500 cash bonus. (The deal was a mess—the agent was a savior.)

Use your imagination.

■

How to Find a House

There's a bit of folk wisdom which says: "He who looks the least finds the most." While we don't recommend this as a literal prescription for finding a house, it's larger meaning does make sense.

Perhaps the best way to understand this phrase is to study its inverse: He who looks the most (and most desperately) finds the least. Think about the last time you lost your keys. You probably dashed about anxiously, muttering all sorts of unpleasant things, and still didn't find them. The frustration following this failure may have left you angry and exhausted. Only when you slowed down, took a deep breath and let your mind relax were you able to walk right to them.

For too many people, a house search resembles the anxious key search. After a short burst of almost frantically looking at house after house that doesn't measure up, or that they can't afford, they feel tired or desperate or both. Although it's often easier said than done, it's important to recognize that exhaustion and desperation are signs that it's time to take a nap, not look at more houses. Unfortunately, few people disengage at this stage. Many simply search more frantically, and all too often, buy a house. ("This place may not be great, but I've got to have something.") The result is rarely positive.

How, then, should you look for a house? In Chapter 1, Describe Your Dream House, you did an important part of the job by creating your House Priorities Worksheet. Now you need to devise a plan to find a house that matches as much as possible. Your first task is to pay close attention to your time and financial constraints. For example, the house search of a well-paid executive with money in the bank, who needs to relocate over the summer so her kids' schooling won't be interrupted, should differ tremendously from that of a sporadically-employed foreign language translator who likes his apartment but eventually wants to buy a modest place with a small down payment and affordable monthly payments.

BUNGALOW

HOUSE HUNTING TIPS

Here's advice from seasoned house hunters on how to make the most of your search:

- Know what you want and can afford before you start looking. Don't waste your time on houses that don't fit your needs and pocketbook.
- Because newspaper ads are often very sketchy and tend to glamorize a house, try to get more information from your agent or the listing agent before visiting an open house. This should save wasted trips.
- Pace yourself; don't try to see more than four houses in an afternoon. Also, try to visit a few houses evenings after work rather than spending your whole weekend hunting.
- Make several copies of a local street map and plot the open house locations to save driving time.
- Come equipped with your own handy dandy home-hunter's kit. Include a notebook, pen or pencil, pocket calculator, tape measure, graph paper and, most important, your House Priorities Worksheet. (See Chapter 1.) Especially if your co-buyer can't come along, bring a camera or video recorder with you. (But be sure to ask the agent or house owner for permission before you start taking pictures or videos.)
- If you're interested in the house, fill out the worksheet carefully. Also, as you walk through, take notes on the layout, condition of major appliances and fixtures, and problems such as stains on the ceiling or cracks in the basement. Use the tape measure to check that the room's dimensions are the same as on the listing sheet.
- Don't let the current decor unduly influence your impression. Remember, the uglier it is, the more likely you are to buy for a reasonable price. Think creatively about what can be changed, and note things that cannot be.

ORGANIZING YOUR HOUSE SEARCH

Set up a file folder on each house that seems like a possible prospect. Include a completed House Priorities Worksheet, the information sheet provided at the open house, the Multiple Listing Service information, if available, ads and your notes. Keeping detailed records may seem like overkill. But as the number of houses you look at grows, it will become the best way to keep track of a myriad of details. And a house you look at and like, but reject because of price, may stay on the market for a few months and have its price lowered. Without a good recordkeeping system, you may end up visiting the same house twice just to refresh your memory.

Your computer can be a valuable tool to keep track of houses. Set up a simple data base for each house with columns for the address, price, number of bedrooms and baths, date, comments or whatever else is important to you. Here's an example:

Address	693 San Lorenzo	411 Solano Avenue	1698 Colusa Avenue
City	Berkeley	Albany	Kensington
Price	$325,000	$249,000	$315,000
Number of bedrooms	3	2	3
Number of bathrooms	1	1	2
Date seen	2/14/95	2/21/95	1/22/95
Comments	Nice home with lots of light	Fixer-upper, but big yard	$14,000 termite report!

Once you enter the information into your database, you can sort the list by price, date, city, address or other variable. Sorting by date would show you which homes have been on the market for a while and which sellers might be good candidates for low offers.

A. The Best Time to Look for Houses

Often, the time to look at houses is irrelevant. A major event in your life such as a new job or need to move your children before the start of school means you must find a new house quickly. For those people with the luxury of timing their purchase, here are a few hints.

- House prices often jump in the spring, absent some major external factor, such as a recession.
- From mid-November through the end of February, the market was once slow. That's not true in all areas. Regardless of the season, look for a seller who needs to move quickly to get an excellent house with a relatively low offer.
- Bad news, such as a local military base closing, can temporarily depress a local real estate market. But you need to move fast to profit. In California's real estate market, house prices often bounce back fast. The big Bay Area earthquake of 1989 is an example; bargains were to be had in some affected areas for a few weeks, but they didn't last long.
- When interest rates are low, there's often more competition for housing. See Chapter 14, Section A, for advice on checking the housing market, and when it favors buyers versus sellers.

B. Check the Classified Ads

All California newspapers publish real estate classifieds, most of which appear on Sundays. The classifieds are usually organized by county or city, and include listings for Sunday open houses.

Get into the rhythm of reading the classifieds. Not only will this help you learn the real estate market, but you'll also spot new listings and price reductions. And don't wait until Sunday to get the Sunday paper—most are available Saturday (or even late Friday night).

If you see a new listing, especially a For Sale By Owner (FSBO), drive by on Saturday. If you like it, knock on the door or call to arrange an early showing. Don't be afraid to be a little assertive—after all, the seller is probably at least as anxious to sell as you are to buy. If the seller has an agent, and you're already working with an agent, make this clear so that you don't jeopardize your representation.

C. Visit Sunday Open Houses

To really get the feel of the market, visit some houses. Start with the Sunday open houses so you can educate yourself without an agent hanging onto your sleeve. Don't be terribly selective at first; your goal is to broadly orient yourself as to general market conditions and current price levels, not to buy the first or second house you see.

Once you have a good idea of local market conditions, it's time to develop a more complete strategy. Attending Sunday open houses is not usually the best long-term way to find a house. The houses tend to be the best—and the most expensive—the broker has; he is trying to attract the highest potential buyer. One exception is For Sale By Owner houses which are primarily marketed via open houses. Another exception is in hot local housing markets, where new listings are frequently held open immediately.

If you visit an open house you like—except for the price—consider making a low offer. For all you know, the seller may have priced the house at $350,000 to test the market, but never really expected to get more than $300,000. Even if the seller says he's not taking low offers, leave your name and phone number and stay in touch. And continue to monitor the classifieds to see if there is a price reduction.

![warning] While you're looking at open houses, real estate agents are looking at you. The primary purpose of open houses is to help agents find more clients, not to sell property. Few open houses are sold to a person who happens to stop by, but lots of new customers are signed up. Be prepared for agents to ask your name and phone number so they can contact you later. If you're already working with an agent, make that clear. Otherwise, just say no, unless you really do like the person and will take the time to check her out. While it's possible to connect with a good agent at an open house, there are better ways. (See Chapter 5, Section F.)

TRACT

HOW TO READ THE CLASSIFIEDS

Anyone who makes a living in the real estate world learns to translate the exaggerated language of classified ads into down-to-earth English. Because most house purchasers aren't around the business long enough to develop this arcane (and only momentarily useful) skill, here is a brief glossary of some of the most common real estate business euphemisms:

Convenient to high school. Youth gangs hang out in your front yard.

Convenient to shopping. For a month before Christmas, your front lawn will become a parking lot.

Cozy. Rooms are the size of closets; closets don't exist.

Fixer-upper or handyman special. Nothing that an experienced four-person construction crew couldn't fix in nine months.

Fruit trees. Impossible to say anything better.

Half-bath. A small closet contains a 60-year-old toilet located three inches from a basin half the size of a tea cup.

Low maintenance yard. Half-dead Bermuda grass interspersed by an occasional patch of pastel-colored gravel.

Modern kitchen. The rest of the house looks like the birthplace of Woodrow Wilson.

Mother-in-law (or in-law) unit. Maybe a starving student would live there, but your in-laws? Never!

Motivated seller. The drug-dealing neighbors have threatened dire bodily harm if complaints are made to the cops.

Needs tender-loving care. Last owner was a recluse with a dozen incontinent dogs.

Not a drive-by. So ugly you have to be dragged by the ear.

Off the beaten path. A bloodhound couldn't find it.

Priced to sell. No one was interested at a higher price.

Quaint. Need you ask?

Starter house. If your alternative is to live in a city shelter, it will look good; otherwise, keep looking.

Water view. Subject to flooding at high tide.

D. Work With a Real Estate Salesperson

In Chapter 5, we discuss how to find and work with a real estate salesperson. We won't repeat that discussion, except to point out that real estate agents and brokers normally have access to houses before they're opened to the public. In some cases, your salesperson will promptly tell you of these houses; at other times, he may not. So, while working with an agent has advantages, there are good reasons to explore additional avenues.

E. Gain Access to the Multiple Listing Service

Multiple Listing Service (MLS) books, which list most houses for sale, are published by local Boards of Realtors for most areas of California. Getting access to information in the MLS is a major advantage of working with an agent. Listings usually include the price, address and a photo (usually overly flattering) of the house, the number and type of rooms, the size of the lot, and other features, such as the kitchen appliances included.

SAMPLE MLS LISTING

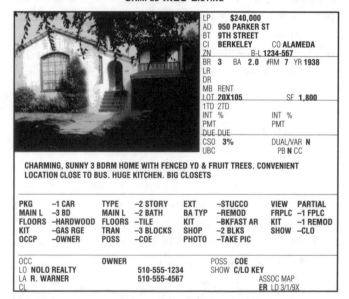

Realtors also publish a Comparable Sales Book (Comp Book), which is sometimes bound into the back of the MLS book. The Comp Book lists most houses sold through the MLS during the previous three months, arranged by city or neighborhood, each with the original asking price and the selling price.

While these books contain a wealth of information, there's a problem: Only real estate professionals associated with a local Board of Realtors are supposed to have them. This is fine if you work with a salesperson associated with a member broker, but what if you don't, and don't want to? You'll have to do without, unless you have a friend in the real estate business who'll let you take a look. Or you can check out MLS-type services online that list homes for sale and even show recent comparable sales. (See Section G, below.) Most of these online services, however, have less information than the traditional proprietary MLS operations of the real estate industry.

If you work with a salesperson with access to the MLS book, ask to see it. Many local Boards of Realtors allow legitimate buyers to look through the books, though you're not supposed to take them out of the room or photocopy pages.

F. How Your Real Estate Agent Can Use a Computer to Help You Find a House

Access to MLS books is a valuable tool for locating likely houses, but it is no longer enough. Today, most new houses are entered onto a computer, printed in the MLS book weekly, and updated in between with supplements called "hot sheets." But in this age of online electronic databases, even "hot sheets" are old news before the ink hits the paper—when a listing agent enters a new house on the MLS computer, all other agents have instant access to it. If you work with an agent, find one with good computer skills, who will check new listings on the computer several times a day. This is imperative in some parts of the state, where the MLS is only available online.

Also, the MLS of many real estate boards includes property photos along with the text information. Realtors can link property addresses to digitized maps, and then print out a customized tour map for their buyers.

Even with a computer, sifting though new listings to locate houses that meet your particular needs is a big job. To save time, an agent can create a computer code to correspond to your specific needs (such as price, location and number of bedrooms) and enter it into the computer. Any new listing that matches the code will be tagged by the computer, providing speedy access to the relevant new listings.

In addition to providing up-to-date sales listings, real estate agents (in some areas) can access a wealth of other data for their clients via their computer:

- the date a particular property was bought and for what price, plus property taxes, legal information and details on the neighborhood
- comparable sales data in bar chart form, with the property address, asking price and final selling price, a format that is much easier to use than pages and pages of print-out, and
- loan origination and mortgage rate comparison programs to speed up loan qualification.

Computer technology is having a tremendous impact on the real estate business:

- Pacific Bell's RealtyLink allows real estate offices to communicate online with lenders, mortgage brokers, title companies, appraisers, and home and pest control inspectors, providing speedy access to property profiles and title reports, appraisals (with photos), loan documents, buyer prequalification requests, computerized loan origination, credit reports and pest reports. RealtyLink also includes a voice mail Audio Tours system for prospective buyers to hear pre-recorded details on homes for sale.
- Photographs, videos and specifications of properties (expensive homes for now) are available on CD-ROM.
- In the not-too-distant future, housebuyers may even be able to take a computerized walk through homes using virtual reality technology.

Real estate agents don't have a monopoly on electronic services. While brokers still have a firm hold on the MLS, that grasp is weakening as more and more online services are

FAR EASTERN

available to consumers. Many shopping centers now have real estate kiosks where you can punch in criteria such as location, price range and number of bedrooms, and then view suitable properties on the monitor. Newspapers are beginning to offer online real estate information, including classified ads, home prices and mortgage information.

Online services available to consumers are discussed below.

G. How Homebuyers Can Access Online Real Estate Services

A wide variety of real estate information and services are available online using a computer, a modem, access software and your telephone line. There are commercial online networks, such as America Online, and electronic bulletin board services (BBSs) like the WELL. Through your computer, you can access mortgage rates, real estate listings, tax information and articles on all aspects of buying a house. You can also post questions and get responses or chat with other computer users and real estate experts on specific housebuying topics.

Here's a brief summary of some of the major services available. While we don't expect you to buy an online service just to obtain real estate information, if you already subscribe, here's how to get the real estate information.

1. America Online (AOL)

AOL offers a comprehensive Real Estate Center with articles and software, amortization programs, lender listings of mortgage rates, real estate listings throughout the U.S., the "Ask OurBroker" board and contributions from Peter G. Miller, author of *The Common Sense Mortgage* and *Buy Your First Home Now* (*Keyword* Real Estate).

AOL also has several real estate message boards where you can discuss and ask questions on all aspects of AOL's information number is (800) 827-6364.

2. CompuServe

CompuServe provides a homefinders' relocation service (*go* HF) offering advice when you move to a new location plus information on specific neighborhoods, including population,

race, age and other demographic data for every U.S. zip code (*go* Neighborhood $$). Housing patterns for the neighborhood are also examined with the status of occupied housing, average home value and rent and the age of housing structures shown on the report. With this information, prospective home buyers can research areas they are considering moving to. CompuServe also has a home forum (*go* HOMEFO), which has spirited messages on buying and selling real estate, and a forum maintained by the California Association of Realtors (*go* CEE). CompuServe's information number is (800) 848-8199.

3. Delphi

Delphi offers a *Mortgage Calculator* which can calculate the term, interest rate, principal or payments on a loan by entering three of the four variables (*go* Bus Mor). Delphi's information number is (800) 544-4005.

4. GEnie

GEnie offers a home and real estate round table which allows users to enter discussions with other like-minded individuals on topics ranging from landscaping to getting a mortgage (*keyword* Home). GEnie's information number is (800) 638-9636.

5. Prodigy

Prodigy offers a collection of *Consumer Reports* articles on real estate topics (*jump* CR Real Estate), columns written by real-estate expert Robert Bruss (*jump* Bruss on Real Estate), plus information on mortgages and rates (*jump* Mortgages). Prodigy's information number is (800) 776-3449.

6. Whole Earth 'Lectronic Link (WELL)

The WELL, one of the most established bulletin boards, offers hundreds of real estate-related topics in a homeowner's conference (go Home) You can ask open-ended questions and anyone can answer. Users get expertise from varied disciplines and viewpoints. For information, contact the WELL at (415) 332-4335.

7. The World Wide Web on The Internet

IRED, the Internet Real Estate Directory (http://www.ired.com/dir/usa/relisuca.htm), lists and evaluates hundreds of real estate web sites all over the world. IRED has a searchable database of over 1,000 questions and answers, and provides information on buying, selling and investing. It's sponsored by Becky Swann and syndicated real estate columnist Brad Inman, who also has an excellent real estate news web site (http://www.inman.com/).

California Living Network (http://ca.living.net/), Listing Link (http://38.246.127.10/states/ca/home.html) have listings of homes for sale throughout the state.

The Multiple Listing Services (MLS) for parts of Los Angeles and Orange Counties are on line at the HomeSeekers Web Site (http://www.homeseekers.com). For San Diego County, go to http://www.homeselect.com/sandiego/region.htm.

There is no centralized San Francisco Bay Area MLS yet. Co-author Ira Serkes has compiled a list of many Bay Area real estate sites at his Serkes Berkeley Real Estate Search Engine (http://www.home-buy-sell.com). This site also includes links to open house ads, city and community information, mortgage calculators, sightseeing and entertainment.

Some web sites show the property address, price, bedrooms, baths and a brief description. Other sites include photos and downloadable flyers created in Adobe Acrobat Format. Acrobat files are in PDF—Portable Document Format. They can be viewed on your computer and printed exactly as if you were handed the flyer.

A savvy real estate agent can put your home buying criteria on line so home sellers with a suitable home will be able to let your agent know about it.

Both the California Association of Realtors—CAR (http://www.car.org/) and the National Association of Realtors—NAR (http://www.realtor.com/) have web sites with research and economic reports, and home and broker searches.

Use one of the search engines for more information. The best are Net Search on Netscape Navigator (http://home.netscape.com/home/internet-search.html), Yahoo (http://www.yahoo.com/) or (http://www.yahoo.com/Business_and_Economy/Real_Estate/), and Lycos, Inc.—the Catalog of the Internet (http://www.lycos.com/).

Alta Vista (http://altavista.digital.com/) and HotBot (http://www.hotbot.com/) search the web and index all words on web sites, so try these for specific searches of keywords such as Realtor, Real Estate, or Relocation (i.e., Berkeley Realtor)

H. Enlist the Help of Personal Contacts

If you know people who live or work near where you want to buy, ask them to become house scouts. This approach can be quite effective because when people plan to move, friends, neighbors and business associates almost always know about it before a house is put on the market. If you locate 25 to 50 house scouts, and each knows 50 to 100 people well enough to hear about moving plans, you should get advance notice of any planned moves of 1,250 to 5,000 people.

Approach your friends and acquaintances in a formal, structured way. You want them to understand that you're seriously requesting their assistance, not just fantasizing about owning a new home. Here is how to do it:

- Prepare a cover letter containing a brief—perhaps humorous—description of exactly what you want your scouts to do. Generally, this should encourage your scouts to spread the word about your needs, and, of course, to call you immediately if they spot a likely house, especially if they hear about it before it goes on the market. Attach your House Priorities Worksheet.

- Send your letter and worksheet to friends and fairly close acquaintances. Include local business people with whom you have a friendly relationship. Doctors, lawyers, dentists and insurance brokers are particularly good sources of information. They routinely have advance information about impending moves. While they can't breach confidentiality by tipping you off to a medical or legal problem which may require someone to move, they can certainly ask their client if it's okay to mention the move to you. We know one woman who learned about a house when she was in the hospital giving birth. The attending nurse knew a family planning to move, and introduced the family to the new mother, who bought the house.

- If your house search turns out to be prolonged, contact your scouts with periodic progress reports and reminders that you need help.

Dear Friends:

We Have a Problem and Need Your Help!

We've been house hunting for months, but without much luck. We're looking for a 3 or 4 bedroom home in Piedmont or the Montclair District of Oakland. Our lender tells us we can pay up to $450,000.

It's important that the house be light and airy, with a private back yard that is (or can be) closed in for our old hound, Faithful Fred. We've attached a sheet listing the most important attributes of our ideal house.

Do you know of anyone thinking of selling? Can you help in one or more of the following ways?

• Keep your eyes open for suitable houses already on the market.

• Look for for sale by owner houses that we might otherwise miss. (These don't appear in real estate business listing books and are often hard to find.)

• Tell your friends, neighbors and business associates—they'll probably hear about a house from someone moving long before it's listed with a broker.

• Tell doctors, dentists, lawyers and other service providers who are often the first to know when people plan to move.

If you hear about or spot a house that seems even remotely likely, give us a call pronto, at 555-4377.

Thanks for your help.

Dennis and Ellen Olson

P.S. As soon as we move in, we plan to throw the best 60s Motown dance party you've ever been to for all our house scouts. And, whoever tips us off to the house we buy will be promptly invited to dinner for four at your choice of Chez Panisse in Berkeley or Masa's in San Francisco.

PAUL AND BARBARA:
OUR HOUSE SCOUTS CAME THROUGH!

After the birth of our second child, we searched for a bigger house in our general area for almost a year, to no avail.

One technique we used was to tell as many people as possible about our search. One day a friend went for her annual teeth cleaning and her dentist mentioned that he was retiring in about six months and moving out of town. Our scout asked if he and his wife planned to sell their home, which they did. She mentioned us to the dentist, and then relayed his invitation for us to call and set up an appointment to look at his house. We did, and loved it.

We suggested to the dentist and his wife that if we could agree on the price, we could jointly handle the entire sale without real estate agents. They named a moderately high, but fair, price, and we said yes. It turned out, however, that they had promised to list the house with a real estate broker friend. They

wanted to honor that promise and so they paid her a 3% commission in exchange for helping with the contract, inspections and closing.

We not only got a great house, we got a great deal. If we hadn't heard about the house and it was put on the market months later, the combination of fast-rising local prices and the need to pay an additional $15,000 in real estate commissions would have increased the price by $50,000 or more, effectively putting it out of our price range.

I.   Do Your Own House Scouting

In addition to enlisting the help of friends, you can do much looking on your own.

1.   Canvass Neighborhoods

While it may be a little aggressive for some tastes, we know people who have found houses simply by notifying every owner in the area of their interest in their neighborhood. If you have the time, the best way to do this is to hand carry a flyer door-to-door and hang signs on notice boards in laundromats and grocery stores. One friend found a good house in a highly desirable and sought-after neighborhood a few days before it would have been listed by posting an "I want to buy a good house at a fair price" card in the local butcher shop.

Another possibility is to mail a friendly letter containing your house specifications to everyone in a particular area after getting the names and addresses from a "reverse directory" at the public library. This type of directory is organized by street address and phone number rather than by last name.

2.   Look for Houses That May Be on the Market Soon

Driving around neighborhoods and looking for run-down houses (peeling paint or weeds in the front yard, no curtains in the window) is one way to find houses that may soon be for sale. For many reasons (foreclosure, ill health, divorce) run-down properties, especially rentals, are often available for purchase, even though they aren't formally listed. If you locate a likely house, ask neighbors if they know whether the house is for sale and the name and phone number of the owner. You can also find the owner's name at the County Assessor's or Recorder's Office, or from a local title or escrow company. Be careful, however; many run-down homes or "for sale" signs in an area may mean it's deteriorating.

HOW TO RESEARCH PROPERTY OWNERSHIP

Property ownership data collected from tax assessor's records is available at most title companies on microfiche. In addition, some title companies have online access to computer databases containing property ownership information, and will provide free access to this information if you plan to use their insurance and closing services.

The data is organized by property address, owner's last name, assessor's parcel number or map corresponding to assessor's parcel number to simplify retrieval.

To determine ownership, look up the property address on the fiche. You'll find the owner's name and where her tax bill is sent (probably where she lives), the parcel number and deed of trust recording information.

One way to use the microfiche is to pick several streets where you want to live and scan the records for the names of owners who don't live on the premises (out-of-town or out-of-state owners are best). They may be the most motivated to sell, and to sell at a good price. Ask the title company to print the owner's addresses onto 8½" x 11" paper so you can photocopy them directly onto mailing labels.

---

3. Advertise for Sellers

Why not let sellers find you by placing a classified ad listing your requirements? Especially if you need help with financing and want the seller to take back a second mortgage, or if you are looking for a house with very particular characteristics (for example, wheel chair accessibility or within one block of public transit), placing your own ad may be an efficient way to narrow down the possibilities. Whatever your requirements are, make

sure you state them clearly or you are likely to be inundated with calls.

4. How to Approach an Owner You Don't Know

The reason you want to know about houses that may soon be for sale is to contact the owner, preview the house and, if you like it, make an offer before it's listed. This is often easier said than done. Many older people are harassed by aggressive real estate salespeople who knock on the door or send mailings, all but asking if they aren't ready to die or move to a retirement home. One of the author's elderly relatives, who lived in a beautiful ocean front house in Laguna Beach, was contacted by over 20 real estate salespeople in her 84th year. (And still, many real estate people wonder why the profession has a relatively poor public image.)

Many people, especially those moving because of health, financial or marital problems, aren't likely to appreciate an aggressive potential buyer. We're all territorial, and most of us will dig in our heels when faced with someone who seems to be trying to hustle us out of our own home.

It's best to approach a potential seller as politely and nonaggressively as possible. If you have a mutual friend (perhaps a house scout), ask him to introduce you. If this isn't possible, write the owner a friendly note (use a nice card) saying you've heard she might be moving, and if so, would she be willing to show you her house. Explain your own needs in a friendly and open way. Follow up with a phone call a few days later. If you meet with resistance, back off.

If you get to see a house, and you like it, you'll naturally want to know how much the seller wants. It's fine to ask, but don't be pushy. She may not have thought about it and if she thinks you're trying to "steal" her home, you'll probably never hear from her again. Do mention that if a sale can be conducted without brokers (or with one broker who gets a 2%-3% com-

INTERNATIONAL STYLE

mission instead of the customary 6% or 8%, or who works by the hour), the seller will save a good bit of money.

J. Enlist More Than One Agent to Help You Search

Another house search strategy is to notify all brokerage companies in your area of your needs, rather than to work with one agent. Mail each company your House Priorities Worksheet. Include a cover letter stating your price range and asking any agent to call you if he or she knows of any property that fits. Emphasize that you don't want to be called about houses that don't closely conform.

Broadcasting your needs far and wide, as opposed to working with the agent, is also a good idea because some large brokers try to sell houses within their own offices before listing them on the MLS. This is done to avoid splitting the commission with an office that produces a buyer. So if you're not already hooked up with an agent, and a real estate office has a property that seems to meet your needs, the office can consider you its customer, and work with you over other prospective buyers who already have an agent.

There's a disadvantage to working this way, however: Your agent becomes a dual agent when he sells you one of his office listings, (Chapter 5, Section B discusses dual agents.)

Be clear about your existing relationship with real estate salespeople. If you're already working closely with an agent, say so. In this situation, only salespeople who represent sellers will contact you. If you aren't already working closely with a salesperson, all agents knowing of houses that fit your needs may contact you, as they're eligible for a commission if you buy.

JUNE AND MARTY: PERSISTENCE PAID OFF

Our search started in August; by January we'd seen 100 houses and were too tired to look at any more, even if it meant moving to a motel.

To get a bit of order in our lives, we listed (in alphabetical order by street) *all* the houses we'd seen. We included comments on each house—price, area, amenities—and sent the list to 30 real estate offices in our area, with a cover letter stating what we were looking for. The list let them know what we'd already seen and why each house wasn't suitable. We asked any agent or broker who knew of a house which met our needs to contact us.

Apparently, few agents wanted to work with finicky buyers like us, as only one responded. He told us he knew of three houses which might be suitable. He was right. We made offers on two, and one was accepted. Our experience convinced us that half the battle of finding a good house is to find an agent who really understands his clients' needs.

K. Find Foreclosures, Probate Sales and Lease-Option Properties

In Chapter 3, we discuss finding properties subject to foreclosure and probate sale, and houses you may be able to lease option.

HOW TO FIND UNLISTED HOUSES

To find houses that are not on the market, but might be available, old Multiple Listing Service books may be helpful. Look at a few months of MLS books from a year or so ago, checking for houses which didn't sell and were taken off the market. For any house that looks good (and isn't terribly overpriced), approach the owner to see if he'd be interested in selling. (See Section I, above, for how to research property ownership and approach an owner you don't know.) You might find a great house just before the seller puts it back on the market. Assuming the seller doesn't have to pay a real estate commission, you could get it at a very attractive price.

L. Shop via TV

In most urban areas, anyone with a TV can shop for a house via video classified advertising programs. Compared to reading a printed ad, viewing a house really is worth a thousand words. Some programs feature still photographs of the interiors and exteriors of homes. Others are more elaborate video productions, which not only show the house, but a bit of the neighborhood as well.

These programs have a number of advantages. Not only can you see a lot of houses quickly and gain some idea of prices and types of houses offered in many different neighborhoods, but viewing houses this way can save you the time involved in driving to houses that are plainly not your cup of tea.

Unfortunately, the huge downside to video real estate shopping is that most programs are only a half-hour or hour, which means they show relatively few houses. Once you eliminate houses in areas and price ranges you aren't interested in, there often isn't much left. Also, because putting a house on TV is costly, the houses shown tend to be high priced. Even if a bargain does sneak in, you probably won't get it, as these shows are watched by many thousands, and in some instances, hundreds of thousands, of people.

M. Finding a House When You're New to an Area

If you're completely unfamiliar with the area you're moving to, you're at an obvious, and serious, disadvantage—you don't have the basic information normally considered essential to locating a good house, in a congenial location, at a fair price. Most house buying books recommend that you solve the problem by finding a good salesperson to work with, who'll spend the extra time necessary to orient you. Frankly, we don't believe doing this will necessarily solve your "new kid on the block" problem. Even the best salesperson will be hard put to figure out which communities you'll feel most comfortable in. Getting a real sense of what houses are worth may also be difficult , but a good market analysis (see Chapter 15) can help. If you move to Los Angeles from Seattle, you'll find that a house worth $200,000 in Washington costs several times that in Los Angeles. But is the L.A. house worth $450,000 or $575,000? Relying on the advice of a salesperson who only gets paid if you buy the house is just plain dumb.

There is one exception: Some brokers train their agents to be "re-location specialists." While they can't know your personal desires, they have thorough knowledge of schools, community services and neighborhood features, and if you're clear about what you want, they should be able to answer your questions or send written information such as local maps and home price information.

A sensible alternative to trying to find a house in a hurry in a new area is to leave your furniture in storage and rent a furnished place until you have a sense of your new turf. Sure, this means moving twice, but it's better than paying too much for a house in an uncongenial area that you may have difficulty reselling when you want to move, which is likely to be soon.

Talk to friends, co-workers, shopkeepers, homeowners and anyone else familiar with where you're moving to before settling on a geographic area. If possible, take advantage of the valuable information available from online services. (See Section G, above.) Emphasize the personal by telling them who you are and what you like. You want to know the specific towns and neighborhoods where you'd fit in. In our view, it's more important to live in such an area than in the perfect house. If you doubt this, think about where you live now. Aren't there towns within a five-mile radius that have okay houses, but where you'd prefer not to live?

Once you settle on a community, the best way to find an agent is through personal contacts. Begin with anyone you know who appears to have good sense, including co-workers on a new job or classmates in a new school. If you don't have even these connections, start with the owner of the coffee shop where you eat breakfast. The important thing is to ask sensible people for referrals until you get one that sounds right. Although recommendations are obviously hard to assess when you don't know the referrer well, this approach is better than looking in the Yellow Pages. When you get the names of several real estate people, talk to each one, following the approach recommended in Chapter 5.

N. Finding a New House

We discuss new houses in Chapter 7. One point worthy of mention here is that to get a good deal on a new house, you need to understand and follow the market for some time. New developments, and new sections of old developments, are continually coming on the market. The best tend to sell quickly; the worst hang on for months. It's extremely difficult to accurately judge the new house market in a weekend, or even a week. The best approach is to follow it for some time, making a careful list of all new projects in the geographical area that interests you. ∎

New Houses, Developments and Condominiums

If a new house is definitely not for you, skip this chapter. But if you're open to buying a new house, read on for common problems and pitfalls, and for suggestions on ways you can save time, aggravation and money. Also, while much of this chapter focuses on new houses, there's lots of useful advice for people buying a condominium or a property governed by a homeowners' association and CC&Rs.

A. Pitfalls and Pluses of Buying a New House

Buying a newly-built house in California usually means purchasing in a tract development. In some ways, this is more like buying a new car than an existing house, because:

- Your choice is limited to relatively few models.
- The seller is a commissioned sales representative trained in carefully orchestrated sales techniques designed to make as much money as possible. (We use the terms seller, builder and developer interchangeably in this chapter to refer to the person, or company representative, who has built the houses and is trying to sell you one.)
- You'll be lured to the development based on a seemingly impossibly-low price, then shown model houses which are typically loaded with expensive extras (Jacuzzi, fireplace, big master bedroom). As with autos, it's easy to get so caught up in admiring the amenities that you lose sight of your goal to buy a well-designed product at a good price.
- Many developers make their profit by selling you add-ons and upgrades which are commonly overpriced; other developers price their houses high to start with and will resist calling in their workers to install anything extra.
- The seller may provide discount financing and toss in valuable extra features if houses are selling slowly, but will charge you top dollar, with no extras, if the market is hot.
- You'll be asked to sign a contract written primarily to benefit the seller, on a take-it-or-leave-it basis, with little opportunity to negotiate over most terms.
- Once you place your order, you have little control over when your house is delivered, unless you buy a model already in inventory.
- If the house turns out to be a lemon, getting problems fixed is extremely difficult, and getting your money back next to impossible.
- Some new houses are auctioned. The idea is to whip up a buyer's feeding frenzy and sell a house for more than would be possible without the auction. As a general rule, good houses in prime developments don't have to be auctioned. If a developer is auctioning lots of houses, it may be a red flag that the houses don't offer a good value. (See Chapter 3, Section D18, for more on why auctions are rarely a good way to buy a house.)

Does this mean you should forget about buying a new house? No. New houses often have many advantages over comparable older houses, such as:

- **Price.** In areas where land is still affordable, such as the Central Valley and Sierra foothills, many houses are built on relatively large chunks of land, meaning a relatively low per-house land cost. In addition, because many houses are built at once, building supplies are purchased in bulk, bringing construction costs down. Townhouses especially, which use less land and cost less to construct than stand-alone houses because of common roofs and walls, are often very reasonably priced. In addition, when new houses don't sell, developers are often under pressure from lenders to raise money quickly. They often do this by cutting prices fairly radically.
- **Amenities.** Many new house developments include pools, tennis courts, golf courses and meeting rooms. This is great, as long as any user fees are reasonable. Check to be sure.
- **Less immediate maintenance and fix-up work.**
- **Lower utility bills.** New homes are usually more energy efficient than older homes, but nonetheless, ask the builder to estimate the gas and electric bills.

ART DECO

- **Restrictive rules**. "Covenants, Conditions and Restrictions" (CC&Rs) regulate many aspects of community life, especially the look of yards, driveways and the outsides of houses. If you appreciate order, this will be an advantage. (See Section G for more on CC&Rs.)

NEW HOUSE CONTRACTS: SPECIAL CONSIDERATIONS

As we mention in Chapter 16, you can use our contract when buying a new house. But you will want to complete it very carefully, to allow for homeowners' association membership, optional add-ons and warranties. You may also want to obtain and review copies of documents relating to the construction of the house. Other clauses unique to new houses relate to developer delays, deposits on optional items and development and improvement plans in undeveloped areas.

B. Choose the Developer, Then the House

The most important factor in buying a new house is not what you buy (that is, the particular model), but rather whom you buy from. Or, put bluntly, to get the best deal, don't buy a house—buy its builder. Think of it this way: If a builder does poor quality work, overcharges for extras and is chronically late, a great-looking house will lose its charm fast. You're much better off buying a solid house, delivered on time, from a quality builder who stands behind his work.

Knowing who builds the best houses in a particular area is easier to find out than you might think. Usually few developers build in a particular locale and their reputations are well-known. To check out a particular builder, talk to:

- **Existing owners in the development you're considering (or in a recently completed development by the same builder)**. If they like or hate the developer, you probably will too. The homeowners' associations will be an especially good source of information because they often hear about, and sometimes coordinate, complaints from buyers. (In one survey, more than 25% of California homeowners' associations responded that they have either filed suit against or seriously considered suing their developer because of defective workmanship.)

- **An experienced contractor**. Have him look at other houses the developer is building. It's hard to tell a lot about how good the construction techniques were on a finished model; it's much easier if someone with experience can get access to a house as it's being built.

- **County planning or building office staff who deal with local developers**. For the best results, ask your questions positively. "Do Brady & Jones finish their projects on time, with few complaints?" will probably be answered candidly, while "Is it true Brady & Jones is a real schlock outfit?" might not be. Be warned, though, that in a few counties the building staff may have a "sweetheart" working arrangement with the builder, so don't use this as your only source of information.

- **Real estate agents who've worked in the area for some time**. While agents won't usually deal directly with new house sales (see Section C below), they will likely have handled the resale of other houses built by the same developer, and will know developers' reputations.

- **The Contractors State License Board and the local Better Business Bureau for any complaints filed against the developer**. The Board will tell you of any complaints filed against a developer only when the complaint has been fully investigated and referred for legal action. Remember, however, that the lack of complaints doesn't necessarily say anything positive about the builder.

 DON'T BOTHER CALLING THE CALIFORNIA DEPARTMENT OF REAL ESTATE

Don't waste your time. In our experience, this agency is substantially worthless when it comes to providing honest consumer information.

C. Using a Real Estate Agent or Broker

Chapter 5 discusses the legal and practical issues of working with a real estate broker or salesperson. Unfortunately, those rules don't necessarily apply when purchasing a new house.

- Developers with hot properties don't want to pay a commission or referral fee to a real estate salesperson representing the buyer. Instead, developers hire their own sales staff (who only represent them) and rely on advertising programs to produce prospects. Not surprisingly, local real estate people, knowing they won't earn a commission, won't show these houses, and may even bad-mouth an entire development in an effort to divert you to houses where commissions are being paid.

- Developers with slow-selling projects may cooperate with local real estate salespeople. This can extend to offering prizes and other come-ons to the salesperson who brings in the most potential buyers. Thus, you may be dragged to completely unsuitable developments for the sole (but unstated) purpose of qualifying the salesperson for a drawing for a trip to Mexico.

MARCIA AND DREW: BOY, WERE WE NAIVE

We visited a model home; we liked it and the financing the builder offered. We told the salesperson we had some design changes in mind and were assured that the developer was fair and flexible, and would work everything out as we went along. We took him at his word and signed on the dotted line. Within a few days, problems began. For one, we wanted to eliminate some completely nonfunctional pillars in the living room. The builder said "no way." We then asked for different bathroom counter tops, and offered to pay the extra. Again, we got no cooperation and had to hire an outside contractor to remove the countertop and install the one we wanted. Whatever we requested turned out to be either impossible or prohibitively expensive. When we asked to see the original salesperson who had promised us "total cooperation," we learned that he was now working as a scuba diving instructor in Hawaii.

I guess you can say we learned the hard way. If we ever again buy a new house, you can be sure we'll be better scouts and come prepared.

- Some developers cooperate with agents under their own (often unusual and not widely published) rules. For example, a developer might not pay a commission if you first visit without your agent, even if your agent is involved in every subsequent step of the purchase, but would pay one if the salesperson was with you when you first registered. Knowing this, the agent with whom you are working is economically motivated to steer you away from any such tracts you've visited on your own and towards one with rules which will result in a commission if you buy.

In short, the traditional seller-pays-the-real-estate-agent-commission model works poorly for new house sales, even when salespeople are eligible for commission. This doesn't mean it's necessarily best to go it alone, especially if you are new to the new house trade. If you want professional help in evaluating or negotiating the purchase of a new house, hire an agent familiar with the local new housing scene by the hour before you sign a contract. (See Chapter 5, Section D.) Then do most of the leg work yourself—before you're locked into a contract—using the agent as an expert sounding board and counselor.

See if the developer will give you a break in the sales price, or provide upgrades such as higher quality carpet, if he doesn't have to pay a real estate agent's commission.

BE SURE TO FIND OUT HOW MANY HOUSES OR CONDOS ARE OWNER-OCCUPIED

When you're considering a house in a new development or a condominium, find out early on what percentage of the units are owner-occupied. The higher the percentage, in general, the better maintained is the development or building. Owners have more at stake (resale value of their property) than do renters, who are more transient.

This information may also affect your ability to get a competitive loan from a conventional lender. If you are buying in a new development, lenders often require at least 50% owner occupancy before granting a loan. In a condominium building, many lenders make loans only where two-thirds or more of the owners occupy their units. If you don't qualify for a loan as a result of low owner occupancy in a new development, you may need to arrange financing with a developer, perhaps on less favorable terms. In a condo, you may still be able to borrow from a conventional lender, but you may have to put down 20-30%.

Another concern is that if you're considering buying a condo in a building that has commercial owners as well as residential (this would be the case, for example, if the residences were built above several stores), a lender may balk at giving you a loan if a substantial portion of the total space is occupied commercially. You may have to assume any loan of the seller of the unit you are buying. If the terms aren't great, your only hope is refinancing in the future.

D. Financing a New House

The discussions on how to determine how much house you can afford (Chapter 2) and the various ways to finance your purchase (Chapters 8 through 13) apply to buying new, as well as existing, houses. A few noteworthy differences, however, exist:

1. Help Arranging a Loan

Often, developers of new housing will help you locate financing by referring you to a local bank or savings and loan that has already appraised the property or to a loan broker. As discussed in Chapter 13, a lender will both check your creditworthiness and appraise the house to see if it's worth what you agree to pay. Normally, you pay for the appraisal, which is supposed to be an objective assessment of the house's value. Then the lender lends you a percentage of the appraised value. For new houses, however, a lender often does a blanket appraisal of all development houses and agrees to approve loans for creditworthy borrowers up to a set amount. If you borrow from one of these lenders, no new appraisal will be necessary. A developer cannot, however, insist that you accept financing through this network. To get the best deal, be sure to comparison shop.

2. Government-Housing Programs

Some builders may have their developments qualified for special government loan programs such as the Federal Housing Authority. For more on this, see Chapter 11, Government-Assisted Loans.

3. Buydowns and Other Direct Financing Subsidies

In slow markets, developers may increase buyer affordability through a "buydown" of the mortgage. Stripped of jargon, this means the developer pays a part of your monthly mortgage for a set period of time. For example, if you find a house with $1,200 in monthly carrying costs, and you have $300 a month of other debts, you'll need a family income of at least $4,550 per month to qualify. If the builder pays $150 a month toward your mortgage for five years, you'll only need a gross income of $4,100 a month to qualify. (This assumes a debt-to-income ratio of 33%. Many lenders want this ratio to be between 28% and 38%.)

More commonly, the builder will buy down your mortgage by subsidizing the interest rate you pay. One way is through the 3/2/1 subsidy, where the developer subsidizes part of your mortgage for three years, decreasing the subsidy each year. The table below shows how a buydown for a $100,000, 30-year loan at a fixed rate of 10% might work.

Why would a developer buy down your mortgage? When sales are slow, unsold inventory accumulates. Developers must continue to pay interest on the money borrowed to finance construction. Selling a house, even if it means helping pay your mortgage to do it, reduces this burden. Sure it re-duces the developer's profit as compared to selling all houses with no subsidy, but when this isn't possible, profits (albeit lower ones) depend on moving homes.

HOW A BUILDER BUYDOWN WORKS

	Your interest rate	Your payment	Mortgage subsidy from full 10% fixed rate
Year 1	7%	$665.30	24%
Year 2	8%	$733.76	16%
Year 3	9%	$804.62	8%
Years 4-30	10%	$877.57	(none)

If a buydown such as a lower initial interest rate is offered but you don't need it to afford the house, consider asking for something else instead, just as you might when buying a new car for cash at a time when a dealer is offering low interest loans. For example, you might offer to purchase for a lower price, thereby lowering the down payment, or ask for extra features such as a deck or better quality light fixtures at no extra cost. In short, the buydown is a tip off that the market is soft and you have room to bargain for a better deal one way or another.

Another reason for substituting a lower price for the buydown is that many buydowns take back many of the benefits they claim to provide—they give you a mortgage which has a higher-than-market interest rate after the buydown period is exhausted. Or, put another way, the underlying mortgage interest rate is higher than you could get on the open market.

If you can choose between a buydown of your mortgage and a significantly lower price, a reduced price (resulting in a smaller mortgage) will normally save you more if you plan to own the house for a long time. If you intend to own the house for only a few years, however, a short-term mortgage buydown is probably better, as you'll pay less during this period. (To help with the calculations, See *The Banker's Secret,* Marc Eisenson; order information is in Chapter 2, Section E.)

 BEFORE PURSUING A BUYDOWN, ASK YOURSELF WHAT HIDDEN COSTS ARE INVOLVED

Many buydowns provide you with an inferior mortgage, with the result that you save less than you think. For example, if the buydown mortgage is non-assumable, and requires you to pay higher than normal points and the underlying mortgage is an ARM with negative amortization (see Chapter 10), you obviously have gotten a lousy deal.

E. Optional Add-Ons and Upgrades

Many developers, whether selling $150,000 houses or $750,000 houses, advertise their houses at comparatively low prices to get you to come out and have a look. The moment you become seriously interested, you can be pretty sure that the price will go up as the developer will try to sell you high profit extras, such as:

- added features (an extra fireplace, deck or bedroom)
- upgrades (replace sliding doors with French doors, install better quality carpet, replace linoleum or formica with tile), or
- design changes (greenhouse windows, extra electrical outlets, or security and alarm systems).

Buying extras and upgrades can enable you to semi-custom design your home at a reasonable price. (This is especially true if the builder will accommodate structural design changes, as is often done with up-market houses.) Many buyers appreciate a wide choice of kitchen cabinets, floor coverings, air conditioning systems, windows, skylights and sprinkler systems. You may even be able to add on a room or two at a reasonable cost. But before you get too carried away, pull out your House Priorities Worksheet (Chapter 1). What do you really need to add to meet your needs, and how much will it cost? Use this figure to compare one new house to the next. Think ahead; if, for example, you plan to upgrade to a fancy stove in a year or two, find out the manufacturer's specifications, leave space for

it and have the necessary large hood and oversized gas lines installed now.

Be sure you investigate all payment options. Typically, some upgrades must be paid for up-front, while others can be added to the price of the house and paid for over time—obviously a much more affordable option if you're on a budget. If you do agree to pay a substantial amount of extra cash, make sure the funds are deposited in an escrow account, to be released when the work has been done.

 If you cancel your contract, some builders will not refund the deposits you paid for optional items. If you plan lots of expensive upgrades, try to negotiate the right for a full (or at least partial) refund if the options (for example, a new security system) haven't been bought or installed, or the right to keep any optional items which you've paid for and haven't been permanently installed.

Upgrades can add 5-20% or more to the cost of a new home. On more expensive houses, this can amount to $20,000, $50,000, or even $100,000. To get the most for your money, follow these steps:

1. **Make sure prices are fair.** Some house developers are more ethical in pricing extras than others. Steer clear of those who deliberately use poor quality materials in highly visible spots in their models, almost forcing you to upgrade to over-priced substitutes. Always confirm, in writing, what you are getting at what price, and whether the developer will allow you to make changes on your own and give you an allowance for materials and labor not used (kitchen cabinets, floor coverings). This can commonly be an issue if you don't like the developer's standard kitchen cabinets, floor coverings, or bathroom fixtures, or the optional upgrades he offers, and want to separately purchase and install these items yourself.

   To double check the prices of extras, visit consumer-oriented showrooms, do-it-yourself home stores and home improvement shops. Also check home improvement magazines.

2. **Negotiate the cost of extras.** Don't be shy about negotiating over the price of extras, even if the developer tells you they're etched in marble. In fact, as with a car, negotiating over extras is often easier than negotiating over the purchase price. Consider asking for one free extra for every two you buy. For example, if you pay top dollar for good carpets, tile and kitchen cabinets, ask the developer

to throw in a better stove at no charge. This is particularly reasonable if the developer does not credit you with its cost for the original item (a plastic countertop) when you upgrade. Also, as mentioned in our discussion of price above, don't be afraid to ask for the right to purchase and install extras or upgrades on your own. If you're considering adding an expensive option such as an oak staircase, built-in window seats or a deck, you may get a better deal from an outside contractor.

HELEN: HOW I GOT THE CARPET I WANTED

I bought a new house in El Sobrante, which came with low-quality carpeting. The developer offered two better grades, but I didn't like either—they were over-priced and still not really top grade. Thus, my offer to purchase was contingent on the developer installing the carpeting of my choice, at no charge. He balked, but I pointed out that he was planning to install carpet anyway, so what was the difference? He finally agreed, and also agreed to give me the carpeting that came with the house. (Why I had to bargain for this is a real mystery, as, of course, I'd paid for it.) At any rate, I purchased my own carpet at a local warehouse for $3,800 and had it delivered. The developer installed it. I then sold the original carpet through a classified ad for $1,500. Not only did I save several hundred dollars over the cost of upgrading to the developer's supposedly top-quality carpet, but I also got the carpet I wanted.

3. **Inspect model houses carefully.** Be sure that the linoleum, tile, rugs and kitchen cabinets are of good quality, and that they're the ones you'll get if you buy a house. Many new house contracts contain a clause saying that the model's features are not necessarily the features you'll receive—you are guaranteed only the functional equivalent of what you see, which will almost always be different and will cost the builder far less. If you suspect this problem, shop elsewhere or make a list of the precise features you're concerned about (include makes and models) and include it in your contract.

Model homes will almost always have the best of everything, including mirrored closet doors designed to make the rooms seem larger. Don't be fooled into expecting that your home will have the same details. If in doubt, get your understanding in writing or included as a contingency in your purchase contract. And be sure to look at an "unfinished" model, to see exactly what you're buying.

4. **Take care of the essentials before negotiating the flashy add-ons.** Be practical. More electrical outlets, a fence around the yard (especially if you have children or pets) and, in many areas, air conditioning, are day-to-day necessities, while a wood-burning fireplace and hot tub are not.

5. **Get it in writing.** When dealing with a developer's sales representative, get all promises as to what will be done, and when, in writing. If you haven't yet signed the purchase contract, make sure it includes all agreed-upon changes. If the developer's contract allows him to install appliances or use materials different from those in the model, establish exactly what you will get and when. If you've already signed the contract, and you later negotiate for changes, write them down in a separate document.

Developers often resist writing things down, wanting you to rely on oral promises. ("Sure, the deck will be built by March 1.") Oral commitments are notoriously unreliable and, in practice, almost impossible to enforce.

Below is an example of what a supplementary written agreement should cover.

SAMPLE SUPPLEMENTARY AGREEMENT

February 1, 199X

On January 12, 199X, Alex Stevens, Sales Manager for ABC HomeCrafters, presented me with a contract to purchase the house at 8 Warden Crescent. After a discussion I agreed to sign this contract with the following conditions:

- ABC HomeCrafters agrees to install a drainage system along the rear property line, according to the specifications set out in Attachment A to this agreement, and a redwood deck with railing behind the kitchen, according to the specifications set out in Attachment B. In exchange, I agree to pay $11,000 above the amount agreed to in the purchase contract dated January 17, 199X, by March 10, 199X.

- Work on the drainage system and deck, plus all landscaping called for in the purchase contract, will be completed on or before November 1, 199X. If any work is not completed by this date, we agree that the money to cover the cost will remain in escrow until the work is completed.

_2/1/9X_   _Patricia Nelson_
Date   Patricia Nelson

_2/1/9x_   _Alex Stevens_
Date   Alex Stevens, for ABC HomeCrafters

F. Choosing Your Lot

In some popular new house projects, you'll need to select a lot before the house is constructed or when construction has just started. This can be tricky, as many builders won't even allow buyers on site for insurance reasons. And even if they will, it can be hard to make an accurate assessment as to what the area will ultimately look like, especially if it's full of earth movers and construction equipment. Still, if you take your time and really study the developer's maps, paying particular attention to the elevation of various parcels and traffic flow patterns, you should get a pretty good picture of what a particular house will be like when the development is complete. Here are some things you will want to consider:

- **Privacy.** Study the elevation of the lot. Will passers-by on the street, or neighbors, be able to look into your windows? If so, will they be viewing rooms where you particularly want privacy?

- **Driveway.** Will you have a clear view down the street? It's dangerous to pull out into the middle of a blind curve.

- **Noise.** A lot at the end of a cul-de-sac will be quieter than one on a main access road, especially if you're on a hill or a corner.

- **Flooding.** Lots on the tops and sides of hills are usually dry. Lots at the bottom are often more prone to flooding, especially if they're near a stream.

Getting a good lot at a good price is often a matter of timing. The best locations in each price range usually go first. Most developers offer waiting lists for popular locations where houses are under construction. In deciding whether to take an okay lot in a section now being built, or to wait and hope for a better location in the next section, consider the following:

- Salespeople who receive a full commission if you buy now—as opposed to a small cut if you put down a deposit on a house that won't be built for a while—will sometimes overpraise existing lots and emphasize possible

ENGLISH VERNACULAR

difficulties and delays in connection with sections where future building will occur. If, however, you state that you'll buy in the yet-unbuilt area or not at all, these difficulties are likely to quickly evaporate.

- Developers often, but not always, build the more desirable sections of a tract first. This excites buyers' interest and moves in many people quickly, creating a positive atmosphere for later sales. Once a development is judged a success, the poorer quality lots can be unloaded, often for considerably higher prices than they might otherwise have brought.

- In large developments where new sections open periodically, the longer you wait, the more choice you'll have. This strategy may cost you dearly, however, if the development is popular, because in this situation the developer will surely mark up prices for newly-built houses, which will likely mean that the resale price of existing houses will also increase. On the other hand, you may end up getting a great deal if the original houses in the development were overpriced, sold slowly and went down in value.

- Sales in yet-to-be-completed sections of developments often fall through, and good houses may reappear on sales lists, sometimes just before closing. So, if you can commit quickly, you may save time and money by staying in touch with a developer and being ready to move fast when a good deal presents itself.

If you're buying a lot in an undeveloped area, be sure you get the developer's written confirmation of promised improvements, such as sidewalks and parks.

Tips on Getting a Good Lot at a Favorable Price

A big portion of the cost of a new house is the land it's built on. Developers price new house lots according to their perceived desirability; a house next to a golf course or waterway will obviously cost far more than one that overlooks a storage area. Dividing lots into broad price categories is usually imperfect, however. For example, there may be a big difference between the best lot in the most expensive category (A) and the worst lot in the second best category (B), but the worst lot in the A category and the best in B category will vary much less.

CLUES TO GOOD CONSTRUCTION AND AMENITIES

The more you pay for a house, the more—and better quality—amenities you should expect. Allowing for the fact that you can't expect the Taj Mahal if you only pay for a low-cost townhouse, here are some things to look for:

Air conditioning

If you live in a hot area, be sure the central air conditioning is adequate. In many tracts in the Central Valley, air conditioning units that supposedly meet minimum standards don't do the job.

Building site

Review a copy of the soils and engineering report, which the builder should have available, and the Transfer Disclosure Statement. (See Chapter 19, Section B.) You are obviously not interested in buying a house that is likely to flood, slide off a hill, or which is built in immediate proximity to an earthquake fault. If you think the report is incorrect—that is, it says the soil is in better condition than it appears, or fear the consequences of earthquake or flood—check U.S. Geological Survey maps for soil stability and earthquake and flood zones. Federal or state agencies should have this and other impartial information. (See Appendix 1, Welcome to California, for other sources.) You may want to arrange specialized inspections. (See Chapter 19, Section I.)

Carpets and drapes

Look for good quality. Poor quality carpets and drapes are often an indication that the house itself is poorly built.

Electrical outlets

How many outlets are in each room? You'll want at least four, with plenty of phone, cable TV and computer jacks. If the builder is scrimping on small items like these, watch out—unless you are deliberately buying a "stripped-down" house and appreciate the fact that many small savings are reflected in the low price.

Energy efficiency

Insulation is measured by an "R" factor. In cool areas of California, look for development that exceeds R19, the minimum standard. Good insulation now will save you enormous heating bills later. Make sure the air conditioning and heating systems are the most efficient.

Entryways

Are the front and back porches covered? Stepping directly into the rain is a nuisance, but eliminating porches saves developers a few dollars.

Floor

The best, but most expensive, floors are hardwood or ceramic tile. Make sure any plywood floor has two layers.

Foundation

Poured concrete is superior to concrete block.

Inside doors

It's usually worth paying extra for solid core doors if they don't come with the house. If they do, the developer is making a quiet but effective statement that he builds a quality product.

Kitchen cabinets

If you're paying top dollar, you want hardwood cabinets, not plywood. Again, this is a good tip-off as to whether you're dealing with a quality developer.

Soundproofing

Make sure you won't hear neighbors or highway noise. In developments where houses are only a few feet apart, or you're on a busy street, this is particularly important. If some houses in the development are already occupied, check this out with the occupants.

Yard

An underground watering system is a good sign that the builder is committed to quality. Given a choice, it's more efficient and convenient, and often less expensive to install an underground watering system before the yard is graded. Also, starting a lawn from sod is normally better than starting from seed.

G. Restrictions on the Use of Your Property: CC&Rs

New house developments and community associations such as condominiums include, as part of the deed to the property, a number of restrictions on how the property can be used and the responsibilities of the homeowners. These are called covenants, conditions and restrictions (CC&Rs). CC&Rs commonly limit the color or colors you can paint your house (often brown or gray), the color of the curtains or blinds visible from the street (usually white), and even the type of front yard landscaping you can do. Some go as far as to require that garages that face the street be kept neat, prohibit basketball hoops in the driveway or front yard and prohibit parking R.V.s and boats in the driveway.

Some developments have so many restrictions that it's almost as if your house is part of a common park, over which you have little say. For example, with some CC&Rs, you don't have the right to cut your lawn, plant a tree or tend flowers; instead, you pay a monthly fee to a gardening company which does the mowing and maintains other landscaping. Typical CC&Rs in a condo have similar restrictions—especially regarding window coverings and maintenance of lawns and gardens. In addition, condo CC&Rs often restrict the size, number or even acceptability of pets.

Getting relief from overly restrictive CC&Rs after you move in isn't usually easy. You'll likely have to submit an application (with fee) for a variance, get your neighbors' permission, and possibly go through a formal hearing at which you may not succeed. And if you want to make a structural change, such as enlarging a window, building a fence, or adding a room, you'll likely need formal permission from the association in addition to complying with city zoning rules.

1. Role of Homeowners' Associations

Some CC&Rs—especially with condos—put costly decision-making rights in the hands of a homeowners' association. These associations can assess mandatory fees for common property maintenance, which can get expensive in housing developments if a pool, golf course or other recreational facilities are included. Many associations in housing developments let their boards raise regular assessments up to 20% per year and levy additional special assessments, for a new roof or other capital improvement, with no membership vote. Also, associations can decide to sue a developer or city and assess you a mandatory share of the legal fees. In condos, especially buildings with fewer than 15 units, however, the condo association can act to modify the CC&Rs or take legal action only by unanimous consent of all owners.

DOES THE ASSOCIATION HAVE ADEQUATE RESERVES?

In condominiums, the money in reserves must cover repairs to all common spaces—roof, garage and the like. While a $50 or $200 per month homeowner's fee may seem steep when added to your mortgage, insurance and taxes, you are better off with a fee that's too high, not too low. Low fees often equal inadequate reserves. When something needs repair, and the reserves are too low, the owners must pay. Usually the association authorizes the repair and bills the owners through a special assessment. If your co-owner(s) don't have the money, you may have to pay their share or face a lawsuit or other collection efforts by whoever did the repairs.

In some housing developments, homeowners' associations are well run and enhance living conditions. Many residents, especially those who buy in an effort to build equity and move on, appreciate the fact that most associations are very sensitive to making decisions which will enhance the value of the properties. Unfortunately, however, some associations are poorly run. Often the majority of residents aren't interested in management details, which can mean a small group of activists gains control and imposes restrictive and sometimes expensive rules and policies. These can lead to bitter squabbles, where neighbors fight each other, using the association as their arena, and splinter groups war with boards of directors. A misman-

PUEBLO

aged or underfinanced association can go bankrupt and lose assets such as cash reserves.

AVOIDING DISPUTES WITH THE HOMEOWNERS' ASSOCIATION

Don't discount the possibility that all sorts of problems may happen in a development you buy into. A University of California study in the late 1980s showed that 30% of California homeowners' associations were sued (or almost sued) by disgruntled homeowners, primarily when homeowners asserted their rights to live as they pleased and associations enforced a telephone book full of rules. The result was costly legal bills as owners battled homeowners' associations in court and a decrease in property values. To minimize these lawsuits, effective January 1994, state law requires homeowner associations and their members to attempt arbitration or mediation when there is a dispute over the CC&Rs. (Civil Code § 1354.)

STEVE AND CATHERINE: STUDY YOUR CC&RS

After burning out looking at over-priced quaint old houses, we decided to check out new ones. We found the ideal house in a beautiful development in Sonoma County. And the price was right too. "What's wrong?" we asked ourselves.

We didn't have to wait long for the answer. "Here are your CC&Rs," the sales agent said as she handed us a package about an inch thick. Arrgg. No way will I live in a place governed by dozens of rules and a homeowner's association. Case closed.

But wait. Why did we like this house? It was near a school, and our son had about five years to go before he graduated from high school. Then we could move to our dream rural hilltop. In truth, we were very interested in enhancing short-term property values. Suddenly, the CC&Rs looked quite different. By preserving the attractive character of the development, the CC&Rs might be our friend, not our enemy.

So with some trepidation, we bought. Surprise! Over four years later, we're still happy with how the CC&Rs work. They provide a framework for resolving minor neighbor disputes and have set maintenance standards that keep our community looking spiffy. So far, we've not been set upon by power-hungry CC&R enforcers. And as we hoped, property values are soaring.

2.   How to Check Out a Development or Condo

While development or condo living is not for everyone, many people like the idea that rules govern the conduct of their neighbors and are happy to obey the rules themselves. If you now live in an area where people fix their cars in the driveway until midnight, and the house on one side of you hasn't been painted in 15 years and the one on the other side is bright purple, a little order may be welcome. If so, you'll want to investigate further. Here are some tips.

- Get a copy of the CC&Rs and relevant documents that govern any development or condo you're interested in. Many listing agents selling condos will not give out CC&Rs until you have submitted an offer—with a contingency that the CC&Rs are okay, of course.

- Read the CC&Rs carefully and decide whether the rules are compatible with your lifestyle. Believe it or not, some are so detailed they even regulate the maximum weight of your dog. (This, in fact, is quite common with condos.)

- If you're on a tight budget, check the homeowners' association membership fees and assessments and how easy it is for the board to increase these amounts. (Remember that lenders will review these assessments when qualifying you for a loan.) Review past budgets, and check the history and amount of fee and assessment increases. Also, find out how much money is in the reserve account.

- Developments with few community extras, such as pools, golf courses, recreation centers, boat docks and the like are much less likely to face large homeowners' association fee increases.

- Find out how much parking is available, if there's an extra charge, and where and how parking spaces are assigned.

- Make sure the association has adequate liability and property insurance. Find out if the development is involved in litigation. If the association is suing the developer, for example, you may have difficulty getting a loan.

- If you ever plan to rent your house or condo, pay close attention to rules affecting tenants and your liability for their actions.

- If parts of the development have been occupied for a while, attend a homeowners' association meeting and talk with the officers. If that's not possible, ask to see the written minutes of recent association meetings and what the key issues are. Either way, you'll get a good sense of how the association works. Some associations enforce every rule with the enthusiasm of a Marine drill sergeant; others are run in a far more relaxed way.

See Clause 10 of our offer form in Chapter 16, which requires your review and approval of items such as CC&Rs and homeowners' association budgets.

RESOURCES ON CC&RS AND HOMEOWNERS' ASSOCIATIONS

Many homeowners' associations belong to organizations which publish a wide variety of useful materials. These include:

- Executive Council of Home Owners (ECHO), 1602 The Alameda, Suite 100, San Jose, CA 95126. (408)-297-3246.
- Community Associations Institute, (CAI) 1630 Duke St., Alexandria, VA, 22314. (703) 548-8600.

CC&Rs and bylaws must conform to the California Corporations Code, Sections 5001 through 10014. You can find the Corporations Code in any law library and in the business or government section of many public libraries. Also, the Community Associations Institute (address above) publishes a guide to California statutes affecting community associations and a regular newsletter updating legal issues in the state.

The Homeowner's Association Manual, by Peter Dunbar (Suncoast Professional Publishing) is a practical guide for operating homeowners' associations.

to walk away or assign your contract to another buyer. Again, get it in writing.

Developer delays can cause serious problems, especially with your mortgage loan. As discussed in Chapter 13, Obtaining a Mortgage, lenders normally won't lock in (guarantee) a particular interest rate for more than about 30 days, although you can sometimes get an extension if you pay a higher fee up front. Thus, if the closing on your new house is delayed several months at a time when interest rates are rising, you'll end up paying a higher rate and, in volatile economies, may no longer be eligible for the loan. If you have to cancel your contract because interest rates have jumped so much that you can't afford the house, you'll most likely have to forfeit your deposits to the builder. In this situation, try (in writing) to have the deposits returned to you, or at least have the matter submitted to arbitration. Or better yet, insist that your contract with the developer contain a financial penalty if the house isn't ready in time.

If you're a current homeowner, you also face the problem of selling your existing house so you can move into your new one when it's ready. In Chapter 14, we discuss the problems inherent in purchasing one house and selling another. When you aren't sure exactly when a new house will be ready, your best bet is to sell the old one with a contingency that allows you to either delay the closing on your old house or, if the closing goes ahead, to continue to live in it (and pay rent) for as long as possible. If you have a choice, it's possibly better to delay the

H. Dealing With Delays

If you agree to buy a house that isn't finished (or even started), you'll be asked to sign a very one-sided contract. You'll be given numerous deadlines (to make deposits, agree to design changes, get loan approval, list and sell your present house, and close escrow), while the developer will be given great leeway—sometimes up to a year from the target date—to deliver the house. Do what you can to change this. Most important, you want to establish some reasonable date at which you can cancel the contract and get all of your money back if the developer doesn't deliver your house. For example, if the developer promises the house will be done June 1, it's not reasonable to cancel the whole deal if he finishes on June 2. But what about August 1 or November 1? At some point, you should be entitled

BACK TO THE FUTURE

closing because mortgage interest is deductible but rent is not. Also, you will be paying rent based on the purchaser's monthly carrying costs, which will almost always be higher than yours, assuming you sold the house for more than you paid for it.

The buyer of your old house will probably want some limitation (say 60, 90 or 120 days) on your right to remain living there. Assuming you have to accept this, you may, of course, still find yourself living in a motel if completion of your new house is seriously delayed.

If you rent, especially if you have a month-to-month tenancy, you're in a better position. When your new house is ready, give your landlord 30 days' written notice of when you plan to move out. Even if you have a lease of a year or more, you're probably in pretty good shape. Breaking a lease isn't normally a problem in most areas of California. Although you're liable to pay the rent for the entire lease, your landlord is legally responsible to try to re-rent your place, and to subtract the new tenant's rent from what you owe. In California's tight rental market, a landlord can usually quickly re-rent a unit at a higher rate, which means you get out of a lease early, at no cost. See *Tenants' Rights,* by Moskovitz & Warner (Nolo Press), for steps to take to assure that your landlord re-rents a place promptly.

I. Inspect the House Before Closing

The biggest complaint of people who live in newly-built developments involves the developer's failure to do all the things she promised in the purchase contract in a timely fashion—such as installing small items like shower heads, cabinet hardware and closet fixtures, repairing or replacing malfunctioning appliances, heaters or air conditioners, or completing promised landscaping. Sometimes more serious problems occur such as shoddy construction, the omission of a room in the plan or an extra room built illegally. For example, an in-law unit must meet certain requirements to be legally rented. You'll face a nightmare if it falls short.

The best way to protect yourself is to include a contingency in your contract allowing you to conduct inspections during specific phases of construction as well as before escrow closes. (See Clause 9 of our offer form). You can then refuse to close escrow until everything is complete and to your satisfaction. Otherwise, once escrow closes, you take occupancy and the developer pockets her money, the developer has little incentive to finish anything quickly or correctly.

Don't rely only on local building inspectors' approval. (One local building inspector we know failed to notice that the builder completely ignored the blueprints, omitted rooms and used all different materials to do the job. He did notice the lawsuit filed against him—and the builder.) To make sure you're getting the best quality construction, hire professionals experienced in checking out new homes to inspect the site at key points in the building process, such as during the framing of walls, doors and floors. While it will cost you extra, hiring professional inspectors is the best way to assure quality construction. *Your New House,* by Alan and Denise Fields (Windsor Peak Press) includes an excellent discussion on scheduling inspections during home construction.

You'll also want to hire a professional inspector before closing. You should also do your own final inspection. Bring a tape measure, note pad and pencil. Be as methodical as you can—open every cupboard door and window, turn on every faucet and test every appliance. You may learn that the upstairs bathroom has no hot water or that the builder completely forgot your air conditioning. Also, see Chapter 19, Sections H and I, for tips on professional and do-it-yourself home inspections.

Hang tough and resist promises that if you'll move in now, the developer will fix all problems promptly. ("We'll install the washroom sinks the day they arrive, and start the landscaping as soon as the rainy season ends.") It's amazing how much work can be completed before closing, and how quickly "impossible to get" parts can appear if you refuse to close until everything is done.

But what if you're living in a motel (or will be soon) if you don't move in? If significant and costly work remains, insist that the necessary funds be placed in a trust account after escrow closes. Then ask for a written agreement providing that if the work is performed on time, the money will be released to the developer, but if it isn't, the funds go to you to hire someone else to do the work. If the developer refuses, at the least make a list of what needs to be done, assign a completion date to each, and have it signed by the developer. (See the sample, below.)

⚠ READ DISCLOSURES CAREFULLY

Sellers must make a number of disclosures when property is transferred in California, including the condition of the house and property, the existence of CC&Rs and homeowners' association, and lawsuits involving the development. (See Chapter 19, Section B discussion of the Real Estate Transfer Disclosure Statement.)

SAMPLE AGREEMENT TO COMPLETE WORK

To: John Addison, Acme Development

From: Abigail Williams

Re: 11 Tulip Drive

Date: December 1, 199X

On December 17, 199X, escrow is scheduled to close on the house I am planning to buy at 11 Tulip Drive. The price I am paying includes a high quality sod lawn. In exchange for my promise to go ahead with the closing, Acme Development agrees to complete all yard grading and drainage work, and to install this lawn by March 15, 199X.

I'm sending you two signed copies of this memo. Please sign one on the "Agreed to by" line and return it to me by December 10, 199X.

Sincerely,

Abigail Williams

Agreed to by:_____

John Addison, Sales Manager, Acme Development

J. Guarantees and Warranties

You've probably heard horror stories about new houses that began to disintegrate the day the buyer moves in. This shouldn't be a problem if you buy from a reputable developer. To protect yourself further, ask if the developer provides any guarantees. Even better is a new house warranty provided by third-party insurers. Let's look at each.

Developer guarantees. Most developers give a one-year guarantee on new houses. The better guarantees include all workmanship and materials. In addition, appliances will be new and will come with their own warranties. Get all model and serial numbers, and a copy of each appliance warranty.

One problem with developer guarantees is that you have only the developer's promise that a problem will be fixed. If the developer goes out of business, as many have in the last few years, you're out of luck. In fact, some guarantees are completely worthless, as unscrupulous developers deliberately put themselves out of business. They create a corporation when they begin working on a particular development and then dissolve the corporation when they complete the work in that particular development. When problems arise, there's no one to turn to to make a claim on the guarantee, and you have no one to sue, as you cannot sue a dissolved corporation. Also, most developer guarantees are worded vaguely, guaranteeing "acceptable standards of workmanship and material." This is hard to enforce if a developer doesn't voluntarily stand behind his work.

CONSUMER ACTION LINES MIGHT HELP WITH CONTRACTOR COMPLAINTS

If you can't get a developer to make good on a new home guarantee or warranty, take your problem to a consumer action line. Offered by many radio and TV stations and newspapers, the best have volunteers who will look into your problem and, if they're convinced you've got a legitimate beef, will go to bat for you against the developer. If this fails and the problem costs less than $5,000 to correct, consider suing the developer in small claims court. See *Everybody's Guide to Small Claims Court,* by Ralph Warner (Nolo Press).

Insurance company warranties. Some developers purchase new home warranty policies from independent insurance companies, which are far better than developer guarantees. Typical policies cover workmanship and materials for one year, plumbing, electrical, heating and air conditioning systems for two years, and major structural defects for ten years. Definitions of defects in material and workmanship, and your rights, are spelled out in much more detail than in developer guarantees. And most third-party policies contain fair dispute resolution procedures if you're dissatisfied with an insurer's response to a claim. Clause 10, Section E, of our offer form (Chapter 16) includes a contingency that the seller provide you with a written warranty covering certain items.

If your developer doesn't—or won't—offer third-party insurance coverage, you can purchase your own house warranty. Be sure you're aware of all restrictions, deductible dollar limits of coverage, and dispute resolution procedures. (See Chapter 19, Section L, for more on home warranties.) ∎

Financing Your House: An Overview

If you've already arranged to finance your house, skip ahead to Chapter 14.

Let's start with the bold truth—despite the fact that mortgage interest rates are at reasonable levels, arranging to finance a house can be depressing. To qualify, you must normally come up with a good-sized chunk of cash for the down payment. Then you need to borrow a huge sum of money and make monthly payments for what seems like the rest of your life. And finally, if you don't want to end up with a lousy deal, you must understand seemingly endless details about mortgages.

Obtaining a mortgage is often perplexing. Literally thousands of real estate lenders offer a variety of products with different interest rates, up-front costs and fine print terms. That's where this chapter and the five that follow come in. Chapters 8 through 13 provide the basic information necessary to sensibly finance the purchase of a house. If you carefully read all our material before making important decisions, you'll be equipped to obtain a good mortgage at a competitive price.

A. How Mortgage Lenders Think

The more money you have for a down payment, the higher your personal income and the lower your debts, the more mortgage options you'll have and the better deal you're likely to get. You'll be a likely candidate for a favorable mortgage loan if:

• You invest a lot of your own money in the down payment. People rarely default on their loans when they have a large personal stake in the property.

• You do well financially and have limited long-term debts. The affluent usually repay their loans, often ahead of time.

• You have an excellent credit history. People who have paid their bills on time for many years are likely to continue to do so. The reverse is also true.

• You are purchasing property that is clearly worth (can be sold for) more than the loan amount. The lender feels secure that if you default, the property can be sold for more than enough to repay the loan. Unfortunately, the converse is true.

From the lender's perspective, the only problem with these criteria in making loans is that every other lender also uses

them. This puts those with terrific credit in an excellent bargaining position because they have many more choices than those with poor or average credit. Fortunately, it also means that lenders have plenty of funds left over to lend to the more typical house purchaser. Unfortunately, the less money you have to put down, the lower your income and the greater your debts, the more likely you will have to accept a mortgage (if you can get one at all) with some undesirable features, such as high interest rates, substantial points, private mortgage insurance or a requirement that you get a co-borrower.

B. Who Lends Mortgage Money?

Many entities, including banks, credit unions, savings and loans, insurance companies and mortgage bankers, make home loans in California. Large lenders tend to work statewide, while smaller ones specialize in narrower geographical areas, types of housing or types of mortgages. Which lenders loan in a particular community and on what terms changes frequently as new companies appear, old ones merge and market conditions fluctuate. Fortunately, because mortgage rates are widely published (see Chapter 13), and many types of loans are standardized no matter who the lender is, comparative shopping is not difficult.

Government-guaranteed loans (see Chapter 11) offered by the Federal Housing Administration (FHA) and U.S. Depart-

CUPOLA COTTAGE

ment of Veterans Affairs (VA) are also options for people purchasing affordably-priced houses in many areas of California. By and large, only moderate priced houses (almost always below $200,000) qualify. In some cities, this includes the majority of houses; in others, hardly any.

Given the numbers of lenders, borrowers and mortgage possibilities, the constantly changing mix of money available and interest rates, there's no magic formula to choosing a mortgage. You must learn the pros and cons of the major types of mortgages available and then compare. As you sift through all the financing details in the next five chapters, remember this important truth: There's no one universally-desirable mortgage, only one that will help you buy the house you want with maximum efficiency at a minimum cost.

DON'T OVERLOOK PRIVATE FINANCING

To bypass lender rules and restrictions, many home buyers borrow some or all mortgage money privately, that is, from parents, other relatives and friends. (Chapter 12 covers private mortgages.) This is the most cost-efficient mortgage of all, but receives little press coverage, at least in part because institutional lenders advertise widely and buyers often forget the alternatives.

C. Standardized Loans—Fannie Mae, Freddie Mac and the Secondary Mortgage Market

Most financial institutions that lend money (banks, credit unions, savings and loans) don't keep most of the loans they make in their portfolio, but rather, sell them to investors on the "secondary mortgage market." Several large institutions, including the Federal National Mortgage Association (FNMA—Fannie Mae) and Federal Home Loan Mortgage Corporation (FHLMC—Freddie Mac), buy a large portion of these mortgages. Ginnie Mae, part of the U.S. Department of Housing and Urban Development (HUD), is also part of the secondary mortgage market for FHA and VA mortgages.

But the secondary mortgage market buys only mortgages that conform to their financial qualification standards and rules regarding maximum size loan. (See Chapter 2.) The result

is that most lenders follow these rules and many mortgages are remarkably similar. For example, Fannie Mae and Freddie Mac buy no loans exceeding $207,000 for a single family house, which is why lenders in newspaper real estate sections often quote interest rates for loans up to this amount. Fannie Mae and Freddie Mac loan limits change annually. $207,000 was the limit in late 1996.

If you need a mortgage larger than $207,000, you probably need what's called a "jumbo" loan, which typically has a slightly higher interest rate than Fannie Mae or Freddie Mac loans.

HOW THE POLITICAL CLOUT OF BIG BANKS COSTS YOU PLENTY

Freddie Mac and Fannie Mae loan limits are way too low in California, where high house prices mean that mortgages commonly exceed $$207,000. So why aren't the limits increased to a more realistic number? One reason is that some lenders who write jumbo loans on more expensive houses oppose any increase. Opposition would make sense if loans in the $200,000-$300,000 range were riskier than smaller loans. But for lenders who loan only to good credit risks and insist on an adequate down payment, jumbo loans aren't riskier. The lenders oppose the increase because low Freddie Mac and Fannie Mae loan limits mean bigger profits when selling high interest jumbo loans.

D. Mortgage Types

Mortgages come in many varieties and are covered in the chapters that follow. Here's an overview.

1. Traditional Mortgages

Fixed Rate Mortgage. The interest rate and the amount you pay each month remain the same over the entire mortgage term, which is traditionally 15, 20 or 30 years. A number of variations are available, including short-term fixed rate mortgages, five- and seven-year fixed rate loans with balloon payments at the end, and two-step mortgages with a lower than normal fixed rate for the first few years, which later steps up to the prevailing market rate after the initial period (often five years) ends. (See Chapter 9.)

Adjustable Rate Mortgage (ARM). The interest rates on these mortgages fluctuate according to interest rates in the economy. Initial interest rates are often substantially lower than for fixed rate mortgages, but if general interest rates go up, so too will ARM rates. Several types of ARMs are available, including an ARM-fixed rate hybrid mortgage. (See Chapter 10.)

2. Creative Financing Techniques

Second Mortgage. This is an additional loan (made by the seller or another lender) when the first mortgage loan and down payment amount fall short of the total purchase price. (See Chapter 12.)

Assumed Mortgage. The buyer takes over the unpaid balance and terms of a seller's loan on a house. Most fixed rate mortgages are not assumable, while most ARMs are. (See Chapters 9 and 10.)

Mortgage Buydowns. These are traditionally used as part of new house sales. (See Chapter 7, Section D.) The developer prepays part of the purchaser's mortgage payment for one or more years to make the purchase more affordable. Recently, some lenders have provided buydowns for fixed rate loans on existing houses.

E. Comparing Fixed Rate and Adjustable Rate Mortgages

It's almost impossible to consider getting a mortgage without comparing a fixed rate mortgage to an adjustable rate mortgage (ARM). We discuss the many types of each (and even hybrids that change from one to the other after a period of years) in the next few chapters; for now, here's a brief overview of the pros and cons of each.

With an ARM, you pay a lower interest rate at the start. This interest rate will go up for several years or more, because ARMs are always offered at a discounted interest rate. Once the discount is eliminated and your ARM reaches its real level, it may fluctuate, depending on whether interest rates in general go up or down. When interest rates increase, your mortgage payments may increase. When interest rates decline, so might

your monthly payments. To avoid constant and drastic fluctuations, ARMs typically regulate (cap) how much and how often the interest rate and/or payments can change in a year and over the life of the loan.

With a fixed rate mortgage, you pay the same amount each month for a set period of years, no matter what interest rates in general do. If you borrow $200,000 for 30 years at 7.5%, and interest rates soar to 15%, your interest rate stays at 7.5%. This sounds good and safe, and if you're concerned with payment instability, this can be a real plus.

But fixed rate loans have a down side. In some cases lenders (such as portfolio lenders, which don't sell their loans on the secondary mortgage market) set more stringent qualification standards for fixed rate mortgages than for ARMs. And you can expect to pay a significantly higher initial interest rate for a fixed rate mortgage—as much as 3.5 percentage points, or over 80% more—than you would at first pay with an ARM. Also, if interest rates in general drop, your mortgage interest rate won't. With a 7.5% fixed rate mortgage, you'll continue to pay 7.5% unless you refinance your loan and incur the up-front costs (points and other loan fees) of getting a new one.

Interest rates on ARMs are initially lower than fixed rates at least in part because ARM rates go up when interest rates in general do. This results in shifting a portion of the risk of rising interest rates from the lender to the buyer. Because fixed interest rates can't rise, no matter how general interest rates behave, lenders set fixed loan rates higher as a cushion against the possibility that interest rates will go up to the point that their cost of money may approach or exceed what they receive in interest.

Your choice of a fixed or adjustable rate mortgage should really depend on the interest rates and mortgage options available when you're buying a house. When the first edition of this book was published in 1990, we strongly recommended a fixed rate mortgage, unless you planned to own the house for such a short period (often less than three or four years) that any substantial rate increases built into an ARM simply wouldn't have time to materialize. But in the mid 1990's, ARMs have been priced to better compete with fixed rate mortgages and in other ways have become more consumer friendly. So the choice between a fixed rate mortgage and an ARM has become less clear.

Our best advice is for you to read the material that follows carefully and do your best to apply it to your own situation. Also, remember that lenders not only lend money to purchase homes; they also lend money to refinance homes. If you take out a loan now, and several years from now you're not happy with it, refinancing will probably be an option.

IN CALIFORNIA A MORTGAGE IS REALLY A DEED OF TRUST

When you borrow money from a lender to finance a home, the legal instrument recorded at the County Recorder is a deed of trust, not a mortgage. We use the term mortgage throughout this book, however, because it's the word in common use. For purists, here's the difference. When you execute a deed of trust, you give the trustee (often a title company) the right to sell your property, with no court approval, if you fail to pay the lender on time. By contrast, a mortgage normally involves only a borrower and a lender, and depending on the laws of the state where the property is located, often requires a more complicated judicial foreclosure proceeding if payments aren't made.

Here is deed of trust language translated into English.

Beneficiary. The lender (financial institution that loans you the money) is the beneficiary of the deed of trust; if you default and the trustee sells the house, the beneficiary is paid from the proceeds.

Promissory note or written evidence of a debt. When you borrow money from a lender, you sign a promissory note obligating yourself to repay the loan over a specific time period at certain terms. Normally, the note is secured by a deed of trust in which you agree that the house itself is collateral (security) for repayment. If the note isn't repaid, the collateral (house) can be sold, with the portion of the proceeds necessary to pay off the note (or as much of it as possible) going to the lender.

Trustee. The trustee, usually a title insurance company, doesn't exercise any control over the house as long as you keep payments current. If you default, however, the trustee can sell the house and use the proceeds to pay off the trust beneficiary (the lender).

Trustor. The trustor is the borrower—that's you, the buyer of the house. As trustor, you legally own the house, but sign a deed of trust giving the trustee the power to sell the house and turn the proceeds over to the beneficiary (the lender) if you default on the loan.

ADVANTAGES OF ADJUSTABLE RATE MORTGAGES

- Lower initial interest rates
- May be lower points than a fixed rate mortgage for the same loan amount
- Lower initial monthly payments
- May be easier to qualify for when initial interest rates (even factoring out first year discount rates) are far lower than fixed rate mortgages
- May allow you to qualify to purchase a considerably more expensive house than with a fixed rate mortgage
- After automatic increases for the first three to five years are factored out (remember, initial ARM interest rates are discounted), interest rates will decrease should general interest rates drop
- Sure to be cheaper than fixed rate loan if you live in the house less than about five years and your ARM has no negative amortization feature (see Chapter 10), because you get all the benefit of the initial lower interest rate
- Assumable by a qualified purchaser when you sell
- May fit specific investment strategies. For example, if you stand to get an inheritance soon and will use it to pay down your mortgage, why not get an ARM with a lower initial interest rate? Or if you have an investment opportunity that's likely to bring a hefty return, you might prefer an ARM if the lower interest rate qualifies you to borrow more (debt-to-income ratios are explained in Chapter 2), which in turn frees up money to invest elsewhere.

ADVANTAGES OF FIXED RATE MORTGAGES

- Monthly payments don't change, even if interest rates rise.
- You get the peace of mind of knowing exactly how much your total mortgage will cost.
- Short-term fixed rate loans, fixed rate loans with balloon payments or interest rate adjustments after three, five or seven years, and mortgage buydowns offer extremely competitive rates and are attractive to people who will move or pay off their mortgages soon.

F. Finding the Least Costly Mortgage—Points, Interest Rates and Other Lender Fees

There are a variety of fees—and fee amounts—associated with getting a mortgage. Loan application fees (typically $500-$700) cover the lender's cost of processing your loan. In addition, many lenders charge a fee for checking your credit. And if you make a low down payment, you'll likely be required to purchase private mortgage insurance. These items and others, such as the fee to appraise the house you want to purchase, are called closing costs and typically add 2%-5% to the cost of your mortgage. (See Chapter 18 for a full description of closing costs.) Some lenders don't charge all these fees; those that do charge varying amounts.

Because points comprise the largest part of lender fees, and are required by virtually all loans written by institutional lenders in California, it's important to understand how they work. One point is 1% of the loan principal. Thus, your fee for borrowing $250,000 at two points is $5,000 ($250,000 x 0.02 = $5,000).

In theory, the buyer or seller can pay points. In practice, the seller rarely does. If the California housing market changes, and a big surplus of sellers—and lots of unborrowed mortgage money—emerge, loans without points or with sellers paying points, may be more common. Typically, however, you will be charged points as a condition of getting a mortgage. One reason why lenders insist on points is that for those who sell their loans on the secondary market, points are their main source of profit.

There is normally a direct relationship between the number of points lenders charge and the interest rates they quote for the same type of mortgage, such as a fixed rate. The more points you pay, the lower your rate of interest, and vice versa. For example, you might be offered a 30-year fixed rate loan of $200,000 with 2 points ($4,000) at 7.875% interest, or the same loan with no points at 8.375%.

One method to compare loans with different points is to use the Annual Percentage Rate (APR) which lenders must disclose to borrowers under federal law. (See Chapter 13.) The APR can be misleading, however, as its method of calculating the cost of a loan as a yearly rate assumes that the loan will not be paid off until the loan term ends. While most loans are for 30 years, people generally pay off their loans before the loan term ends because they either move or refinance sooner. Also, different lenders have various ways of calculating costs included in the

APR, so that a loan for the same dollar amount and number of points may have different APRs with different lenders.

So before comparing points to interest, factor in how long you plan to own your house. The longer you live in your house (or pay on the mortgage), the better off you'll be paying more points up front in return for a lower interest rate. On the other hand, if you think you'll sell or refinance your house within two or three years, we strongly recommend that you obtain a loan with as few points as possible.

You can compare various combinations of interest rates and points (assuming all other up-front fees are the same or nominal) on a 30-year fixed rate loan by using the table below to determine at what year the trade-off between points and interest is about even. The table (When to Pay Additional Points for a Lower Interest Rate) assumes the current interest rate, including the effect of points, is 8.75%. The results will not be appreciably different as long as interest rates are between 5% and 15%.

TAX DEDUCTIBILITY OF POINTS

When you get a mortgage with points, lenders will either reduce the loan by the amount of the points charged—which means on a $250,000 loan at two points ($5,000) you'd be advanced $245,000, not $250,000—or give you the full loan amount and require payment to cover the points at the closing.

Points are tax deductible. Also, the IRS allows buyers to deduct points paid for them by the home sellers—in addition to points buyers themselves pay for a mortgage. This IRS ruling is retroactive, starting with homes purchased in 1991.

For more information on the tax deductibility of points, call the IRS at (800) TAX-FORM.

G. What Mortgage Is Best for You?

As you should now understand, there's no best mortgage. The type of mortgage you can and should get is only one piece in your house purchase puzzle. In the next five chapters, we'll give

WHEN TO PAY ADDITIONAL POINTS FOR A LOWER INTEREST RATE

Let's compare a fixed rate, 30-year mortgage at 8.25% interest and 2.5 points with one at 8.75% and no points.

Step 1: Calculate the difference between the points on the two loans; here, it comes to 2.5 points (2.5-0).

Step 2: Calculate the difference between the interest rates; here, one mortgage charges 8.25% interest and the other 8.75%; the difference is 0.5% or 1/2%.

Step 3: Use the table to determine the number of years at which both loans are equal. According to the table, if you are paying 2.5 more in points for a 1/2% lower interest rate, at 7.2 years both loans are about equal. If you plan to have the loan for more than 7.2 years, it makes economic sense to pay the extra points to get the lower interest rate.

Interest Rate Reduction	Additional Points													
	.25	.5	.75	1.0	1.25	1.5	1.75	2.0	2.25	2.5	2.75	3.0	3.25	3.5
1/8%	2.3 yrs	5.3	10.0	23.5	No matter how long you plan to have the loan, don't pay the extra points.									
1/4%	1.1	2.3	3.7	5.3	7.2	10.0	13.5	21.0						
3/8%	0.7	1.5	2.2	3.1	4.2	5.3	6.5	8.0	9.8	12.0	15.0	21.0		
1/2%	0.5	1.1	1.6	2.3	2.9	3.6	4.4	5.3	6.2	7.2	8.5	9.8	11.4	13.5
5/8%	0.4	0.8	1.3	1.8	2.3	2.8	3.3	3.9	4.6	5.3	6.0	6.8	7.7	8.7
3/4%	0.3	0.7	1.1	1.4	1.8	2.3	2.7	3.2	3.6	4.1	4.7	5.2	5.9	6.5
7/8%	0.3	0.6	0.9	1.2	1.6	1.9	2.3	2.6	3.0	3.4	3.8	4.3	4.7	5.2
1%	0.3	0.5	0.8	1.1	1.3	1.6	2.0	2.3	2.6	2.9	3.3	3.6	4.0	4.4

you lots of facts relevant to efficiently putting every piece in place. In this chapter, however, it makes sense to ask yourself five questions as part of developing an overview of the decision-making process.

1. How Much House Can You Afford?

Chapter 2 gives detailed instructions on determining the maximum amount a lender will let you borrow to purchase a house, based on your income, down payment and other factors. If you haven't yet done so, read Chapter 2 and complete the calculations. You also need to add in closing costs, which normally amount to 2%-5% of the cost of a house. You should get a good idea of whether the house you want is within your financial reach or whether you'll have to stretch your finances.

Making the determination as to how much house you can afford is directly related to choosing a mortgage. The more you

can easily afford a particular purchase (that is, your debt-to-income ratio is low), the more likely you can qualify for a good mortgage at a competitive interest rate.

2. Is Your Income Likely to Increase Soon?

If your income is relatively modest now but is sure to go up soon, you may have another choice if you wish to buy a relatively expensive house—a hybrid mortgage. It lets you make lower fixed rate payments now, but turns into an adjustable rate mortgage at a preestablished time, such as seven years. This gives you short-term security at a locked-in interest rate, but, of course, has the downside that if interest rates go way up, you'll bear the brunt when the loan becomes adjustable. (For more on hybrid mortgages, see Chapter 10, Section I.)

Another possibility is the graduated payment mortgage (GPM). Available from only a few lenders, it provides low interest rates in the first few years in exchange for stepping up to a higher rates later. It's different from a hybrid mortgage in that the higher rates of a GPM are preestablished, not tied to the prevailing market rate at the time of the rate change. (Chapter 9, Section H, discusses GPMs.)

3.   How Much Down Payment Can You Make?

As we discuss in Chapter 4, the minimum down payment is typically 10% of a house's purchase price. A few affluent buyers pay much more, sometimes 100% of the purchase price, borrowing no money at all. There are exceptions, however, including 3% and 5% down First Time Buyers programs (described in Chapter 4) and government loans (see Chapter 11) which specifically allow for a very low, or even no, down payment loan. On most purchases, however, lenders require 10%-25% down to insure resale of the home and recoupment of their investment if you default.

The larger your down payment, the less you must borrow, and therefore the lower your monthly payments. Low monthly payments mean a favorable debt-to-income ratio, which increases your mortgage choices. A large down payment also often means lower up-front fees and a slightly lower rate of interest. There are also arguments against making a larger down payment than required. We discuss the pros and cons in Chapter 4.

4.   How Long Do You Plan to Own Your Home?

The length of time you plan to own your house is very relevant to which type of mortgage you choose. Over time, most ARMs will charge an interest rate about the same as a fixed rate loan, if interest rates remain steady. If general interest rates go up or down, an ARM will fluctuate accordingly. If you plan to own your house for only three to four years, however, the fact that an ARM's initial interest rate is lower and it takes time for it to

increase to its maximum preprogrammed rate means an ARM is the better deal. And because interest rate increases are capped (they can go up only a certain amount each six months or year), this is true even if interest rates go up in the interim.

5.   What Do You Predict for the Economy?

If the U.S. (or developed world, as no nation economically stands alone anymore) suffers terrible economic times, the Federal Reserve Bank typically responds by lowering interest rates substantially to spur the economy. This means that if you have an ARM, your mortgage interest rate will stay close to where it is now, or go down.

As explained in Chapter 10, ARM interest rates are set by adding a lender's profit margin to a financial interest rate index. Because ARMs are heavily discounted at the outset, however, their interest rates are essentially preprogrammed to increase, even if general interest rates (as measured by the ARM index) remain the same. It takes a large drop (about 25%) in general interest rates to counteract the built-in increase. So even if general interest rates drop by 10%, your mortgage rate will increase, but the drop will be factored in and the increase will be less than if the drop didn't occur. If you have a convertible ARM (see Chapter 10) and convert to a fixed rate mortgage when rates drop, you may benefit even more, assuming they eventually go back up.

If inflation becomes more of a danger, however, interest rates are likely to increase. In this situation, ARM interest rates will surely go higher, perhaps much higher, than those for fixed rate mortgages.

Where does this leave us? In a state of uncertainty—no one knows whether interest rates will go up or down. This uncertainty leads many people to prefer fixed rate mortgages; others, however, conclude that because initial ARM interest rates are currently little more than half of those for fixed rate loans, it makes sense to grab an ARM and hope for the best. ■

Fixed Rate Mortgages

A generation ago, mortgage rules were simple—interest rates were fixed in advance and repayable in equal monthly installments over a term of 15 to 30 years. The mortgage lender, usually a bank or savings and loan on a main corner, downtown, required that the purchaser make a down payment of 20% or more, have steady income and a good credit rating.

> **EXAMPLE:** Norma and Jill borrow $100,000 on a fixed rate mortgage at 8% interest for 30 years. Their monthly payments are $734. Over 30 years, their total obligation will be $264,156. (Note that they pay $164,161 in interest.) No matter what the economy does in the meantime, these amounts won't vary, unless Norma and Jill pay off the mortgage early, in which case they will save some of the interest portion of their debt.

Today there are many more mortgage options, including relatively new (and more affordable) types of fixed rate mortgages.

A. Should You Choose a Fixed Rate Mortgage If You Can Afford One?

Many people ask if they should get a fixed rate mortgage if they can afford one. The answer is a qualified yes; you will want a fixed rate mortgage if you plan to own the house for an extended period. A fixed rate mortgage offers two main advantages:

- The amount you must pay is established in advance and can never increase. The amount can decrease, however—if you pre-pay your fixed rate mortgage, you can substantially reduce the loan balance and cost of interest at any time.
- You may save on interest costs. Even though many ARMs offer a substantially lower initial rate of interest, the total interest paid on a fixed rate mortgage may be less than on an ARM, if interest rates go up substantially and stay up for an extended period. This is because the interest rate on ARMs is preprogrammed to increase over a few years' time to a market rate which is about the same as that for fixed rate mortgages. If market rates go up, the interest rates on ARMs will rise even higher than the preprogrammed amount. (See Chapter 10 for a discussion of the pros and cons of ARMs.)

You may want to forego a fixed rate mortgage, however, if:

- You'll be moving to another house or refinancing within three to four years. As mentioned, in the long run, the ARM rate will eventually increase to a level about the same as for a fixed rate mortgage and will go higher if interest rates go up. In the short run, however, ARM rate increase caps mean ARM rates will stay below those of comparable fixed rate mortgages. How long will it take for the ARM to cost you more than a fixed rate mortgage? Many ARMs are quite a bit cheaper for the first few years and then increase to a level close to that for fixed rate mortgages some time between 24 and 36 months. If you add in the time value of money you save at the beginning of an ARM (that is, if you plan to invest your savings), the break even point will happen substantially later.
- You believe that interest rates are likely to fall substantially. If they fall like a stone (which is unlikely absent a severe depression), ARM rates will stay close to their initial level, or perhaps even drop. By contrast, if you have a fixed rate mortgage, you'll have to refinance to take advantage of lower rates, which means paying a new round of points and fees. (Of course, if rates have gone down substantially, it will be well worth your while to refinance.)

CARPENTER GOTHIC

MONTHLY PAYMENTS FOR
FIXED RATE MORTGAGE

As of late 1996, 30-year fixed rate mortgages of $207,000 are available from institutional lenders for about 8% with 2.125 points; larger "jumbo" loans carry a slightly higher interest rate. Often, loans made by family members have a lower rate of interest. In Chapter 13, we discuss how to shop competitively for a fixed rate mortgage.

Interest Rate	Loan amount				
	$100,000	$150,000	$200,000	$250,000	$300,000
6.5%	632	948	1,264	1,580	1,896
7.0%	665	998	1,330	1,663	1,996
7.5%	699	1,049	1,398	1,748	2,098
8.0%	734	1,101	1,468	1,834	2,201
8.5%	769	1,153	1,538	1,922	2,307
9.0%	805	1,207	1,609	2,012	2,414
9.5%	841	1,261	1,682	2,102	2,523
10.0%	878	1,316	1,755	2,194	2,633
10.5%	915	1,372	1,829	2,287	2,744
11.0%	952	1,428	1,905	2,381	2,857
11.5%	990	1,485	1,981	2,476	2,971
12.0%	1,029	1,543	2,057	2,572	3,086
12.5%	1,067	1,601	2,135	2,668	3,202
13.0%	1,106	1,659	2,212	2,766	3,319
13.5%	1,145	1,710	2,219	2,864	3,436

ROUGH AND READY COMPARISON OF A FIXED RATE MORTGAGE AND AN ADJUSTABLE RATE MORTGAGE

Assume you're borrowing $250,000 for 30 years. Here's how the initial payments on a 4% adjustable rate mortgage and a 7.5% fixed rate compare:

7.5% Fixed	$1,748
4% ARM	1,194
	$ 554 difference each month

The fixed is 46% higher than the adjustable to start with. But this advantage won't last long. Assume the ARM is tied to a financial index which has an average interest rate of 4% over the next four years and that the lender collects a margin of 2.5% above this index interest rate. Assume also that the ARM can never increase more than six interest points (a life-of-the-loan cap. Adjustable rate mortgage margins, indexes and caps are all discussed in Chapter 10.) By the beginning of the second year, the interest rate on the ARM loan would be 6.5%; a comparison could look like this:

7.5% Fixed	$1,748
6.5% ARM	$1,580

If the index interest rate rises to the life-of-the-loan cap by the end of the four years (a full six interest points above the initial interest rate), the ARM owner would be paying 10% interest. A comparison would look like this:

7.5% Fixed	$1,748
10% ARM	$2,194

B. Not All Fixed Rate Mortgages Are the Same—Down Payments, Points, Interest Rates and Other Variables

Although the concept of a fixed rate mortgage is easy to grasp—you pay the same amount each month for a set period of years, no matter how market interest rates change—purchasing a good one involves comparing several features. In addition to interest rates, you need to consider the amount required for a down payment, points and sometimes private mortgage insurance (PMI). By understanding each, you can compare fixed rate loans to each other and to ARMs.

MOVEABLE HEARTH

REFINANCING: THE EFFECT ON POINTS AND INTEREST RATES

Whether to opt for a loan with more points and a lower interest rate over fewer points and higher interest doesn't only depend on how long you'll own the house, but on how long you'll own the loan (or, perhaps we should say, how long the loan will own you). Refinancing your house with a new loan to get a better interest rate has the same effect as selling the house and buying another. Your old loan is gone and you'll need to pay new points for a new one.

If interest rates are fairly high when you look for your initial loan, and you expect them to drop before long, you're a candidate to refinance soon. You'll want to shop for a loan with the fewest points, even if this means paying slightly higher interest. Having paid few up-front points, you're in great shape to refinance when interest rates drop.

---

1. Down Payments

In Chapter 4, we discuss the considerations in making a down payment within the generally required range of 10%-20%. While some fixed rate mortgage lenders require a 20% down payment, many will accept 10% or 15%, if you can afford the payments, based on your debt-to-income ratio. (See Chapter 2, Section B.) If you put 10% down, many lenders won't let the ratio of your monthly carrying costs to your income exceed 28%-34%, especially if you have other long-term debts. In addition, the lender is likely to charge a higher interest rate or more points, or require that you pay for private mortgage insurance.

If you put down 20%, an allowable debt-to-income ratio will be in the range of 33%-38%, and possibly higher if you have no other long term debts. If you put 25%-40% or more down, you'll likely be treated as an easy qualifier. This means that your current income need not meet as strict debt-to-income ratios as long as your credit history is sound and the condition of the property you're buying is good or better.

If you can make a down payment of only 10%-15% and are determined to get a fixed rate mortgage, you'll probably need

to buy a less expensive house or get a gift from a family member so that you need to borrow less. The less you borrow, the lower your monthly payments and the easier it will be for you to qualify within the generally allowable 28%-38% debt-to-income ratio discussed in Chapter 2.

EXAMPLE: Beth and Sam want to buy a house in Laguna Beach for $425,000. Their combined income is $120,000, and they've put $72,000 aside. Their long-term debts consume $650 per month. They want to put 15% or $63,750 down (to leave money for private mortgage insurance and closing costs). They have a problem. A 30-year fixed rate loan for $361,250 at 7.5% means monthly payments of $2,526, which brings their monthly carrying costs to $3,074 (not including the cost of private mortgage insurance). Adding the $650 (their long term debts) results in a total monthly obligation of $3,724, or 37.2% of their monthly income, which exceeds the debt-to-income ratio their lender will allow. Despite their enviable income, Beth and Sam probably won't qualify for a fixed rate loan from most lenders. To qualify, they need to put 20% down ($85,000) and get a $340,000 mortgage. This would reduce the monthly carrying costs plus other long-term debts to $3,569, and reduce the debt-to-income ratio to 36%, probably acceptable to many lenders with a 20% down payment.

2. Private Mortgage Insurance

Buyers are commonly required to purchase private mortgage insurance (PMI) when they make down payments of under 20%. We discuss PMI in Chapter 4, Section C.

3. Points and Interest Rates

Points are up-front charges made by a lender as a condition of lending money. One point equals 1% of a loan. You want a loan charging the lowest possible interest rate and the fewest points. Typically, however, you'll face a points-interest rate seesaw; when one goes down, the other goes up for the same-sized loan. In Chapter 8, we discuss the relationship of points to interest rates. At its simplest, it's better to pay more points and less interest if you plan to keep a mortgage for more than four years and vice versa if you plan to move on or refinance sooner.

C. Avoid Mortgages With Prepayment Penalties

At some time, you may decide to pay off your fixed rate mortgage early, either to save interest on your original mortgage or to refinance if interest rates drop. You want to be able to do this without paying the lender a penalty for the privilege. Generally, this isn't a problem, as loans rarely contain a penalty for early payment (called a prepayment penalty). If you find a loan that's otherwise desirable, but has a prepayment penalty, keep shopping. And, if for any reason, you're tempted to take a loan with a prepayment penalty, read the fine print carefully, including:

- the time period during which a lender may charge a prepayment penalty; make sure the penalty applies only in the first year or two of the loan.
- the maximum charge for prepaying a mortgage, and
- the periods, if any, when prepayment may be made without a penalty.

D. Fixed Rate Mortgages' Lengths and Payment Schedules

Not all fixed rate mortgages last for 30 years; shorter terms are available. Are they advantageous? As described below, it depends.

1. Short-Term Fixed Rate Mortgages vs. Prepaying Your Mortgage

Standard mortgages are scheduled to be paid off in 30 years. Today, lenders commonly offer mortgages for shorter terms at favorable interest rates because the faster the loan is paid off, the lower their risk of interest rates jumping or buyers defaulting.

Are short-term mortgages beneficial to you, the borrower? Not necessarily. True, interest rates on short-term fixed rate mortgages are significantly lower than long-term fixed rate mortgages. This represents a good savings if you qualify for a short-term mortgage and are sure you can pay off the mortgage within the short time frame.

Take a $100,000 fixed rate loan at 8%. As the chart below shows, you'd pay $956 per month if you pay it off over 15 years and $734 per month on a 30-year term. You'll end up paying $90,000 less in interest with a 15-year mortgage. A 15-year loan will have a better interest rate—often one-half of a percentage point less—than the same 30-year mortgage. You might also prefer a 15-year mortgage if, within the next 15 years, you plan to retire or your children will start college and you want the discipline of being required to pay off your mortgage by then.

But you can achieve exactly the same savings and benefits by voluntarily paying more principal each month on a longer term loan. The advantage of prepaying a long term mortgage is its flexibility—you don't legally obligate yourself to the higher payment, so you can change your mind and pay less if need be.

Even prepaying a small amount per month makes a large difference in your total payments. For example, by paying an extra $50 per month on a 30-year, 8% fixed rate $100,000 mortgage, you'd repay the loan in 24 (not 30) years and save nearly $40,000 in interest. If you don't want to pay a little extra each month, consider making a yearly lump sum payment—perhaps when you receive your tax refund or some other periodic funds—to reduce the principal.

If you plan to prepay a mortgage, remember this rule: No matter how much extra you pay in one month, you still must make at least the regular payment the next month. You can't prepay a large sum one month and then pay nothing until this extra amount is balanced by your monthly payment obligations.

THE BANKER'S SECRET

A few places before we've mentioned *The Banker's Secret,* easy-to-use software that quickly calculates how much money and how many years you cut off a mortgage by prepaying. A book is available with the same title. Whether you pay a little extra each month, make an occasional large lump sum payment, or both, *The Banker's Secret* will keep you on top of things. For price and order information, contact Good Advice Press, P. O. Box 78, Elizaville, NY, 12523, phone: (800) 255-0899.

SHORT-TERM LOANS: SAVINGS ON A $100,000 MORTGAGE

Term	6% Int.		7% Int.		8% Int.		10% Int.		12% Int.	
(Years)	Mo. Pmt.	Total Paid	Mo. Pmt.	Total Paid	Mo. Pmt.	Total Paid	Mo. Pmt.	Total Paid	Mo. Pmt.	Total Paid
10	1,110	133,225	1,161	139,330	1,213	145,560	1,322	158,640	1,435	172,200
15	844	151,894	899	161,789	956	172,080	1,075	193,500	1,200	216,000
20	716	171,943	775	186,672	836	200,640	965	231,600	1,101	264,240
30	600	215,838	665	239,509	734	264,240	878	316,080	1,029	370,440

THE GRADUATED EQUITY MORTGAGE (GEM)

The Graduated Equity Mortgage (GEM) is fairly rare these days, but it's worth exploring because it offers a slightly different twist in cutting total interest costs, and is another option, especially if you expect your income to increase. Marketed under different names and variations, it works like this: Monthly payments are calculated (amortized) as if the loan would be paid off over a long term, typically 30 years. But the loan is paid off sooner by gradually increasing monthly payments according to a pre-set formula, such as 5% per year for five years, at which point the payments stabilize.

GEMs substantially cut total interest costs and are often paid off in about half the normal time, such as 15 instead of 30 years. But GEMs, like other short-term loans, obligate you to make higher payments than you would otherwise have to make. If you can't make the higher payments, you'll need to refinance, which won't be easy if you're hurting financially or if interest rates have gone up substantially.

With bi-weekly mortgages, you make the equivalent of 13, not 12, monthly mortgage payments per year. On a 30-year $100,000 fixed rate loan at 8%, your monthly payments are $734 and the total cost of the mortgage is $264,240. With a bi-weekly mortgage, you pay $367 every two weeks and pay off your mortgage in a little less than 23 years, at a cost of $217,998, saving over $46,000 in interest.

All this sounds good until you realize that most lenders charge an extra fee to handle this type mortgage. There are exceptions, though, so it always pays to shop around, assuming you have the self-discipline, it's better to pay monthly, prepaying principal whenever you can. If you follow this approach and put any extra money available early in a month in an interest-bearing money market account, you'll accomplish a slightly better result.

2. Weekly and Bi-Weekly Mortgages

Many lenders offer fixed rate mortgages (and ARMs) that require weekly or bi-weekly (rather than monthly) payments. Others require an extra payment or two during each year. With these plans, you pay less interest over the life of the loan because the loan term is shortened and the lender gets the money sooner.

PAYING $100,000 FIXED RATE LOAN AT 8% BI-WEEKLY AND MONTHLY

Year	Balance at End of Year	
	$367 every 2 weeks	$734 every month
0	$100,000	$100,000
1	98,397	99,165
2	96,661	98,260
3	94,781	97,280
4	92,744	96,219
5	90,538	95,070
10	76,430	87,725
20	24,040	60,478
23	1,748	47,078
24	0	41,850
30	0	0

E. Most Fixed Rate Loans Aren't Assumable

An assumable loan is one which a buyer can take over from a seller. Fixed rate loans in California (except government-guaranteed loans) are generally not assumable by a buyer. If you have a fixed rate loan and sell your house, you must either pay it off and have the buyer take out his own loan, or get the lender's permission for the buyer to assume yours. The latter rarely occurs, for obvious reasons; the buyer won't want the loan if it's above the current market rate, and the lender won't allow it to be assumed if it's below. If interest rates are about what they were when the loan was initially written, however, some lenders (especially one who hasn't sold the loan to a third party) may let a buyer with a good credit history assume it. This saves the buyer some up-front money in points and loan origination fees.

Some real estate professionals advise against fixed rate mortgages because they're not normally assumable. If interest rates skyrocket in the future, they argue that selling a house will be difficult because buyers won't qualify for a new mortgage and won't be able to assume yours. By contrast, because ARMs are assumable by a creditworthy buyer, having one will make it easier to find a purchaser, because the ARM interest rate will likely be capped at a more affordable level than the new inflated market rate.

But we don't believe this possibility is enough to prefer an ARM over a fixed rate mortgage because:

- Interest rates are unlikely to go up and stay up at extremely high levels, as they did in the early 1980s. Even if they do, you may not want to sell (especially if you have a good fixed rate loan), because you'll have trouble financing a new house.
- Even if you must sell when interest rates are extremely high, other creative financing strategies will surely be available, such as your carrying back a good-sized second mortgage at a more reasonable interest rate or otherwise helping the buyer finance the purchase.
- If you live in your house for a long time, and have paid off a substantial amount of your mortgage, little will be left for a subsequent buyer to assume. A buyer assuming your loan balance will need a large amount of secondary financing; if this is only available at a very high rate of interest, he won't be able to afford the purchase.

F. Short-Term Fixed Rate Mortgages With Balloon Payments

Most people get a new mortgage within five to seven years either because they move or refinance. Recognizing this, lenders have begun to offer shorter term mortgages. One of these is a five- or seven-year fixed rate mortgage with payments figured (amortized) as if the mortgage would last 30 years.

The five-year mortgage is sometimes called a 5/25 and the seven-year version a 7/23, with the first number referring to the original "known" interest rate period and the second number referring to the remainder of the 30-year term. At the end of the five- or seven-year period, you must pay off or refinance the remaining balance, which of course will be huge.

EXAMPLE: Gina and Tony get a $200,000 five-year fixed rate mortgage at 7%, with payments amortized over 30 years. Their monthly payments are $1,331 for 60 months. At the end of 60 months, they will still owe their lender $188,264, which they must pay off or refinance.

The advantage of choosing this type of mortgage over a conventional 30-year fixed rate mortgage is a significantly lower interest rate. Because the lender is tying up money for only a fraction of the 30-year period, interest rates may be as much as one whole point less (7¼% if regular fixed rate mortgages are 8%).

But you are taking a risk to get the lower interest rate—that is, if interest rates are sky high when the balloon payment comes due, you will have to refinance at a higher interest rate, or pay off a huge lump sum. This is not as big a problem with the seven-year version (7/23) which usually spans an interest rate cycle. Most fixed-rate mortgages with a balloon payment have a reset feature or a "conditional refi" (refinancing) with a 5% cap for the remainder of the term which limits your risk. Check with the lender, and read disclosure material carefully, to understand how this feature works.

If you will move within a few years anyway, or stand to inherit a substantial sum, other types of loans are worth considering.

G. Two-Step Mortgages

A two-step mortgage has two fixed periods and one rate increase between them. Two-step mortgages are very similar to 5/25 or 7/23 mortgages (see Section F, above), but start at a slightly higher interest rate.

With a two-step mortgage, after the original five- or seven-year period is up, you are not expected to pay off your loan, refinance it, or use the reset/"conditional refi" aspect. Instead, there is a one-time adjustment based on an index like the National Mortgage Contract Rate, plus a margin (such as 2.25%). This adjustment brings the mortgage close to then prevailing fixed rate mortgage rate. In a way, the two-step is really more like an ARM with only one adjustment.

After the adjustment, the two-step mortgage's interest rate remains stable for the 23- or 25-year balance, unless you move or refinance sooner. The advantage of a two-step over the reset 5/25 and 7/23 mortgages is that you are assured of a fully 30-year loan with no balloon payment.

> **EXAMPLE:** Tom and Sheila purchase a $150,000 two-step mortgage at 6.5%. With the loan amortized to be paid off in 30 years, they pay $948 per month for the first seven years. Then the rate steps up or down to the prevailing 30-year fixed rate amount. If that rate has jumped to 8.25%, Tom and Sheila will pay $1,098 per month for the next 23 years.

H. Graduated Payment Mortgage (GPM)—A Fixed Rate Mortgage With a Low Initial Interest Rate

A Graduated Payment Mortgage (GPM) is an increasingly rare, but attractive, option for people whose income is rising and who want the certainty of a fixed rate mortgage but who don't qualify because their current income is too low. If you can find one, a GPM is better than an ARM because GPM payment levels are established in advance and cannot go up to the high levels ARMs almost always reach.

GPM payments are set artificially low in the first years of the mortgage (making it easier to qualify), then increase gradually at set amounts at set times. Lenders are most apt to qualify people for a GPM whose income is likely to increase soon, such as a doctor completing a residency. Most lenders are fairly strict ("cynical" might be a better word), however, and are likely to be more conservative about your future prospects than you are, especially if you're over age 40, the point at which lenders claim income potential has normally peaked.

A typical 30-year GPM requires initial loan payments of about 60%-80% of that for regular fixed rate loans. Payments then increase 5% each year for five years, and remain at that level for the remaining 25 years. Because GPMs are slightly riskier than fixed rate mortgages for lenders, the interest rate charged is slightly higher.

A negative feature of GPMs is that, in the early years, payments don't cover the interest due on the mortgage, which means the amount you owe increases (negatively amortizes). Eventually, when your payments increase (usually in the sixth year), this process begins to reverse.

Negative amortization is also a feature of a few ARMs. With adjustable rate mortgages, the consequences of negative amortization can be far more serious than with GPMs. This is because you don't know in advance when and how much your interest rate (and thus total payments) will go up. With a GPM, however, you know from the start exactly how much and when negative amortization will occur and when it will disappear. (For a discussion of negative amortization, see Chapter 10, Section C.)

 PAUL AND JUDY:
CONVINCING A LENDER THAT WE QUALIFIED FOR A GPM
We decided to buy a bigger house, and were convinced that a fixed rate mortgage was the only way to go. We simply didn't want to worry about mortgage payments rising significantly.

We knew we'd have a problem qualifying, even though the equity in our existing house was enough for a 20% down payment. Our problem was that Paul made a fairly hefty child support payment each month to support his kids from his first marriage. This debt, plus the carrying costs for the house we wanted to buy, meant our debt-to-income ratio was close to 40%.

Then we found a lender who offered GPMs and thought, perfect—the lower interest rate would let us qualify, and our increasing income would allow us to easily make higher payments later. Unfortunately, the lender disagreed, stating that because we're each established in our careers, our income wouldn't go up enough for us to make the larger payments later. We knew this wasn't true. Judy's company was growing fast, and she was in line for more responsibility and a higher salary. The only reason she wasn't already there was that she was out of the work force for seven years while our kids were very young.

So we asked Judy's boss for help. He not only put through a decent-sized raise immediately, but contacted the bank and explained that Judy was on the fast track for promotion. We also re-emphasized to the bank that Paul's children would be on their own in three to four years, further increasing our net income. We got our GPM.

I. Buydown Mortgages— The Seller Subsidizes Your Payments

A buydown mortgage (sometimes called a compressed buydown) usually works like this: The lender or seller subsidizes the mortgage for the first years of the loan by paying part of the mortgage payment. Because the buyer's monthly payment is lower, her debt-to-income ratio decreases and the house purchase is more affordable.

Buydowns are most common when a new house developer wants to move new houses that are selling slowly. (See Chapter 7, Section C.) They are gaining in popularity for existing houses as well. In this situation, a lender sometimes offers a slightly lower initial interest rate to help you to qualify for a loan in exchange for charging higher interest later. Depending on the number of steps (two- or three-year buydowns), a borrower might qualify at and pay 7% the first year, 8% the second year, and 9% thereafter, when a standard 30-year fixed rate mortgage might be 8.25% at the same cost in points. ■

Adjustable Rate Mortgages

Thousands of financial institutions offer ARMs, with varying interest rates, features and prices. While ARMs may be an excellent way to finance a home, especially if you're on a tight budget, they can be dangerous if you don't know exactly what you're getting. Fortunately, once ARM language is deciphered, obtaining a good one is less difficult than you might imagine. We'll show you how in this chapter and in Chapter 13 we'll explain how to measure the true cost of a mortgage, adjusting for interest, margins, index and finance charges.

A. Are ARMs a Decent Consumer Choice?

In most years, the choice is clear. Fixed rate loans offer a better consumer value if you can afford one. That's been much less true in the mid-1990s, however, because ARMs have been very cheap—some offering initial interest rates little more than half those of fixed rate mortgages. The reason is that ARMs are tied to short-term interest rates (often three months to one year), which are at low levels not seen since the early 1960s, while fixed rate mortgages are tied to longer-term rates (usually seven to ten years on a 30-year bond). Because of the huge

MISSION REVIVAL

federal deficit and the continuing belief of financial markets that when inflation lies ahead, long-term interest rates need to remain comparatively high.

Initial ARM interest rates are lower than fixed rate mortgages. After a few years, however, when you pay the fully indexed ARM interest rate, this will not always be true unless interest rates drop substantially or your index adjusts more slowly than most mortgage indexes. (The 11th Federal Home Loan Bank District's Cost of Funds, for instance, adjusts more slowly than Treasury Bills, CD rates and LIBOR rates.) Even if the ARM rate does go slightly above the fixed rate, it will take as many as seven years before your total interest cost is higher.

Look at it this way. Assume you have an ARM with an initial interest rate of 4%, and a margin of 2.75 percentage points above a one-year U.S. T-bill index. If the T-bill rate is 3.5% when you take out the loan, and is still 3.5% four years later, then, under your ARM, the interest rate would increase to 6.25% (the 3.5% index plus the margin of 2.75 percentage points), still less than the going rate of 7.5% for fixed rate loans. If you have a periodic cap (no negative amortization), the rate can't jump all at once. Depending on the exact amount of your periodic interest rate cap, the initial 4% rate would typically take two years to reach 7.5%. In the meantime, you would save money. And, of course, it would take several more years of paying higher interest rates to eat up this savings.

If interest rates generally go up, an ARM won't be quite such a good deal. True ARMs have a life-of-the-loan cap, which places a top limit on your interest rate—often six or seven interest points above the starting interest rate, for a total of about 10% on an ARM with an initial interest rate of 4%. This means if the T-bill rate goes up, and remains up for a long time, you could be paying 10% interest on an ARM, when you could have gotten a fixed rate loan for 7.5%, with no risk of further increase.

ARMs can be a good deal in a number of situations if you find one with favorable terms (no negative amortization) and if:

- the lower interest rate for the ARM makes it possible for you to buy a house
- you need money for other purposes—say to start a small business—so that making a lower down payment and financing with a low interest ARM makes sense, or
- you plan to move or refinance in the next three to five years. Because your initial ARM interest rate is lower than

ARM TERMS DEFINED

Before committing to purchase an ARM, be sure you understand the following mortgage terminology.

Adjustment period

The time between interest rate or payment changes. Most loans have monthly, semi-annual or annual adjustment periods. Annual or semi-annual are preferred; try to avoid monthly adjustment periods, if possible.

Caps

The term "caps" refers to two different concepts. One is how much your interest rate can go up or down over the term of your mortgage (life-of-the-loan cap). The other is how much it can go up or down at each adjustment period.

Life-of-the-loan cap (or overall cap)

This is the maximum (usually five to six percentage points) that the interest rate can increase or decrease (floor) over the life of the loan. For example, if the interest rate starts at 4%, and the life-of-the-loan cap is six percentage points, your interest rate can never exceed 10%. (Although arithmetic dictates that your loan could decrease to -2%, ARM loans always include a floor provision, usually of 1%.) The overall cap may be based on an ARM start rate—for example, an ARM that starts at 4% and has a floor of two percentage points, has a life-of-the loan cap of 6%. The overall cap may also be an absolute rate—for example an ARM that starts at 4.125% may simply have a life-of-the-loan cap of 10.625%.

Payment cap/negative amortization

A payment cap limits the dollar amount your monthly payment can change at each adjustment period, usually once a year by 7.5% of the previous payment; a $1,000 loan minimum payment can increase to $1,075 or decrease to $925. The term payment cap (as opposed to periodic cap) is usually a clue that the loan has negative amortization. This means that while the minimum payment you must pay is capped, your total debt may go up or down. If your capped monthly payments don't cover the fully indexed interest rate (this is described just below), the difference will be added to your loan balance. That is, after you make your minimum monthly payment, your mortgage debt will increase, not decrease.

Periodic cap

This limits the amount the interest rate of an ARM can change at each adjustment period. With a periodic cap, your interest rate might go up as much as 1% every six months or 2% annually—with your payments increasing accordingly—but that is the limit of your obligation. Your debt continues to amortize, or go down. What you pay is what you owe.

Index

A market-sensitive financial yardstick to which ARM interest rates are linked. For example, mortgage interest rates could be tied to the weekly average of one-year U.S. Treasury Bills or, less often, the London Interbank Offer Rate (LIBOR), or the six-month CD rate, or the 11th Federal Home Loan Bank District Cost of Funds. An index computed by averaging rates over a fairly long term (such as 26 or 52 weeks) will move up or down more slowly than one tied to daily or weekly spot rates.

Margin

The factor or percentage a lender adds to your index interest rate to arrive at the interest rate you pay or the market rate. Most initial interest rates are set at, or below, the index interest rate (with no margin added). This means that, subject to the periodic or payment caps, ARM interest rates will automatically rise in the first several years to reach the market rate, unless the index interest rate falls substantially during this period.

Fully indexed rate

An ARM's true base interest rate after all initial discounts are filtered out. The fully indexed rate is calculated by adding the margin to the index. If your loan is based on the 11th Federal Home Loan Bank District Cost of Funds (COF) with a 2.5% margin, your fully indexed rate is 7.5% when the COF is 5%.

a fixed, an ARM is cheaper than a fixed rate loan for the first few years. After two or three years, you'd be paying the same interest rate you'd have with a fixed rate mortgage. ARMs usually have no prepayment penalty, so you can refinance every two to three years and simply get another ARM with a low initial rate. But if you refinance, you'll have to pay the cost of points and fees, which reduces the attractiveness of this option.

If you believe general interest rates will fall substantially, should you jump for an ARM? Not necessarily. If rates fall, the interest rate on your newly purchased ARM will still go up for the first few years because the original ARM rate is heavily discounted. When the lender's margin is added to the financial index, your payments will be substantially higher. If interest rates fall in the meantime, your payments will go up more slowly, but given the built-in interest rate increase, general interest rates will have to drop 25% or more before the amount you pay falls below your first year rate. True, a fixed rate mortgage won't go down at all, but in the event interest rates in general fall 25% or more, you can refinance your existing mortgage at the new lower fixed rate. Yes, you'll have to pay fees and points, but for long-term owners it will be well worth it to lock in the lower rates.

LOOK BEYOND DISCOUNTED RATES

Many lenders heavily advertise very low initial ARM rates that are a great deal less than the fully indexed rate. Because the overall cap is a stated amount over the initial discounted rate, however, the start rate is an important figure. For several reasons, however, discounted rates aren't the only criteria to consider when choosing an ARM:

- They don't last long (usually six months).
- The interest rate on which your loan qualification (debt-to-income ratio) is figured is often the first year rate, not the discounted rate, so discounted rates don't necessarily help with loan qualification.
- Lenders who offer very attractive initial rates often get their money back by including less attractive ARM features in the fine print, such as higher periodic interest rate caps or even negative amortization.

EXAMPLE: You get a $200,000, 30-year ARM with an initial interest rate of 4.5%, and a 2.5 percentage point margin over the index of 4%. Your loan will rise to 6.5% after the initial discount ends, even if the index your rate is tied to remains steady. After that, the rate will continue to rise until it reaches its fully indexed rate (when the margin is added to the index).

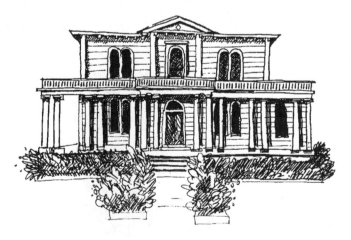

ITALIANATE

B. Loan and Payment Caps

The term "cap" sounds simple. If you have a 5% ARM with a five percentage point life-of-the-loan cap and a two percentage point one-year periodic cap, no matter how high general interest rates rise, your mortgage can't go above 10%, and can't increase to more than 7% after one year. Right? Yes, but that's far from the entire story. Confusing finance world terminology assures that caps aren't this straightforward.

First, be aware of the term "5% life-of-the-loan cap." Five percent and five percentage points are very different. Five percentage points raise an interest rate of 5% to 10% during the life of a loan, a 100% increase. A five percent cap would raise that 5% loan to only 5.25%.

Most ARMs also cap the maximum amount your interest rate can go up in a particular adjustment period (periodic caps). Most will have a cap of between one and two percentage points per year (often adjusted every six months). For a loan with an initial rate of 5%, a one percentage point cap means the rate can rise to 6% in one year.

C. Negative Amortization

Depending on the type of ARM you have, if mortgage interest rates go way up in a year, you may not be protected from the increase above the periodic cap. Buried in the fine print of a few ARM contracts, in confusing language, is a negative amortization (sometimes referred to by lenders as a "deferred interest" or "interest advances") provision. It's a system that takes away most of the advantages of the yearly cap.

Negative amortization loans can be confusing. They may have two (sometimes three) payment streams/options:

1. A minimum payment (often at the deeply discounted initial rate) which can go up or down by 7.5% (payment cap) and is adjusted annually. Usually this minimum payment covers only what you are required to pay the lender each year and your debt goes up. What you owe keeps increasing as if there was no cap. The interest you don't pay is tacked on to the balance of your mortgage, at which point interest begins to accrue on the unpaid interest. This is what is known as negative amortization. The crucial feature of a loan with negative amortization is that if your payments don't cover the fully-indexed mortgage interest rate (the index rate plus the margin), what you owe on your total mortgage will increase even though you made all required payments.

2. Payment based on the fully indexed interest rate, or the index plus the margin. This changes monthly after an initial three-to-six month period. If you pay this rate, you cover all the interest, but there is no amortization. Your indebtedness remains the same.

3. Payment that includes a reduction in principal and covers the fully indexed rate. This means that you are amortizing your loan each month as you would with a fixed rate mortgage or no-negative amortization ARM.

When there is more than one payment possible, each option is shown and you make the payment you want, with negative amortization being one of the options.

Some ARMs with negative amortization require that if the total amount owed gets too big (usually if your total loan balance increases to 7% to 25% over the original loan amount), you must pay off the full increase, or the lender will reamortize your loan so that the new, larger balance must be repaid over the remaining years of the loan. Not only can you end up owing more than the amount of the original loan—sometimes even more than the value of your house—in some extreme cases you may have to come up with additional cash, or risk foreclosure.

EXAMPLE: Because of negative amortization, your $100,000, 30-year ARM loan balance increases by 10% to $110,000. Depending on the terms of your mortgage, your lender can require a lump sum payment of the $10,000, or, if you can't come up with the money, will re-amortize the loan so that your payments are increased to pay the loan off over the remaining years on the loan term.

Can anything good be said about negative amortization? A little. If interest rates drop, negative amortization will begin to work in your favor. Your interest rates will go down faster than those on an ARM without negative amortization.

Lenders who offer loans with negative amortization normally charge a slightly lower initial rate, and usually have lower margins, than do those lenders who market ARM loans without negative amortization. Even so, we believe the difference isn't large enough to compensate for the added risk. Indeed, most lenders don't mention negative amortization, except in the fine print of their contracts, knowing that most borrowers will say "hell no" if they really understand how it works.

To find an ARM without negative amortization, call a few major California banks. Many now realize that negative amortization loans are "anti-consumer," and so they've stopped, or at least cut back, selling them. Many savings and loans, however, still commonly offer ARMs with negative amortization, primarily for income property, where the more even payments of these types of loans are good for cash flow. ARMs with negative amortization are not recommended for the average homeowner.

How an ARM Works

A homebuyer obtains a $200,000 ARM from Happy Savings & Loan, with no negative amortization. Here's how her payments would look if her loan reached its life-of-the-loan cap.

Initial Interest Rate	4%
Lender's Margin	2.75 percentage points
Index	Average of 6 Month T-Bill. Begin @ 5%; increase one percentage point every six months
Life-of-the-Loan Cap	11%
Periodic Cap	One percentage point every six months (true periodic cap)

Months of Loan	Interest	Payment	Loan Balance
1-6	4%	$ 955	$198,257
7-12	5%	1,064	196,812
13-18	6%	1,180	195,622
19-24	7%	1,301	194,646
25-30	8%	1,428	193,849
31-36	9%	1,560	193,202
37-42	10%	1,695	192,678
43-48	11%	1,835	192,256

After four years, the homeowner has paid $66,114 and owes a balance of $192,256. The interest rate cannot rise any more, however, because the rate has reached the life-of-the-loan cap. Now assume interest rates rise for two years and then remain stable for four years:

Months of Loan	Interest	Payment	Loan Balance
1-6	4.00%	$ 955	$198,257
7-12	5.00%	1,064	196,812
13-18	6.00%	1,180	195,622
19-24	7.00%	1,301	194,646
25-30	7.75%	1,394	193,808
31-36	7.75%	1,389	192,974
37-42	7.75%	1,382	192,143
43-48	7.75%	1,377	191,316

After four years, the homeowner has paid $60,255 and owes a balance of $191,316.

BEWARE OF LENDER INTEREST SHELVING

Another ARM feature to watch out for is "shelving" (or "warehousing"). Although not as bad as negative amortization, it lets lenders recover interest rate increases above the periodic cap if interest rates subsequently go down. For example, if a periodic cap prevents interest rates from going up more than 1.75 points in the first year, but the index goes up three points, the amount between the cap and the index (which would have contributed to negative amortization were that allowed) is instead "shelved" by the lender and added on later if interest rates drop substantially. Currently, most ARMs don't have this feature, but check to be sure.

D. ARM Indexes and Margins

By now you understand that when interest rates go up, so do ARM payments. Different ARMs, however, are tied to different financial indexes, some of which fluctuate up or down more quickly than others.

Indexes that lenders often use include those tied to the rates paid on three-month, six-month or one-year United States Treasury Bills (called "T-bills"). Other common indices use the rate at which American T-bills are sold in Europe (LIBOR), the six-month CD rate, which is based on a mixture of long- and short-term treasury securities called the "moving treasury average," and the Cost of Funds of the 11th Federal Home Loan Bank District. Lenders don't simply loan you money at the interest rate of the index, which is only slightly above what they pay their own CD depositors. Instead, lenders tack on two to three interest points (called a margin) to cover their costs and to make a profit.

Because you're sure to be concerned that your loan payments might jump fast, you want an ARM tied to a financial index that is likely to fluctuate more slowly than the daily ups and downs of the financial market. Look for a loan where the lender computes interest rates based on an average of the index calculated over a number of weeks. For example, averaging a 26-week index means it will take a while before a quick spurt in interest rates moves the average significantly higher. The most volatile indexes (and therefore the worst if interest rates spike up) are computed on daily or weekly "spot basis." These indexes will go up quickly if interest rates jump. Sure, they can go down fast, too, but if you're on a tight budget and can't afford a big increase, we don't believe they're worth the risk.

Historically, LIBOR rates have been the most volatile, while the 11th Federal District Cost of Funds has been the least. T-bill and CD rates have fallen in between.

Don't get so caught up in the index that you forget to look at the margin, the number added to the index to arrive at the interest rate you are charged. In the current market, we believe that a margin of 2.5 to 2.75 points (for a six-months ARM) is a fair deal, and 2.625 to 2.875 points for a one-year ARM, adding a larger margin isn't. This is because a small difference in the margin can translate into substantially higher loan costs.

On a 30-year, $130,000 loan, with a 2.5 percentage points margin, when the index is 5% your interest rate will be 7.5%, and your payments $909. With a 3 percentage points margin, your interest rate will be 8% and your payments $954, or $45 more per month. Over a 30-year mortgage you'd pay $19,440 more if the interest rate remained at 8%.

E. Assumability

Most ARMs are written to allow credit–worthy purchasers to assume them from the seller. After the interest rate discounts offered in the first few years are eliminated, ARMs track current interest rates, and lenders have nothing to lose by someone assuming your loan. In contrast, fixed rate mortgages (except those that are government-backed) are not normally assumable and usually must be paid off in full when a house is sold. (See Chapter 9, Section E.)

Should you make it a high priority to find an assumable loan? Most of the time, no. Many purchasers will want a fixed rate loan and won't want to assume your ARM. And even if they want an ARM, they will normally be able to get a new one at an initial rate lower than your current one. Only if interest rates skyrocket, as they did in the early 1980s, and you have an ARM with a fairly tight life-of-the-loan cap, will a subsequent purchaser want to assume it. This, of course, is because your ARM will then be cheaper than a new loan. Should this occur, and if your ARM is still large, it will be easier to sell your house than if you have a fixed rate mortgage.

F. Prepayment Penalties

Most ARM loans written in California on single family homes don't have a prepayment penalty. (Some zero-point ARMs have a three-year prepayment penalty for large prepayments, although some exemptions apply.)

With no penalty, you can make an extra payment or increase your payment, occasionally or regularly, and reduce considerably the amount of interest you pay. (Chapter 9, Section D, discusses the advantages of prepaying your mortgage.) Also, if interest rates remain stable or increase, you can refinance your ARM; after three to five years, ARM interest rates can go up to unattractive levels.

G. Convertibility

A convertible ARM acts like any other ARM, with one big difference. Interest rates are initially tied to the fluctuations of an interest-sensitive index (plus the lender's margin, of course). But a buyer can change to a fixed rate mortgage after a certain period of time, for example two to five years, during a specified period (called the conversion window—it usually lasts about two weeks, around the anniversary of the loan), without having to pay new loan fees or points.

Convertible loans can be a good idea if, because of high short-term interest rates, fixed rate mortgage interest rates drop, in which case a purchaser with an ARM may want to convert to a fixed rate mortgage to lock in the lower interest rate.

A convertible mortgage costs about one-quarter point more at origination than a nonconvertible ARM. Also, you must usually pay a conversion fee of around $250 to $400; some lenders charge a high conversion fee of 1% of the loan balance on a fixed rate mortgage.

Paying extra for convertibility obviously makes little sense if you plan to move or refinance soon. If you plan to own a house over a long term, however, convertibility is more attractive. In making the assessment, remember that if you buy a non-convertible ARM and interest rates fall, you can refinance at a new favorable fixed rate. Yes, you'll have to pay new points and fees, but if we're really in a recession, the Federal Reserve will have likely made the supply of money abundant, and fixed rate mortgages may be relatively low.

H. Hybrid Adjustable Rate Mortgage

Some lenders offer an ARM-fixed rate hybrid mortgage. This loan features an initial fixed rate (often for three, five, seven or even ten years) which later converts to an ARM. You get the security of fixed rate payments in the early years and risk paying more later, when, hopefully, you'll have more income, or will have refinanced.

This mortgage is especially popular with people who don't expect to own their houses beyond the point when the conversion to an ARM occurs. Because of life's unexpected happenings, however, look carefully to see that once the loan turns into an ARM, it's a good quality one. Specifically, check the caps, the index and margin used, and whether or not there's negative amortization. Some hybrid mortgages allow the lender to adjust upwards at an unreasonably high rate of three points as opposed to a more typical one-to-two point interest rate increase cap. Fortunately, this is only a one-time increase at the time the loan goes from a fixed rate mortgage to an ARM. Thereafter, the frequency cap should be no more than 1% every six months or 2% every year.

I. Summing Up—What Good ARMs Look Like

Shopping for a good ARM is a lot like shopping for a good suit. You want good quality at a good price, not the cheapest or flashiest threads on the market. When it comes to ARMs, we recommend that you get the best margin and index you can, and be skeptical about initial discounted rates. Look for an ARM that conforms to these guidelines:

- A margin that is as low as possible, such as 2.5 percentage points for a six-month ARM or 2.75 percentage points for a one-year ARM.
- An ARM tied to an index that will adjust for inflation relatively slowly, if you expect rates to increase. Again, historically this has been most often the 11th Federal District Cost of Funds. If possible (and it often isn't), avoid ARMs tied to much shorter periods, such as an index tied to a monthly spot interest rate.
- A periodic cap that limits interest rate increases to no more than two interest rate percentage points per year.
- Interest rates can only be changed once a year, or, if you can't find one of these (they are scarce), once every six months.
- The maximum interest rates can increase over the life of the loan is six interest points. If you accept a loan that can go up more, make sure it has other desirable features that make the trade-off worthwhile.
- No negative amortization.
- The right to prepay the loan in full or in part without penalty, and the right of a subsequent qualified buyer to assume your loan at the same interest rate you'd be paying, rather than the then-current market rate. These features are normal. ∎

Government-Assisted Loans

Four government-assisted mortgage programs (and some local financing programs) are available to help Californians buy homes. These programs are administered by:

- U.S. Department of Veterans Affairs (VA)
- Federal Housing Administration (FHA)
- California Housing Finance Agency (CHFA)
- California Department of Veterans Affairs (Cal-Vet).

The VA and FHA are federal programs that have been used by millions of homeowners throughout the U.S. for many years. The CHFA program primarily provides mortgage financing for first-time California house purchasers in designated areas, and for qualifying first-time buyers who wish to buy outside these areas. The Cal-Vet program provides low down payment mortgage loans to qualifying California veterans.

These programs differ significantly in the types of homes that qualify, loan conditions and fees, but have a common purpose: to help an average family buy a modest house to live in, with a very low down payment. Unfortunately, because the maximum loan amounts for all four programs are relatively low, they're of primary benefit if you're buying in areas of California where house prices are moderate or low. (You may be able to combine a VA loan, however, with additional financing to buy a more expensive house.) But generally, if you're looking in one of California's more affluent communities, government-assisted loans won't be much help.

For information beyond this chapter, contact the particular government agency (addresses throughout this chapter) or a loan broker or real estate agent familiar with government loan programs.

A. Veterans Affairs Loans

VA loans are available to men and women who are now in the service and to veterans with an other than dishonorable discharge who meet specific eligibility rules, most of which relate to length of service. Certificates of Eligibility are available from a VA office.

The VA doesn't make mortgage loans, but guarantees part of the house loan you get from a bank, savings and loan or other private lender. If you default, the VA pays the lender the amount guaranteed. The maximum guarantee is based on the size of the loan. In late 1996, the maximum VA guarantees were as follows:

MAXIMUM VA GUARANTEES

Size of Loan	Maximum Guarantees
$50,750 or less	50% of loan
$50,750-$144,000	40% of loan, up to $36,000
$144,000-$203,000	25% of loan, up to $46,000

If a veteran has obtained a VA loan guarantee previously, he can use the difference between the previously guaranteed amount and the current level.

There is no maximum size for a VA loan, except the loan may not exceed the VA's Certificate of Reasonable Value (CRV), based on the VA's appraisal of the property. A lender can lend as much as it wants. In the following situations, however, the purchaser will need to come up with a cash down payment, in addition to the VA loan guarantee:

- The loan exceeds $203,000 (maximum VA loan purchased by the secondary loan market).
- The sales price of the house exceeds the VA's Certificate of Reasonable Value. All VA purchase contracts give the buyer the right to cancel the deal if the contract price exceeds the CRV.

The VA's guarantee effectively replaces the down payment on houses up to $203,000. You still must repay the whole loan; the guarantee protects the lender against loss and makes it easier for veterans to get favorable loan terms.

Eligible VA borrowers must have a good credit history and demonstrate an ability to pay monthly carrying costs on the house, plus other monthly obligations, using approximately 41% or less of their monthly income.

As a general rule, most mortgage companies make VA loans, but many banks and savings and loans don't. Contact a regional office of the VA for a list of lenders active in the program. Only fixed rate mortgages are available. Buydowns are an option in some new housing developments; with them, a builder pays part of your mortgage for the first few years. (For more information, see Chapter 7, Section D.)

You must pay the VA an administrative fee for the loan, ranging from 1.25% to 2.0% of the total borrowed, depending upon the amount of the down payment; members of the Reserves and National Guard pay a higher fee. The interest rate is often slightly below the market rate and the lender may try to compensate by requiring more points.

ELIGIBILITY RULES FOR VA LOANS

You should qualify for a VA loan if your military service meets the requirements of one or more of the following:

Wartime Service

You served at least 90 days on active duty during:

- World War II (September 16, 1940 to July 25, 1947)
- Korean Conflict (June 27, 1950 to January 31, 1955)
- Vietnam Era (August 5, 1964 to May 7, 1975), or
- Persian Gulf Conflict (Reservists and National Guard members activated during the Persian Gulf Conflict on or after August 2, 1990).

If you served fewer than 90 days, you may be eligible if you were discharged because of a service-connected disability.

Peacetime Service

You served at least 181 days continuously on active duty, and your entire service fell between:

- July 26, 1947 and June 26, 1950
- February 1, 1955 and August 4, 1964, or
- May 8, 1975 and September 7, 1980 (if enlisted) or October 16, 1981 (if an officer).

If you served fewer than 181 days, you may be eligible if you were discharged because of a service-connected disability.

Service after September 7, 1980 (enlisted) or October 16, 1981 (officer)

If you began service after these dates, but are no longer in the service, you must have:

- completed 24 months of continuous active duty
- completed at least 181 days of active duty with a hardship discharge, a discharge for the convenience of the government or been determined to have a compensable service-connected disability, or
- been discharged due to a service-connected disability, no matter how long you served.

Active Duty Service Personnel

If you're now on active duty, you're eligible after having served 181 days of continuous duty, regardless of when your service began.

Reserves and National Guard

Members of the Reserves and National Guard who are not otherwise eligible and who have completed six years of service and have been honorably discharged or are still serving, may be eligible for VA loans. Disabled reservists do not have to complete six years to qualify.

Others

Many other people are eligible, including an unmarried surviving spouse of an eligible veteran who died as the result of a service-connected disease or injury. In addition, the spouse of a member of the armed services listed as missing in action or as a prisoner of war is eligible, as are certain U.S. citizens who served in the armed services of allied governments during WWII.

REGIONAL VA OFFICES

U. S. Department of Veterans Affairs
Federal Building
11000 Wilshire Blvd.
Los Angeles, CA 90024

U. S. Department of Veterans Affairs
Federal Building
1301 Clay St.
Oakland, CA, 94612

U.S. Department of Veterans Affairs
2022 Camino Del Rio North
San Diego, CA, 92108

All the offices share the same phone number—(800) 827-1000. For general VA mortgage information, ask for VA Pamphlet 26-4, "Guaranteed Home Loans for Veterans" and VA Pamphlet 26-6, "To the Home-Buying Veteran." To get a Certificate of Eligibility, complete VA Form 26-1880, "Request for Determination of Eligibility and Available Loan Guarantee Entitlement." Also ask for the list of participating lenders.

VA loans are much easier to negotiate than they were even a few years ago, when the VA limited the interest rate a lender could charge and would not approve loans on which the borrower paid points. Points and other closing costs are now freely negotiable between buyer and seller, and buyers are free to choose whatever loan rate they want.

NEW HOUSING AND VA LOANS

For most loans for new houses, the VA inspects construction at various stages to ensure compliance with the approved plans. The builder must provide a one-year warranty that the house is built in conformity with the approved plans and specifications. If the builder provides an acceptable ten-year warranty, the VA may only require a final inspection. (See Chapter 7, Section I, for more on inspections of new houses.)

ASSUMING A VA LOAN

You do not need to be a veteran to assume a VA loan on an existing house, as long as you are a creditworthy purchaser and meet VA standards. This means a fixed rate loan is assumable at its original interest rate, which can be a bargain if rates have increased.

The credit eligibility requirements for buyers seeking to assume VA loans are fairly strict. If a buyer assumes a VA loan, the veteran remains liable for the payments unless the VA approves the buyer and the assumption agreement, and issues a release of liability. This release protects the seller in case the buyer (or any other future owner) defaults. The seller can not, however, reuse the full eligibility until the old (now assumed) loan is fully paid off.

B. Federal Housing Administration Financing

The Federal Housing Administration (an agency of the Department of Housing and Urban Development) insures loans made to all U.S. citizens and permanent residents who meet financial qualification rules. Under its most popular program, if the buyer defaults and the lender forecloses, the FHA pays 100% of the amount insured.

This loan insurance lets qualified people buy affordable houses. The major attraction of an FHA-insured loan is that it requires a low down payment, usually about 2%-5%. FHA also counts nontraditional sources of income for your monthly payments or down payment, including overtime and bonus income, and money from a community savings club (popular ways of saving money in many minority communities). Qualified veterans may be eligible for a reduction in the minimum down payment. A 10% down payment is required on newly-constructed houses (less than a year old), unless the builder provides the buyer a ten-year approved home warranty, or if it is a project that has had prior HUD approval. The minimum down payment for property acquired at HUD foreclosure sales is 3% of the sale price. (Chapter 3, Section D8 discusses government foreclosures.).

In many areas of California where housing is reasonably affordable, such as parts of the Central Valley, the FHA program is used by a majority of purchasers. Even in urban coastal areas, the FHA program is widely used to insure loans in areas where housing prices are moderate.

FHA MORTGAGES CAN BE EASY TO QUALIFY FOR

John Murphy, Branch Manager of Benicia, California's AccuBanc/Medallion Mortgage Company, which generates hundreds of FHA mortgages per year, puts it this way: "FHA is truly an excellent choice for many people having trouble qualifying for a conventional mortgage. In large part, this is because FHA's qualification rules are much more flexible than those of conventional lenders, who must follow Freddie Mac and Fannie Mae guidelines if they wish to sell their mortgages in the secondary mortgage market." (See Chapter 8 for more on Freddie Mac and Fannie Mae.)

The current FHA loan limits vary by county. The maximum limits in California are $155,250 for single family houses and $198,550 for duplexes. Loan limits increase from time to time. Check with a regional FHA office to see what's current.

The FHA insures a variety of loans, including fixed and adjustable rate mortgages and Graduated Payment Mortgages. The FHA's most popular loan is the fixed rate mortgage (often called a Section 203-B loan). It:

- Requires a down payment of 2%-5% of the sales price. Buyers must use their own funds (not secondary financing) for the down payment. In some limited circumstances, second mortgages may be used along with an FHA loan to finance the balance.
- Requires mortgage insurance which costs 2.25% of the loan if you finance it over time. If you pay closing costs, the up-front portion of the mortgage insurance can be added in determining cash to close. Contact your local FHA office for details.
- Is assumable by a creditworthy buyer who is not an investor.
- Has no prepayment penalty (although you may have to submit a notice of intent to prepay 30 days in advance).
- Is fully guaranteed. Thus, lenders often qualify people for FHA loans whose incomes and down payments are too small for non-FHA guaranteed loans.
- Has more flexible qualification rules than other loans. For example, under FHA rules, a relative can often take title with you as a co-borrower. This lets people qualify who might otherwise be ruled out by past credit problems, by short-term employment at their current job or because they failed to meet required income-to-debt ratios.
- Is open to all U.S. citizens and resident aliens, regardless of income.

Like most government benefits, FHA loans have downsides:

- **Low Loan Limits.** Although loan limits vary throughout California, they're low everywhere. In many communities, virtually no houses are priced low enough to qualify. Realistically, the FHA program is primarily used by first-time purchasers for affordable housing in areas such as the Central Valley, Sierra foothills, and Northern tier counties. In some affluent communities, it isn't used at all.
- **Mortgage Insurance.** You must pay mortgage insurance equal to 2.25% of the amount borrowed. While it can be paid over the term of the loan, it adds to the mortgage total. In addition, there is a monthly fee of about .5% of the monthly loan payment. However, in almost all cases,

the combined payment if far less with an FHA loan then the monthly rate on a conventional mortgage.

- **Condition of the Property.** Fixer-uppers and properties needing significant repair won't qualify for the standard FHA loan program. If you want to buy a house in need of repair, any work recommended by FHA appraisers or by a licensed pest control inspector must be done before the sale closes. Fixer-uppers might, however, qualify for the FHA's Rehabilitation Loan Program (Section 203-k). The details of this program are beyond the scope of this book. Contact the FHA for more information.
- **Appraisals.** An FHA-approved appraiser must establish a fair market value for a house. FHA appraisers are strict, but reasonably fair. If the appraisal is less than what you pay for the house, the difference must be made up in cash, not by the FHA loan. A clause must be inserted in all sales contracts giving the buyer the right to cancel if the appraisal value is lower than the agreed-upon sales price.
- **General Red Tape.** It is often said that FHA loans are subject to inordinate bureaucratic snags and delays. This isn't always true. In the hands of an experienced mortgage company or other FHA loan originator, FHA loans can be processed in about the same time as conventional loans.
- **Buyer's Debt-to-Income Ratio.** To obtain an FHA loan, your debt-to-income ratio will be computed similarly to the method discussed in Chapter 2. The FHA wants to see that carrying costs (mortgage principal and interest, property tax and insurance) generally do not exceed 29% to 34% of income and that your total long-term debts of ten months or more (including housing) don't exceed 41%.

EXAMPLE: Juve and Zoe are in their late twenties. They currently earn a combined income of $45,000 per year. Juve, who has just finished school, has been working at a new job for four months. Zoe, who also works, has a spotty credit history dating back two years prior to her marriage to Juve. The couple wishes to buy a starter house for $122,000, with a 10% down payment. Because of Juve's short-term job history, they may not qualify for a loan from a conventional lender. Under the FHA program, however, they probably qualify. Even if they don't, they can arrange for a creditworthy co-borrower to help them. For example, if Zoe's dad, who has a good income and credit history, will place his name on the ownership (title) papers with Juve and Zoe, they'll qualify easily.

U.S. DEPARTMENT OF HOUSING AND URBAN DEVELOPMENT REGIONAL OFFICES

Contact a regional office for more information on FHA loan programs and a list of approved lenders.

1630 E. Shaw Avenue, Suite 138, Fresno, CA, 93710-8193, (209) 487-5033

1615 W. Olympic Boulevard, Los Angeles, CA, 90015-3801, (213) 251-7095

777–12th Street, Suite 200, Sacramento, CA, 95814, (916) 498-5220

2365 Northside Drive, Suite 300, San Diego, CA, 92108, (619) 557-5305

Philip Burton Federal Building and U.S. Courthouse, 450 Golden Gate Avenue, San Francisco, CA, 94102-3448, (415) 436-6550

Office of Native American Programs, (415) 436-8211

Box 12850, 34 Civic Center Plaza, Santa Ana, CA, 92712-2850, (714) 957-7333.

C. California Housing Finance Agency Programs

The California Housing Finance Agency (CHFA) provides mortgage financing for first-time homebuyers (or people who haven't owned a home in three years) who want to buy a previously-occupied affordable house. The "first-time" requirement is waived if you are purchasing in a CHFA state-designated "target area," typically a low-income area, some of which have serious social problems.

CHFA funds are limited and tend to be most commonly available for people who wish to purchase in target areas, though CHFA makes loans to eligible purchasers in non-targeted areas. Unlike the VA and FHA programs, CHFA will only help if your income doesn't exceed the maximum income limit established for the county where the house you want to buy is located. Currently, these income limits are less than $50,000 in most counties, but check with CHFA, as the limits change fairly rapidly. Also income limits are higher if you purchase in a CHFA "target area."

Because mortgage money comes from the sale of tax exempt bonds, interest rates are lower than those offered by conventional lenders. Depending on the county, qualifying house prices are usually between $100,000 and $250,000.

CHFA requires that you make a minimum 3% down payment plus closing costs and have sufficient income to make payments. CHFA debt-to-income standards are a little more relaxed than the normal 28%-38% ratio discussed in Chapter 2.

CHFA Funds for New Houses: In some parts of California, CHFA funds are available to help eligible buyers purchase new houses, instead of being restricted to only those previously approved by CHFA. Contact the CHFA for more information.

CALIFORNIA HOUSING FINANCE AGENCY OFFICES

For up-to-date information about the CHFA program and a list of approved lenders, contact:

1121 "L" Street, 7th Floor, Sacramento, CA 95814, (916) 322-3991, or

5711 Slauson Avenue, Culver City, CA, 90230, (310) 736-2355.

D. Cal-Vet Loans

This program provides mortgage loans to qualified California veterans who served during designated "war periods." Cal-Vet loans are made directly by the program, not by private mortgage lenders. Actually, Cal-Vet doesn't make loans. They purchase the property and "sell" it to the veteran on a Contract of Sale. The title vests with Cal-Vet until the Contract of Sale is paid off. This is one of the few uses of Contract of Sale (or Contract for Deed) left today.

The buyer must usually put 5% down. The maximum loan amount for a single family house or condominium is $250,000. An additional $5,000 loan may be approved for houses with solar energy heating.

The interest rate on Cal-Vet loans is 8% with a 30-year repayment period. This is for an adjustable, not fixed rate, mortgage. Also, the interest rate is based upon the continuing costs of bonds sold to support the program. Any increase or decrease in the interest cost will affect existing loan contracts, as well as new ones. Ninety days' written notice must precede any changes in the interest rate.

Cal-Vet allows a buyer to secure a second mortgage from another lender to close the gap between the amount of the Cal-Vet loan and the amount needed to finance the house. The total amount of financing (the second loan plus the Cal-Vet loan) cannot exceed 90% of Cal-Vet's appraised value of the property.

If any part of a Cal-Vet loan is prepaid in full within two years of its origination, you face a prepayment penalty equal to 2% of the original loan amount.

Cal-Vet also makes low down payment construction loans to eligible veterans to build a single-family home.

ELIGIBILITY RULES FOR A CAL-VET LOAN

Application for benefits must be made within 30 years from the date of release from active duty, except until January 1, 1993, when veterans who qualify for funding with Veterans' Revenue Bonds will be eligible to apply regardless of the date of release. To qualify for revenue bonds, the veteran (and spouse, if applicable) must either be a first-time homebuyer or be purchasing in a targeted area. Veterans released from active duty for fewer than 30 years who do not qualify for revenue bonds will be funded with general obligation bonds, which are limited to veterans with active duty prior to January 1, 1977.

To qualify for a Cal-Vet Loan you must meet one or more of the following requirements:

Wartime Service

You must have been released from active duty under honorable condition, and served at least 90 consecutive days on active duty unless discharged sooner because of a service-connected disability. At least one day of active duty must have been during one of these qualifying "war" periods:

- Operation Restore Hope–Somalia (December 5, 1992 - date yet to be determined)
- Persian Gulf Conflict (August 2, 1990 - date yet to be determined)
- Operation Just Cause–Panama (December 20, 1989 - January 31, 1990)
- Vietnam Era (August 5, 1964 - May 7, 1975)
- Korean Conflict (June 27, 1950 - January 31, 1955)
- World War II (December 7, 1941 - December 31, 1946)
- World War I (April 6, 1917 - November 11, 1918)

Peacetime Service

Your peacetime service was done in a campaign or expedition for which a medal has been authorized by the government of the United States, and the veteran was awarded this medal.

Career Officers

Applicants serving in the military for an indefinite period of time (career officers) may also be eligible. A statement of satisfactory performance from the military is required.

Other

The unremarried spouse of an eligible veteran who has died, is being held as a prison of war or is missing in action may be eligible in some circumstances.

CAL-VET LOAN OFFICES

Toll-free information: (800) 952-5626

Internet: http://www.ns.net/cadva/

1100 Mohawk Street, Suite 260, Bakersfield, CA, 93309, (805) 395-2869

2520 Stanwell Drive, Suite 160, Concord, CA, 94520, (510) 602-5070

1752 East Bullard Avenue, Suite 102, Fresno, CA, 93710, (209) 445-5466

2001 Solar Dr., Suite 135, Oxnard, CA, 93030, (805) 983-7477

2115 Churn Creek Rd., Redding, CA, 96002, (916) 224-4955

25884 Business Center Dr., Suite F, Redlands, CA 92374, (909) 478-7513

2710 Gateway Oaks Dr., North Bldg., Suite 190, Sacramento, CA, 95833, (916) 263-4010

268 West Hospitality Lane, Suite 105, San Bernardino, CA, 92408, (909) 383-4282

5095 Murphy Canyon Road, Suite 340, San Diego, CA, 92123, (619) 627-3966

12070 Telegraph Road, Suite 210, Santa Fe Springs, CA, 90670, (310) 944-3585, or (818) 575-4838 (L.A. County), (714) 761-0109 (Orange County)

19TH CENTURY PALM

E. Municipal Financing Programs

A few California cities and counties offer various forms of financial assistance with down payments, primarily to first-time home buyers who are buying modestly-priced properties. Often, these are the result of the city or county selling bonds for low "municipal rates" and passing the savings on to local purchasers. Call your city or county housing or planning office and inquire about any programs in your area. Programs come and go fairly quickly because below-market rate mortgage money tends to get committed very quickly. Here are some examples of municipal programs:

- Low-interest down payment loans and subsidies (in the form of second mortgages) to qualified first-time home buyers.

- Requirement that some local developers provide down payment assistance as a condition of municipal approval of the project.

- Participation in the federal Mortgage Credit Certificate (MCC) program, which gives income-eligible, first-time home buyers who receive a certificate from a participating lender, an IRS tax credit equal to 20% of the mortgage interest payments made on a home. This credit is in addition to standard tax deductions available to homeowners and, in effect, makes it easier to qualify for mortgage loans by increasing a borrower's after-tax income. The MCC program is not available with bond-backed loans such as CHFA or Cal-Vet, but may be used with FHA, VA and privately-insured loans. ■

12

Private Mortgages

Financial institutions and government programs are not the only sources for mortgage loans. A great deal of mortgage money is supplied by private sources—parents, other relatives, friends. Borrowing money privately is usually the most cost-efficient mortgage of all.

EXAMPLE: Ted and Harry plan to buy a $300,000 house. They have $50,000 in savings and equity in their present house. Harry's family is financially well-off, and offers them a 6%, fixed rate, 30-year mortgage for the remaining $250,000. A similar bank loan would carry an interest rate of 8% with 2.5 points ($6,250) and other fees of $1,000. In addition to saving on fees and points, Harry and Ted will pay Harry's family $1,499 per month, whereas they'd pay a bank $1,834 per month. This means they will save $120,600 over 30 years.

The principal advantages of a private mortgage are:
- **Low interest.** Friends and relatives often charge 10%-30% less than conventional lenders charge. Flexible repayment structures (such as paying interest only, or less, for a few years) are also possible.
- **No points or loan fees.** Institutional lenders normally charge thousands of dollars in up-front points and fees. You avoid these costs by borrowing money privately.
- **Easier qualifying.** Private lenders don't insist on your meeting rigid debt-to-income ratios. You qualify as long as you and the lender are satisfied that you'll pay back the loan.
- **Saving on private mortgage insurance.** If you borrow 80% or more of the house purchase price from a bank or other lender, you will have to pay private mortgage insurance. (See Chapter 4, Section C.) By borrowing privately, you avoid this cost.
- **Minimal red tape.** To borrow from an institutional lender, you must fill out an application form and provide documentation verifying every item on the form. Then you must wait for approval. To borrow money from a friend or relative, you just give the lender a promissory note reflecting the interest rate and terms for repayment, along with a mortgage (deed of trust) on the property, which the seller records at the County Recorder's Office.
- **Fast qualification.** If you've arranged private financing in advance and are ready to close quickly, sellers who are under time pressure to sell will often accept a slightly lower offer. By financing privately, you're likely to save money on the house price itself.

- **No lender-required approval of house's physical condition.** Private lenders don't usually require that a house's defects be repaired before closing. Institutional lenders do, and either the buyer or seller must produce the needed cash. This can be difficult to do, which means desirable houses with physical problems are hard to sell. If the sales price drops, a purchaser with private financing can buy at a favorable price and fix the (sometimes exaggerated) defects later. (See Chapter 3, Section D7, for more on this.)

The three broad approaches to borrowing all or most of the money necessary to buy a house privately are:
- Borrow from friends or relatives. (In Chapter 4, we discuss gifts from family and friends. In Section A below, we're primarily concerned with loans.)
- Borrow from the seller (Section C, below).
- Borrow from a non-institutional private lender (Sections B and D, below).

A. Get a Loan From Friends or Relatives

Borrowing money presupposes knowing someone who will lend it to you. If you're certain that you can't borrow money from anyone you know, skip this section.

Both lender and borrower can benefit by dealing with each other rather than an intermediary such as a bank. This isn't surprising given how much a financial institution's overhead costs and its profit needs increase the cost of the money it lends.

To consider whether private financing, either in whole or part, will work for you, ask yourself two questions:
- Is a parent, grandparent, other relative, close friend or business acquaintance financially well off?
- Does that person trust you?

If the answer to both of these is "yes," follow up with two more:
- Of those people who have the ability to help, who is most likely to extend you a helping hand?
- Of those who have the ability to help, who tends to make reasonably conservative investments, such as bank CDs and money market funds, not speculative investments, such as stocks, commodities or commercial real estate?

This last question is important because people who invest conservatively are more likely to be interested in lending mortgage money at an interest rate higher than they get now. By contrast, people who invest aggressively in an effort to achieve larger returns won't be as impressed by the prospect of getting an interest rate a little better than a bank would pay (though they may lend anyway, for personal reasons).

If a relative or friend has the ability to help you, don't automatically assume that she will. The hardest part about borrowing money is convincing the lender that her investment will be safe.

⚠ BEWARE OF IMPUTED INTEREST

The IRS assumes that mortgage lenders receive reasonable interest on every loan and assesses taxes accordingly. This is true even if the lender charges no interest or low interest to a family member or friend. The "imputed" interest rate charged by the tax man for loans of more than $10,000 changes, but generally is between 4% and 9%. So even if your generous friend or relative charges you less, the IRS requires her to report interest income at that rate. If she doesn't, is audited and the IRS discovers the omission (a very unlikely scenario), the IRS will readjust her income using the imputed interest rate, and charge her the tax owed on the readjusted income plus a penalty.

1. Approaching Friends, Relatives and Other Private Lenders

Start with the idea that you're not asking for charity. You're offering a business proposition—a loan at a fair rate of interest, secured by a first mortgage. Understand that trust is the key to getting any business deal to work, whether it's buying a pound of fish or borrowing $250,000. Would you bring your car to a mechanic who did a lousy job for a friend, leave your coat with a dry cleaner who ruined your aunt's favorite dress or buy a second pound of fish from a shop that previously sold you a rotten one? No, because you no longer trust the merchant.

Your relative or friend will probably take a similar approach. If he has the money to lend, and knows you're trustworthy, chances are he'll make a loan. If for some reason he doesn't trust you—you've racked up large credit card bills, bounced checks or maybe even forgot to return a lawn mower—he'll probably back off quickly. Keep in mind that trust isn't the same as love. We all know people we love dearly but wouldn't trust with a $20 bill.

So, are potential lenders likely to trust you? If you can unequivocally say "yes," terrific. If it's "no," or "maybe, with coaxing," consider what you can do to improve their view of your reliability. If you currently owe money to a relative or friend, pay it back in full before proposing a new loan. If you were wild in your younger years, but are now staid and responsible, make sure your parents spread the word to wealthy Uncle Harry before you show up on his doorstep asking to borrow $180,000.

Once you decide who to ask, think carefully about how to raise the subject. Never surprise a potential lender by blurting out a request at a social event or other inappropriate occasion. Make an appointment, even if you see the person regularly and the formality seems odd. Give the person a general idea of what you want to talk about, but save the details. For example, you might say "Grandpa, I'm trying to buy a house and I'm reviewing a number of ways to finance it. Can we sit down and talk soon?" If Grandpa never seems to find the time, you have your answer. If he says, "how about Tuesday?," be on time and prepared to make an effective presentation.

🏠 MORT: MY GOOD FRIEND HELPED ME

Several years ago, Mort found a house he wanted to buy. Although he had enough equity in his existing house and savings in the bank to make a good-sized down payment, he needed much more to finance the entire purchase. Just as Mort was starting to collect mortgage information from lenders, his good friend Babette stopped by for coffee. Upon hearing about the new house plan, Babette volunteered to lend Mort $200,000, to be repaid over 20 years, at a very competitive interest rate, secured by a first mortgage.

Why would Babette make this generous, unsolicited offer? Certainly, the trust and good regard accumulated over a 20-year friendship was important. Financial factors were also important. Babette had just retired and was living off the interest from her investments and she wanted a higher rate of return on her money than she currently received from CDs.

They quickly struck a bargain. Mort got a fixed-rate, 20-year loan at 6.5% (about 1.5 percentage points lower than the going rate at the time), with no points, appraisal fees or credit checks. He saved close to $10,000 on the fees alone, and $170,435 in interest over the life of the loan (assuming he would have taken out a 30-year fixed rate loan). He also saved the hassle and time of filling out a loan application.

But what was in it for Babette? She got a 6.5% interest rate on her money at a time when CDs were paying 5%. She also got a first mortgage on the house. Should Mort default, Babette can easily foreclose, have the house sold and recover the balance of her loan, plus the costs of sale.

2. Making an Effective Loan Presentation

The best way to approach anyone for a loan, whether it's a local bank officer or your Aunt Penelope Rose, is to put together a business-like proposal containing the following information:

- How much you wish to borrow.
- The interest rate you propose to pay. It should normally be higher than what financial institutions currently pay their investors, and lower than what you'd pay to an institutional lender. Find out what CDs pay and fixed-rate mortgages cost. Propose paying a little less than half the difference. For example, if fixed-rate mortgages cost 8%, and banks pay 5% on CDs, you might propose paying 6.5% for a private house loan.
- The loan terms you propose. This should include the length of the mortgage and the amount of the monthly payments. Use the amortization table in Chapter 2 or *The Banker's Secret* discussed there to come up with exact figures. If you and your mom want to compare the monthly payments on 15-, 20- or 25-year loans at 6%, 6.5% or 7% interest, *The Banker's Secret* will quickly give you the information.
- A copy of the family financial statement you prepared in Chapter 2, listing your sources of income, existing debts and other financial information.
- A copy of a recent credit report from a credit reporting agency. In Chapter 2 we discuss how to get one.
- An estimate of the purchase price of the house you want to buy. This won't be exact unless you've already made an offer and had it accepted, but do your homework. Be ready to show the potential lender your house profile sheet from Chapter 1 and a fairly tight estimate for such a house. In Chapter 15 we explain how to use the sales prices of comparable houses to develop this information. If the potential lender wants to make sure the house you find will be worth what you want to pay, offer to get it appraised prior to purchase.
- The amount you have available for a down payment. If it's 20% or more, point out that you're investing more than enough of your own money to guarantee that the lender will have little risk of loss, even if you default. (Chapter 4 discusses down payments.)
- Your debt-to-income ratio. As discussed in Chapter 2, financial institutions want to see that your monthly carrying costs don't exceed 28%-38% of your monthly income. Even though a friend or relative probably won't insist on rigid qualification rules, this can be very important to demonstrate that you'll have enough income to comfortably make the payments.

When you meet with the potential lender, present your proposal in general terms first. This gives the other person a chance to back off gracefully, whatever his reason. If you sense this happening, say "thanks for listening" and change the subject. Remember that people have many reasons for not lending money—don't take "no" as a personal rejection.

If the person shows some interest, be brief but organized in presenting the details. Give the potential lender ample time to ask questions and don't expect a decision on the spot. Be prepared to leave photocopies of all documents.

HOW A LARGE DOWN PAYMENT MINIMIZES THE LENDER'S RISK

If you miss payments, the mortgage holder or lender has the legal right to have the property sold through foreclosure. Proceeds (after the costs of sale are subtracted) go to the first mortgage holder. If you have more than one mortgage, the mortgages are numbered in the order in which they were taken out. The lower the number (first being the lowest), the more likely the mortgage holder will be paid if you default.

If the sale price doesn't cover the mortgage debt, the mortgage holder doesn't get all that is owed. For this reason, lenders want the house to be worth considerably more than what they lend. Even allowing for the fact that houses usually sell for relatively low prices at foreclosure sales, most lenders feel safe in lending 80% of appraised value, with the buyer making a 20% down payment.

---

3. Responding to a Proposed Lender's Questions and Concerns

First, and most important, if you plan to approach a relative who doesn't have much business savvy, consider whether the loan makes sense for that person. For example, if Aunt Muriel's health is such that she may need most of her money in the next few years, don't borrow from her, even if she'll lend it. She's better off having access to her money, even if she gets a lower interest rate in the meantime.

Often, friends or relatives will be concerned about what happens to their investment should you become ill or disabled and can't pay them back, or if you (or another breadwinner) die and your family can't make the payments. The lender fears being caught in a situation where she needs her money repaid, but doesn't want to foreclose on a distressed family member or friend to get it. One way to deal with this concern is to agree to purchase both life and disability insurance on yourself and any other co-buyer, and to keep the insurance in force until the loan is repaid. Term life insurance for younger people, particularly, will cost little. A good disability policy which will pay a large proportion of your monthly salary should you be unable to work is more expensive, but worth it. Make sure your policy pays at least 60% (more is better) of what you would have received had you been able to work.

4. Finalizing the Loan

If your presentation is successful, and your friend or relative agrees to lend you the needed money, you need to prepare the paperwork. You can do this yourself or get help. Here's what's needed:

- A promissory note for the amount of the loan, including the rate of interest, repayment and other terms. (Nolo's *Simple Contracts for Personal Use,* by Elias and Stewart, contains promissory notes.)

ADOBE

- A mortgage, or, to use the technically correct term, a deed of trust. A tear-out one, with instructions for its use, is in *The Deeds Book,* by Randolph (Nolo Press). Or, as part of the closing process on the house you buy, simply pay the title (or escrow) company a modest fee to prepare and record a deed for you.

⚠ Some people skip the preparation and recording of a deed of trust, reasoning that a promissory note is enough. It isn't. The lender isn't fully protected—from either subsequent lenders or purchasers—unless a formal notice of the loan is recorded.

B. Shared Equity Transactions

If you're considering borrowing privately, you may also be open to purchasing a house with an investor. In this scenario, instead of going to mom and asking to borrow $200,000, you ask a private investor to contribute toward the purchase and share equity in the house as a co-owner. When the house is ultimately sold, she'll make a profit on her portion. We are not advocates of shared equity transactions because an inherent conflict exists between the buyer-investor and the buyer-resident. For more information, see Chapter 3, Section D11, where the pros and cons of shared equity transactions are discussed.

C. Second Mortgages—Financing by Sellers

It's not uncommon for the seller to finance part of the purchase price of a house. This is often called "seller financing," a "seller take back" or a "seller carry back."

In theory, if a seller has no immediate need for money, he can transfer his house to you and receive nothing in return but your promise to pay in the future, secured by a mortgage. This is similar to borrowing the entire purchase price from a friend or relative, except the seller provides the money you need.

In practice, however, because most sellers have no personal reason to help you, they usually want their money at the time of sale. This means the seller will insist that your down payment and amount borrowed add up to the sales price. Still some sellers will finance at least a portion of your purchase price themselves. In this situation, a conventional lender has usually agreed to lend you a substantial portion, such as 75%, of the needed money secured by a first mortgage. The seller provides a much smaller portion, say 10%, of the total secured by a second mortgage, with the buyer putting 15% cash down.

Here are some of the reasons a seller may provide a second mortgage:

- **To sell a house which has been on the market for a long time.** Taking back a second mortgage makes a house easier for a buyer to finance and therefore for the seller to sell. If the buyer's down payment plus first mortgage loan from an institutional lender doesn't total the sales price, the buyer can use the seller financing to make up the difference.

  EXAMPLE: You have $33,000 for a down payment on a house listed at $280,000. You qualify for a mortgage of $224,000 from an institutional lender, leaving $28,000 necessary to complete the deal (allowing $5,000 for closing costs). Your seller is retired and living off investments. He agrees to take back a second mortgage for the remaining $28,000, at a competitive rate of interest.

- **For tax reasons, to spread the seller's receipt of the profits realized from the house sale.** If the seller didn't live in the house she is selling, or does not plan to purchase a more expensive one within 24 months, she'll owe taxes for the year she sells. (See Chapter 14, Section C, for more on tax laws.) Depending on her tax bracket, she may benefit by receiving a portion of these profits in future years, particularly if she's retiring and her income will drop from the 33% or 28% bracket to the 18% bracket.

ALL AMERICAN

- **For investment purposes.** A seller may take back a second if you'll pay a higher rate of interest than banks do on CDs, short-term U.S. Government securities and money market funds. Because second mortgages are riskier than firsts, it's sometimes considered reasonable for the buyer to pay a fairly high rate of interest. A seller with a hard-to-sell-house, however, may need to offer a second at a lower-than-market interest rate to try and move the property.

SECOND MORTGAGES: A BUYER'S WISH LIST

- A reasonable interest rate
- Low initial payments so as to not jeopardize first mortgage financing
- No prepayment penalty
- No balloon payment for at least five years and the automatic right to extend the loan if it's impossible to refinance to pay the balloon in full on the due date
- The right to have a subsequent creditworthy buyer assume the second mortgage.

Seller financing can be as flexible as the buyer and seller agree. Many sellers will accept promissory notes with variable payment structures or interest rates. You can have low interest rates in the first year or two, with increases later. Or you can provide for fixed monthly payments with a floating interest rate. If the interest rate goes up, the amount not covered by the payments is added on to the end of the mortgage.

In short, all sorts of second mortgage interest rate scenarios are possible, depending on the needs and relative bargaining powers of the buyer and seller. The higher the rate you are willing to pay, though, the more likely the seller is to say yes.

A serious problem with second mortgages is that the monthly payments on the second are likely to be so large that the buyer no longer qualifies for a first mortgage under standard debt-to-income ratios. After all, if she wasn't having affordability problems in the first place, she could borrow more on a first mortgage and wouldn't need a second.

Fortunately, second mortgages can be structured to deal with this problem. For one, a seller can accept a Graduated

Payment Second Mortgage (GPM), a type of fixed rate mortgage, under which the buyer pays a low rate of interest for a few years, with pre-programmed increases over time. (Chapter 9, Section H, discusses GPMs.)

Another scenario is for the buyer to make very low monthly payments on the second mortgage for several years, paying off the entire balance with a large balloon payment at a specific future date (often three to ten years after the sale). Under optimum circumstances, the house's value and buyer's income will have risen before the balloon payment is due, so he can refinance the first mortgage, using a portion to pay off the second. (See Chapter 9, Section F, for more on balloon payments.)

To allow for the possibility that the buyer's income and the house's value may increase more slowly than expected, institutional lenders usually require that at least five years of interest-only payments pass before the balloon payment is due on the second mortgage. The buyer should also insist on an option to extend if he can't refinance the first mortgage. Also, if possible, the first mortgage should be written to allow for refinancing or borrowing more against the property as its value goes up, without having to again pay points, loan fees and the like.

⚠ DON'T OVEREXTEND YOURSELF

The need to arrange a second mortgage with a large balloon payment tells you that you're stretching your finances close to the breaking point and betting heavily on future property value appreciation to pull you through. Also, be aware that interest rates may increase substantially by the time the balloon payment is due and you need to refinance. Consider whether you're in danger of purchasing more house than you can reasonably afford and should pull back and look for a more affordable one.

⚠ WATCH OUT FOR WRAPAROUND NOTES

Some sellers will offer a wraparound note ("wrap"), also known as an All Inclusive Trust Deed (AITD). It "wraps around" existing financing; you pay the seller, and they pay the other note holder.

Be wary! You're usually much better off paying the first mortgage holder directly and having the seller simply carry back a second. A seller offers a wrap because he receives a higher interest yield for the total loan than you would pay by negotiating the two mortgages separately.

PREPARING A SECOND MORTGAGE

Step 1: Determine the terms of the second, including the dollar amount, length of the loan, interest rate and repayment terms. If you think you may be able to repay the loan ahead of schedule, make sure the second mortgage doesn't include a prepayment penalty (discussed in Chapter 9, Section C). Normally, the buyer and seller bargain over the terms of the second mortgage during the negotiating process. Many buyers will benefit from the advice of a savvy real estate expert here.

Step 2: Be sure the lending institution which will provide the first mortgage knows and approves of the terms and conditions of the second.

Step 3: Prepare the necessary paperwork—the buyer's promissory note for the amount of the second mortgage, containing all mortgage terms. Nolo's *For Sale by Owner*, by George Devine, includes a promissory note for a second mortgage. Relatively straightforward arrangements can be handled by the title or escrow company which is doing the closing. For more complicated mortgages, including those with an adjustable interest rate, you may need the help of an experienced real estate lawyer. In addition, the title or escrow company should prepare and record a second mortgage (a "deed of trust") at the County Recorder's Office.

Step 4: Make sure your purchase contract contains all the terms and conditions of the second mortgage (required by Civil Code §§ 2956 through 2967.) Clause 1 of our contract (see Chapter 16) includes seller financing disclosures. If you use our contact, modify any terms that may differ.

EXAMPLE: Sally and Burt want to buy a $300,000 house outside of Fullerton. They have $70,000 from savings and a gift from Sally's mother. Their combined monthly income is $4,700. Unfortunately, the best deal they can get is an ARM for $200,000 at 7.5% for 30 years. They're $30,000 short. They look for a cheaper house, but hate everything they see. They really want the $300,000 house.

Sally and Burt approach Patience, the seller, and propose that she take back a second mortgage for the $30,000. Because she needs to move fairly quickly, and there are no other likely buyers, Patience agrees. She offers Sally and Burt a five-year interest-only (Sally and Burt will pay Patience only interest—no principal) second at 10% interest, which will result in payments of $333.33 per month. Unfortunately, however, Sally and Burt no longer qualify for the first mortgage as the monthly payments for the two mortgages exceed the institutional lender's debt-to-income ratio. They go back to Patience and propose a seven-year second, with interest-only payments of 5% for the first two years. Beginning in the third year, the payments would increase 20% per year for five years. At the end of the seventh year, Sally and Burt would owe the balance in a balloon payment.

D. Second Mortgages—Financing by Private Parties Other Than the Seller

Sellers aren't the only people who can provide second mortgages. Relatives and friends can make second loans, and some private investors will as well. Loan brokers can bring prospective borrowers and prospective second mortgage lenders together for a fee. In addition, private lenders advertise in the "Trust Deeds for Sale" section of newspaper classifieds, promoting the fact that they have money available to invest in seconds.

Finally, as a last resort, many commercial lenders, often called "home equity lenders," make second mortgage loans. They charge high points, loan fees and interest, however, and their deals are rarely attractive. ∎

Obtaining a Mortgage

The previous five chapters describe the kinds of mortgages—and their pros and cons—available to house buyers. You should have a good idea as to the type you want—and can afford. Now it's time to actually get a mortgage. When shopping for a home loan, remember that you're a customer willing to pay good money for a good product and decent service. Forget about the words "lender" and "borrower," which tend to cast you in the role of a powerless supplicant begging for a loan. Thousands of companies (savings and loans, banks, mortgage companies and credit unions) make house loans in California. If you're eligible for a mortgage from one lender, many others will also be glad to have your business. If you don't like the treatment you get from one lender, go elsewhere.

It's no secret that buying a house is a big financial stretch for many Californians, especially first-time homebuyers. This is a polite way of saying you may have trouble qualifying for a loan. While we can't manufacture greenbacks for you, we can give you some helpful advice.

If you have credit problems, take the steps to clean up or rebuild your credit before, not after, you apply for a mortgage. Lenders will do a careful check of your credit history before approving a loan. Any problems may delay—or even jeopardize—your loan. For advice on dealing with credit problems, review Chapter 2, Section F6. Other helpful chapters are:

- Chapter 3, for strategies on closing the affordability gap
- Chapter 4, for creative ways to raise money for your down payment
- Chapter 11, for getting a loan with government assistance, and
- Chapter 12, for approaching relatives and friends to ask for help.

Assuming you're in decent financial shape, your next task is to clearly understand that real money can be saved if you carefully shop for a mortgage. Everything else being equal, even a one-quarter percentage point difference in interest rates can mean savings of thousands of dollars over the life of a mortgage.

A. Gather Information on Mortgage Rates and Fees

Gathering information about current mortgage interest rates is essential, whether you'll be working with a loan broker (Section B) or shopping for mortgages on your own (Section C).

Fortunately, this need not be a daunting task, as mortgage interest tables are printed in the Sunday real estate sections of many metropolitan newspapers. These tables include current mortgage interest rates, points and fees charged by various lenders for different types of mortgages.

HOW TO COMPARE MORTGAGE RATES BY APR

Advertised rates may not always be based on the same factors—one lender's 8.5% interest rate may actually be a better deal than another's 8.3%. The lower rate, for example, might not include points while the higher one does. In an attempt to allow buyers to compare loans, federal law (Regulation Z) requires all lenders to state the Annual Percentage Rate (APR) and to include fees and points. When these fees are figured in, the APR is usually 0.25% to 0.30% higher than the advertised rate for 30-year loans

Assume, for example, you're considering a $100,000 loan at 8% for 30 years. If there were no loan fees, the APR would be 8%. If there are 2 points, the APR would be 8.21%, because you'd receive only $98,000 after the $2,000 in points was subtracted.

⚠ Even APR comparisons aren't perfect. Depending on how lenders write loans, identical packages can end up with slightly different APRs. In addition, APR comparisons assume you'll pay off the loan over its entire term, and thus amortize the fees and points over this period. But most people move or refinance sooner, with the result that a loan with lots of points may be more expensive than one with fewer points (and a higher interest rate), even though the APR is the same. Also, APR comparisons don't take into consideration the tax deduction you get on mortgage interest and points. Your loan will cost you more or less depending on your tax bracket. (To compare points and interest rates, see Chapter 8, Section F.) APR discussions also omit closing and transaction costs, which can vary slightly.

While mortgage interest tables include only a small percentage of the total mortgages on the market, they can give you a good feel for the current price range, especially if you ignore the mortgages with the lowest rates. These are usually offered by small companies which write very low risk mortgages in relatively affluent areas, or are available only for already-approved loans which will close in ten days, and so they're listed more as a form of advertising to attract customers. And remember, just because a low interest loan is available, there's no guarantee that you'll qualify for it or that it has all the features you want (or that it won't have some features you don't want, such as negative amortization or a prepayment penalty).

In addition to newspaper listings, some commercial networks' online services and local bulletin boards provide computerized comparative mortgage rate information. (See Chapter 6, Section G, for details.) As with newspaper listings, these data bases carry only a fraction of the mortgage options available.

B. Work With a Loan Broker

Another approach to looking for a loan (after doing your own preliminary work) is to hire a loan broker, a person who specializes in matching house buyers and appropriate mortgage lenders. If you qualify financially, a savvy loan broker can find you a competitively-priced mortgage that meets your needs. This is often fairly easy, because brokers subscribe to one or more computerized services which list most loans currently offered in a particular area. Ask to see a current printout so you have access to the same information the broker does.

Loan brokers must have a real estate broker's license, (although someone who works for a broker needs only a salesperson's license).

Loan brokers usually receive two types of compensation:

- A commission from the lender that is a portion of the points you pay on your loan. If there are no points, the lender pays the broker and recoups this payment by charging the borrower a higher interest rate.
- A processing fee, ranging from $200 to $500. Some brokers charge this processing fee upfront; others only at the close of escrow.

The broker is legally required to disclose both the amount and source of his compensation to the borrower.

Financial institutions accommodate loan brokers because lenders want more loan business and will pay a middle person a commission to get it. In addition, because loan brokers do much of the paper preparation work, they often save lenders time in loan transactions.

Working with a loan broker has its pros and cons. On the positive side, it's often easier and more effective than looking for the cheapest rates yourself. If you are a first-time home buyer or simply don't have the time to shop for mortgages, you'll appreciate the help a loan broker can provide, such as:

- reviewing your financial profile and, if necessary, counseling you on steps to improve it (such as those discussed in Chapter 2) before applying for a loan
- providing information about types of mortgages which meet your needs
- identifying the financial institutions that offer the type of mortgage you want and are likely to qualify for
- helping you prepare the papers needed to apply for a loan (if you don't use a loan broker, you'll do this directly with the financial institution), and
- talking to the loan officers on your behalf, to anticipate and solve any problems.

The down side of using loan brokers include:

- You must be sure that the person you work with knows what he's doing and that you can trust his recommendation.
- Not all loan brokers handle government loans (Chapter 11) or work with all lenders.
- A few loan brokers have been known to prefer financial institutions that treat them well (pass on more points or offer attractive prizes or gifts), but don't necessarily offer you the lowest or best rates.
- You may be able to find the best mortgage on your own. In fact, some lenders keep their best loans in house. That means, they are available only if you contact the lender directly—these loans are not made available to loan brokers.
- A few loan brokers (like some banks) use bait-and-switch advertising to recruit customers—that is, they claim they can arrange better loans at lower rates than is actually possible. You can minimize your risk by checking out mortgage rates and features before contacting a broker.

California has thousands of loan brokers; some work alone, others in fair-sized companies. To find a good one, ask friends, relatives and acquaintances for a recommendation. If you're working with a real estate agent, he'll surely have a suggestion, but before relying solely on her word, make a few phone calls and check out the referral. Some loan brokers are known on the local grapevine to be more helpful, creative and trustworthy than others.

If you have a problem with a loan broker or a bank loan department, you can file a complaint with the Department of Real Estate. (See Chapter 5, Section B, for phone numbers of local offices.)

WHY USE A LOAN BROKER?

We asked Michael Cohen, a loan broker with Schnell Investment Company in Berkeley, California, who a number of Nolo Press employees have used with terrific results and who helped us greatly with this book, "Why use a loan broker? Why add yet another personality to an already complex transaction, when it is so easy to go directly to your neighborhood savings and loan or bank?"

Here's what he said:

The main reasons are flexibility, service and security. Any one lender has only a few products to offer. By contrast, a well-connected mortgage broker may place loans with 50-60 lenders, including large S&Ls, small local banks or mortgage bankers representing insurance or pension fund investors.

A loan broker representing many institutions has many program options, pricing trade-offs and underwriting variations to offer. This may include access to swing loans, commercial and multifamily loans, construction and "rehab" loans. In addition, a good loan broker can counsel the borrower on loan qualification strategies and financing alternatives. She'll also spot potential problems early on and suggest a way to resolve them. This may mean the difference between getting the loan or not. If one lender doesn't come through (despite the loan broker's advocacy efforts), the broker may be able to place the loan elsewhere. In these uncertain days when banks are combining into larger and more distant, faceless monoliths, working with an actual person may provide you with better service.

One final word: The loan broker doesn't get paid by the lender unless the loan closes. Therefore, it's in the broker's enlightened self-interest to see that the loan is approved and the borrower is satisfied. Unlike a clerk who earns a salary in any event, a savvy loan broker never forgets that ultimately it is the satisfied borrower who provides the fee for the broker's services.

ANTONIO & GRETEL: WORKING WITH A LOAN BROKER

We'd made an offer on a house that several other people wanted. We knew that in order to be considered seriously we needed to show the sellers we could afford the purchase. We'd heard that a particular bank was a quick qualifier for adjustable rate mortgages and charged no application fee for ARMs.

Sure enough, within a few days, for no cost, we were told we qualified for a loan. This satisfied the sellers who accepted our offer (rejecting another attractive one because the people couldn't secure financing).

Now we had time to shop for a good loan. We went back to the "quick qualifier" bank and pointed out that their rates seemed to be on the high side. They said take it or leave it; we left. On the recommendation of friends, we called a local loan broker. Though this took some time, we came out of it with an excellent fixed rate loan. (He also showed us ARMs at much lower rates than offered by the "quick qualifier" bank.)

Our loan broker was helpful in another way. As Gretel had been a freelancer for part of the previous three years, we had to demonstrate earning capacity. The loan broker suggested to us that Gretel not only gather her tax returns for the past several years, but also that she get letters from her major clients stating her projected income for the foreseeable future.

C. Interview Lenders

An alternative to working with a loan broker is to comparison shop for a loan on your own. Even if you plan to work with a loan broker, doing your own research can help make sure you're getting the best deal and educate you about market conditions so you can work more efficiently with a broker.

One good way to mortgage shop is to interview several lenders. Start by identifying lenders offering loans appropriate for you, based on newspaper listings or ads or recommendations from your real estate agent or a friend, relative or employer. If you regularly do business with a bank or other financial institution, it makes sense to include that bank, if it offers reasonably competitive loans. Obtain all written material describing available mortgages from lenders you have identified as possibilities. To the extent possible, gather all information on the same day, so you can do an accurate comparison.

After reviewing the lenders' written material, make an appointment to meet a residential real estate loan officer or to speak with one on the telephone. If you, or a relative or close friend own a business and has an ongoing relationship with a bank, ask for an introduction to a real estate loan officer. You may get some extra personal time and attention this way.

When you call to schedule an appointment or obtain information, be sure to verify that the lender offers the type of loan you want. Loan rates, fees or requirements for points may have changed since the newspaper you read went to print.

When you visit or speak to a lender, your goals are to review the following materials with the loan officer:

• The various mortgage plans available, including the required down payment, APR, interest rate, points, loan origination fees, credit check charges and appraisal fees. If you've read the written material, what the loan officer tells you should come as little surprise.

• The family financial statement you prepared in Chapter 2. Based on this, the loan officer should be able to give you a good idea of the type of mortgage you qualify for.

• All details important to you. For example, if you plan to make a low down payment, find out whether private mortgage insurance (PMI) is required. If you're considering an ARM loan, ask about periodic caps, life-of-the-loan caps, negative amortization and the like.

⚠ Keep in mind that the financial institution you talk to first—or even second—may not be the cheapest or best for you. If a loan officer tries to thrust a loan into your hands, politely state that you still want to look at other loans. Be sure to ask if the loan officer is paid any commission for mortgage loans he makes. Some loan officers make a commission on the number or dollar amount of loans they make; this may affect what loans they recommend.

D. Complete the Mortgage Rates and Terms Table

This chapter includes a two-page Mortgage Rates and Terms Table to keep track of information you collect on different loans. (Appendix 4 includes a tear-out copy.)

This form is important for three primary reasons:

1. Filling it out requires that you understand the details of every loan you consider. You'll have no surprises later.

2. Having this information will be an invaluable aid to your memory; days or weeks later you can check what you've been offered.

3. Assuming you get information about more than one loan, it will let you efficiently compare features.

⚠ **BE CAREFUL OF MORTGAGE SHOPPING BY PHONE**

If a loan sounds too good to be true, it may be. Some lenders quote super low interest rates, just to get you to fill out an application. Only when you're far along in the process, do you find out that the low interest or no-points rate you were quoted was only guaranteed for a few days or only available to buyers with unblemished credit histories. At this point, it may be too late to back out of the deal, and you're stuck with a more expensive loan. Whether you're gathering loan information by phone or in-person, always ask upfront about any special conditions or requirements.

HANDYMAN'S DREAM

MORTGAGE RATES AND TERMS TABLE

Lender	_____	_____	_____
Loan agent	_____	_____	_____
Phone number	_____	_____	_____
Date	_____	_____	_____

1. General Information

Fixed or adjustable	☐ F ☐ A	☐ F ☐ A	☐ F ☐ A
Fixed rate mortgage interest rate	_____ %	_____ %	_____ %
Government financing	☐ Y ☐ N	☐ Y ☐ N	☐ Y ☐ N
Minimum down payment	_____ %	_____ %	_____ %
PMI required	☐ Y ☐ N	☐ Y ☐ N	☐ Y ☐ N
Impound account	☐ Y ☐ N	☐ Y ☐ N	☐ Y ☐ N
Term	_____ Years	_____ Years	_____ Years
Assumable	☐ Y ☐ N	☐ Y ☐ N	☐ Y ☐ N
Prepayment penalty	☐ Y ☐ N	☐ Y ☐ N	☐ Y ☐ N
Negative amortization (adjustables only)	☐ Y ☐ N	☐ Y ☐ N	☐ Y ☐ N
Rate lock-in available	☐ Y ☐ N	☐ Y ☐ N	☐ Y ☐ N
Cost to lock-in	21 Days $_____	21 Days $_____	21 Days $_____
	30 Days $_____	30 Days $_____	30 Days $_____
	45 Days $_____	45 Days $_____	45 Days $_____

2. Debt-to-Income Ratios Information

Allowable monthly carrying costs as % of income	_____ %	_____ %	_____ %
Allowable monthly carrying costs plus long-term debts as % of monthly income	_____ %	_____ %	_____ %
Maximum loan you qualify for based on debt-to-income ratios	$_____	$_____	$_____

3. Loan Costs

Number of Points	_____	_____	_____
Cost of Points	$_____	$_____	$_____
PMI	$_____	$_____	$_____
Additional loan fee	$_____	$_____	$_____
Credit report	$_____	$_____	$_____
Application fee	$_____	$_____	$_____
Appraisal fee	$_____	$_____	$_____
Miscellaneous fees	$_____	$_____	$_____
Estimated total loan costs	$_____	$_____	$_____

4. Time Limits

Credit/employment check	_____ Days	_____ Days	_____ Days
Lender appraisal	_____ Days	_____ Days	_____ Days
Loan approval	_____ Days	_____ Days	_____ Days
Loan funding	_____ Days	_____ Days	_____ Days
Loan due date each month	_____	_____	_____
Grace period	_____ Days	_____ Days	_____ Days
Late fee	_____ % Pmt	_____ % Pmt	_____ % Pmt

5. Other Features [such as a discount if you have an account with a certain bank, or a lender buydown (discount) of interest rate on initial payments]

	_____	_____	_____
	_____	_____	_____

_____	_____	_____	_____
_____	_____	_____	_____

6. Fixed Rate Two-Step Loans

Initial annual interest rate	_____%	_____%	_____%
Over how many years	_____ Years	_____ Years	_____ Years

7. Fixed Rate Balloon Payment Loans

Interest rate	_____%	_____%	_____%
Monthly payment	$_____	$_____	$_____
Term of loan	_____ Years	_____ Years	_____ Years
Amount of balloon payment	$_____	$_____	$_____

8. Convertible Loans

Earliest conversion period	_____ Months	_____ Months	_____ Months
Conversion window	_____ Weeks	_____ Weeks	_____ Weeks
Index: 11th District COFI	☐ _____%	☐ _____%	☐ _____%
6 Mo. T-Bills	☐ _____%	☐ _____%	☐ _____%
1 Yr. T-Bills	☐ _____%	☐ _____%	☐ _____%
6 Mo. LIBOR	☐ _____%	☐ _____%	☐ _____%
Other _____	☐ _____%	☐ _____%	☐ _____%
Margin	_____%	_____%	_____%
Conversion fee	$_____	$_____	$_____

9. Adjustable Rate Mortgages (ARMs)

Index: 11th District COFI	☐ _____%	☐ _____%	☐ _____%
6 Mo. T-Bills	☐ _____%	☐ _____%	☐ _____%
1 Yr. T-Bills	☐ _____%	☐ _____%	☐ _____%
6 Mo. LIBOR	☐ _____%	☐ _____%	☐ _____%
Other _____	☐ _____%	☐ _____%	☐ _____%
Margin	_____%	_____%	_____%
Convertible	☐ Y ☐ N	☐ Y ☐ N	☐ Y ☐ N
When	_____ Year	_____ Year	_____ Year
Initial interest rate	_____%	_____%	_____%
How long	____ Mos. ___Yrs.	____ Mos. ___Yrs.	____ Mos. ___Yrs..
Interest rate cap (with negative amortization) or	_____%	_____%	_____%
Interest rate cap (without negative amortization)	_____%	_____%	_____%
Adjustment period	_____ Months	_____ Months	_____ Months
Life-of-loan (overall) cap	_____%	_____%	_____%
Initial payment	_____ Months	_____ Months	_____ Months
Payment cap	_____%	_____%	_____%
Payment cap period	_____ Months	_____ Months	_____ Months
Highest payment or interest rate in: 6 months	___% $_____	___% $_____	___% $_____
12 months	___% $_____	___% $_____	___% $_____
18 months	___% $_____	___% $_____	___% $_____
24 months	___% $_____	___% $_____	___% $_____
30 months	___% $_____	___% $_____	___% $_____
36 months	___% $_____	___% $_____	___% $_____

10. Hybrid Loans

Initial interest rate	_____%	_____%	_____%
Term as a fixed rate loan	_____ Years	_____ Years	_____ Years
Interest rate at first adjustment period	_____%	_____%	_____%

A COMPARISON OF SIX MORTGAGES

By now, you may be completely overwhelmed by the chapters on mortgage financing, thinking "I like the stability of a fixed rate mortgage, but the initial low cost of an ARM is tempting." Before finalizing your decision, compare six $150,000 mortgages through seven years (the typical length of time a homeowner keeps a mortgage). For information on margins, indexes and life of the loan caps, see Chapter 10.

Mortgage type	Interest rate	Start of mortgage		After 7 years	
		Annual % rate (APR)	Monthly payment	Total payment	Total paid on principal
30-year fixed	7.625%	7.925	$1,062	$89,182	$12,002
15-year fixed	7.25%	7.717	$1,370	$115,021	$50,476
1-year ARM; after 1 year, rate increases with 2.625 margin, 3.5 index, 10.625% life of the loan cap	4.625%	4.853	$772	$99,765	$11,552
3-year ARM; after 3 years, rate increases with 2.625 margin, 5.25 index, 11.875% life of the loan cap	6.375%	6.643	$936	$99,192	$10,149
5-year ARM; after 3 years, rate increases with 2.625 margin, 5.25 index, 11.875% life of the loan cap	7.25%	7.540	$1,024	$91,586	$11,142
Two-step; fixed for 7 years; changes to ARM with 2.25 index and 5.0 life of the loan cap	7.125%	7.412	$1,011	$84,889	$13,016

As the chart shows, a 15-year fixed rate mortgage pays down the $150,000 balance the quickest. If you can't afford this loan's higher monthly payments, be comforted in knowing that in this example, the differences among the other mortgages are not that great.

Tear out the Mortgage Rates and Terms Table in Appendix 4. Make several photocopies. Then complete one for each lender which offers you a mortgage which meets your basic priorities.

Instructions for Completing Mortgage Rates and Terms Table

Heading

At the top of the table, enter the lender's name (such as Bank of Richmond), the name of the loan agent you met or spoke with, his phone number and the date of your meeting or telephone conversation.

Section 1: General Information

Enter the type of loan: fixed or adjustable; the rate, if it's a fixed mortgage; whether it qualifies for government financing (if that's a need you have); the minimum down payment required; whether private mortgage insurance (PMI) is required, and if so, whether you'll need to set up an impound account; the term (number of years of the loan); whether it's assumable;

whether it has a prepayment penalty; whether it has negative amortization and if so, whether it lets you (and for how much) lock-in at a certain rate. (These terms are discussed in Chapters 8, 9 and 10, and in Section E below.)

Section 2: Debt-to-Income Ratios Information

Then enter information on your debt-to-income ratios (see Chapter 2 to refresh your memory). Here you need to indicate the percentage of your income each lender allows for the monthly carrying costs to obtain the mortgage, and for monthly carrying costs plus monthly payments on other long-term debts. Then, based on these debt-to-income ratios, enter the maximum loan each lender will make.

Section 3: Loan Costs

If possible, enter the costs associated with getting the loan—the number of points and their cost, PMI, additional loan fee, credit report, application fee, appraisal fee and other miscellaneous costs. Then total them up. Your estimate will have to be rough because most lenders won't estimate closing costs until they start processing your loan. Even then, the costs are still estimates. You won't know the actual total of loan costs until you review the final papers you need to close escrow.

Section 4: Time Limits

You want to know how long it will take to process your loan application, and if it's approved, come up with the money (called "funding the loan"), enabling you to close the deal. Enter this information in the fourth section. Also, pay attention to the following items:

- the date each month your payment will be due; the first of the month is standard, although some portfolio lenders set the fifteen of the month
- how many "grace" days you have (after which the payment is considered late—15 days is standard), and
- the fee for late mortgage payments.

Section 5: Other Features

If the loan has any special features, such as discounted points if you have a savings account with the bank, indicate them.

Section 6: Fixed Rate Two-Step Loans

If you look at any fixed rate loans which step up to a higher rate after several years, indicate the initial annual percentage rate and for how many years it stays in effect.

Section 7: Fixed Rate Balloon Payment Loans

If you are considering a fixed rate loan for a short period (often three, five or seven years) that ends with one large balloon payment, indicate the interest rate and monthly payment, the term of the loan and the amount of the balloon payment.

Section 8: Convertible Loans

If you look at any convertible loans (these begin as an ARM and can be converted to a fixed rate mortgage), be sure to note the earliest conversion period and the conversion window (specified period during which you may convert). For example, many convertible loans let you convert after two years, but only during a specific two-week period. Also indicate the index, the margin and the fee charged for converting.

If you know you don't want an ARM, skip the rest of the Mortgage Rates and Terms Table. Otherwise, enter in Section 8 the information necessary to compare ARMs. If any terminology is confusing, see Chapter 10, Adjustable Rate Mortgages.

Section 9: Adjustable Rate Mortgages (ARMs)

First, enter the adjustable loan criteria—what index it's tied to, the amount of the margin, whether it's convertible, and if so, when.

Next, write down interest rate information—the initial rate, how long it lasts, the interest rate cap, the adjustment period and the life-of-the-loan cap. Be sure you understand whether the interest rate cap is a true periodic cap (caps both what you pay and what you owe) or is a payment cap which lets the amount you owe increase (negative amortization).

Finally, enter the payment information—the initial payment, payment cap and payment cap period. Also calculate your worst case scenario: the highest interest rate and monthly payments possible with the adjustable rate loan offered for different time periods.

Section 10: Hybrid Loans

If you are interested in an ARM that has a fixed rate for the first few years and then becomes adjustable, enter the information here. Pay particular attention to how much the interest rate can jump at the first adjustment period.

NEW HOUSE FINANCING

In buying a new house, the developer will very likely try to steer you to a particular lender. You may be told that the property has already been appraised and that, as a result, you'll save on fees and other red tape. Maybe so, but carefully check to see if the rate and loan terms you're being offered by the developer's chosen lender are competitive. Often, you can beat these prices. (For more on financing new houses, see Chapter 7, Section D.)

E. Apply for and Get a Loan

Once you've made an offer on a house and have identified what seems to be the best mortgage for you, it's time to apply for a loan. Despite the ads that tout "overnight approval," you should allow a reasonable period for approval (or denial) after you complete a loan application. Before final loan approval (called funding the loan), the lender must verify all your financial, employment and credit information, arrange an appraisal of the property and prepare the necessary paperwork. Normally, this process takes about three to six weeks, unless you have a high income and plan to make a substantial down payment, in which case approval should be faster. And in times of high volume, the process may take longer than six weeks.

The timeline at the end of this chapter shows all the steps involved from loan application to close of escrow.

1. Speeding Up Loan Approval

You'll save a lot of time in the loan application process by completing the family financial statement in Chapter 2 and determining your debt-to-income ratio. Find out the lender's qualification standard before you start filling out loan applications so you don't waste time applying for loans you clearly won't qualify for. If you've gotten a prequalification letter from a lender or loan broker (discussed in Chapter 2, Section G), you may have already pulled together much of the information you need.

Here are some other tips for faster loan approval.

Ask your lender what information they require for your loan application, and then have it available for your first meeting. Typically, lenders need the following documents to process your application:

- the purchase contract for the house you want to buy
- a legal description of the property
- the listing agreement or sales contract if you are selling a house
- source of down payment, including documentation for any gift funds involved
- the last two years' tax returns and W-2 forms
- pay stubs for the last two pay periods
- proof of nonsalary income such as rental income or alimony
- three months of bank statements for every account you have
- proof of assets such as pension funds, stock or life insurance, and
- names, addresses and phone numbers of recent employers.

Neatly write or type every section of the application. Don't leave any blanks! If some item doesn't apply, write "not applicable" or "N/A."

Tell the truth. Don't exaggerate your earnings or hide negative credit information—the lender will find out anyway. And if so, this misrepresentation (or fraud) may automatically cancel your loan application.

Show you're creditworthy. If you're concerned that something on your application may work against you—for example, you had major credit problems three years ago—attach a brief written explanation, such as how you've since rebuilt your credit. See Chapter 2, Section F, for advice on checking your credit file and cleaning up your credit rating.

⚠ Be suspicious if a lender turns down your loan or charges a higher interest rate or more points because your credit is bad. Make sure you see a written copy of the negative information and that you're not being hoodwinked by a dishonest lender.

Hand-deliver paperwork. To speed up the process, offer to hand carry forms to your employer and banks, verifying your employment and deposit information.

Monitor the process. If you're under time pressure to close by a certain date, or have a limited time when interest rates are locked in (see Section 3, below), be sure to keep close tabs on the process. Make sure your loan officer has all the information he needs to process your loan application. Keep in regular touch and document all phone and written communications with the lender.

2. Getting the Lender's Commitment

If a lender says that you qualify for a loan, ask for a "commitment" or "loan qualification" letter, stating the size and type of the loan and the interest rate you qualify for. The commitment letter may specify that certain conditions be met before final loan approval—for example, that you pay off a long-term debt or that the house appraises for at least the loan amount. As a precaution, don't remove financing contingencies from your offer (see Chapter 16) until these conditions have been met.

3. Locking in Interest Rates

It's important to understand that even a commitment letter isn't the same thing as a guarantee to borrow at a particular interest rate or particular terms. If interest rates go up, the lender will demand that you pay the higher amount, unless you've received a "lock-in" or "rate lock." If you haven't, and interest rates rise, the lender will recalculate your debt-to-income ratio to see if you still qualify at the higher interest rate.

A rate lock is a guarantee by a lender to make a loan at a particular interest rate, even if the market changes. Most rate locks are good for about 21-30 days after your loan is approved, and usually apply to a specific house. (You can often arrange for a rate lock for longer, but you'll have to pay for it, usually in the form of higher points—as much as 1/5 to 3/8 of a point more.) One reason you'll have to pay more is that when a lender locks in a rate, it has made a commitment to deliver the loan to Freddie Mac, or Fannie Mae, or another investor. If the lender doesn't deliver—that is, you don't buy the house—the lender still must pay a fee to the investor. Also, because of volatility in the market, Freddie Mac and Fannie Mae set a higher price on loans to be delivered later—for example, within 60 days versus 10 days.

A rate lock is particularly valuable when the house is in escrow and you are on a tight budget, as it protects you from the possibility that a hike in interest rates will result in your no longer qualifying to make the purchase. If you are not worried about increasing rates, you'll probably want to skip obtaining a lock-in and hope rates go down so that you'll get the benefit of the lower rate.

If you don't close escrow by the rate lock deadline, you'll lose this interest rate and may need to pay more. In the worst case scenario, if interest rates are too high with this particular lender, you may need to start the whole loan application process over with another lender.

GOTHIC REVIVAL

⚠ **BEWARE OF STRATEGIES UNSCRUPULOUS LENDERS MAY USE TO AVOID MEETING A RATE LOCK**

If your lender requires additional (and often very picky) documentation at the last minute—for example, details on a minor credit problem or more income data if you're self-employed—be leery. To avoid these kinds of delays, make sure all your information is complete when you apply for a loan. Get the rate lock agreement in writing. Keep in touch with the lender so you can head off any problems. Finally, file a complaint with a regulatory agency (see sidebar below) if the deal threatens to come undone.

F. Get Your House Appraised

A few weeks after you apply for a loan, the lender will arrange for an appraisal of the property, to make sure it's worth the amount you want to borrow. The buyer typically pays a fee for the appraisal as part of the closing costs, usually $300 to $400 depending upon the size and price of the house and property. Some government loan programs, such as FHA, set their own appraisal procedures. (See Chapter 11.)

The appraiser will measure, photograph and inspect the property inside and out, and estimate the value of the property based on recent documented prices of comparable sales within a few blocks of the house, adjusting for differences in size and features among the properties.

If the appraisal comes in at or above the amount of money you need to borrow, and everything else checks out, your loan will be approved. There may be problems, however, if the appraisal comes in low. In this case, your first step should be to get a copy of the appraisal; if you pay for the appraisal, the lender is legally obligated to give you a copy. If you've collected your own comparable sales data before determining your offer price (see Chapter 15, Section E), you should be able to justify a higher appraisal price to the lender. Consider asking for a second appraisal.

Here are your options if you can't get a higher appraisal:
- back out of the deal—assuming financing contingencies in your contract allow this (see Clause 1 of our offer form in Chapter 16)
- come up with more money for a down payment
- get the seller to lower the price or take back a second mortgage (discussed in Chapter 12, Section C), or
- look for another lender.

A HYPOTHETICAL TIMELINE:
FROM LOAN APPLICATION TO CLOSE OF ESCROW

Let's assume you submitted an offer to purchase a home to a seller and it was accepted on January 1.

The application process should proceed roughly as follows:

January 2-3	You submit loan application; lender runs credit check immediately and reviews with you any negative information.
January 3-4	Day after running credit check, lender sends out requests for verifications of your employment and deposit accounts, if necessary. Lender orders appraisal of the house.
January 2-5	Within 72 hours of when you submitted your application, lender must send you loan disclosures (annual percentage rate and other information) and good faith estimates of closing costs.
January 10-18	One to two weeks after lender arranges for appraisal of property, it's completed.
January 10-February 1	One to four weeks after lender sends out verifications, employer and banks return them.
January 12-February 4	Two to three days after verifications have been returned, lender assembles a loan package. Loan underwriter compares loan package to lender's guidelines. If it fits, underwriter sends package to supervisor and others for approval. If it doesn't fit, but is in the ballpark, underwriter sends package to others for second opinion. If it totally fails to fit guidelines, loan is rejected.
January 13-February 6	Lender loan committee gives final approval, sometimes with certain conditions (such as pay off a long-term debt).
January 14-February 9	One to three days after loan approved (or condition removed), lender types up loan papers.
January 15-February 10	One day after lender types up loan papers, escrow holder prepares final closing papers for you and seller.
January 16-February 11	One day after escrow holder prepares final closing papers, you and seller go to escrow holder to sign all papers.
January 17-February 13	One to two days after you and seller sign escrow papers, loan package is sent to lender for final review and funding check.
January 18-February 15	One to two days after loan package is sent to lender for final review and funding, a check is sent to escrow holder or local bank. (Closing may be delayed until check is deposited into local bank or otherwise clears.)
January 19-February 16	Escrow closes! Congratulations.

CUPOLA COTTAGE

WHERE TO COMPLAIN ABOUT PROBLEMS WITH A LOAN APPLICATION

If you have a problem with how your loan application was handled—perhaps you felt fees were excessive, the appraisal unfair, or the rate lock guarantee unmet—document your concerns. If you can't work things out with the lender, be prepared to file a complaint with a regulatory agency. Where you complain depends upon the type of financial institution—for example, whether it's a state-charted bank or a savings and loan. To find out where to complain, start with the Department of Real Estate (Chapter 5, Section B includes a list of local offices) and the Department of Consumer Affairs (800-344-9940). If you feel the lender discriminated in the loan application process, contact the Department of Fair Employment and Housing at (800) 884-1684.

Buying a House
When You Already Own One

→ Homeowners looking to buy who can afford to own two houses at once (even if for just a short period), don't need to worry about perfectly timing their purchase and sale transactions and can skip this chapter. You can also go on to Chapter 15 if you're a first-time buyer, although this chapter might give you some tips to protect yourself if you buy from someone looking to purchase a new house.

If you already own a home and plan to sell it before buying another, questions of timing inevitably arise. Is it better to sell your old house before buying a new one? Or should you focus primarily on buying, even if it means that you may have to sell your present house quickly to close on the new one?

If you sell first, you'll be under time pressure to find another house quickly. This is stressful, and rarely results in your finding a truly good house at a reasonable price. Even if you do find a great house, you're likely to overpay in an anxious effort not to lose out to another purchaser.

On the other hand, buying a new house first and then scrambling to sell your old one is no fun either—especially if you're trading up substantially and need to sell your old house for top dollar to make the down payment on the new one. As any experienced real estate agent will confirm, selling a house fast and getting the best possible price are normally mutually exclusive concepts. Too often, you're under time constraints to close on the new house, and will accept a lower than optimum price on your old house in order to make a quick sale.

Is there a good solution to the problem of whether to buy or sell first? Or is this just one of life's miserable little enigmas to which there is no good answer? Fortunately, this chapter gives you constructive steps to minimize the psychological and financial downside of selling one house while buying another.

NOLO'S BOOK FOR HOME SELLERS

Nolo Press publishes *For Sale by Owner,* by George Devine, a co-author of this book. *FSBO* (pronounced "fizzbo") provides practical, easy-to-use forms and the legal, financial and real estate knowledge needed to sell your house—on your own or with the help of a broker. With the help of *FSBO,* many homeowners find it relatively easy to sell their own houses and use the money saved as part of their down payment to trade up to a nicer one. See the back of this book for information on ordering *FSBO.*

MARY ADVISES: LISTEN TO GRANDPA

In selling my house and buying another, I remembered my grandfather saying always "buy low and sell high." To accomplish this, he explained, you must get time on your side. People pay top dollar when they're pressed for time and get a bargain when they can be patient.

So, the question became, how could I apply Grandpa's advice to my situation? To avoid selling my house in a hurry in order to pay for a new one, I called my dad and asked for a short-term loan. He helped some. Next I called my uncles and a college roommate who has a knack with money. Together they agreed to advance me the rest of what I needed for a few months. Combined with my own savings, this let me make a very chunky down payment (55% of the purchase price) on a new house without the need to sell the old one. I then listed my existing house for sale at an aggressive price, perfectly prepared to have to wait for a while, and maybe even to take less. Instead, I immediately got a full price offer. I was so surprised, I almost forgot to say "yes." By preparing to be patient, I sold for about $25,000 more and bought for about $35,000 less than if I'd been in a hurry.

A. Check the Housing Market Carefully

Before you put your house on the market or commit to buying a new one, carefully investigate the sales prices of houses in the markets where you'll be selling and buying. It's essential that you have a realistic idea of how much you'll get for your house, and how much you'll pay for the one you buy as part of developing a strategy to sell high and buy low. (See Chapter 15 for more information on accurately pricing a house.)

⚠ It's an understatement to say that market conditions in California change frequently. Don't assume you know how to price your house, even if you bought it just last year.

Don't be surprised if your investigation leads you to conclude that you couldn't afford to buy your own home, never mind the house of your dreams. At this stage, you may join hundreds of thousands of other Californians and decide to remodel or add to your current house, not move. This can make good sense, because the cost per square foot of remodeling is often below the cost per square foot of purchasing new space. (For more on remodeling, see Chapter 3, Section C.)

If, after investigating prices, you decide to go ahead and buy a new house, you next must focus on whether the market is "hot" (favors sellers) or "cold" (favors buyers). As we discuss in Chapter 15, judging the relative temperature of the market is important to buyers and sellers, and is crucial for people who are both. Your dual position lets you adopt a strategy of protecting yourself in your weaker role while letting your stronger role take care of itself.

1. Strategies in a Seller's Market

If sellers have the advantage in the communities or neighborhoods where you both now own and plan to buy, it follows that selling your current house will likely be easier than buying a new one. Thus, you want to compete aggressively in purchasing a new house, while insisting on maximum flexibility as to the date you move out of your present house.

You can guarantee yourself this leeway by stipulating that the sale of your current house be contingent upon your finding and closing on a new one. When a buyer makes an offer on your house, include in your written counteroffer a provision spelling this out. Although few buyers will agree to an open-ended period, some will be so anxious to buy your house that they'll agree to delay the closing until you close on a new house or until a certain number of days pass, whichever comes first. (See Chapter 16, Putting Your Offer in Writing, for more on offers and counteroffers.)

EXAMPLE: Roberta wants to move closer to her job. Both where she now lives and where she hopes to call home are hot (seller's) markets. She puts her current house on the market, making it clear that any sale will be contingent upon her closing on her new house. A number of potential buyers surface, and the highest bidder is agreeable to waiting a reasonable time, but balks at an open-ended contingency. Roberta, who does not want to lose the deal, agrees to move out either when she closes on another house, or after 120 days pass from the closing on her present house, whichever occurs first.

Although she remains under a degree of time pressure, four months should be enough time to find a good new place, especially given that she got such a great price on the sale of her old one.

IS THE MARKET HOT OR COLD?

This summary tells how to take the temperature of a particular housing market (see Chapter 15, Section F, for more details):

- If, in a given geographical area, considerably more people are looking to buy than are looking to sell, it's considered a seller's market. Prices tend to rise (often quickly), and buyers must bid competitively (read: high) and have their financing lined up in advance to succeed.
- If sellers predominate in an area, as can happen in areas of high unemployment or skyrocketing interest rates, the market favors buyers. In a buyer's market, sellers often must court buyers by lowering prices and offering innovative financing packages that often include the seller taking back a second mortgage. (See Chapter 12, Section C.) In new housing developments, sellers often offer to pay a portion of the buyer's monthly mortgage. (See Chapter 7, Section D.)

California has historically been a seller's market, due to a relatively strong economy, high immigration and slow growth and environmental concerns that limit new house construction in many areas. In the early 1990s, however, this has changed, and prices have declined in most of the state. In the next few years, no one can guarantee that any particular area will be either a buyer's or a seller's market. Local factors, such as earthquakes, riots and fires in the early 1990s, can make California houses hard to sell in affected communities. Also, in times when interest rates are relatively low, or just after house prices have already dropped, a short-term seller's market may exist.

Because markets can change so fast (for example, in the spring of 1994, over half of San Francisco's neighborhoods switched from buyers' markets to sellers' markets after buyers had had the upper hand for quite some time), it's crucial to have current information. Pay careful attention to newspapers, radio and TV reports on upward and downward trends in local real estate markets. If prices in your area are stable or heading downward, you can be pretty sure you are in a buyer's market.

RENTING YOUR OWN HOUSE

When you sell your house contingent upon moving into a new one, you have two options if you need more time to move. One option is to become a tenant in your old house if you continue to occupy it once the sale closes. Here are a few hints on how to handle this:

- You and the new owner should sign a written rental agreement. A tear-out copy is available in *The Landlord's Law Book: Rights & Responsibilities,* by Brown and Warner (Nolo Press). The rental term should be for seven days, not one month. This means you pay rent each week and must give seven days' written notice to move out. In landlord-tenant lingo, you make the rental period week to week, not month to month. Alternatively, you could pay by the month but modify the rental agreement to let you give seven days written notice to move, rather than the normal 30 days.

- Your weekly rent should be about 25% of the buyer's monthly carrying costs (mortgage principal and interest, taxes and insurance). This will be considerably higher than what you paid to live in that house (your old mortgage), but the interest you earn on the cash proceeds of the sale will offset this to a degree. In addition, it will probably be less than if you had to move to a temporary place, and it saves you the trouble of moving twice.

Another option is to delay the closing if possible. As long as you are confident the buyer won't try to back out, this can make sense for two reasons. As an owner, you can deduct mortgage interest and property taxes; as a tenant, you can't. As a tenant, your rent will be figured at the new owner's higher costs. Of course, you will have a pile of money in the bank from the sale, but its true value won't equal your higher costs as a tenant.

2. Strategies in a Buyer's Market

In a buyer's market, where sellers outnumber buyers who can afford to purchase houses, you're in a stronger position as a buyer than as a seller. Consider protecting yourself by making your offer to buy a new house contingent upon your selling your current one. (See Clause 10 of our offer form in Chapter 16.) A seller having a hard time finding a buyer is likely to accept this contingency, even though it means waiting for you to find a buyer.

When you make an offer to purchase contingent on selling your present house, be ready for the seller to counter with a "wipe-out" clause. This lets the seller accept your offer, but keeps the house on the market, with the requirement that he give you written notice if he receives another offer he wants to accept. Then, within 72 hours (or whatever length of time your agreement says) you must satisfy all contingencies and proceed with the purchase, or your offer is wiped-out, and the seller can proceed with other offers.

In this situation, a wipe-out clause is not unreasonable, as the seller needs some way to get out of a deal if you never sell your house. We discuss wipe-out clauses in more detail in Chapter 18, After the Contract Is Signed.

EXAMPLE: Ronald and Phil live in a small California town hard hit by lumber mill closings. They'd like to purchase a larger house than the one they already own, and houses are moving slowly. Although Ronald and Phil, both teachers, haven't lost their jobs due to the mill closings, the town's economic problems have made it difficult for them to sell their house and afford a new one. So, when they find a house they want to buy, they make their offer contingent upon their selling their old house. The seller accepts, but insists on including a 96-hour wipe-out clause to take effect 30 days after the contract is signed. This means that once 30 days pass, the seller can accept other offers, contingent upon giving Ronald and Phil 96 hours notice to satisfy (or eliminate) the requirement that they sell their existing house and go ahead with the deal.

AMERICAN NOMADIC

Sometimes, the offer is made contingent upon arranging financing. This usually has the same effect as making your offer contingent on selling your present house. Unless you have large savings, a lender won't normally approve financing on a new purchase until the sale of the old house is made and the down payment money is in hand, or at least until the lender is confident that your present house is priced fairly and will sell soon.

SAVE MONEY ON REAL ESTATE COMMISSIONS

If you're selling and buying in the same area, consider using the same real estate agent to sell your current house and buy a new one. If you do, you may well be able to save money on the typical 6%-8% commission sellers pay the listing agent by negotiating a lower rate. Remember, even a 1% or 2% savings is a lot of money.

B. Bridge Financing: How to Own Two Houses Briefly

Unfortunately, no matter how carefully you time things, you may not perfectly dovetail the sale of one house with the purchase of another. You may own no houses, in which case you'll have money in the bank and will need a temporary place to live, or you may own two houses at once. The following suggestions should help you pull this off:

- **Raise as much money as possible to put towards the down payment on a new house.** Most people have some money saved to combine with the profit from the sale of an existing house to make the down payment on the new one. If your savings, without the sale, put the second house within reach, maximize your cash by charging living expenses, getting an advance from your employer or selling personal possessions you no longer need. Although the interest on credit cards is high, you'll be able to pay bills off promptly when your existing house sells. If you raise a good amount of money this way, consider combining it with the next option.
- **Borrow down payment money from family or friends.** Point out that you need help for only a short period and offer a competitive interest rate. In Chapters 4, Raising Money for Your Down Payment, and 12, Private Mortgages, we discuss borrowing from private sources. Keep in mind that it's easier to borrow short-term money than to borrow a large sum for 20 or 30 years. If, for example, your parents have money put aside for retirement or your sister is saving to take a year off from work, either may be willing to tap savings to help you for the short time it will take to buy one house and sell another.
- **Get a bridge loan from a financial institution.** If you have no other choice, you can normally borrow money from a financial institution to "bridge" the period between when you close on your new house and when you get your money from the sale of your old one. This simply amounts to getting a short-term home equity loan on your existing house, using it toward the down payment on your new house and repaying it when your first house sells.

We say "no other choice" because bridge loans can be very expensive. Lenders often charge a host of up-front points or fees for credit checks, appraisals, loan originations and physical inspections. These can amount to 5% to 15% of the amount borrowed. On $50,000, that's $2,500 to $7,500. This wouldn't be unreasonable if you needed the money for a long time and spread the cost over many years. It's very expensive, however, if you only need money for a few months.

If you follow this approach, give the lender a promissory note, secured by a second mortgage (deed of trust) on your new house. This arrangement will mean no monthly payments are due until your first house sells and thus no negative effect on your debt-to-income ratio. This is an area where a loan broker who specializes in matching house buyers and appropriate mortgage lenders should be able to help. (See Chapter 13, Section B.)

ENGLISH VERNACULAR

WHAT TO LOOK FOR WHEN SHOPPING FOR A BRIDGE LOAN

- The lender from whom you obtain your financing for your new house may offer you a less expensive home equity bridge loan than other lenders. Ask about this possibility before committing to a long-term mortgage.
- When applying for a bridge loan, ask the lender to waive inspection and appraisal of your existing house. If the equity in that house is much larger than the bridge you need, the lender may do this. Also ask that the lender not charge points.
- If you purchased or refinanced your existing house only a few years past, find your paperwork. Some lenders will accept a recent appraisal, physical inspection or title report in lieu of charging you for new ones.
- If you don't know whether you'll need a home equity bridge loan until the last minute, see if you qualify for a stand-by personal line of credit. Although interest rates are higher than on a bridge loan (and non-deductible), up-front costs are minimal.
- Consider working with an experienced loan broker. (See Chapter 13.)

JENNY AND GREGG: WE HAD TO ACT FAST

We found the house to buy so fast, we were late in getting in gear to sell our existing house. Things were threatening to get out of control. We knew the sellers of the house we planned to buy wanted a quick, easy sale, and we would look good to them only as long as we appeared ready to close. If we tried to make the purchase contingent on our selling our existing house, they'd lose interest and put the house on the market, raising the price beyond what we could afford.

Instead, we agonized for a bit and said "yes." Immediately we put our existing house on the market. Unfortunately, it was harder than we expected to sell at the high price we wanted. We faced the possibility of owning two houses at once. Rather than panic and sell our existing house cheap, we lined up a bridge loan from a bank, but held off making the final commitment, which would have cost a lot in fees. We then lowered our asking price slightly, to awaken buyer interest. It worked. The house

sold at a still very good price, in time for us to make the closings simultaneous. We may have done better if we took the bridge loan and held out for a higher price, but with two kids and two jobs, the last thing we wanted to worry about was owning two houses.

RANDY & SHEILA: SELL YOUR FIRST HOUSE BEFORE YOU BUY ANOTHER

We bought a nice house near the top of the market in 1992. A few years later, we needed to move about 50 miles to be nearer to Randy's new job. We quickly found a great house and happily made an offer, thinking we would get the equity out of our existing old house and put it in the new one. Fortunately, we made the offer contingent on the sale of our old house. I say fortunately because our existing house turned out to be unsalable at anything near the price we needed to get.

After the bid on the new house fell through, we took the old house off the market. Randy now spends two hours a day on the road commuting. Soon we'll re-start our attempt to move, but this time we'll do our homework and price our house realistically. Then, when we're pretty sure of what it will sell for, we'll look for another.

C. Tax Considerations of Selling One House and Buying Another

Anyone who plans to sell one house and buy another should understand the tax considerations of his actions.

1. Buying a Second House of Equal or Greater Value

If you sell an owner-occupied house at a profit, and buy and occupy a more expensive one, you pay no federal or California tax on the profit now, assuming the sale of the first home and the purchase of the second occur within 24 months of each other. You must, however, report the sale to the IRS on Form 2119, under § 1034 of the Internal Revenue Code. If no broker is involved, you must report the sale on IRS Form 1099B.

This doesn't mean you'll never pay tax on your gain. You'll eventually owe the tax when you sell a house and don't buy one of equal or greater value. (If you are 55 or over, your tax may be reduced by the once-in-a-lifetime $125,000 federal tax exclusion—see Section 3 below.) This delayed tax is often referred to as a "roll over" of gain on your income tax because it lets you roll over the gain on one home into the other. You can do it as many times as you want.

To take advantage of it, keep in mind these points:

- It doesn't matter if the purchase of your next house occurs before or after the sale of the first one, as long as the two events aren't more than 24 months apart. The important date, for tax purposes, is when title is transferred, usually by the recording of the deeds. (See Chapter 18.)

- Any gain you "defer" or "roll over" in intermediate home sales is subtracted from—thus reduces–the basis (discussed below) in your next home. The same is true of any tax benefit you receive for unreimbursed casualty losses on your home.

- You can use the roll over advantage every time you sell a home and buy another within 24 months. But you are limited to using it only once every two years. The only exception to the once-every-24-months rule is if the sale is forced by a job-related move that qualifies under IRS regulations for a moving expenses deduction. (See Appendix 3, Planning the Move, for details.)

2. Trading Down: Buying a Less Expensive House When You're Under Age 55

Selling your house to buy another of lesser value is somewhat unusual, but might occur, for example, if you moved from a high housing cost area, such as San Francisco or Los Angeles, to a lower cost area, such as the Central Valley or Sierra foothills. Because you're not buying a house of equal or greater value, you'll owe some taxes. Essentially, the taxes you'll owe will be the lesser of:

1. the gain (Section c, below) on the sale of the old home, or
2. the amount by which the adjusted sales price (Section d, below) of the old home is more than the purchase price of the new home.

Here is how to calculate these figures.

a. Figure Your Adjusted Cost Basis

To figure your profit (gain) made on the sale of your house, start with how much you paid for it. That figure is the "cost basis."

You arrive at the adjusted cost basis by adding the cost of any capital improvements to the cost basis. At the risk of

oversimplifying slightly, capital improvements are additions to your property that increase its value, that you cannot remove and that have a useful life of more than one year. For example, a swimming pool, carport or new kitchen is a capital improvement, as is a built-in dishwasher, new furnace, or wall-to-wall carpeting. Less obvious examples include upgrades to components of the property, such as replacing galvanized pipe with copper, putting in new insulation or installing circuit breakers to replace a fuse box.

Ordinary repairs and maintenance are not capital improvements. Repairs that do not constitute capital improvements include fixing a broken pipe (even if you patch galvanized pipe with a small piece of copper), painting or replacing linoleum.

EXAMPLE: Joe and Trudy purchased a house in 1973 for $71,000 and made $9,000 worth of capital improvements over the years. Their adjusted cost basis is $80,000.

Original purchase price	$71,000
Capital improvements	+ 9,000
Adjusted cost basis	$80,000

Sometimes it's hard to decide whether a particular expenditure qualifies as a capital improvement. In doubtful cases, check with a tax expert or the Taxpayer Assistance Service of the IRS. Or, if you're in the do-it-yourself spirit, consult the U.S. Master Tax Guide published by Commerce Clearing House (Chicago, IL), available in most libraries.

The basis also adjusts automatically under certain laws. For example, when one spouse dies and leaves a community property house to the other, the basis (for federal tax purposes) of the entire property (the one-half community property shares of both the deceased and surviving spouse) is increased from the original purchase price to its fair market value as of the date of the deceased spouse's death.

b. Figure the Amount Realized

The second step in figuring out the tax you owe is to figure the "amount realized" from the sale. The amount realized is the sales prices minus selling expenses.

Selling expenses include broker's and attorney's fees and transfer taxes. They don't include expenses of fixing up your house to sell it.

To continue our example, let's say Joe and Trudy sell their house for $179,000 and have costs of sale of $227 and a broker's commission of 6%. Their amount realized is $168,773.

Gross sales price	$179,000
Documentary transfer tax	- 197
Document fees (estimate)	- 30
Broker's commission	-10,740
Amount realized	$168,033

c.   Figure the Gain

To calculate the profit on the sale of their house, Joe and Trudy must subtract the adjusted cost basis (section a above) from the amount realized (Section b above).

Amount realized	$168,033
Adjusted cost basis	- 80,000
Gain	$88,033

Unfortunately, they're not done yet. Remember, they'll owe tax on the lesser of 1) the gain and 2) the difference between the "adjusted sales price" and the price of the new house. So they must figure the adjusted sales price.

d.   Figure the Adjusted Sales Price

The adjusted sales price of a house is the amount realized (section b) minus any fixing-up expenses incurred when a house is fixed up to sell. Fixing-up expenses must be for work done during the 90 days before the contract to sell the real property is signed and must be paid for no later than 30 days after escrow closes. They cannot be capital improvements. (See Section a, above).

Let's assume Joe and Trudy spent $3,000 on fixing up their house to sell it, and bought a new house within 24 months for $128,000.

Amount realized	$168,033
Fixing up expenses	- 3,000
Adjusted sales price	$165,033
Price of new house	-128,000
	$37,033

The taxable gain, which must be reported to federal and state tax authorities, is the lesser of:

- $37,033 (adjusted sales price of first house less purchase price of new house); and
- $88,033 (gain on the sale of the first house).

The Internal Revenue Code (§ 1034) and relevant publications (IRS 521 and 523) can be confusing. What makes it clear is actually filling out Form 2119 (or State Form 3535) according to the instructions provided. A completed sample follows. Of course, if you are confused, you should consult a tax accountant.

CALIFORNIA PROPERTY TAX RELIEF

As a result of the California initiative of the mid-1970s, Proposition 13, property taxes are assessed on the value as of March 1, 1975. For people who've owned homes for many years, their values are comparatively low. When they sell that house and purchase another, however, they pay property taxes on the price of the house being bought, which is likely to be higher than the one being sold.

To help older people deal with this, California law lets owners over age 55 (only one spouse of a married couple must qualify), who sell one house and purchase another within two years in the same county to transfer their old tax assessment rate to the new house. Transferring the tax assessment inter-county is possible if you move to a county which participates in the statewide transfer system. The county tax assessor can tell you whether or not your county participates in the system.

To qualify for this tax break, the new house cannot cost more than the amount the first house sold for if the purchase precedes the sale. If the sale is within one year of the purchase, the cost of the new house cannot exceed 105% of the cost of sale (or 110% if two years after). Check with your county tax assessor to see if the law applies when you contemplate your transaction.

Form **2119**

Department of the Treasury
Internal Revenue Service

Sale of Your Home

▶ Attach to Form 1040 for year of sale.

▶ See separate instructions.   ▶ Please print or type.

OMB No. 1545-0072

19**93**

Attachment
Sequence No. **20**

Your first name and initial. If a joint return, also give spouse's name and initial.	Last name	Your social security number
Mo and Esther	Elder	123 45 0678

Fill in Your Address Only If You Are Filing This Form by Itself and Not With Your Tax Return	Present address (no., street, and apt. no., rural route, or P.O. box no. if mail is not delivered to street address)	Spouse's social security number
	1 Jamestown Avenue	
	City, town or post office, state, and ZIP code	
	San Francisco, CA 94124	

Part I   General Information

1	Date your former main home was sold (month, day, year) ▶	**1**	5 / 5 / 9
2	Have you bought or built a new main home?		☑ Yes ☐ No
3	Is or was any part of either main home rented out or used for business? If "Yes," see instructions		☐ Yes ☑ No

Part II   Gain on Sale—Do not include amounts you deduct as moving expenses.

4	Selling price of home. Do not include personal property items you sold with your home	**4**	$ 575,000
5	Expense of sale (see instructions)	**5**	$ 29,413
6	Amount realized. Subtract line 5 from line 4	**6**	$545,587
7	Adjusted basis of home sold (see instructions)	**7**	$ 135,000
8	**Gain on sale.** Subtract line 7 from line 6	**8**	$ 410,587

Is line 8 more than zero?	Yes ▶	If line 2 is "Yes," you **must** go to Part III or Part IV, whichever applies. If line 2 is "No," go to line 9.
	No ▶	**Stop** and attach this form to your return.

9   If you haven't replaced your home, do you plan to do so within the **replacement period** (see instructions)?   ☐ Yes ☐ No
- If line 9 is "Yes," stop here, attach this form to your return, and see **Additional Filing Requirements** in the instructions.
- If line 9 is "No," you **must** go to Part III or Part IV, whichever applies.

Part III   One-Time Exclusion of Gain for People Age 55 or Older—By completing this part, you are electing to take the one-time exclusion (see instructions). If you are not electing to take the exclusion, go to Part IV now.

10	Who was age 55 or older on the date of sale?	☐ You ☐ Your spouse ☑ Both of you
11	Did the person who was age 55 or older own and use the property as his or her main home for a total of at least 3 years (except for short absences) of the 5-year period before the sale? If "No," go to Part IV now	☑ Yes ☐ No
12	At the time of sale, who owned the home?	☐ You ☐ Your spouse ☑ Both of you
13	Social security number of spouse at the time of sale if you had a different spouse from the one above. If you were not married at the time of sale, enter "None" ▶	**13**
14	**Exclusion.** Enter the **smaller** of line 8 or $125,000 ($62,500 if married filing separate return). Then, go to line 15	**14** $ 125,000

Part IV   Adjusted Sales Price, Taxable Gain, and Adjusted Basis of New Home

15	If line 14 is blank, enter the amount from line 8. Otherwise, subtract line 14 from line 8	**15**	$285,587
	• If line 15 is zero, stop and attach this form to your return.		
	• If line 15 is more than zero and line 2 is "Yes," go to line 16 now.		
	• If you are reporting this sale on the installment method, stop and see the instructions.		
	• All others, stop and **enter the amount from line 15 on Schedule D, col. (g), line 4 or line 12.**		
16	Fixing-up expenses (see instructions for time limits)	**16**	$ 40,000
17	If line 14 is blank, enter amount from line 16. Otherwise, add lines 14 and 16	**17**	$ 165,000
18	**Adjusted sales price.** Subtract line 17 from line 6	**18**	$380,587
19a	Date you moved into new home ▶ 6 / 11 / 9 **b** Cost of new home (see instructions)	**19b**	$ 200,000
20	Subtract line 19b from line 18. If zero or less, enter -0-	**20**	$ 180,587
21	**Taxable gain.** Enter the **smaller** of line 15 or line 20	**21**	$ 180,587
	• If line 21 is zero, go to line 22 and attach this form to your return.		
	• If you are reporting this sale on the installment method, see the line 15 instructions and go to line 22.		
	• All others, **enter the amount from line 21 on Schedule D, col. (g), line 4 or line 12,** and go to line 22.		
22	Postponed gain. Subtract line 21 from line 15	**22**	$ 105,000
23	**Adjusted basis of new home.** Subtract line 22 from line 19b	**23**	$ 95,000

Sign Here Only If You Are Filing This Form by Itself and Not With Your Tax Return	Under penalties of perjury, I declare that I have examined this form, including attachments, and to the best of my knowledge and belief, it is true, correct, and complete.			
	Your signature	Date	Spouse's signature	Date
	Mo Elder	3/20/94	Esther Elder	3/20/94
	▶ If a joint return, both must sign.			

For Paperwork Reduction Act Notice, see separate instructions.   Cat. No. 11710J   Form **2119** (1993)

♻ *Printed on recycled paper*   ☆U.S. GOVERNMENT PRINTING OFFICE: 1993-345-331

3. Buying a Less Expensive House When You're Age 55 or Older

If you (or your spouse if you are married) are over 55, and you sell one home and buy another of lesser value, federal tax law lets you exclude from your profit (capital gains) up to $125,000, if the following are true:

- you lived in the house as your principal residence for any three of the past five years (the years need not be the last three, nor consecutive)
- you specifically elect to use the exclusion, and
- you (or your spouse) haven't used the exclusion before, even in a prior marriage.

Note: You cannot use part of the exclusion now and part later, even if you don't use the whole $125,000. It's a once-in-a-lifetime opportunity.

While the $125,000 exclusion is a real benefit for many people, even if you're eligible you may not want to use it just yet. The tax savings may be relatively small and, if you think you'll sell your second house at a great profit some day, you may want to save the exclusion for later use. If you don't plan to buy again, however, use the exclusion now, even if your gain is relatively small.

EXAMPLE: Mo and Esther, both 60, wanted to move from their large house to a $200,000 townhouse. Their house had appreciated considerably in value, and they had put $35,000 of capital improvements in it over the years, but it needed many repairs. They had little money for the repairs, but knew they'd have to be made in order to sell. When Joan offered to buy their home for $575,000 ($475,000 more than the original $100,000 purchase price), they accepted her offer, along with her contingency that Mo and Esther put $40,000 in escrow for necessary repairs. Here is the tax they owe now:

Adjusted cost basis:	
Original purchase price	$100,000
Capital improvements	+35,000
Adjusted cost basis	$135,000
Amount realized:	
Selling price of house #1	$575,000
Costs of sale	-663
Broker's commission	-28,750
Amount realized	$545,587
Gain:	
Amount realized	$545,587
Adjusted cost basis	-135,000
Gain	$410,587
Taxable gain:	
Gain	$410,587
"Over 55" exclusion	-125,000
Taxable gain	$285,587

Now let's assume that Mo and Esther both use the $125,000 exclusion and buy another house for $200,000 within the 24-month period to increase their tax benefits. What they owe taxes on now is the lesser of their taxable gain ($285,587) and the adjusted sales price of the first house less the purchase price of the second one. That figure is as follows:

Taxable gain if second house purchased:	
Amount realized	$545,587
Repairs	-40,000
"Over 55" exclusion	-125,000
Cost of house #2	-200,000
Taxable gain	$180,587

If Mo and Esther had bought a more expensive new house, they could defer the tax on even more gain. ∎

How Much Will You Offer?

This chapter assumes that you've found a house you like and have the financial resources to buy it. Now you must decide how much to offer. We discuss preparing (and, if necessary, withdrawing) an offer to purchase, including the back and forth counteroffer process, in Chapters 16 and 17. Before we get involved with dollars and cents, we give you the basic legal rules for creating a house sales contract.

A. How a Contract Is Formed

A valid contract to transfer ownership requires that one party make a specific written legal offer to buy or sell a particular piece of property and the other person legally accept it in writing. Perhaps the most common misconception is that a seller's listing price is a legal offer. It's not. Legally, a listing price, be it in a newspaper ad or Board of Realtors' Multiple Listing Book, is only a general indication of what a seller will accept. If you see an ad listing a house at a certain price and call up and say "I'll buy it," the seller has no obligation to sell it to you. He may be under pressure to sell at that price, however, because his contract with his broker probably guarantees the broker a commission if the seller gets an offer at the full listing price that otherwise complies with the terms of the listing.

The seller can say the house is no longer for sale or even double the advertised price, as long as he's not doing so to discriminate. (See Chapter 6 for more information on laws prohibiting housing discrimination.)

The first legally binding offer in a real estate sale is usually made in writing by the prospective buyer. Legally binding means that the offer is specific (lays out the price and other terms), and the seller has the opportunity to accept it in writing before either it is withdrawn or the time period for its acceptance runs out.

EXAMPLE 1: Kirk lists his home for sale for $396,000. Kate, who just received a large inheritance, sees the ad, shows up and plunks down the full price in $1,000 bills, along with a written offer to buy. Must Kirk accept her money? No. His listing isn't a legal offer. He can raise the price, remove the house from the market or simply put Kate off for a few weeks while he tries to get a better offer. Is Kate's written offer to purchase binding? Yes. If Kirk accepts the offer within the time Kate gives him, there's a contract, unless Kate had already withdrawn her offer in writing.

EXAMPLE 2: Kate simply stops by Kirk's house and enthusiastically blurts out an offer and Kirk says "I accept." There's still no binding contract. Her offer wasn't in writing, so there was no legal offer for Kirk to accept.

B. Decide How Much You Will Offer

In putting together your actual offer, consider the following factors:
- the advertised price of the house
- what you can afford
- prices for comparable houses
- whether the local real estate market is hot or cold
- whether the house itself is hot or cold
- the seller's needs
- whether the house is uniquely valuable to you, and
- how much you're willing to pay.

Let's consider each in brief.

C. What Is the Advertised Price?

A seller's advertised price should be treated as only a rough estimate of what she'd like to receive. Different sellers price houses very differently. Some deliberately overprice, others ask for pretty close to what they hope to get and a few (maybe the cleverest) underprice their houses in the hope that potential buyers will compete and overbid. In considering the list price of a house you're serious about, take the time to learn about the seller's personality. Here are a few of the more common seller profiles:

Optimistic Charlie. As arrogant as he is optimistic, he tends to believe that everything he's associated with, including his house, is especially valuable. As a result, he's likely to price his house way above what comparable houses are selling for. Some Optimistic Charlies get so carried away they overprice by 30%-40%, although 10%-25% is more typical. They justify demanding an overly high price with the "greater fool" theory: "Maybe I'm asking too much, but what the hell—some idiot might fall in love with the house and pay it." Unfortunately, some Optimistic Charlies are encouraged by brokers or agents so anxious to get the listing that they "romance" Charlie into believing that his house will fetch an inflated price.

Straightforward William. After investigating comparable prices and taking the temperature of the local market, William prices his house at exactly what he believes it's worth, not a dollar more, nor a dollar less. William, who typically hates to bargain, may be as stubborn as a spaniel with his nose in a fresh dish of hamburger if a purchaser offers him less than the asking price. Sometimes he may even accommodate a buyer on other terms of the deal to prove himself right on his pricing decision. For example, if a physical inspection turns up structural problems, William might agree to pay for $25,000 of needed work in the form of a credit in escrow, if the buyer pays the asking price, rather than lower his asking price by $15,000 and have the buyer pay the cost of repairs.

Canny Cynthia. Smart enough to realize that nothing gets the blood of the average American pounding like the notion of a bargain, and knowing that she won't sell at her asking price, Cynthia deliberately underprices her house. Her plan (which often works beautifully because few sellers try it) is to excite a feeding frenzy among bargain hunters, who'll bid against each other so furiously that the winner will pay more than the house is worth. This strategy works particularly well in hot markets, where low prices attract eager buyers. (See Section F on hot and cold markets.)

D. How Much Can You Afford?

Chapter 2 focuses on how to determine how much house you can afford, based on your income, savings and non-housing long-term debts. If you haven't yet read Chapter 2 and figured out what you can afford, do so now. Once you know your maximum, lower the number a little, to allow for the following additional expenses:

Closing costs. Your share will be about 2%-5% of the purchase price. (See Chapter 18 for details.)

Moving expenses. The amount depends on how much stuff you have to move, how far you're moving it and how much you'll do yourself. If you plan on hiring a mover, get an estimate and add about 25%.

Redecorating. Keep a few dollars to redecorate. If the house you buy hasn't had a facelift recently, you'll probably want to paint it at least. Also, if you truly hate the wall-to-wall carpet in the front room and the cerise plastic tile in the bathroom, you'll be grateful if you have a few bucks to make changes before you move in.

Two months mortgage payments. In addition to the down payment and closing costs, the lender will probably want to see that you have two or three months of mortgage payments in the bank.

If the amount you can afford is at least 90%-95% of the seller's advertised price, it's reasonable to make a formal written offer. After all, most houses sell for less, sometimes much less, than their asking price.

E. What Are Prices of Comparable Houses?

Before making an offer to purchase, you should know the recent selling prices of nearby houses similar to the one you're interested in buying. If you've been house hunting for a while, you should have a good feel for comparable prices (called "comps" in the real estate trade). If you've been looking for only a short time, or in other areas, you have some research to do.

To get reliable comparable price data, real estate appraisers have developed the following sensible guidelines to distinguish comparable houses from others:

- A comparable sale should have occurred within six months (the more recent, however, the better). In a market where prices fluctuate fairly fast, comps should be on sales within the last 30 to 60 days. In extremely volatile markets, you'll need to compare prices of houses where sales are still pending.

- A comparable sale should be for a house quite similar to the one you're interested in. This is relatively easy in buildings with condominiums or developments where houses are similar in size, condition, age, construction and layout. Look for houses of similar age, in comparable locations, and with similar number of rooms, square feet and yard size. In the real world, however, comparisons often must be made between houses that are somewhat different. A physically comparable house a few blocks away might be in a better school district or have a great view, which will raise the property's value. The more difference between houses, the less valuable the comparison.

- A comparable sale should be within six blocks of the house you want to buy. The six block area should be shaved if the neighborhood changes significantly in a shorter radius, for example, if a major street, freeway or railroad clearly marks a border between two different residential areas.

⚠ SELLERS AND AGENTS DON'T ALWAYS TELL THE TRUTH ABOUT SALES PRICES

To find out what comparable properties have sold for, why not simply ask the person whose house you are curious about what they were paid? No problem, as long as you take the answers with a grain of salt. To make themselves look good to neighbors or friends, sellers commonly exaggerate what they received, or emphasize the sales price and fail to mention the cost of items they've agreed to repair.

You can also ask a real estate salesperson you're working with for comparable sales data. But this approach, too, has problems. If the agent is being paid on commission, she won't get paid unless you buy a house. Because your offer is more likely to be accepted if you bid high, the agent may put his interests ahead of yours and provide you with comparable sales data to lead you to bid aggressively. If you've hired a broker by the hour, however, he has no stake in whether or not you buy and should provide you with reliable information. (See Chapter 5, Working With Real Estate Professionals.)

EARLY PEARL

HOW TO CHECK PRICES OF CURRENT LISTINGS AND PENDING SALES

A pending sale is one in which an offer to buy and an acceptance to sell have been made, but the transaction is still in escrow. Houses pending sale are listed in the Realtors' Multiple Listing Book and are noted in appraisal reports; however, the actual sales price is not listed until the transaction closes. To find out the prices of houses pending sale, plug into the gossip among real estate agents who work in the area. If you can't, and you're working with a real estate professional (either on commission or by the hour), have him call the broker who represents the seller of the pending sale you're interested in.

While actual and pending sales prices of recently sold homes are the best source of comparable information, asking prices of homes still on the market can also provide guidance. Despite the fact that asking prices don't tell you what a house will eventually sell for, they can give you some idea of the top of the range of market values in your area. As a general rule, asking prices are at least 10% over the market. To find out asking prices, go to open houses and check newspaper real estate classified ads. Your real estate agent should also be a good source of information.

---

1. Realtors' Comp Books

Usually, the best comparable sales data are in a Board of Realtors comp book for the geographical area where you're looking. The comp book is sometimes bound in the back of the Realtors' Multiple Listing Book, and lists the sales price of houses that sold recently. We discuss the Multiple Listing Service, comp books and other services offered by local Boards of Realtors in Chapter 5. Real estate agents aren't supposed to show comp books to people not members of their real estate board, but it's been known to happen.

⚠ In all but very hot markets, there is a real danger of a buyer being romanced by sellers and real estate professionals into relying on outdated "comps" from a past market more favorable to sellers. Instead, you need to aggressively search out recent comps and calculate your offer accordingly.

2.   Property Profiles From Title Companies

If you can't get access to a comp book or a tip on what's in it from an agent anxious for your business, ask a local title company for help. You can either provide them with the street addresses of comparable sales and they'll give you the prices, or ask them to print out information on all sales on certain named streets. You can also get detailed information on specific property (a property profile). Property profiles are often free if you've done business with the title company, or it thinks you may in the future.

3.   Checking Deeds at the County Recorder's Office

Comparable sales information is also available at the County Recorder's Office. You need to know the street name, or the name of the buyer (grantee) or seller (grantor) of a particular property. If you don't know either, you can find out the seller's name at the County Assessor's Office. You then look up the deed in either the grantor or the grantee index.

When you find the deed, note the documentary transfer tax, located in the upper right-hand corner. The basic documentary transfer tax is $1.10 per $1,000 of price, except in cities and counties with local surtaxes. In San Francisco, for example, the tax is $5.00 per $1,000. The sales price is figured from this transfer tax.

> **EXAMPLE:** You want to find the sales price of a house in a city where the documentary transfer tax is $1.10 for each $1,000 of the sale price. The deed for the house shows a documentary transfer tax of $240.90. You divide $240.90 by $1.10 to get 219. Multiplying 219 by $1,000 equals a sales price of $219,000.

You can use this same technique to find out how much the current owner of the property originally paid and when he bought the house.

Keep in mind that the documentary transfer tax does not necessarily reflect the full price paid by the buyer. If the buyer assumed loans held by the seller, this amount won't be included.

4.   Sales Prices From Private Companies

At least two private companies now offer comparable sales prices for some areas of California. For details and fee information, contact:
- Consumer Reports Home Price Service, (800) 775-1212
- Dataquick Information Systems, (800) 999-0152.

F.   Is the Local Real Estate Market Hot or Cold?

In deciding how much to offer for a house, take the temperature of the local housing market. Is it:
- hot—prices are going up?
- cold—prices are dropping?
- lukewarm—prices are relatively stable?

This is important information, as the psychology of scarcity and abundance typically plays a major role in a house's selling price. A market perceived as hot (more buyers than sellers) feeds on itself, and prices continue to rise. The opposite also tends to be true—falling prices triggered by an excess of houses tend to fall further, as sellers scramble to get the best price they can.

HOW PRICES ARE DRIVEN UP IN A HOT MARKET

Imagine that five buyers are interested in the same house in an area where houses sell—and prices rise—fast. Their agents emphasize that good houses are scarce, and that there's a lot of competition for this one. To preempt the competition, several of the agents urge their clients to bid over the seller's asking price. Two do, and the ultimate buyer pays $20,000 more than comparable houses sold for. A few weeks later, other buyers, deciding how much to bid on a similar house, discover this new "comp," and increase their offers based on it. Their agents (who don't get a commission unless their client makes an acceptable bid) emphasize how fast prices are rising and encourage this bidding.

You can often spot broad, area-wide hot or cold trends by reading the real estate sections of local and regional newspapers for a few weeks, where you will find reports of sales price trends. For example, you might read that prices are down 5% from last month. While this is valuable information, you have to look at data from several months to really spot a trend—one month's figures can be skewed up or down if a higher or lower than normal percentage of expensive or starter houses sold that month.

To know what's going on in a particular neighborhood, however, you'll need to closely follow the local residential real estate market for an extended period. This involves visiting lots of houses and reading MLS and comparative sales books. If you don't have time to get this "up to the elbows" sort of knowledge, consult with one or more experienced local real estate people who won't get a commission from your purchase and thus have no economic incentive to exaggerate prices.

To do your own temperature research, keep in mind these rules:

- If 25% or more of the houses sell within a week or ten days of being listed, the market is hot.
- If more than 40% of the houses listed sold for more than the listing price, the market is sizzling.
- If more than half of the houses were on the market a month or more before selling, and most sold for less than their listing price, the market is cool.
- If the supply of houses on the market is steadily increasing, sales are slow, and prices of the houses you're looking at have decreased more than once, the market is cold.

EXAMPLE: Thad can afford a $250,000 house. After a long search, he falls in love with one listed at $225,000, in a marginal neighborhood, adjacent to a much nicer one. A comparable house in the upscale area sells for $375,000. Thad has two worries, both fueled by his infatuation with the house and his idea that the neighborhood where it's located is bound to improve fast. First, he's afraid that someone else will buy the house before he does, and second, he's concerned that because he's so smitten with the house, he'll overpay.

Before he decides how much to offer, Thad should check the temperature of the local housing market. If houses are selling relatively slowly, and the house he wants has been on the market for a month or more, Thad can probably offer less, perhaps even much less, than the asking price. If houses are selling briskly, however, and the house he likes is new to the market (and reasonably priced, given the comparable sales data), he should offer close to the asking price. He may even want to bid slightly more to preempt other offers and avoid a bidding war if houses are selling at a premium within a few days of being listed.

Another good long-term gauge of a market's temperature is the level of current mortgage interest rates. As rates jump substantially (usually one percentage point or more), most housing markets begin to cool—although just as rates begin to rise, people may rush to buy, hoping to lock in before rates climb even higher. Conversely, as rates drop, more people can afford houses and the market perks up.

G. Is the House Itself Hot or Cold?

At least as important as determining the local housing market temperature is figuring out the temperature of the particular house you want to buy. For many reasons, a particular house may be more or less attractive (hotter or colder) than those surrounding it. Here are some questions to ask:

- How long has the house been on the market? If it's more than 30 days, you can probably buy it for less than the asking price.
- Has the asking price dropped? If it has been reduced once and it still hasn't sold (give it a month), the house is an icicle and may be ready for another reduction.
- Does the house have serious structural problems requiring a hefty cash infusion? If so, the house, even if otherwise attractive, may be hard to sell. If you have cash or can finance the purchase privately, the house may be yours. (See Chapter 3, Section D7, for more on buying a house with structural problems.)
- Has the seller, or more likely, the listing agent, tipped you off that a lower offer will be considered? If you're told that the seller needs to sell quickly to close on a new house, because of a divorce or to move far away, you're almost surely being told to try a lower offer. Or, if a real estate agent says the seller "would like to receive," or "hopes to receive," a certain amount, the agent is saying that the seller is being unrealistic and that a lower offer will probably be accepted.
- Has the seller set a cut-off date by which all offers must be made? This can be a good indication that the house is hot

and you may have to bid aggressively to get it. But be careful—the seller and his agent may create a bidding war (called a "feeding frenzy" in the real estate business), or at least the appearance of one. A seller may state that "five offers will be made" (or that "many people are considering bidding"), when only one or two are serious. If you face this, consider hiring a broker by the hour to counsel you and, hopefully, to talk to the seller's agent and find out what's going on behind the scenes. The seller's salesperson may be more candid with another professional than with you.

• Is the house an ugly duckling? In a hot market, interest in an unattractive house is likely to be lukewarm; in a cool market, icy. If you find a dowdy place you know how to turn into a swan, keep your passion to yourself and bid low. (Again, see Chapter 3 for more on buying a homely house.)

• Is the seller discretionary, and will sell only at top dollar, or motivated, and needs to sell quickly? In a slow market, with a great many houses that have been for sale over a long period of time, it's important to understand where the seller is coming from. If you see a house where the price has been reduced substantially after only one month on the market, chances are the owner needs to sell and may reduce the price further to do so quickly. If the house is being sold by an investor, you may find there's less leeway on the price.

ANTICIPATING INTEREST RATE SWINGS CAN SAVE YOU MONEY

If you follow societal economic trends, you may be able to predict interest rate swings in advance. For example, if unemployment is up and other economic indicators (such as housing starts) turn down, it's a good bet that the Federal Reserve Board will lower interest rates and mortgage rates will fall. The idea is to be ready to purchase very soon after interest rates take a substantial drop. It usually takes a few months for sellers to realize that the lower interest rates greatly increase the number of people who can afford to buy, and that this increase means they can often get a higher price. By moving fast, you can pay less for the house, and get a lower interest rate, too.

H. What Are the Seller's Needs?

Historically, the real estate business is structured to keep buyer and seller at arm's length. Although a few main players work better through intermediaries than face-to-face, much of the real estate "distancing" comes from real estate professionals' understandable fear that if buyer and seller make direct contact, they won't need professional middlepeople (brokers and real estate agents). Unfortunately, this industry prejudice toward keeping buyer and seller apart can work to your disadvantage. You want to be able to size up the seller and structure your negotiating strategy accordingly, but obviously you can't if you never meet. (Chapter 17 discusses negotiating strategies when you make an offer to buy a house.)

How do you meet the seller directly to figure out her needs? Sometimes you can make friendly contact at an open house, if she's present. If not, and the house is occupied by the seller, ask to revisit when the seller is likely to be home. Or, follow up with a phone call (or a knock on the door) to ask a few questions that the agent wouldn't be expected to know the answer to. There's the danger that the seller (or more likely her agent, who is sure to put a "do not disturb occupant" sign in front of the house) will be annoyed. But if you're as pleasant as you are persistent, you'll make contact with the seller and, in the process, very likely learn a lot. If you annoy a few agents in the process, so what?

Talking to the seller directly isn't the only way to understand her needs; a savvy salesperson working on your behalf may be able to glean useful information by talking to the seller's agent, such as how much room there is to negotiate on price or other items. Also, you may gain valuable insights by chatting with the neighbors while legitimately checking out the neighborhood. If you have school age children, talk to neighbors with kids about local schools. In casual conversation, they're likely to tell you why the seller is moving and lots of other useful information.

People likely to want to close quickly, even if it means taking a lower price, include:
• a seller who has accepted a job in a different area
• a seller who has made an offer on another house contingent on selling her existing one
• older people selling a long-time family home (sometimes with the help of a younger relative or friend)
• sellers divorcing or going through other major life changes, such as a loss of a job or retirement

- people who've inherited a house they don't plan to live in, and
- sellers needing a new home because of an expanded family.

We are not advocating taking advantage of a seller in distress. But nevertheless, it's only common sense to find out if a seller needs to close quickly. If so, you may find a good house for a very reasonable price.

> **EXAMPLE:** Buck and Bonnie were in the midst of selling their family house to move to a retirement community, when Buck became seriously ill. Bonnie, realizing that the house sale and move was causing Buck considerable stress, concluded that her first priority was to get Buck out of the house alive. She looked for a buyer who could close quickly and wouldn't fuss about details.
>
> Three offers came in. One offeror hadn't pre-qualified with a lender, and Bonnie wasn't convinced he'd get a loan. Another included six contingencies in her offer, two of which called for an inspection as if the house had been nominated for an award in *Architectural Digest*. When rejecting this offer, Bonnie remarked "If I've learned anything in 65 years, it's that no matter how much you think you're going to profit, in the long run it rarely pays to deal with fussy, difficult people."
>
> The third offeror, Janet, bid $20,000 less, but had pre-qualified for a loan and requested only a routine structural inspection. In addition, she made it clear that she'd try to close quickly and would be as helpful and undemanding as possible. (I'll buy the rugs; yes, you can take the drapes; don't worry about the crack in the toilet, or the twisted garage door hinges.) Janet got the house.

I.   Is the House Uniquely Valuable to You?

A house's worth on the market isn't necessarily the same as its worth to you. It may be worth more or less, depending on your needs. A modest house listed at a reasonable price, for example, may be a bargain if you have three kids, the house is in a city that has excellent public schools and the lot is large enough to add on a couple of rooms. The same house, however, may be overpriced for a couple not planning to have children. Don't get so carried away with judging objective marketing considerations that you forget your personal needs. And always remem-

ber that while there are loads of houses on the market, you only need one.

J.   How Much Are You Willing to Pay?

Okay, now for the last and most important consideration before you decide how much to offer. How much money do you really want to pay for the house? While tactical considerations (the temperature of the market, the seller's needs) are important, nothing should outweigh your own honest assessment of how much you are willing to fork over. These days, there are lots of houses on the market and relative bargains are available to people who are willing to be patient and make a number of offers.

ART: I GOT A BARGAIN WITHOUT BEING TOO GREEDY
I wanted to buy a house. But I'm an artist who supplements my income by teaching and I knew I'd have a long search for a house I could afford. Nevertheless, I lined up financing in advance so I could jump on a bargain if one surfaced. To my surprise, one did. An acquaintance got a prestigious four-year fellowship abroad and needed to sell his two-bedroom bungalow quickly. I looked at the house the next day. My guess, based on looking at dozens of houses in the area, was that it was worth close to $180,000 if marketed with real patience. The seller indicated he'd take about $150,000 for a quick sale. I was excited. This was my chance.

Then I heard that another person was ready to make an offer. My spirits fell. I spoke to my dad, who had worked in real estate years before. His advice was not to be too greedy. "Bid a few thousand more than $150,000." I agonized about the exact amount and bid $154,500. I beat the other bidder by $2,500 and got a super house for the price.

> **EXAMPLE:** Jeff and Lia are building up a cash-hungry business and plan to put limited money toward a house. They want a modestly-priced house in an unassuming neighborhood, and will put their excess cash into their business. They hope that the business will produce a profit and let them buy a nicer house in a few years.
>
> While house hunting, Jeff and Lia find a house selling for $50,000 more than they want to spend, but which is a real bargain. For a moment they're tempted—but they

return to their dream of building up their business, and pass up the house.

They make offers on several other houses, but lose out to more aggressive buyers. Finally, between Thanksgiving and Christmas, they find one they really like, with a seller who needs to relocate quickly to take a new job. They make a low-ball offer $60,000 below the already reasonable advertised price. After several counteroffers and some tense negotiations, they raise their offer $15,000 and get a good house at a real bargain.

K. Making the Final Decision

The moment of truth has arrived: It's time to look at the many personal and market factors we discussed and come up with an offer on the house you want to buy. Let us make one final observation and give one bit of advice. First, the observation: Most people who don't frequently buy and sell real property offer and pay too much. Now, the advice: When you reach your decision on how much to offer, consider reducing it a bit. If this means you lose the house to someone willing to bid more, so be it—there are loads more on the market, and with a little work, you may even find a better one.

EXAMPLE: After a long search, Randy and Lee find a house that meets all their needs. It lists for $310,000 and has heating system and roofing problems that will cost $25,000 to repair. It needs about $13,000 of other fix-up work, including an interior paint job, new tile in the kitchen and work on the hardwood floors. They check comparable prices and conclude that if the house were in tip-top shape, it would sell for about $350,000. They next take the temperature of the local housing market. Fewer than 5% of houses sell above their asking prices, and many houses have been on the market for months. Nevertheless, they believe that the house is competitively priced and will probably sell quickly.

Randy and Lee first lean towards offering the full $310,000, in the hope of pre-empting other bids and getting the seller to say "yes" quickly. Then they rethink their strategy and consider offering $298,000. Finally, after looking at how many houses are on the market, they decide to start much lower. They offer $278,800. Although this increases the chance that someone else may get the house, they reason there's only a slight chance of this happening given the structural problems, and figure if they can buy the house for between $290,000-$295,000, they have made a good deal. If not, they'll just keep looking.

⚠ Be sure the house is worth what you're offering. As part of the loan approval process, lenders will arrange a professional appraisal of the property. If you offer substantially more than the house is appraised for, your lender may not approve your loan. Chapter 13, Section F, discusses appraisals and how to handle low appraisals.

DON'T STRETCH YOUR FINANCES TOO FAR

Let us again caution you against stretching your finances too far to buy a house. Many real estate people urge buyers to plow every possible dollar into a house. This can be a mistake, especially if you can easily afford a nice house that meets your needs but pour a lot of money into a fancier one. Once you invest money in a house, it's very difficult and costly to try to get it back out.

Why are we cautious? Anyone familiar with the California housing market knows that family problems are commonly traced to paying too much for houses, leaving inadequate money for other needs. A devastating illness or loss of work means a large house payment will be almost impossible to make. People who refuse to stretch their finances to the limit, however, have money for other uses, including straightening the kids' teeth and taking an occasional vacation.

■

Putting Your Offer in Writing

This chapter shows you how to prepare a written purchase offer. The next chapter discusses how to present it to the seller and suggests good negotiating techniques. Read both chapters carefully before filling out the offer form. Even though a salesperson is probably preparing the paperwork for you, still pay close attention to this material. Many important decisions are made as a part of completing your written offer form, and it's essential that you understand each one and fully protect your interests.

A. What Makes an Offer Legally Valid?

A legal offer must be in writing, delivered to the seller or his agent and contain specific financial and other terms so that if the seller says "yes," the deal can go through. The seller's acceptance, too, must be in writing.

Real estate offers almost always contain contingencies—events that must happen or else the deal won't become final. For example, your offer may be contingent on your qualifying for financing or the house passing certain physical inspections.

Most offers give the seller a short time in which to accept. During this time, you may revoke your offer in writing before the seller communicates an acceptance to you or your agent. (See Chapter 17, Presenting Your Offer and Negotiating, for more on revoking.)

B. Offer Form Terminology

Before you look at the offer form, here are a few words on offer terminology. The important thing to understand is that the same paperwork is called by different names, each with a different legal meaning, depending on when and by whom it's used.

- Making an *offer* is when you fill out a Contract to Purchase Real Property form, such as the one in this book, and give it to the seller.
- A *counteroffer* is used by a seller who accepts some of your terms but modifies others. The seller may respond, for example, with a higher price or a shorter time for you to arrange financing. A counteroffer is often (but not always) done using exactly the same form as the Contract to Purchase Real Property, with the title changed to reflect that it's a counteroffer.

- A *counter counteroffer* is when you accept some of the seller's counteroffer terms, but modify others. Again, you can do this using a slightly modified version of the original offer form if you wish. (The back-and-forth dance can go on for a while with counter counter counteroffers, etc.)
- The offer becomes a legally binding *contract* when you and the seller agree on all the terms in the offer (or counteroffer, etc.) and sign it. You can both sign an offer form, such as the Contract to Purchase Real Property in Appendix 4, or a separate written document stating that all terms of the offer (or counteroffer) are accepted. Not only must you both sign the agreement, you must both also initial every page.

MANY TYPES OF OFFER FORMS

The Contract to Purchase Real Property form in this book includes all terms you need to consider when making an offer on a house in California. Many varieties of printed offer forms are in use in California, in part because many brokers design their own forms. Typically, printed forms look different from ours (and from each other), but cover the same topics. Some contain numerous fine provisions, many designed to absolve all real estate professionals in the transaction (who, after all, buy the forms) from any possible liability.

If you work with a large brokerage firm, you may prefer to use its form. Independent brokers often use forms published by Realty Publications, Inc., the Professional Publishing Corporation or the California Association of Realtors. These forms are all well written and will do the job, but you should still read this chapter to understand what the clauses mean and how to change any you don't like.

EXAMPLE 1: Mitch gives Patricia a written offer to purchase her house for $300,000, which includes seven days to accept. Two days later, Patricia accepts in writing. A contract has been formed.

EXAMPLE 2: Now assume the same offer from Mitch, but before Patricia says "yes," Mitch finds a house he likes better. He immediately calls Patricia's agent and withdraws his offer. While this revokes his offer, he puts his revocation in writing and drops it off at Patricia's agent's office so there can be no misunderstanding. Mitch's offer has now been withdrawn; no contract can be formed between them unless one or the other makes a second offer and the other accepts it in writing.

If this is confusing now, it will become clearer in Chapter 17, Presenting Your Offer and Negotiating.

IF YOU'RE LOOKING TO BUY A NEW HOUSE OR A CONDOMINIUM

The offer form below can be used to make an offer on a new house or condominium. In either situation, however, you'll need to make some adjustments.

With new houses, for example, you'll need to carefully complete Clause 20, Other Terms and Conditions, to allow for homeowners' association membership, optional add-ons and warranties. You might also want to add a contingency to Clause 10, letting you obtain and accept copies of architectural plans, surveys, soil reports, engineering calculations and related construction documents before closing. It may be easier to use the form contract available from the developer, but be sure you understand all its terms and add any terms that are missing. See Chapter 7 for more information on new houses.

With condos, too, you'll want to allow for homeowners' association membership in Clause 20. You might also want to check the contingency to Clause 10 letting you obtain and accept copies of CC&Rs, articles of incorporation, bylaws, rules and regulations in force, three years of financial statements from the homeowners' association, a statement of financial reserves and one year's minutes of the homeowners' association before closing. You will also want statements of outstanding assessments, anticipated assessments or anticipated extraordinary repairs.

C. How to Fill Out the Contract to Purchase Real Property Form

Below is a clause-by-clause review of the Contract to Purchase Real Property form found in Appendix 4. Tear it out and make several copies before you start filling it out.

Heading

Insert the address, including the county. The street number, city, county and state are sufficient—a legal description isn't required. If the property has no street address, describe it the best you can ("the ten-acre Norris Ranch on County Road 305, two miles south of Andersonville").

Next, enter the date you'll make the offer. Then insert the full names of the buyer(s) and their spouses. If you are married but buying a house using only your separate property (property acquired before marriage, by gift or inheritance during marriage or after permanent separation), enter only your name. Normally, however, some community property (property acquired by either spouse during marriage, except gifts or inheritances) is used toward the down payment or monthly payments, which means your spouse's name should also appear on the offer. (For more on this subject, see Chapter 20, Legal Ownership: How To Take Title.)

BUNGALOW

Finally, insert the amount of your offer and deposit, both written out (such as, two hundred and seventeen thousand) and numerically ($217,000). If the seller accepts your offer, he'll expect a deposit as "earnest money." This is usually about 0.5% of the purchase price or, sometimes, a flat $1,000 for middle-priced houses. The seller may counteroffer and ask for more. We advise not going above 1%-2% of the purchase price. Also indicate the form of the deposit (personal check is most common). For general information on how to get your deposit back if the purchase doesn't go through, see Clause 22 below.

1. Financial Terms

Before entering the financing details, specify how many days you plan to give yourself to arrange your financing. If you have to start from scratch (no prequalification letter), expect to spend five to six weeks. If all that remains is an appraisal of the property, expect to have your financing set up in about two or three weeks.

- Item A: Enter your deposit amount (from the heading) and to whom it is made out (the escrow holder). (See Clause 3 for more information on escrow.)
- Item B: It is common for the buyer to increase the amount of the deposit shortly after the offer is accepted, typically seven days, or when you remove the contingencies for the pest control and general contractor inspections. (See Clause 9 for more information on these inspections.)
- Item C: Specify your proposed down payment balance—your total down payment less your deposit and deposit increase.
- Items D-G: Because the seller has a legitimate interest in finding out, before accepting your offer, if you can afford the house, here you get into financing nitty-gritties. List the amount of each loan in the left column and detail the financing to the right. If you already have your financing lined up, this will be easy. Otherwise, you'll have to make an educated guesstimate. If a paragraph doesn't apply, enter N/A (for not applicable) in the blank.

If the first (and perhaps only) loan you propose is a new first mortgage, complete Section D, specifying the minimum number of years, type of financing, maximum interest rate and other requirements, such as the maximum life-of-the-loan cap on an ARM and maximum number of points you're willing to pay. If you're applying for a government loan, be ready to demonstrate to the seller that you're eligible.

If the first loan you propose to use to finance your purchase is the seller's existing loan, complete Section E. Here you specify whether you'll assume the loan (take over the payments, and become responsible for the loan, with the lender's approval) or buy subject to an existing loan (make the payments without taking over formal responsibility—quite unusual). Also name the seller's lender, the approximate remaining balance, the current interest rate, the type of loan and the approximate number of remaining years. Whatever you don't know leave blank—the seller or his agent can help you complete it.

If you propose using a second loan to help pay for the house, complete either Section F or G, depending on whether it's a new loan or an existing loan. One common proposal is for you to borrow money from the seller; another is for a friend or relative to put up the money for you. Whatever you propose, be sure to spell it out clearly. Sections F and G mirror Sections D and E above.

- Item H: Enter the total of the left column. This number is your offer price.
- Item I: If you plan to include conditions in your offer related to financing, initial here and at your conditions at Clause 20. Otherwise, write N/A. Examples of financing conditions include:
  - Making the offer contingent upon receiving an appraisal for the purchase price. This can protect you if you think your offer is well above what the property is worth.
  - Your obtaining a bridge loan.

BACKWOODS EGYPTIAN

CONTRACT TO PURCHASE REAL PROPERTY

Property address, including county: _____

_____ .

Date: _____, 19_____

(Buyer) _____ ,

makes this offer to purchase the property described above, for the sum of _____

_____ dollars ($_____). Buyer includes a deposit, in the amount of

_____ dollars

($_____), evidenced by ☐ cash ☐ cashier's check ☐ personal check ☐ promissory note ☐ other.

1.   Financial Terms

This offer is contingent upon Buyer securing financing as specified in Items D, E, F & G below within _____ days from acceptance of this offer.

$ _____   **A. DEPOSIT TO BE APPLIED TOWARD THE DOWN PAYMENT**, payable to (Payee) _____ ,

_____ , to be held uncashed until

the acceptance of this offer. If this offer is accepted, the deposit shall be delivered to Payee and applied toward the down payment.

$ _____   **B. DOWN PAYMENT INCREASE**, to be paid into escrow ☐ within _____ calendar days of acceptance, or

☐ on or before _____ .

$ _____   **C. DOWN PAYMENT BALANCE**, to be paid into escrow on or before the close of escrow.

$ _____   **D. FIRST LOAN—NEW LOAN.** Buyer shall obtain a new loan, amortized over not fewer than ____ years. Buyer's financing shall be:

☐ Conventional (name of lender, if known) _____

☐ Private (name of lender, if known) _____

☐ Government (specify): ☐ VA ☐ FHA ☐ Cal-Vet ☐ CHFA

☐ Other: _____

Buyer's mortgage shall be

☐ at a maximum fixed rate of _____%

☐ an adjustable rate loan with a maximum beginning rate of _____%, or

☐ (fill in any other requirements here) _____

_____ .

$ _____   **E. FIRST LOAN—EXISTING LOAN.** Buyer shall ☐ assume ☐ buy

subject to an existing loan under the same terms and conditions that Seller has with _____

_____ , the present lender.

The approximate remaining balance is $ _____ , at the current rate of interest of _____ % on a

☐ fixed ☐ adjustable rate loan, for a remaining term of approximately _____ years, secured by a First Deed of Trust.

$ _____   **F. SECOND LOAN—NEW LOAN.** Buyer shall obtain a new loan, amortized over not fewer than _____ years. Buyer's

financing shall be:

☐ Conventional (name of lender, if known) _____

☐ Private (name of lender, if known) _____

☐ Government (specify): ☐ VA ☐ FHA ☐ Cal-Vet ☐ CHFA

☐ Other: _____

Buyer's mortgage shall be ☐ at a maximum fixed rate of _____ %, ☐ an adjustable rate loan with a maximum

beginning rate of _____%, or ☐ (fill in any other requirements here) _____

_____ .

2. Occupancy

Indicate whether or not you intend to occupy the property as your primary residence. The seller is interested in this information because if you don't plan to occupy the property, you may have a harder time securing a loan for your purchase.

3. Escrow

Escrow is the process in which a disinterested third party, usually a title or escrow company, transfers the funds and documents among the buyer, seller and their lenders, following instructions provided by the buyer and seller. (Escrow is described more thoroughly in Chapter 18.)

In this clause, put the name and address of the escrow holder you choose. Although you do not actually open an escrow account until the seller accepts your offer, it's wise to do some preliminary investigation in advance, so that you will have at least a tentative idea as to the company you will use. If you are buying and selling a house in the same area, you will want to use the same escrow holder to coordinate the closings on both properties.

The seller may disagree with your choice and list another escrow holder in the counteroffer. Unless you are truly attached to "your" escrow holder, go with the seller's. If you're buying a new home, condominium or foreclosure, the seller will usually have already opened escrow and will require you to use their title or escrow company. Title fees are usually competitive, but you should ask the seller to pick up the difference if their escrow company charges more.

Also, specify how soon escrow will close after the seller accepts your offer. Be sure to give yourself ample time to remove all contingencies, such as arranging financing and inspections. The escrow instructions authorize the escrow company to give the seller your money and give you the deed to the property, and are usually delivered a few days before the closing date. Chapter 18 contains details on opening and closing escrow and tips on choosing a closing date.

4. Prepayment Penalty and Assumption Fee

This standard clause simply states that if the seller's existing loan has a prepayment penalty (it probably won't) and the seller is paying off the loan now, before the end of the full term

of the loan, he'll pay the penalty. It also states, however, that if the seller's existing loan has a prepayment penalty and you assume the loan, you assume the responsibility for any prepayment penalty assessed after the close of escrow. This could occur if you sell the house, refinance the loan or prepay before its term runs out.

5. Expenses of Sale

Here you check off those items you agree to pay for, those you want the seller to pay for, and those you propose to split with the seller. Don't feel compelled to check every item—a lot depends on the particular house and market. As regards to inspections, Clause 9, below, contains a list of the ones you may want to require. Review Clause 9 and then list the ones you think you need at items J-M above.

Also, you may want the seller to purchase a home warranty (see Chapter 19, Check Out a House's Condition), especially if you're concerned about hidden problems with heating, electrical or plumbing systems, or with certain appliances on the property. If so, indicate here that the seller pays and list what you want covered. At Clause 10, below, check item E, and also list what items you want covered.

Use the chart below, Who Pays for What, as a guide to how expenses are commonly divided; it's quite all right for you and the seller to agree differently.

6. Property Tax and Insurance Prorations; Non-Callable Bonds

This clause allocates payment of property taxes, insurance policies carried over from seller to buyer, rents, interests and any homeowners' association dues or regular assessments. Each owner pays only for the period of actual ownership. For example, if property taxes are $1,000 for a fiscal year beginning July 1, and escrow closes on the next April 1, the buyer's prorated share is $250 for the last quarter of the year (April, May and June), while the seller's share is $750 for the three previous ones (July through March).

This clause also allocates payment of homeowners' association special assessments. If the seller will pay only what is due until the close of escrow and then the buyer will pay the rest, select the first box. If you propose another arrangement—such as the seller paying 100% of any outstanding assessments, select the second box and write in the specifics.

$ _____   **G. SECOND LOAN—EXISTING LOAN.** Buyer shall ☐ assume ☐ buy subject to an existing loan under the same terms and conditions that Seller has with , the present lender. The approximate remaining balance is $ _____ , at the current rate of interest of _____ % on a ☐ fixed ☐ adjustable rate loan, for a remaining term of approximately _____ years, secured by a Second Deed of Trust.

$ _____   **H. TOTAL PURCHASE PRICE, EXCLUDING EXPENSES OF SALE AND CLOSING COSTS.**

$ _____   **I. OTHER. (See Paragraph _____ of this contract for additional terms and conditions.)**

LOAN APPLICATION. Buyer shall submit complete loan application and financial statement to lender(s) within 5 days after acceptance. If Buyer, after making a good-faith effort, does not secure financing by the time specified, this contract shall become void, and all deposits shall be returned to Buyer.

GOVERNMENT FINANCING. In the event of FHA or VA financing, Buyer shall not be obligated to complete the purchase, nor shall Buyer forfeit the deposit, if the offer price exceeds the property's FHA or VA appraised value. Buyer shall, however, have the option of proceeding with the purchase from any above-named lender or a different lender without regard to the appraised value.

EXISTING LOAN. If Buyer is assuming any loans or purchasing the property subject to any loans, Seller shall, within 7 days after acceptance, deliver to Buyer copies of all applicable notes and deeds of trust, loan balances and current interest rates. Buyer's obligation under this contract is conditioned upon Buyer's written approval of the documents within 7 days after receipt. If Buyer does not accept the documents, either party may terminate this contract.

SELLER FINANCING. The following terms apply only to financing extended by Seller.

1. The rate specified as the maximum interest rate in D or F, above, shall be the actual fixed interest rate for seller financing.
2. The loan documents shall be prepared in the form customarily used by Escrow Agent, identified in Clause 3.
3. The promissory note and deed of trust shall include the following:
    a. Request for Notice of Default on senior loans.
    b. Seller's right to have Buyer execute and pay for a Request for Notice of Delinquency.
    c. Acceleration clause making the loan due, at Seller's option, upon the sale or transfer of the property.
    d. Title insurance coverage insuring Seller's deed of trust interest in the property.
    e. Late charge of 6% of the amount of any installment received more than 10 pays after the date it is due.
    f. Obligation of Buyer to maintain fire and extended insurance with Seller named as loss payee at least to cover lesser of replacement of improvements or the liens on the property.
4. Seller shall obtain at Buyer's expense a tax service to notify Seller in the event of a property tax delinquency by Buyer.
5. If the property contains 1-4 dwelling units, Buyer and Seller shall execute a Seller Financing Disclosure Statement as provided by the arranger of credit as soon as is practicable prior to the statements reflecting Buyer's financial condition in such detail as is customarily required by institutional lenders. Seller shall keep these documents confidential and use them only to approve Buyer's creditworthiness. Seller shall notify Buyer in writing within 7 days after receipt of Seller's approval or disapproval of Buyer's credit.
6. Buyer shall notify Seller in writing within 7 days after receipt of the Seller Financing Disclosure Statement of Buyer's approval or disapproval of the financing terms offered by Seller.

2. Occupancy

Buyer ☐ does ☐ does not intend to occupy the property as Buyer's primary residence.

3. Escrow

Buyer and Seller shall deliver signed escrow instructions to _____

_____ , escrow agent

located at _____

_____ , within

a reasonable time before the close of this sale. Escrow shall close within _____ days of acceptance of this offer. The escrow fee shall be paid by Buyer.

WHO PAYS FOR WHAT

Item	Who usually pays	Comments
Escrow fees	Buyer customarily pays in northern California, seller in southern California	Not uncommon for fees to be divided
Title search	Buyer customarily pays in northern California, seller in southern California	Buyer benefits—not unreasonable for buyer to pay
Title insurance for buyer/owner	Buyer customarily pays in northern California, seller in southern California	Buyer benefits—not unreasonable for buyer to pay
Title insurance for lender	Buyer	Buyer benefits—buyer should pay
Deed preparation fee	Buyer	Buyer benefits—buyer should pay
Notary fee	Buyer usually pays for grant and trust deeds; seller usually pays for reconveyance deed on the property	Grant and trust deeds help buyer purchase and finance property; seller receives reconveyance deed when paying off existing mortgage
Recording fee	Buyer usually pays for grant and trust deeds; seller usually pays for reconveyance deed on the property	Grant and trust deeds help buyer purchase and finance property; seller receives reconveyance deed when paying off existing mortgage
Attorney's fee (if attorney hired to clarify title)	Whoever hired attorney	
Documentary transfer tax	Seller usually pays except in probate sales where buyer is legally required to pay	
Pest control inspection report	Buyer usually picks inspector and pays for inspection in northern California; seller often has property inspected before listing it for sale in southern California	In southern California, lenders usually won't process buyer's loan application without termite inspection because termites are a serious problem; if seller didn't do inspection, buyer should to assure that report meets buyer's standard
General contractor report	Buyer usually picks inspector and pays for inspection	Buyer should pay to assure that report meets buyer's standard
Roof inspection report	Buyer usually picks inspector and pays inspection	Buyer should pay to assure that report meets for buyer's standard
Other inspections	Buyer usually picks inspector and pays inspection	Buyer should pay to assure that report meets for buyer's standard
One-year home warranty	Seller	Sometimes seller offers to purchase a policy when he lists the property—if he doesn't, buyer can purchase one if desired or negotiate this as part of the contract
Real estate tax Fire insurance Bond liens (unless able to be paid off)	Buyer and seller usually prorate as of the date the deed is recorded (see Clause 5)	Both parties benefit; should be prorated

4.   Prepayment Penalty and Assumption Fee

Seller shall pay any prepayment penalty or other fees imposed by any existing lender who is paid off during escrow. Buyer shall pay any prepayment penalty, assumption fee or other fee which becomes due after the close of escrow on any loans assumed from Seller.

5.   Expenses of Sale

Expenses of sale, settlement costs and closing costs shall be paid for as follows:

	Buyer	Seller	Shared Equally	
A.	☐	☐	☐	Escrow fees
B.	☐	☐	☐	Title search
C.	☐	☐	☐	Title insurance for buyer/owner
D.	☐	☐	☐	Title insurance for buyer's lender
E.	☐	☐	☐	Deed preparation fee
F.	☐	☐	☐	Notary fee
G.	☐	☐	☐	Recording fee
H.	☐	☐	☐	Attorney's fee (if attorney hired to clarify title)
I.	☐	☐	☐	Documentary transfer tax
J.	☐	☐	☐	Pest control inspection report
K.	☐	☐	☐	General contractor report
L.	☐	☐	☐	Roof inspection report
M.				Other inspections (specify):
1.	☐	☐	☐	_____
2.	☐	☐	☐	_____
3.	☐	☐	☐	_____
4.	☐	☐	☐	_____
N.	☐	☐	☐	One-year home warranty (specify covered items): _____
				_____
				_____
O.				Other (specify):
1.	☐	☐	☐	_____
2.	☐	☐	☐	_____
3.	☐	☐	☐	_____
4.	☐	☐	☐	_____

6.   Property Tax and Insurance Prorations; Non-Callable Bonds

Seller shall be responsible for payment of Seller's prorated share of real estate taxes and assessments accrued until the deed transferring title to Buyer is recorded. Buyer understands that the property shall be reassessed upon change of ownership and that Buyer shall be sent a supplemental tax bill which may reflect an increase in taxes based on property value.

Any premiums on insurance carried over from Seller to Buyer and any homeowners' association dues and regular assessments, interests, rents shall be prorated, that is, Seller shall pay the portion of the premiums and fees while title is in Seller's name and Buyer shall pay the portion of the premiums and fees while title is in Buyer's name.

Homeowners' association special assessments shall be ☐ paid current by Seller (payments not yet due shall be assumed by Buyer without credit toward the purchase price) or ☐ _____

_____

Buyer agrees to assume non-callable assessment bond liens (those which cannot be paid off by Seller) as follows: _____

_____

_____

This clause also provides that the buyer assumes any "non-callable" bond liens—bonds to finance local improvements such as curbs, gutters or street lights. The seller may not even know whether the house has any such liens, but they'll show up on the title report.

Often bonds must be paid off when a house is sold, but sometimes they can't be—that is, they're "non-callable." In that case, the buyer assumes responsibility to pay the lien, but the cost of doing so is credited by the seller to the buyer in escrow. Unless a title search has already been done and you know specifically what non-callable bond liens are on the house, ask the seller for help in filling this in or leave it blank.

7. Fixtures

Fixtures are items permanently attached to real property, like built-in appliances or bookshelves, wall-to-wall carpeting, chandeliers, drapes and landscaping. Fixtures come with the house unless you and the seller agree that the seller can remove them. If the seller wants to take something considered a fixture, such as a built-in stove, and you agree, list it here.

8. Personal Property

Everything other than real property and fixtures is personal property. Personal property doesn't come with the house unless the seller agrees in writing to include it. If the seller promises to include items such as rugs, beds or appliances that aren't built-in, list them here.

9. Inspection Contingencies

Offers to purchase a house almost always contain contingencies, conditions that either the seller or buyer must meet (or the other party must waive) before the deal will close. Many relate to inspecting a house. (See Chapter 19, Check Out a House's Condition, for details.)

In Clause 9, you specify what inspections on the house you want done—and MUST approve of—before you will complete the purchase (close escrow). You also note how soon after the acceptance of the offer the inspections must be done. Normally, allowing 20 working days is reasonable. Requiring all the inspection contingencies listed in Clause 9 is unusual. Often, only a general contractor and pest control report are asked for unless the buyer suspects problems requiring an inspection by a specialist. As a very rough rule, you normally want to require more inspections when a house is older and expensive or vulnerable to special problems, such as near an earthquake fault or slide zone.

With new houses, you may want to schedule inspection during key phases of construction, plus a final inspection, in Clause J. (See Chapter 7, Section I, for inspecting new houses.)

Item K lets you include inspections that may be important to you, such as a home security inspection. In some neighborhoods, local police departments will visit individual homes to evaluate security and recommend improvements. (For details on home security surveys and other aspects of neighborhood crime prevention, see *Safe Homes, Safe Neighborhoods*, by Mann with Blakeman (Nolo Press).)

Clause 9 also lets you cancel the contract if any of the inspection reports are not to your satisfaction. Most buyers negotiate with sellers to correct—or to compensate them for correcting—the problems before canceling the contract. One approach to negotiating is to insist that the seller obtain a home warranty covering the problem.

19TH CENTURY PALM

7. Fixtures

All fixtures and fittings that are permanently attached to the property or for which special openings have been made, are included, free of liens, in the purchase price, including built-in appliances, electrical, plumbing, light and heating fixtures, garage door openers/remote controls, attached carpets and other floor coverings, screens, awnings, shutters, window shades, blinds, television antennas/satellite dishes and related equipment, private integrated phone systems, air coolers/conditioners, pool/spa equipment, water softeners (if owned by Seller), security systems/alarms (if owned by Seller), attached fireplace equipment, mailbox, in-ground landscaping including trees/shrubs, EXCEPT: _____

_____

_____

_____

8. Personal Property

The following items of personal property, free of liens and without warranty of condition (unless otherwise provided), are INCLUDED in the sale:

☐ Stove ☐ Oven ☐ Refrigerator ☐ Washer ☐ Dryer ☐ Freezer ☐ Trash Compactor ☐ Dishwasher

_____

_____

_____

_____

9. Inspection Contingencies

This offer is conditioned upon Buyer's written approval of the following inspection reports. All inspections shall be carried out within _____ days of acceptance of the offer. Buyer shall deliver written approval or disapproval to Seller within 3 days of receiving each report. If Buyer does not deliver a written disapproval within the time allowed, Buyer shall be deemed to approve of the report.

Seller is to provide reasonable access to the property to Buyer, his/her agent, all inspectors and representatives of lending institutions to conduct appraisals.

☐ A. Pest control report, covering the main building and ☐ detached garage(s) or carport(s); ☐ the following other structures on the property:

_____

_____ . Buyer may elect to pay for all, a portion or none of the cost of the work recommended by the report.

☐ B. General contractor report as to the general physical condition of the property including, but not limited to, heating and plumbing, electrical systems, solar energy systems, roof, appliances, structural, soil, foundation, retaining walls, possible environmental hazards, location of property lines, size/square footage of the property and water/utility restrictions.

☐ C. Plumbing contractor report.

☐ D. Soils engineer report.

☐ E. Energy conservation inspection report in accordance with local ordinances.

☐ F. Seismic safety report.

☐ G. Environmental hazards inspection reports including, but not limited to, asbestos, radon gas, lead-based paint and hazardous wastes.

☐ H. City or county inspection report.

☐ I. Roof inspection report.

☐ J. General contractor report at the following phases of construction (specify) _____

_____

_____

☐ K. Other (specify) _____

_____ .

If Buyer and Seller, after making a good-faith effort, cannot remove in writing the above contingencies by the time specified, this contract shall become void, and all deposits shall be returned to Buyer.

10. Other Contingencies

This offer is contingent upon the following:

☐ A. Buyer receiving and approving preliminary title report within _____ days of acceptance of this offer.

TIME ALLOWED FOR REMOVING CONTINGENCIES

Most offers call for the removal of contingencies within 30 to 60 days after the seller's acceptance. There are no hard and fast rules, however; you and the seller should decide depending on your time constraints and how long it will realistically take to remove each. If the house is in great physical shape, 30 days should be adequate to remove all contingencies relating to its physical condition. The seller might even reasonably request that physical inspection contingencies be removed within 7-14 days. This makes sense from a seller's point of view; sales that fall apart often do so because inspections turn up defects and buyer and seller can't agree on who will pay for repairs.

A contingency based on your selling an existing house or obtaining a loan you haven't yet applied for (this is spelled out as a contingency in Clause 1) will normally need 30-90 days for removal. If any contingencies aren't met in the specified time, the deal is over unless you and the seller agree in writing to extend the contingency release time.

Chapter 18 discusses how to remove contingencies and includes a contingency release form and a form to extend time to satisfy a contingency.

10. Other Contingencies

In Clause 10, you specify the other contingencies that must be met before you will close.

- Item A is needed for all houses. You want to make sure title (legal ownership) is good, that is, no one has a lien on the house or claims an easement. (See Chapter 18, After the Contract Is Signed, for a discussion of these terms and preliminary title reports.) In most cases, the buyer orders the report within 3 days of acceptance.
- Item B is for condos and houses in developments. In Chapter 7, we discuss how developments and condo associations have fairly detailed rules which apply to all owners. So if you buy a new house, one in an existing housing development or a condo, make sure the seller provides you with all the rules and regulations, financial documents and other pertinent paperwork—and study them carefully. Several of these disclosures are required by the statutory disclosure statement discussed in Chapter 19.
- Item C is perhaps the most common non-inspection contingency. In hot (sellers') markets, sellers often reject offers with this contingency, but recently, in areas of the state where sales have slowed, sellers are accepting it more often. If you need to sell a house before buying another, read Chapter 14, Buying a House When You Already Own One.
- Item D comes up in two situations. In the first, you are buying property you plan to occupy, which currently has tenants. (This may especially be the situation if you are buying a condo.) You buy subject to tenants' rights. Many tenants will move on their own. In rent control areas (see Clause 13), however, a long-term tenant with low rent may resist. After escrow closes, you may have to bring an eviction action on the grounds that you intend to occupy.

  The other situation is when the place you are buying has tenants living in it who you intend to let remain after the sale (for example, you're buying a duplex or house with an already rented in-law unit). Under state rental laws, you inherit not only the tenants, but also the rental agreements. If you feel those agreements are unreasonable, you'll want to be able to get out of the contract. For example, if the tenants have a 30-day rental agreement, they must be given 30-days' notice before moving out. There may be further restrictions in communities with rent control laws requiring the landlord to show "just cause" to evict. (See Clause 13 for more on rent control.)

  If you're buying property subject to tenants' rights or rental property, see *The Landlord's Law Book, Volume 1: Rights and Responsibilities*, by Brown and Warner (Nolo Press).
- Item E lets you request that the seller provide you with a written warranty covering certain items. If you check this item, be sure to check "Seller" under item N in Clause 5, Expenses of Sale. Before insisting on a home warranty, be sure to read Chapter 7, Section J, and Chapter 19, Section L.
- Use Item F for any other contingency that may be important to you. If you trying to buy a condominium, for example, you may want to make the purchase contingent

☐ B.   Seller furnishing declaration of restrictions, CC&Rs, bylaws, articles of incorporation, rules and regulations currently in force, other governing documents, one year's homeowners' association minutes, financial statements of the owners' association for the past three years, a statement of reserves, assignment of parking spaces within _____ days of acceptance.

☐ C.   Sale of Buyer's current residence, the address of which is _____

_____ , by_____ ,19____

☐ D.   Seller furnishing rental agreements within _____ days of acceptance

☐ E.   Seller providing Buyer with a home warranty to cover the following: _____

_____

_____

☐ F.   Other: _____

_____

_____

_____

_____

_____

Buyer shall deliver written approval or disapproval to Seller within 3 days of receiving each report, statement or warranty. If Buyer does not deliver a written disapproval within the time allowed, Buyer shall be deemed to approve of the report, statement or warranty. If Buyer and Seller, after making a good-faith effort, cannot remove in writing the above contingencies, this offer shall become void, and all deposits shall be returned to Buyer.

11. Condition of Property

Seller represents that the roof, heating, plumbing, air conditioning, electrical, septic, drainage, sewers, gutters and downspouts, sprinklers, as well as built-in appliances and other equipment and fixtures, are in working order. Seller agrees to maintain them in that condition, and to maintain all landscaping, grounds and pools, until possession of the property is delivered to Buyer. Seller shall, by the date of possession, replace any cracked or broken glass.

12. Foreign Investors

If Seller is a foreign person as defined in the Foreign Investment in Real Property Tax Act, Buyer shall, absent a specific exemption, have withheld in escrow ten percent (10%) of the gross sale price of the property. Buyer and Seller shall provide the escrow holder specified in Clause 3 above with all signed documentation required by the Act.

If Seller has a last known address outside of California or if Seller's proceeds will be paid to a financial intermediary of Seller, under California Revenue and Tax Code, Buyer, unless an exemption applies, must deduct and withhold 3-1/3% of the gross sales price from Seller's proceeds and send it to the Franchise Tax Board.

13. Rent Control

The property ☐ is ☐ is not located in a city or county subject to local rent control. A rent control ordinance may restrict the rent that can be charged for this property, limit the right of the owner to evict the occupant for other than "just cause" and control the owner's rights and responsibilities.

14. Title

At close of escrow, title to the property is to be clear of all liens and encumbrances of record except those listed in the preliminary title report and agreed to be assumed by Buyer. Any such liens or encumbrances assumed by Buyer shall be credited toward the purchase price. If Seller cannot remove liens or encumbrances not assumed by Buyer, Buyer shall have the right to cancel this contract and be refunded his/her deposit and costs of inspection reports.

15. Possession

Buyer reserves the right to inspect the property three days before the close of escrow. Seller shall deliver physical possession of property, along with alarms, alarm codes, keys, garage door openers and all other means to operate all property locks, to Buyer: ☐ at close of escrow ☐ no later than _____ days after the close of escrow.

If Buyer agrees to let Seller continue to occupy the property after close of escrow, Seller shall deposit into escrow for Buyer a prorated share of Buyer's monthly carrying costs (principal, interest, property taxes and insurance), for each such day, subject to the terms of a written agreement, specifying rent or security deposit, authorizing a final inspection before Seller vacates and indicating the length of tenancy, signed by both parties.

on the homeowners' association authorizing pest control and general inspections of the common area. (In larger buildings, especially, contractors infrequently have access to common areas.)

Clause 10 also lets you cancel the contract if the contingencies are not filled to your satisfaction.

 MAKE YOUR OFFER CONTINGENT UPON YOUR PURCHASE OF HAZARD INSURANCE, PARTICULARLY IF YOU ARE IN A HIGH RISK EARTHQUAKE OR FIRE AREA

California home buyers are finding it increasingly difficult to purchase hazard insurance, with appropriate coverage (especially for earthquakes) at affordable rates. (See Chapter 18, Section C, discussion of hazard insurance.) To protect yourself, use Item 10F to make your purchase contingent upon your applying, and receiving a commitment in writing, for hazard insurance on the property as required by your lender. Ask for as much time as possible to remove this contingency, at least 30 days if possible, depending upon your particular situation.

11. Condition of Property

In Clause 11, you require the seller to assure you that certain mechanical systems and appliances are in good working order and to keep them that way until you take possession of the property. You are also requiring the seller to replace any broken glass by the time you take the property.

12. Foreign Investors

To comply with a federal law called FIRPTA (Foreign Investment in Real Property Tax Act, Internal Revenue Code § 1445), the seller must complete a form (available from an escrow or title company, or the IRS) stating whether he's a foreign investor as defined by that law. If he is, you must withhold in escrow 10% of the sale price of the house and fill out and file some papers with the IRS. The escrow agent can help you.

If the seller is located outside of California or the proceeds of the sale will be paid to an intermediary of the seller, you must withhold and send some money to the Franchise Tax Board (California's taxing authority). Again, the escrow agent can help you.

13. Rent Control

About 15 California cities have rent control ordinances, which may restrict the rent the owner can charge a tenant, as well as control the owner's rights and responsibilities. While this is most relevant with multi-unit buildings, it can decrease the value of houses likely to be rented in the future. Even if you're not planning to rent your home now, conditions change and you may rent it out in the future.

Check the appropriate box at Clause 13.

CALIFORNIA RENT CONTROL CITIES		
Berkeley	Los Angeles	San Jose
Beverly Hills	Los Gatos	Santa Monica
Cotati	Oakland	Thousand Oaks
East Palo Alto	Palm Springs	West Hollywood
Hayward	San Francisco	Westlake Village

14. Title

This standard clause assures you that title to the house will be in good order ("clear") when you take possession. If the seller is unable to clear up difficulties before the close of escrow, you have the right to get out of the contract. We discuss checking out the title in Chapter 18.

15. Possession

This clause lets you have one last look at the property right before the close of escrow to make sure the seller (or tenant) didn't damage the place before moving out and that all promised repairs have been done to your satisfaction. It also specifies when you can move in and finally steam off the dreadful green wallpaper. (See Chapter 7, Section I, and Chapter 18, Section E, for more information on final inspections.)

Although you'll probably want to take possession on the same day escrow closes, be prepared to give this up during your negotiations. Many sellers who are buying another house insist on not moving out until 60-90 days after escrow closes, in exchange for paying you rent. Some sellers who are renting new places won't want to move out until the first of the month when their lease begins—they, too, will pay you rent.

Should you agree that the seller can stay on after closing, we suggest you and the seller sign a written rental agreement specifying a daily rent or security deposit, authorizing a final inspection and indicating the term (length). (See Chapter 14, Section A, for resources on rental agreements.)

For now, the contract states that you expect a per day charge of *your* prorated monthly carrying costs. The seller may not want to pay that much, especially if *her* monthly carrying costs were far less than yours will be—as will be the case with a long time owner. When you get around to writing up the agreement, we suggest you come up with an amount that's fair for both of you, such as 0.5% of the cost of the house, which is $500 on a $100,000 house.

If the seller needs only a few days and has been a pleasure to work with, it's not worth the aggravation of charging a fee and writing up an agreement. Be a sport. But if the seller needs to stay for more than just a few days and then turns uncooperative when it's time to leave, you may need to formally evict her. (See Chapter 21, Section B)

16. Agency Confirmation and Commission to Brokers

This clause lets you and the seller confirm your relationships with your agents. Long before you fill out this offer form, if you are working with an agent you would have completed a Confirmation: Real Estate Agency Relationships form, which contains the identical information as Clause 16. (See Chapter 5, Working With Real Estate Professionals, for more information.) It doesn't hurt to repeat the information in the offer form.

Clause 16 also clarifies who pays which broker, and how much. Your options are outlined in Chapter 5. The notice is required by law (California Business and Professions Code § 10147.5).

17. Advice

This clause means that you are not liable for giving tax or legal advice to the seller, the seller isn't liable for giving that information to you and the real estate agents aren't liable for giving that information to you or the seller.

SUPPLEMENT TO REAL PROPERTY PURCHASE CONTRACT

The material set out below is hereby made a part of the offer dated _____,19____ from (Buyer) _____

_____ to

(Seller) _____

for the purchase of the real property located at: _____

_____

Additional terms: _____

_____

_____

_____

_____

Buyer _____   Date _____

Buyer _____   Date _____

18. Backup Offer

Check this clause only if the seller has already accepted another offer to buy the property and your offer is a backup offer. If your backup offer is eventually accepted, this clause gives you 24 hours to approve the deal in writing from the time you're notified of the acceptance in writing. This lets you make more than one backup offer without being obligated to purchase more than one house if your offers are simultaneously accepted.

19. Duration of Offer

Here, you give the seller a deadline to accept your offer. If he doesn't accept by that time, your offer automatically expires unless you extend it in writing. (See Chapter 17, Presenting Your Offer and Negotiating, on how to extend an offer. Chapter 17 also covers revoking your offer before the seller accepts or the deadline expires.) If the seller tries to accept your offer after it expires, shrug your shoulders and say, "Sorry, you're too late," unless you still want the house.

In deciding how much time to give the seller, pay close attention to the seller's needs and your negotiating strategy. If you think the house is a bargain and there are no other potential buyers around, give the seller very little time—just a few hours. Similarly, if you're bidding high to preempt other bidders, give the seller a very short time.

But if you're bidding low on a number of houses with the hope of eventually picking up a bargain, leave your offer open for a considerably longer time. If you're somewhere in between these extremes, give the seller about one to three days to respond. If you're making a backup offer, you need to let time pass for the other deal to fall through, thus 60-90 days is a good length. We discuss this issue in more detail in Chapter 17.

20. Other Terms and Conditions

In this space, list any terms or conditions not covered in the contract. If there's not enough space, write "Summarized on Supplement to Real Property Purchase Contract" and type up a form such as the one below.

Examples to include in Clause 20 or a supplemental offer include:

- acknowledgment that the property contains illegal units

- details outlining a probate or foreclosure sale (you will need help from a real estate agent in either of these situations)
- specification of who will pay to pump and certify a septic system or connect a sewer
- acknowledgment that the buyer is a licensed real estate agent, and
- contingency that buyer sees and approves prior years heating bills, if you are worried about heating a very large house.

21. Risk of Damage to Property

This paragraph states that you assume the risk of damage to, or destruction of, the property after you get title to it. If the house is damaged or destroyed before then, you may be able to get out of the deal, depending on the extent of the damage, as a percent of the purchase price.

You fill in that amount in the two blanks. We have left them blank because the amount entered differs substantially around the state. The statewide real estate contract published by the California Association of Realtors uses 1%. On the other hand, the form published by the San Francisco Association of Realtors uses 5%. Find out local custom before entering an amount.

22. Liquidated Damages

This clause deals with what happens if you back out of the deal with no good reason. If you refuse to go through with the sale because a contingency can't be fulfilled, the seller must return your deposit. (See Chapter 18, Section B6.) But if you back out simply because you change your mind, or don't try in good faith to fulfill a contingency (for example, you don't even apply for a loan), it's considered a default and the seller need not return your deposit. This approach makes sense; the seller should be compensated if you simply decide not to go through with the purchase for a reason not covered in the contract.

This clause treats your deposit as "liquidated damages," meaning you and the seller agree in advance on the maximum amount of the damages if you default. By setting the maximum amount in advance, you and the seller can save both time and money by avoiding court or arbitration, and you are protected from the risk of a court or arbitrator awarding the seller a larger amount.

16. Agency Confirmation and Commission to Brokers

The following agency relationship(s) are confirmed for this transaction:

Listing agent: _____ is the agent of:

☐ Seller exclusively   ☐ Buyer and Seller

Selling agent: _____ is the agent of:

☐ Buyer exclusively   ☐ Seller exclusively   ☐ Buyer and Seller

Notice: The amount or rate of real estate commissions is not fixed by law. They are set by each Broker individually and may be negotiable between the Seller and Broker.

Buyer and Seller shall each pay only those broker's commissions for which Buyer and Seller have separately contracted in writing with a broker licensed by the California Commissioner of Real Estate.

$_____ or _____% of selling price to be paid to _____

by ☐ Seller ☐ Buyer.

$_____ or _____% of selling price to be paid to _____ by

☐ Seller ☐ Buyer.

17. Advice

If Buyer or Seller wishes advice concerning the legal or tax aspects of this transaction, Buyer or Seller shall separately contract and pay for it.

18. Backup Offer

☐ This offer is being made as a backup offer. Should Seller accept this offer as a backup offer, the following terms and conditions apply:

If Seller accepts this offer as a primary offer, he/she must do so in writing. Until that time, Buyer's deposit check shall be held uncashed.

Buyer has 24 hours from receipt of Seller's written acceptance to ratify it in writing. If Buyer fails to do so, Buyer's offer shall be deemed withdrawn and any contractual relationship between Buyer and Seller terminated.

19. Duration of Offer

This offer is submitted to Seller by Buyer on _____, 19_____, at _____ ☐ a.m. ☐ p.m. , Pacific Time, and will be considered revoked unless a copy of this contract with Seller's signature accepting it is delivered in person, by mail or fax and personally received by Buyer or Buyer's real estate agent not later than _____ ☐ a.m. ☐ p.m. on _____, 19_____, or, if prior to Seller's acceptance of this offer, Buyer revokes this offer in writing.

20. Other Terms and Conditions

_____

_____

_____

21. Risk of Damage to Property

All risk of loss to the property which occurs after this offer is accepted shall be borne by Seller until title has been conveyed to Buyer. Any damage totaling _____% or less of the purchase price shall be repaired by Seller prior to the transfer of title. If the land or improvements are destroyed or material damaged in an amount exceeding _____% of the purchase price, Buyer shall have the option of either terminating this agreement and recovering all deposits made or purchasing the property in its then condition.

22. Liquidated Damages

If Seller accepts this offer, and Buyer later defaults on the contract, Seller shall be released from Seller's obligations under this contract. By signing their initials here, Buyer (_____) and Seller (_____) agree that if Buyer defaults, Seller shall keep no more than three percent (3%) of the purchase price stated above if the property is a dwelling with no more than four units, one of which Buyer intends to occupy as Buyer's residence.

California law generally prohibits sellers from keeping more than 3% of the agreed-upon sale price as liquidated damages. (Civil Code § 1675.) But this doesn't mean that the seller gets the full 3%. The seller generally must prove that her damages somehow relate to that amount. In some situations, where you back out early on and the seller immediately gets another acceptable offer, her damage is zero—and she won't be entitled to anything, and certainly not 3% of the sales price.

The provision must be in at least 10-point boldface type and signed or initialed by you and the seller. This makes it clear that you've actively chosen to include the provision and know that you are not required to do so.

23. Mediation of Disputes

This clause lets you first try to settle any disputes that arise under the contract by non-binding mediation. Mediation is a process where you and the seller pick someone to help you reach a mutually agreeable decision. The result is never imposed on either party. Mediation is cheap, fast and without the emotional drain and hostility of litigation. We highly recommend it.

Anyone can be a mediator, although it's best to have someone familiar with the real estate business. The person you choose should be fair minded and work well with people. Don't suggest your agent or the seller's agent. Both of you have an interest in getting someone you agree is impartial. The escrow holder may be willing to recommend (or at least informally suggest) someone as a mediator if you and the seller are having trouble agreeing.

RANCH

24. Arbitration of Disputes

If you want any disputes to be decided by arbitration, you must include this exact clause in your contract. If you opt for it, you choose to resolve your dispute by arbitration should your attempt to settle any dispute informally or by mediation not succeed. You give up your right to a court trial. We recommend choosing arbitration. Like mediation, it's cheaper, faster and less hostile than litigation.

In arbitration, you submit your dispute to one or more arbitrators for a decision. Under this provision, the arbitration will be governed by rules of either the American Arbitration Association, a respected organization in the field or the Judicial Arbitration and Mediation Services, Inc., a California dispute resolution organization made up of many former California judges.

The rules of both AAA and JAMS provide that the parties may get a lawyer to represent them (but don't have to) and that the decision is final—neither party can appeal it to a court. Some commentators (and, of course, most real estate lawyers) recommend against this clause, believing you have a better chance of winning big by going to court. We don't agree. Relying on the American court system to produce an efficient, cost-effective result of a dispute is usually naive.

25. Attorneys' Fees

In our contract, the losing party in arbitration or litigation (you could wind up in litigation if you choose arbitration and the seller doesn't agree, or vice versa) is responsible for their own—and the other side's—attorneys' fees and court costs. This clause is standard.

26. Entire Agreement

This clause, which states that this contract is the entire agreement between you and the seller, and that all modifications to the contract must be in writing, is a statement of the law that oral real estate agreements are simply not enforceable. If you're relying on anything the seller has told you, get it in writing.

Seller shall retain the right to proceed against Buyer for any other claim or remedy Seller may have, other than for breach of contract. In the event of a dispute, funds deposited into escrow are not released automatically and require mutual, signed release instructions from Buyer and Seller, a judicial decision or an arbitration award.

23. Mediation of Disputes

If a dispute arises out of, or relates to, this agreement, Buyer and Seller ☐ agree ☐ do not agree to first try in good faith to settle the dispute by non-binding mediation before resorting to court action or binding arbitration. Mediation is a process in which parties attempt to resolve a dispute by submitting it to an impartial, neutral mediator who is authorized to facilitate the resolution of the dispute but who is not empowered to impose a settlement on the Buyer and Seller.

To invoke mediation, one party shall notify the other of his/her intention to proceed with mediation and shall provide the name of a chosen mediator. The other party shall have seven days to respond. If he/she disagrees with the first person's chosen mediator, the parties shall ask the escrow holder to choose the mediator or to recommend someone to choose the mediator. The mediator shall conduct the mediation session or sessions within the next three weeks. Before the mediation begins, Buyer and Seller agree to sign a document limiting the admissibility in arbitration or a lawsuit of anything said or admitted, or any documents prepared, in the course of the mediation.

Costs of mediation shall be divided equally between Buyer and Seller.

_____ Buyer   _____ Seller

_____ Buyer   _____ Seller

24. Arbitration of Disputes

Any dispute or claim in law or equity between Buyer and Seller arising out of this contract or any resulting transaction which is not settled by mediation shall be decided by neutral, binding arbitration and not by court action except as provided by California law for judicial review of arbitration proceedings.

The arbitration shall be conducted in accordance with the rules of either the American Arbitration Association (AAA) or Judicial Arbitration and Mediation Services, Inc. (JAMS). The selection between AAA and JAMS rules shall be made by the claimant first filing for the arbitration. The parties to an arbitration may agree in writing to use different rules and/or arbitrator(s). In all other respects, the arbitration shall be conducted in accordance with Part III, Title 9 of the California Code of Civil Procedure.

Judgment upon the award rendered by the arbitrator(s) may be entered in any court having jurisdiction thereof. The parties shall have the right to discovery in accordance with Code of Civil Procedure § 1283.05. The following matters are excluded from arbitration hereunder: (a) a judicial or non-judicial foreclosure or other action or proceeding to enforce a deed of trust, mortgage, or installment land sales contract as defined in Civil Code § 2985, (b) an unlawful detainer action, (c) the filing or enforcement of a mechanic's lien, (d) any matter which is within the jurisdiction of a probate or small claims court, and (e) an action for bodily injury or wrongful death, or for latent or patent defects, to which Code of Civil Procedure § 337.1 or § 337.15 applies. The filing of a judicial action to enable the recording of a notice of pending action, for order of attachment, receivership, injunction, or other provisional remedies, shall not constitute a waiver of the right to arbitrate under this provision.

Any dispute or claim by or against broker(s) and/or associate licensee(s) participating in this transaction shall be submitted to arbitration consistent with the provision above only if the broker(s) and/or associate licensee(s) making the claim or against whom the claim is made shall have agreed to submit it to arbitration consistent with this provision.

"NOTICE: BY INITIALING IN THE SPACE BELOW YOU ARE AGREEING TO HAVE ANY DISPUTE ARISING OUT OF THE MATTERS INCLUDED IN THE 'ARBITRATION OF DISPUTES' PROVISION DECIDED BY NEUTRAL ARBITRATION AS PROVIDED BY CALIFORNIA LAW AND YOU ARE GIVING UP ANY RIGHTS YOU MIGHT POSSESS TO HAVE THE DISPUTE LITIGATED IN A COURT OR JURY TRIAL. BY INITIALING IN THE SPACE BELOW YOU ARE GIVING UP YOUR JUDICIAL RIGHTS TO DISCOVERY AND APPEAL, UNLESS THOSE RIGHTS ARE SPECIFICALLY INCLUDED IN THE 'ARBITRATION OF DISPUTES' PROVISION. IF YOU REFUSE TO SUBMIT TO ARBITRATION AFTER AGREEING TO THIS PROVISION, YOU MAY BE COMPELLED TO ARBITRATE UNDER THE AUTHORITY OF THE CALIFORNIA CODE OF CIVIL PROCEDURE. YOUR AGREEMENT TO THIS ARBITRATION PROVISION IS VOLUNTARY."

"WE HAVE READ AND UNDERSTAND THE FOREGOING AND AGREE TO SUBMIT DISPUTES ARISING OUT OF THE MATTERS INCLUDED IN THE 'ARBITRATION OF DISPUTES' PROVISION TO NEUTRAL ARBITRATION."

Buyer's(s') Initials _____/_____   Seller's(s') Initials _____/_____

25. Attorneys' Fees

If litigation or arbitration arises from this contract, the prevailing party shall be reimbursed by the other party for reasonable attorneys' fees and court or arbitration costs.

26. Entire Agreement

This document represents the entire agreement between Buyer and Seller. Any modifications or amendments to this contract shall be made in writing, signed and dated by both parties.

27. Time Is of the Essence

Time is of the essence in this transaction.

28. Disclosures

_____ By initialing here, Buyer requests a copy of the Real Estate Transfer Disclosure Statement.

_____ By initialing here, Buyer requests copies of geologic, seismic and flood hazard disclosures.

_____ By initialing here, Buyer requests a copy of *The Homeowner's Guide to Earthquake Safety*.

_____ By initialing here, Buyer requests a copy of *Environmental Hazards: A Guide for Homeowners and Buyers*.

_____ By initialing here, Buyer requests a lead-warning statement.

_____ By initialing here, Buyer requests a copy of the following disclosures: (specify) _____

_____

29. Buyer's Signature

This constitutes an offer to purchase the above listed property.

Selling Broker _____   Buyer _____

By Selling Agent _____   Buyer _____

Broker's Address _____   Broker's Telephone _____

_____   Broker's Fax _____

_____

Date: _____ , 19_____

30. Seller's Acceptance

The undersigned Seller ☐ accepts ☐ accepts subject to the attached counteroffer the foregoing offer and agrees to sell the property on the terms and conditions stated above.

Seller agrees to pay compensation for services as follows:

☐ _____ % of the sales price or ☐ $ _____ to (Listing Broker) _____

_____

☐ _____ % of the sales price or ☐ $ _____ to (Selling Broker) _____

_____

payable on recordation of the deed or other evidence of title. If the sale is prevented due to the default of Seller, the commission shall be paid at default. If the sale is prevented due to the default of Buyer, the commission shall be paid only if and when Seller collects damages from Buyer.

Listing Broker _____   Seller _____

By Listing Agent _____   Seller _____

Broker's Address _____   Broker's Telephone _____

_____   Broker's Fax _____

_____

Date: _____ , 19_____

27. Time Is of the Essence

This standard clause emphasizes the importance of the dates you and seller agree to. It means that a missed deadline by either party is considered a substantial breach of the contract, which can result in the other party being given money damages or being allowed to cancel the contract.

PUT AWAY YOUR STOP WATCH
Despite this provision, the trend in recent legal decisions is to reject cries of "he breached the 'time is of the essence' clause" for a delay of a few hours or days, unless you can show that you have suffered, or will suffer, damages as a result.

28. Disclosures

This clause is included to be sure that you get all disclosure statements legally required or necessary for the property you are buying. While the seller has a legal obligation to make certain disclosures, requesting the disclosures in this clause will remind the sellers of their obligation if you haven't yet received any disclosures.

Each disclosure statement is describe with more detail in Chapter 19.

29. Buyer's Signature

By signing this clause, you agree to make this offer that will become a binding contract if accepted by the seller. All buyers must sign. In addition, if you're married, your spouse must also sign, unless you're purchasing the house with your separate property. If you have a broker have the broker (or agent) sign it too, and put her address, phone number and fax number (if any). Also include the date and time the offer is made (presented to the seller).

30. Seller's Acceptance

If the seller signs, she accepts your offer as it stands. If the sellers are a married couple, they both must sign, even if one spouse claims the house is separate property. A title company won't want to get involved in the complexities of California community property law and will want to see both signatures. ■

Presenting Your Offer and Negotiating

This chapter discusses presenting your offer to the seller and, if necessary, negotiating the price and other terms. If you haven't done so already, read Chapter 16, Putting Your Offer in Writing.

IF YOU'RE LOOKING TO BUY A NEW HOUSE
This chapter focuses on negotiating to purchase an existing house. We discuss negotiating with the developer to purchase a new house in Chapter 7.

A. State Your Intent to Make an Offer

Once you decide to make an offer, your real estate agent usually presents your offer, in person, to the seller's agent (or to the seller directly if the house is a for sale by owner). The seller or her agent will either:

- set up an immediate appointment to receive your offer (this is common in cooler markets), or
- tell you the date and time when multiple offers will be formally accepted. (This happens in hotter markets when the seller expects more than one offer. But be wary: Some sellers try to create the false impression that they are surrounded by a gaggle of eager buyers in an effort to get you to bid high.)

Once an offer has been made, the negotiating begins. The seller rejects, accepts or counteroffers through her agent. If she counters, you can accept it, reject it or have your agent present a counter counteroffer. The negotiations continue, until either a deal or an impasse is reached.

Buyers don't usually go with the agent to present the offer or negotiate. This approach can work well if you have excellent rapport and your agent truly understands your priorities. Unfortunately, you face the danger that an agent who starts out as your messenger ends up making substantive decisions, while you become increasingly isolated. Thus, we believe it's best to insist on being present at all conferences—especially if the seller is present.

Be prepared for the fact that most real estate people believe it's foolish for buyers to be present at negotiations. Some fear that you'll muck up the process; others resent interference with their usual practices. They are a bit like doctors who, years ago, had 110 reasons to bar fathers from the delivery room. But it's your purchase, not the agent's and you can call the shots if you want to.

DON'T REVEAL YOUR OFFER TOO EARLY

If the seller asks questions about the terms of your offer before you meet, it's usually best to politely decline to answer until you can make a formal presentation. This is especially true if your offer is on the low side, or contains a number of contingencies. Once you're in the same room, it's harder for the seller to dismiss your offer out of hand, and you can build rapport and ask for a counteroffer. Also, if you can get the negotiating process started, and the seller likes you, she may be willing to accommodate your needs. An offer revealed prior to the formal presentation may be used by the seller or her agent to try and get you, and others, to bid higher. If the seller persists in negotiating by phone, point out that legally binding offers must be in writing, and insist on meeting.

B. Present Your Offer

Offer conferences and meetings may take place at a real estate office or the seller's home. The mood at the offer conference will be business-like, especially if it's at a real estate office. If you're at the seller's house (especially if it's a for sale by owner), however, it may be more relaxed, complete with coffee and cake.

No matter what the mood, you have two goals, in addi-tion to presenting your offer:

- To fully understand the seller's needs so you can adjust your offer to meet them, without compromising your own objectives.
- To convince the seller that you can afford to buy the house and are a reasonable person to work with.

You want to convey to the seller that you are reasonably knowledgeable about the real estate market—though you don't want to come on like a sharp operator or know-it-all lawyer (especially if you are a lawyer).

Approach the seller in a straightforward, friendly manner. As an opener, say something nice about an aspect of the house that reflects the owner's personal taste, such as the garden or artwork. But don't gush about the house or the neighborhood—you'll only drive up the price. On the other hand, don't criticize the wallpaper, carpets or anything else that reflects the seller's taste. You're more likely to alienate the seller than get her to lower the price—you may even blow the whole deal. The linoleum and kitchen cupboards you call old-fashioned or tacky are part of his life. A seller you offend may find a reason to reject your bid.

Bring a prequalification letter for an amount that shows you can afford the home. It's okay if the amount you are prequalified for is above the amount of your offer. A seller would rather see that you have a cushion—and that your loan application will be approved—than that you can just barely afford the amount you are offering to pay. (See sidebar, What to Bring to the Offer Conference, below.)

Another way to establish your economic bona fides is to casually mention your job, or jobs, such as "One reason we like this house is that it's a convenient commute to both of our jobs—Sidney is a law librarian and works at the county courthouse and I'm a nurse at the hospital, which is only about 20 minutes away."

Let the seller know you can afford the purchase, but don't act like you just won the lottery or came from rich Uncle Charley's funeral. Particularly avoid discussing all the expensive improvements you plan to make. If the seller knows you have an extra $25,000 to put into the house after you buy it, the price is likely to go up.

Even though you have decided on the terms you need, it's not too late to glean some useful information from the seller. You learn nothing by monopolizing the conversation; encourage the seller to talk. If the seller needs to move quickly to close on another house, relocate before school starts or cope with a divorce, you may be able to get a better price if you can close quickly.

If you get information from the seller that surprises you and you want to modify your offer, ask to speak privately with your real estate agent. Sometimes this may mean no more than walking around the block. At other times, you may need to recess for hours or even days, if you want to get legal, tax or other specialized advice.

WHAT TO BRING TO THE OFFER CONFERENCE

You should bring the following materials to an offer conference:

1. A completed offer. (See Chapter 16, Putting Your Offer in Writing.)
2. Proof that you can afford the purchase. In order of effectiveness, they are:
   - a preapproval or prequalification letter from a financial institution, stating that you're eligible for a loan, or a qualification letter from a local loan broker, stating that you qualify for a loan large enough to finance the purchase (see Chapter 2, Section G)
   - a credit report from a credit-reporting agency, or
   - a family financial statement. (See Chapter 2, Section B).
3. A brief letter about yourselves and why you like the house (as long as it's not too gushy).

BACK TO THE FUTURE

C. Pick a Negotiator

Who is your best bet to negotiate? The most skilled negotiator available—someone who is detail-oriented, has a good nose for value, strong communication skills and common sense. This could be you, the agent you're working with or someone else altogether.

 GOOD BOOKS ON NEGOTIATING

Successful Real Estate Investing in the 90s, by Peter Miller (Harper Collins).

Getting to Yes: Negotiating Agreement Without Giving In, by Fisher and Ury (Penguin Press).

1. Should a Real Estate Professional Negotiate for You?

If you have good negotiating skills—perhaps from on-the-job experience—you will likely represent yourself just fine.

If you doubt your own negotiating skills and believe your agent is a good negotiator, however, consider letting him handle the offer presentation and negotiation, unless you're working with a seller's agent—that is, your agent will be paid by, and has a fiduciary duty to, the seller. (See Chapter 5, Working With Real Estate Professionals.) In this case, the potential conflicts of interest are too great to risk. If, however, your agent is a buyer's agent or dual agent you're in better shape.

Regardless of whom the agent legally represents, remember that any agent paid by commission has a direct personal stake—his fee—in your buying the house. To get the deal to go through (to get a commission), he may counsel you to offer too much, or may not risk bargaining with the seller to the lowest possible price. But don't automatically reject your agent as negotiator because of this possible conflict—quite a few agents put personal pride as negotiators and their professional reputation first and do negotiate to the last dollar, even at the risk of losing their commission.

Another—and often better—approach is to hire a knowledgeable real estate broker by the hour to negotiate. As we discuss in Chapter 5, because she is paid by the hour, regardless of whether or not the deal closes, there is no inherent conflict of interest.

One more thing—only real estate agents and attorneys may legally be paid for negotiating on your behalf.

ENGLISH VILLA

AN ALTERNATE STRATEGY: YOU STAY IN THE BACKGROUND

If you have total confidence in your negotiator, consider staying away from the negotiating sessions. An advantage to this is that your negotiator can propose options you don't have to accept, while, at the same time, learn valuable information. For example, if your negotiator offers to pay an extra few thousand dollars in exchange for the seller taking a $10,000 second mortgage and the seller expresses interest, you must still say "yes" or "no" before there's an actual deal. Now that you know that the seller will take a second mortgage, you may decide to ask for an even larger one, or offer to pay less of a price premium in exchange.

SUCCESSFUL NEGOTIATING OFTEN TAKES TIME

Recently, California real estate prices have dropped. Some houses have been on the market for many months—that is, it's a buyer's, not a seller's market. Knowing this, a savvy purchaser will make a low—but not ridiculous—first offer. Assuming the seller counteroffers, the buyer will raise the initial offer slightly. Even if the seller counters again and claims he will not go lower, the buyer will take her time and reluctantly again counter, raising her previous offer only slightly—and certainly not up to the seller's bottom line. Although the buyer risks that her tough negotiating stance will backfire, if she waits patiently she'll eventually get a great price.

---

2. Negotiating Tips

Whomever you designate as your negotiator—usually you, your co-buyer or your agent—should call the tactical shots. Don't argue with or correct your negotiator in the seller's presence. It's fatal to have two people on the same side pulling in different directions. If you think things are veering off track, ask for a private caucus.

Make sure negotiations don't turn into a power struggle or get hung up on unimportant issues. You're much more likely to get the house if discussions are cordial, not hostile. Aggressiveness is at least as likely to turn the seller off as it is to get him to agree to your demands.

Even if you love the house, be ready to break off negotiations if the price and the other terms aren't right. There *will* be other houses.

STARTING OFF ON THE RIGHT FOOT

Don't overlook the basics when you arrange to meet with a seller to negotiate:
- Show up on time.
- Dress reasonably, but conservatively. Downtown business clothes aren't necessary, but the seller wants to see that you're not a flake.
- If you don't own a decent car, borrow one (or accompany your agent, who is guaranteed to have a sober four-door sedan).
- Leave your kids at home.

D. The Seller's Response to Your Offer

At the offer conference, the seller and her agent will read your offer. They normally focus on:

- **Price** [Top of our offer]. If it's in the ballpark of what the seller expected, the negotiation process will likely begin. If it's way out of line, the seller is likely to reject your offer on the spot, unless you indicate a willingness to bargain.
- **Financing** [Clause 1 of our offer]. A surprising number of people who have little hope of lining up financing make offers; the seller will look at your financing information and will reject on the spot if it seems unrealistic.
- **Contingencies** [Clauses 9 and 10 of our offer]. If the seller wants to sell fast, he'll be particularly concerned with any difficult or time-consuming contingency, such as your need to sell an existing house.

Depending on these factors, and whether or not anyone else has made a better offer, the seller's formal response will be to:
- accept your offer on the spot
- reject your offer on the spot
- request more time to consider your offer and respond before it expires
- tell you that other offers will be coming later and that he'll respond after all offers are in
- let you know that someone else has already bid more and ask you if you want to raise your offer, or
- present you with a counteroffer, accepting some of your terms and changing others—this usually happens later, but some sellers make written counteroffers on the spot; just as your offer must be in writing to be legally binding, so, too, must the seller's counteroffer.

Let's now briefly look at each of these possible responses.

 CHUCK AND MING:
BUYING A GOOD HOUSE IN A BAD WAY

Chuck and Ming spot a house they like. Frederick, their agent, arranges with the sellers' agent, Shirley, to present the offer to the sellers, Mike and Gail, at 11 a.m. the next day. Chuck and Ming arrive on time but Frederick is 20 minutes late. Everyone else sits around awkwardly, waiting for him to appear.

Finally, still puffing from running up the walk, Frederick bursts in and immediately slaps Chuck and Ming's offer in front of Mike, Gail and Shirley, barely taking time to say hello. The offer is $15,000 less than Mike and Gail's listed price, but Chuck and Ming love the house and will meet the asking price, if necessary.

Shirley asks Chuck how they like the house. Ming interrupts saying they really love it. Shirley then asks Ming if they've had a chance to look at other homes in the area. Ming says yes, they're exhausted from looking at dozens of others.

Shirley nods at Mike and Gail and they excuse themselves. They're hardly out of the room when Chuck and Ming criticize Frederick for being late; he, in turn, expresses anger at Ming for not keeping her mouth shut and letting a more knowledgeable person do the negotiating.

In the meantime, Shirley, Mike and Gail are pleased; Ming and Chuck have offered a good price, they can obviously afford the purchase and the only contingency is a routine inspection. The offer is so solid, Mike and Gail probably would have accepted it as is, but based on Ming's revelations about how they love the house, Mike and Gail decide to hold out for more.

They counteroffer $13,000 higher than Chuck and Ming's offer. By this time, Chuck and Ming have figured out that they handled the negotiation poorly. Still, they love the house and decide to continue to negotiate. They counteroffer at $6,000 more than their first offer, and Mike and Gail respond with a counter counteroffer of $11,000 more. A deal is finally struck for $9,000 above the first offer.

Ming and Chuck conclude they slightly overpaid. In truth, they overpaid by a lot. Mike had already sold his business and bought another 300 miles away, so he and Gail were anxious to sell. If Chuck and Ming had made a slightly lower initial offer and appeared unwilling to raise it, Mike and Gail would have sold for $20,000 less than they received.

1. The Seller Accepts on the Spot

If the seller says "yes" to your offer, make sure he immediately follows up by putting it in writing. An oral acceptance is not legally enforceable. Also, be sure he says yes to every term of your offer. If he accepts all but one, even something as minor as who pays for the title search, it isn't an acceptance, but a counteroffer which you, in turn, can accept or reject.

The seller can accept by using an Acceptance of Purchase Offer form or by completing the acceptance blank at the bottom of your Contract to Purchase Real Property form.

2. The Seller Rejects on the Spot

If the seller rejects your offer, try to get it in writing. An oral rejection can cause problems if your original offer gives the seller additional time to accept. In theory, the seller could change her mind and accept your offer in writing two days later when you may no longer want the house. If the seller refuses to go to the trouble of putting her rejection in writing, simply withdraw your offer using a written Revocation of Offer to Purchase Real Property form. (See Section G, below.)

Occasionally, a buyer feels he can modify whatever term it is that caused the seller to reject the offer. For example, if a seller says no because your offer includes a contingency to first sell your existing house and you're willing to immediately remove the contingency (because you can get bridge financing from a lender or a loan from a parent), present a second written offer, either on the spot or at a subsequent appointment.

Normally, however, if the seller thinks a deal can be made, she'll counter your offer, not reject it outright. Most outright rejections happen when the seller already has a better offer or thinks the buyer's offer is ridiculously low or otherwise weak.

ARE YOU CONCERNED ABOUT DISCRIMINATION?

What are your rights if the seller refuses your offer and then promptly sells to another buyer at the same or a lower price, or on less favorable terms? If you think the seller's decision not to sell to you was based on your race, ethnic background, religion, sex, sexual orientation, marital status, age, family status or disability, the seller may be violating laws prohibiting discrimination. Contact the California Department of Fair Employment and Housing. (Check the Government Pages of your phone book for the nearest office.)

---

3. The Seller Asks for More Time

A seller may put off making an immediate decision. She may anticipate other offers, want to verify your financial information or be a procrastinator. It's reasonable (although not required) to give the seller one to three days to decide whether to accept, reject or counter your offer. (See Clause 19 of our offer form in Chapter 16.) If the seller wants more time than you have specified in your offer, and you want to oblige, complete an Extension of Offer to Purchase Real Property form. (A tear-out copy is in Appendix 4.)

If you make a take-it-or-leave-it offer to force a quick decision, you won't want to give the seller extra time. This preemptive bid strategy is a good one in a hot (seller's) market, if you bid aggressively on a new listing (maybe even overbid the asking price) in an effort to grab the house fast. In addition, the strategy may be necessary if you're interested in more than one house, and want to force a quick decision on one in order to bid on another if the first seller says no.

EXAMPLE 1: Nan and Philip locate a pleasant house in Los Angeles priced at $350,000. Many buyers are interested in the house due to a recent fall in interest rates and the perception that prices are about to jump. Checking comparable prices, Nan and Philip conclude the house may even be underpriced. To try to preempt other bids, they offer $360,000, and state that their offer must be accepted upon presentation. The seller asks for a 48-hour extension. Nan and Philip, who are determined not to raise their bid, refuse. The seller, fearing to lose the deal, counteroffers for $370,000. Nan and Philip bend slightly and counter counteroffer at $364,000. They get the house.

EXAMPLE 2: This time, Ed and Sara find the same house. They too realize that it may go for more than the asking price. But because they have limited financial resources, they have decided on a different overall house purchase strategy from Nan and Philip. They plan to bid low on several houses, hoping to pick up a bargain from a seller who either needs to sell quickly and doesn't receive other bids, or who has accepted a high bid which subsequently falls through at a time she really needs to close fast. Thus Ed and Sara offer $335,000 on the L.A. home, and leave the offer open for two weeks, knowing it's likely to be accepted only as a last resort. Ed and Sara have no chance of getting the house, unless the deal with Nan and Philip falls apart.

Note: If Ed and Sara change their mind or find another house before their offer expires, they can withdraw their offer in writing at any time before it's accepted.

4.   The Seller Is Waiting for Other Bids

If a seller is expecting other offers, she's unlikely to make a decision until all offers are in, unless she receives one so good she feels she'd better say yes pronto. If you want the house, there's nothing you can do but wait, unless you want to force the matter by making an attractive offer that requires an immediate decision.

Some unscrupulous sellers exaggerate the interest in their house (or even create a fake bid) in an effort to cause a bidding frenzy. Inventing bids is fraud and ground for loss of license when done by a real estate professional, but it's been known to happen.(Both § 10176 of the Business and Professions Code and § 2785(a) of the Department of Real Estate Regulations prohibit this type of fraud.)

5.   The Seller Has Received a Higher Bid

A seller may say that he's already received a higher offer and that you'll need to raise yours if you want to be seriously considered. Ask to see the higher written offer, so you know what you're bidding against, and then ask the seller to give you a written counteroffer. Without the counteroffer, you're in the silly position of bidding against yourself.

The seller is unlikely to show you the competing offer; instead, his agent is likely to point out that you have no right to see a potential contract to which you are not a party. Even so, it doesn't hurt to ask, and by doing so, you may cause an inexperienced seller or salesperson to expose the fact that the other offer isn't written or is weak.

If you're shown another offer contract, don't stop reading when you find out the amount offered. Put yourself in the position of the seller, and check to see if the financing is solid, and whether there are any contingencies that make the offer chancy. If the offer is full of contingencies, or seeking financing that may not come to fruition, the seller may accept your more solid, lower offer.

If the higher offer has real potential, and the seller counters your offer at, or above, the amount of the other offer, consider three things in deciding whether to pay that higher amount:
- how much you can afford
- how much you believe the house is worth, and
- your overall house purchase strategy.

Don't get so caught up in negotiating that you make a decision you'll regret later. It's usually best to avoid bidding wars—some of the best deals are the ones you don't make. If you do bid higher, take time away from the negotiating table to carefully consider each increase. A house you concluded was worth $600,000 on Sunday is unlikely to be worth $700,000 on Tuesday, just because another buyer wants it. Above all, never let an offer conference take on the atmosphere of a poker game, where a bid is quickly offered, countered and then raised. In this type of atmosphere, you are sure to pay too much.

EXAMPLE: Sandy bids $200,000 on a house listed at $223,000 that she believes is fairly priced. When two other people offer $206,000 and $210,000, Sandy makes one final effort for the house. She bids $216,000, with the hope that her fairly good-sized increase will scare off the competition. It does, and she gets the house for $7,000 less than she concluded it was worth. Sandy successfully combined two strategies. She bid low to test the market, and she preempted the competition by raising her initial bid substantially.

6. The Seller Responds With a Counteroffer

Offers, even very attractive ones, are rarely accepted exactly as written. More typically, the seller responds with a written counteroffer accepting some, even possibly most, of the offer terms, but proposes certain changes. If the seller orally states his counteroffer, insist that it be put in writing before you consider or discuss it.

a. Major Provisions of a Typical Counteroffer

Most counteroffers correspond to these provisions of an offer:
- **Price.** Unless your offer meets or exceeds the asking price, the seller may counteroffer, asking for more money. If your initial bid was low, and you decide to increase it (in a counter counteroffer or by accepting the counteroffer):
  - Make the increases small.
  - Try to get something in return for each increase. For example, ask the seller to pay for certain repairs, throw in a major appliance or take back a second mortgage at a favorable interest rate.
  - Be ready to break off negotiations if the price and the terms aren't right.
- **Financing.** If the seller believes your financing is impractical, she'll likely propose a change. Similarly, if you offer to put 10% down, with the seller taking back a second mortgage, and she wants all of her equity in cash, she'll counteroffer.
- **Occupancy.** If your offer doesn't give the seller enough time to move out, she'll lengthen it in her counteroffer.
- **Your selling a current house.** If your offer is contingent on selling a current home, the seller may reject this in a counteroffer if the market is hot and he believes he can easily find another buyer. Or he may counteroffer with a wipe-out clause (see Chapter 18, Section B5) which would let him supersede your offer with another if closing is held up by your unsuccessful attempt to sell. If you agree to a wipe-out clause, the seller must give you a reasonable amount of time to remove the contingency and go ahead with the deal, before he can sell to someone else.

- **Inspections.** A seller's counteroffer for dealing with inspections may suggest a shorter period of time, eliminate one or more of your proposed inspections, or offer the house for sale "as is," meaning he won't pay for any defects the inspections turn up. While it's reasonable for you to complete inspections in a timely manner, it's completely unreasonable (and a red flag indicating likely physical problems) for the seller to limit the type of inspections you can conduct, insist that you purchase "as is," or require that you agree to pay in advance for problems that haven't yet been discovered.

b. Sample Counteroffer

A written counteroffer need not restate the entire offer. It can propose changes and then accept all other terms of the offer. The following counteroffer may be used by either the seller or buyer when only limited changes are proposed in the counteroffer (or counter counteroffer). (A tear-out copy is in Appendix 4.)

A seller can also counteroffer using a detailed offer form, like the one in this book. If he does, study it carefully—no two forms are the same. Be sure that the counteroffer clauses don't affect you differently than your form did. Consider hiring an experienced broker or real estate lawyer to review the paperwork. If one provision of the counteroffer is unacceptable and you no longer want the house, do nothing. A counteroffer not accepted by the deadline simply expires.

> **EXAMPLE:** Leili offers to buy Tony and Jackie's house for $180,000, leaving the offer open for 48 hours. They counteroffer just before the deadline, asking for $210,000 and permission to remove some built-in bookshelves. In addition, they require Leili to drop her contingency to sell her existing house first. Tony and Jackie give Leili 12 hours to accept the counteroffer. Leili, who has found a house she likes better, does nothing and the counteroffer simply expires.
>
> Had Tony and Jackie made the counteroffer immediately after Leili's offer, Leili (assuming she was still set on buying the other house) should revoke her offer in writing to prevent the possibility that Tony and Jackie might recall their counteroffer and accept her original offer before the end of the 48 hours.

COUNTEROFFER [COUNTER COUNTEROFFER]

Date:_____

Time: _____ ☐ a.m. ☐ p.m.

In response to the offer [counteroffer] to purchase real property at (address) _____

_____ ,

dated _____, 19____, _____

_____ , Buyer [Seller] submits the following counteroffer [counter counteroffer]:

_____

_____

_____

_____

All other terms of the offer [counteroffer] remain the same. This counteroffer [counter counteroffer] expires on _____, 19 ____

at (time) _____ ☐ a.m. ☐ p.m. unless Buyer [Seller] delivers a written acceptance to Seller [Buyer] or his/her agent before then.

_____   _____
Signature   Date

_____   _____
Signature   Date

ACCEPTANCE

The undersigned Buyer [Seller]   ☐ accepts   ☐ accepts subject to the attached counteroffer

the foregoing offer and agrees to sell the property on the terms and conditions stated above.

Seller agrees to pay compensation for services as follows:

☐ _____ % of the sales price or ☐ $ _____ to (Listing Broker) _____

_____

☐ _____ % of the sales price or ☐ $ _____ to (Selling Broker) _____

_____

payable on recordation of the deed or other evidence of title. If the sale is prevented due to the default of Seller, the commission shall be paid at default. If the sale

is prevented due to the default of Buyer, the commission shall be paid only if and when Seller collects damages from Buyer.

Buying [Listing] Broker _____

By Buying [Listing] Agent _____

Buyer [Seller] _____

Buyer [Seller] _____

Broker's Address _____

_____

Broker's Telephone _____   Broker's Fax _____

Date: _____ , 19_____

E.   Negotiate by Counteroffers

For many sales, the written offer-acceptance process is completed relatively quickly: The buyer makes an offer, the seller suggests a few changes, the buyer agrees. Sometimes, however, the process drags on, with counteroffers, counter counteroffers and counter counter counteroffers flying back and forth for days, or even weeks. This can work well, if you and the seller narrow your differences with each counteroffer. But don't get so caught up in negotiating that you pay more than the house is worth, or otherwise make a bad deal.

If you participate in a counteroffer dance, make sure:

- all counteroffers are in writing
- you and the seller meet all deadlines
- all counteroffers contain a time limit by which responses be accepted, and
- you and the seller keep clear on what's being offered and what's being accepted. At some point, using short counteroffer forms which don't restate the entire offer will become confusing. Before that happens, use a new Contract to Purchase Real Property form, such as the one in Appendix 4. Retitle it "Counteroffer" ("Counter Counteroffer" or whatever), state the terms you and the seller have agreed on and make appropriate changes.

 CHRISTINA:
I'M GLAD OUR FIRST FEW OFFERS FELL THROUGH

A few months ago, my husband and I got a strong case of househunting fever. After eight years of renting a small apartment in a noisy downtown neighborhood, we were sick of the graduate student lifestyle. Now that we were both busily employed at good jobs, we wanted a larger place with more grass and trees—someplace good to raise the kids we planned to have in a few years. We had saved enough for a down payment on a $200,000 house.

Our first weekend househunting, we fell in love with a beautiful house in a nearby suburb. It had everything we wanted, but, was $30,000 above out maximum price and it needed some major structural work. The sellers were anxious to sell quickly for full price and "as is," because they had already bought a second house.

We made the classic mistake of thinking this house was the only one in the world; we counteroffered for days, trying to think of ways to get the extra money, move quickly and the like.

Our real estate agent, who was anxious for a quick sale, fanned the flames. When this deal fell through, we repeated the same mistake with the next house. A few weeks later, we finally came to our senses and realized there were lots of houses out there. We got a new agent, slowed down our house search, and became more realistic—after, all, we were in no real hurry to move. Once we relaxed, we found a lovely place—much nicer than the first one—for $15,000 less than we expected to pay. Now our advice to others is get out of the fast lane, enjoy the process and you'll almost surely spend less than you assume you will.

F.   An Offer Is Accepted—A Contract Is Formed

A contract is formed when either the buyer or the seller accepts all of the terms of the other's offer or counteroffer in writing within the time allowed. After this happens:

- Make photocopies of the contract; give one to the buyer and one to the seller. If short form counteroffers were used to change a long offer, all contract terms won't be stated in one document. It's best to retype all the accepted terms onto one form.
- The buyer should give the seller's agent a deposit check made out to an escrow or title company in the amount called for in the contract. Usually this is $1,000 or, on more expensive houses, a percentage of the price.
- Keep all paperwork in a safe place.
- Give copies of documents to any real estate agent, attorney or tax advisor who's assisting you.
- Cooperate with the seller to begin escrow proceedings.
- Take steps to begin removing the contingencies—you usually have only a few days to act. At the least, you'll need to arrange inspections and apply for financing if you haven't already done so.

G.   Revoking an Offer or Counteroffer

You may revoke your offer in writing any time before the seller accepts in writing. You needn't state a reason. If you want to revoke an offer (or counter counteroffer), do so immediately. Call the seller or her agent and tell her you're revoking your offer; immediately follow up in writing. The best ways to do this are by fax (follow up by sending the original to the seller or agent), Western Union mailgram (which contains the date and time of sending), hand delivery or overnight mail.

A Revocation of Offer to Purchase Real Property form is in Appendix 4.

H. Making a Backup Offer

If you locate a house you love, but lose out to another bidder, consider making a backup offer. You can do this by checking Clause 18 on our offer form. It gives you the right to say "yes" or "no" in writing within a certain number of hours should the seller inform you in writing that his primary offer has fallen through and he now wants to accept your offer.

Some sellers, confident that the offer they have accepted will go through, won't go to the trouble of accepting backup offers. Others won't bother with them because they know that the buyer's subsequent right to approve means they aren't contracts at all. If a seller won't accept a backup offer but you're interested in the house, stay in touch. If the first offer falls through, you'll be there waiting.

Many cautious sellers are delighted to receive backup offers and accept desirable ones. If a seller accepts more than one, priority is set by the date and time of acceptance. ■

After the Contract Is Signed: Escrow, Contingencies and Title Insurance

Congratulations! Your offer to purchase a house has been accepted. But it's not yet time to buy a new doormat. Many tasks remain before the house is yours—opening an escrow account, removing contingencies, obtaining title insurance and closing escrow—and all are discussed in this chapter.

The time it takes between the contract signing and the close of escrow (real estate speak for your becoming the owner) depends on what remains to be done following the signing. If you have your financing lined up in advance, and the house is in excellent condition, you can expect to own the house in 45 to 60 days. If, however, your offer is contingent upon your selling an existing house, inspection reports disclose lots of physical problems or you need to arrange a complicated financing package, it could take several months, or occasionally even longer.

UNDERSTAND ESCROW BEFORE YOU BEGIN THE PROCESS
Opening and successfully closing escrow involves detailed, picky and often overlapping steps. Before taking any concrete action, read this entire chapter carefully to be sure you understand both the big picture and the small details of the escrow process.

A. Open Escrow

In finalizing the purchase of your house, you and the seller need a neutral third party to:
- hold onto, and then exchange, deeds and money
- pay off existing loans
- record deeds
- prorate the property tax payments, and
- help with other transfer details.

To begin this process, you and the seller "open an escrow account" with a person or organization legally empowered to act as an escrow agent. In many eastern and mid-western states, escrow is commonly handled by lawyers, and is often termed "settlement." Lawyers need not be involved with escrow in California, and usually aren't, unless an unusual problem arises (for example, the seller's title isn't clear), in which case either buyer or seller may wish to consult an attorney.

By custom, escrow is done differently in northern and southern California. The common "dividing line" between northern and southern California escrow approaches is somewhere near the Tehachapi Mountains. Nevertheless, both northern and southern escrow styles routinely appear in the middle of the state, and some northern California escrow agents are beginning to adopt southern California practices.

Northern California. An escrow account is normally opened with a title insurance company (often just called a title company) immediately after the purchase contract is signed. Title companies not only provide the necessary title insurance, but also handle financing arrangements such as collecting your down payment and funds for your lender, paying off the seller's lender, and preparing and recording a deed from the seller to you and a deed of trust for your lender.

Southern California. An escrow account is usually opened by the buyer and seller with an escrow company, which prepares the necessary papers and exchanges the seller's ownership interest for your money after deducting the amount needed to pay off the seller's existing mortgage, past taxes and other liens. Title insurance is obtained from a title insurance company, which isn't usually otherwise involved in the escrow process.

Other Escrow Holders. Although it's unusual, escrow can be legally handled by someone other than a title or escrow company. The buyer or seller's attorney, a real estate broker who has a trust account for supervising escrows or the escrow department of a bank are all legally empowered to do the job.

1. How to Open Escrow

When the seller accepts your offer to purchase the house, you'll normally give your agent a deposit made out to the escrow holder. The deposit is taken to the title or escrow company and an escrow account is opened. Your deposit check will be cashed immediately, so make sure it's good. The deposit will be applied to the purchase price or it will be returned to you if you back out of the deal for a good reason—for example, a contingency can't be met. (See Section B6, below.)

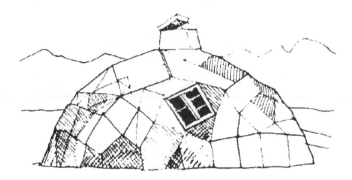

GEODESIC DOME

ESCROW TERMINOLOGY

Here are common real estate terms used during escrow:

Close of Escrow or Closing

The final transfer of ownership of the house to the buyer. It occurs after both the buyer and seller have met all terms of the contract and the deed is recorded. Closing also refers to the time when the transfer will occur, such as, "the closing on my house will happen on January 27 at 10:00 a.m."

Closing Costs

The expenses involved in the closing process. These usually include broker commissions, title insurance, loan fees, lender's appraisal, inspection fees, private mortgage insurance (if required), deed recording and incidental fees charged by the escrow agent and lender. (See Section F, below.)

Closing Statement

A document prepared by the escrow holder containing a complete accounting of all funds, credits and debts involved in the escrow process. Basically this amounts to a statement of the amount of cash the buyer and the buyer's lender have put into escrow, how much the seller has received and how much money was used for other expenses.

Demand or Request for Beneficiary Statement

A letter from the seller's lender to the escrow holder telling how much the escrow holder must send the lender to pay the seller's existing mortgage in full. The lender sends it after being notified by the escrow holder that the seller is selling the house and expects to close escrow by a certain date. If the time between opening and closing escrow is reasonably short, the seller wants to receive the demand fast in order to include the calculations in the closing. If the time between opening and closing will take some time, however, he won't rush the demand. A demand is typically good for only 30 days; if it comes too soon, it will expire before escrow closes and the seller will have to request a second one.

Final Title Report or Final

Just before the close of escrow, the title company rechecks the condition of the title established in the preliminary title report. If it's the same (it usually is), the preliminary title report becomes the final report, and title insurance policies are issued.

Funding the Loan

After your lender issues a loan commitment letter (see Chapter 13, Obtaining a Mortgage), the lender must actually fund the loan—that is, deliver the money to the escrow holder. California law requires that checks and drafts be collected prior to disbursement. This means that to close escrow, funds must be deposited one or more days prior to the close of escrow, except for cash and funds deposited by electronic transfer. To avoid problems and delays, make sure you're in continuous communication with your lender.

Good Faith Estimate or Reg. Z Disclosure

A federal law requiring the lender to disclose to you all the material terms of the loan (such as negative amortization, the annual percentage rate and caps) you are applying for.

Legal Description or Legal

The description of the parcel of land being sold which appears on the deed to the property. It has nothing to do with the buildings, but rather the land itself. The legal may specify Lot and Block numbers or metes and bounds (a complicated exercise in map-reading), none of which should concern you. (If you want to know more about legally describing California real property, see *The Deeds Book,* by Mary Randolph (Nolo Press).)

Loan Commitment

A written statement from a lender promising to lend you a certain sum of money on certain terms.

Opening Escrow

Escrow is opened when you and the seller select an escrow agent to hold onto and transfer documents and money during the house purchase process.

Preliminary, Prelim or Pre

The preliminary title report issued by a title company soon after escrow opens. It shows current ownership information on the property (including any liens or encumbrances on the property). If any problems are found, the seller can take steps to resolve them before escrow closes. The title insurance policy issued at the close of escrow is usually based on this report.

Taking Title

Describes the transfer of ownership from seller to buyer. For example, "The buyer takes title [gets his name on the deed] next Tuesday."

CONSIDER GETTING A POWER OF ATTORNEY
If you or a co-buyer will be traveling, consider filling out a power of attorney so the nontraveling buyer can sign the final papers. Ask your escrow company to draft the power of attorney.

2. How to Find an Escrow Holder

In Clause 3 of our offer contract, you enter the name and address of the escrow holder you choose. In some situations, the seller may disagree. If so, she will list her choice in the counteroffer. As the basic task to be accomplished and prices charged are similar, this should not be an issue to hold up the acceptance of an offer; unless you feel very strongly about using "your" escrow agent or not using the seller's, give in.

How do you know which title company or escrow company to enter on the offer form? As with finding any service provider, it's best to get a recommendation from someone you trust. If you are working with an agent, she'll almost surely recommend a company to handle the escrow. If your agent will monitor the escrow process, it often makes sense to go with her suggestion.

If you are considering several recommended firms, you may be inclined to call around and compare prices. You may save a few dollars, but prices tend to be pretty similar. Because of the small potential savings involved, it normally makes more sense to concentrate on finding a company that offers superior service, especially if you're handling the purchase without professional help. If you are, check to be sure that the escrow company you choose will be supportive.

3. How to Work With the Escrow Holder

What happens after escrow opens depends to a considerable extent on your escrow agent, whether you're in northern or southern California and your contract with the seller. If the contract contains contingencies, the escrow holder may do very little until you and the seller remove them, although many escrow holders in southern California routinely confer with agents, or with sellers and buyers without agents, to make sure steps are being taken to remove contingencies. Southern California escrow holders also frequently try to help resolve any title disputes. (See Section D, below.) Even if your escrow holder is less involved, be sure he gives you a list of what you need to provide, and when you need to do it.

Your salesperson should help to see that the escrow process goes smoothly. If neither you nor the seller is working with a salesperson, however, you'll need to handle the details yourselves. Fortunately, it's not difficult. Make an initial appointment with the escrow agent. Bring the timeline outlined in Chapter 13, Obtaining a Mortgage, with you and use it as your guide to ask questions. Check in regularly—about once a week—to be sure you're doing what's expected and that the process is on track.

If a dispute arises between you and the seller during escrow, don't look to the escrow holder to resolve it—or to transfer the money and deed. The escrow holder is a neutral party. You'll have to solve the problem (see Chapter 21, If Something Goes Wrong During Escrow); until then, the escrow holder sits still. If the dispute drags on long enough, the escrow holder may get tired of being stuck in the middle and may initiate a lawsuit (called an "interpleader") to have the court resolve the dispute and direct the distribution of the deposited money.

4. Ordering Title Insurance

Ordering title insurance from a title insurance company (usually the same company handling the escrow in northern California) is the buyer's responsibility. The title company issues a preliminary title report, and then just before closing, a final title report and two title insurance policies. (Title insurance is discussed in Section D, below.)

5. The Cost of Escrow

Closing costs are typically about 2%-5% of the purchase price, with the lion's share made up of points and other loan fees. Generally, escrow costs, which are considered to be part of closing costs, are under 1% of the purchase price. (In southern California, the costs are divided between the escrow company and a title insurance company. See Section F for a complete list of escrow and closing costs.) Included in the escrow costs are the preliminary and final title reports, recording of the deed, notarization, the title company's fees, the escrow company's fees (if necessary) and two title insurance policies. One policy is for the buyer (CLTA policy) and one is for the lender (ALTA policy). (See Section D for more on title insurance.)

No law specifies who pays escrow costs; you and the seller negotiate as part of the forming of the contract. For our discussion on who *customarily* pays which fee, see Chapter 16, Putting Your Offer in Writing.

B. Remove Contingencies

If your contract contains contingencies, you must remove them in writing and let the escrow holder know they've been removed before the purchase becomes final. Removing the most common contingencies, and extending the time for doing so, are discussed below.

1.   Inspection Contingencies

Most house purchase contracts give the buyer the right to have the house inspected by specified inspectors, and approve the results of their reports, before going through with the sale. (See, for example, Clause 9 of our Contract to Purchase Real Property form in Chapter 16.) To do this, you normally hire professional inspectors. Give them a copy of the seller's Real Estate Transfer Disclosure Statement and copies of any other inspection reports and disclosures the seller provides you. The seller must let the inspectors have access to the house, although you may need authorization from a homeowner's association for the contractor to inspect common areas of a condominium. We suggest that you accompany the inspectors on their rounds. Chapter 19 discusses the seller's legally required disclosures and the house inspection system in detail.

Inspections often find problems. For example, the house may have termite or fungus damage, need new wiring or plumbing, or require roof or foundation repairs. You have various options to deal with such problems:

- If your offer is contingent upon your approving inspection reports, and a report indicates serious problems, you can back out of the deal. (You can, of course, also back out of the deal even before this point, if you are dissatisfied with the seller's disclosures. See Chapter 19, Section B.)
- If the problem was disclosed before you made your offer, however, and you nevertheless offered to purchase the house "as is" (problems and all), you can't legally claim that it must be repaired at the seller's expense before you'll buy.

If a problem was never disclosed, and didn't become evident until after the close of escrow, you face a more complicated situation and possibly a legal battle. (See Chapter 21, Section E.)

Assuming the house needs repairs and your offer wasn't "as is," your first question is do you still want the house if it's repaired? If the problem is extremely serious (the house is in a hazardous slide zone or near an earthquake fault), you may say, hell no, even if the foundation is strengthened. But assuming you still want the house, you and the seller must negotiate over who pays for what. This can be difficult.

 MITCHELL: HOW I USED AN ESCROW CREDIT TO REDUCE MY DOWN PAYMENT

Here's how I negotiated with the seller, who credited me with a fifth of my down payment!

I was going to offer $362,000 for a two-bedroom house on the east side of the San Francisco Bay, but changed my mind after reading an inspection report commissioned by another buyer. It identified leaks in an old roof and pest problems in the foundation. I offered $359,000 and asked for a $5,000 credit for roof work and a $12,000 credit for pest work. We negotiated and the seller agreed to install a new roof, and give me $3,000 toward closing costs and $6,000 for pest work.

The pest problem was old and not getting worse, however, so the repair work wasn't necessary (my lender agreed). Besides, the seller had just had the house painted beautifully, and had the pest work been done, I would have had a problem matching the new paint. In any event, because the work wasn't required, I got to use $9,000 to reduce my out-of-pocket costs for closing and the down payment.

a.   Negotiating the Cost of Repairs

By the time an offer has been accepted and inspections have been done, neither you nor the seller wants to spend more money. At the same time, both of you have already invested considerable time and energy in the transaction and don't want to walk away and start over. If either of you needs the sale to go through to meet other commitments, time pressure (and often, the other's leverage) can cause great stress and resultant short tempers.

From your point of view, you want the seller to pay. After all, you made your offer based on the assumption that the house was sound. Often the seller will agree and pay for most, or even all, problems. This is especially true in the 1990s, as a cooling off of the market has resulted in sellers tending to be more reasonable. But fairly often the seller will ask you to share the costs and threaten to call off the deal if you don't.

In the final analysis, who pays what usually comes down to who is perceived to have more negotiating clout. If the seller thinks she's agreed to sell at too low a price, she'll probably refuse to pay for all or most repairs, believing that if the deal falls through, she can put the house back on the market at a higher price. If you think she is right, you'd be smart to share modest repair costs. If, however, you believe you've offered top dollar for the house and don't think it's worth a penny more, you'll want to insist that the seller pay most or all of the repairs and refuse to finalize the deal if she won't.

b.   Paying for Repairs

A seller willing to reduce the purchase price to allow for the cost of repairs normally does so through an "escrow credit." This means the seller agrees to leave money in escrow from the sale proceeds to cover the amount of the repairs. The exact amount the repairs will cost is normally agreed to by all parties based on contractor's bids. You want to be sure that the cost reflects all needed work using quality labor and materials.

If expensive repairs are needed, the lender often requires that work be done before escrow closes. Assuming the seller has agreed to cover the cost, a portion of the money placed in escrow can be paid to a contractor before the close of escrow, or held by the escrow holder after the sale closes, pending the contractor completing the work. But, if you've agreed to pay for a portion of the repairs, you must come up with the money in addition to the down payment. If this is difficult to do, explore the possibility of having the seller mark up the price of the house by the amount of the repairs. This still results in your paying for the repairs through the higher price, but if the mortgage lender will go along, and if the appraisal value of the house justifies the higher price, you can now borrow 80%-90% of the amount needed. The seller who gets the artificially high price uses the extra money to pay for the repairs as part of the escrow process.

In some situations, especially where repairs aren't major, a lender will let escrow close without requiring the repairs to be made. In this situation, if the seller has agreed to pay a credit

into escrow for the work, the buyer is free to use this money for other purposes, such as contributing to the down payment.

EXAMPLE: Mary agrees to sell her house to Albin for $281,000, after originally asking $290,000. Mary tells Albin that the house is old and may need some repairs, but that she's considered this by accepting $9,000 below her asking price. Nevertheless, Albin's offer is contingent upon his approval of a pest control and general contractor's inspection. The inspections turn up $30,000 worth of beetle damage and drainage problems. Albin refuses to go through with the sale unless Mary credits him $30,000 in escrow for the repairs. She refuses, claiming her price reflected the problems. They negotiate and agree to share the costs, with Mary paying $24,000 and Albin $6,000. The compromise reflects the fact that Albin was ready to walk away from the deal if Mary didn't pay most of the cost. Mary, on the other hand, needed to move and didn't have time to find another buyer in a slow sales market.

A problem remains, however. Albin doesn't have $6,000 to pay his share. This problem is solved when his lender agrees to let the price of the house be raised to $287,000, with Mary now responsible to pay for all repairs. The lender is willing to do this based on its appraisal, which concludes that once the $30,000 of repairs are made, $290,000 reflects a fair market value.

If the lender doesn't require that work be done, and you have enough cash to pay for the repairs yourself, consider asking the seller to reduce the asking price instead of giving you a credit in escrow. This saves you money because escrow and title fees, as well as annual property taxes, are based on the purchase price. Note that the real estate agents involved might not be too pleased because their commissions are also based on purchase price.

c.   Removing Inspection Contingencies

As you satisfy or waive an inspection contingency, you must remove it in writing. Section 4, below, shows how.

 CAROLYN:
CONTINGENCY REPORTS NEED TO BE SPECIFIC
My offer, with an inspection contingency, was accepted. I gave a $1,000 deposit and hired a licensed contractor to do an

---

EXTENDING TIME TO MEET CONTINGENCIES

The material set out below is hereby made a part of the contract dated _____,19 ____ between (Buyer) _____

_____

and (Seller) _____

to purchase real property located at _____

_____ .

The final date for Buyer's removal of all contingencies set out in Clause _____ of the contract, is hereby extended until (month and day) _____

19_____ at (time) _____ ☐ a.m. ☐ p.m.

Signature of Buyer _____   Date _____

Signature of Buyer _____   Date _____

Signature of Seller _____   Date _____

Signature of Seller _____   Date _____

---

inspection. His report found several general problems, and I backed out of the deal. The sellers refused to return my deposit, saying the inspector I hired didn't know what he was talking about. Even though my deposit was still in escrow, the sellers subsequently managed to sell the house by going through a different escrow holder. In the meantime, my money is still in escrow, and I am in the process of going to Small Claims Court to get it back.

One lesson I learned from this is that in the future, if I ever again have to rely on an inspection report to terminate a contingent offer, that report must be very specific as to the problems. It's much easier for a seller to dispute a report which sets out general conclusions.

2. Financing Contingencies

In Clause 1 of our contract, the buyer makes any offer to buy contingent on arranging for satisfactory financing. To remove (release) this contingency you should provide the seller with written evidence that you have obtained financing sufficient to purchase the house, and with a contingency release form. (See Section 4, below.) Evidence of financing is usually a loan commitment letter from a lender or a bank confirmation if you arrange private financing. If you're assuming the seller's mortgage, order the assumption documents from the lender to start the process of taking over the loan.

3. Extending Time to Meet a Contingency

Buyers frequently need extra time to satisfy a contract contingency. Without the extra time, the contract ends (that is, the deal falls through) unless you and the seller agree to extend it. If the seller wants out, he won't extend the time. More commonly, however, the seller wants the deal to go through, but needs reassurance that you're still serious about buying the house. He may demand that you increase your deposit in exchange for granting you an extension. The amounts vary, but to extend a $300,000 offer for a few weeks, $1,000 or so is reasonable.

Any agreement to extend the time to meet a contingency (or to change any other term of the contract) must be in writing and signed. A sample is above; a blank copy is in Appendix 4.

CONTINGENCY RELEASE

(Buyer) _____

of the property at (address) _____

_____ ,

hereby removes the following contingency(ies) from the purchase contract dated _____ , 19_____ :

_____

_____

_____

_____

_____

If this release is based on accepting any inspection report, a copy of the report, signed by Buyer, is attached, and Buyer releases Seller from liability for any

physical defects disclosed by the attached report.

Signature of Buyer _____   Date _____

Signature of Buyer _____   Date _____

Signature of Seller _____   Date _____

Signature of Seller _____   Date _____

EXAMPLE: Julie agrees to buy Shawn's house for $300,000, contingent upon her securing an adjustable rate mortgage at 6% or lower for 80% of the purchase price and selling her own house within 90 days. Julie arranges the financing easily, but is having trouble selling her house. Shawn feels Julie's asking too much for her house. He's also considering putting his house back on the market for $310,000 if Julie doesn't meet the 90-day closing deadline. Julie really wants Shawn's house and knows she's in danger of losing it. She offers him $3,000 cash and agrees to lower her listing price by $15,000 if Shawn will extend her time to purchase (to let her sell her existing house) for another 60 days. Shawn agrees.

4. Releasing Contingencies

As you satisfy or abandon (waive) a contingency, you must remove (or release) it in writing. Don't wait until all contingencies are met to do this. Remove each one as it is satisfied or abandoned. You remove a contingency by executing a contingency release form such as the one above. (A tear-out copy is in Appendix 4.) Give the original to the seller and keep a copy for yourself.

If the release is based on an inspection report, identify the report in the release and attach a copy. Also, date and sign the inspection report and write "Approved as read" on it.

If the seller has agreed to credit you for the cost of any repairs, add the following to the release, after the word "report":

"providing that by _____ __.m. on _____ , 19___, Seller agrees in writing to extend to Buyer an escrow credit in the amount of $_____ against the purchase price to cover the cost of needed repair and rehabilitation work to be paid by Buyer."

SELLER'S DEMAND FOR REMOVAL OF CONTINGENCIES

Under the terms of the contract dated _____, 19___, between (Buyer) _____

_____ and (Seller)

_____ for the purchase of the real property at (address)

_____ ,

Seller hereby demands that Buyer remove the following contingency specified in Clause _____ of the contract:

_____

_____

_____

within ☐ ninety-six (96) hours from receipt of this demand if personally delivered.

☐ five (5) days from mailing this demand if mailed by certified mail.

If Buyer does not remove this contingency within the time specified, the contract shall become void. Seller shall promptly return Buyer's deposit upon Buyer's execution of a release, releasing Buyer and Seller from all obligations under the contract.

Signature of Seller _____ Date _____

Signature of Seller _____ Date _____

Personally delivered on: _____ , 19_____   Mailed by certified mail on: _____ , 19_____

---

5. Wipe-Outs: Demanding the Removal of Contingencies

Some contracts let the seller demand in writing that you remove all contingencies within a certain time (usually between 72 hours to one week). If you can't, the seller can give you written notice that he's ending your contract (wiping it out) and going ahead with a backup offer. Below is an example of the type of form the seller will use. He can send it to you only if a wipe-out clause was included in the original contract. Wipe-out clauses are most common when an offer is contingent upon your selling an existing house or arranging for financing that the seller believes may not come through.

6. When You Can't Fulfill a Contingency

If, after trying in good faith, you or the seller can't meet a contingency, the deal is over. The most common reasons sales fall through are:

- An inspection turns up expensive physical problems and you decide you no longer want the house, or you and the seller can't agree who will pay.
- You're unable to sell your existing house within the time provided.
- You can't secure adequate financing within the time provided.

You and the seller should sign a release canceling the contract and authorizing the return of your deposit. The seller has no right to keep your deposit if the deal falls through for failure to meet a contingency spelled out in the contract. If the seller refuses, or you refuse, to sign the release within 30 days following a written demand, the person who refuses to sign may be liable to the other for attorney's fees and damages of three times the amount deposited in escrow, no more than $1,000 and no less than $100 (Civil Code § 1057.3).

If an inspection turns up negligible problems and you refuse to go ahead with the purchase (or you refuse to proceed for another non-legitimate reason), the seller can keep your

---

RELEASE OF REAL ESTATE PURCHASE CONTRACT

(Buyer) _____

and (Seller) _____

hereby mutually release each other from any and all claims with respect to the real estate purchase contract dated _____, 19 ____

for the property located at: _____

_____

_____

It is the intent of this release to declare all rights and obligations arising out of the real estate purchase contract null and void.

☐ Buyer has received his/her deposit.

☐ Seller has directed the escrow holder to return Buyer's deposit.

Signature of Buyer _____   Date _____

Signature of Buyer _____   Date _____

Signature of Seller _____   Date _____

Signature of Seller _____   Date _____

---

deposit. A seller rarely does keep an entire deposit, however, because he often can't complete a subsequent sale until the escrow with you terminates; this normally can't happen until your deposit is released. Also, state law generally limits the amount sellers can keep if you default. (See Chapter 16, Clause 22, for our discussion of liquidated damages.)

Even if a buyer withdraws for a non-legitimate reason, it's common for the buyer and seller to compromise, with the seller keeping part of the deposit and some of it being returned to the buyer.

Below is a release form; a tear-out copy is included in Appendix 4.

C. Obtain Hazard Insurance

Before finalizing your loan, your lender will require that you purchase hazard insurance to pay the lender in the event your house is damaged or destroyed by fire, smoke, wind, hail, riot or vandalism or another similar act. Don't balk at the insur-

ance. You're going to want what's required and probably more. Virtually all homeowners buy comprehensive homeowner's insurance, not just the minimum required by the lender. In addition to covering your house, homeowner's insurance protects other structures on the property (such as a pool or in-law unit) and your personal property, usually for 50% of the liability limit on your house, unless you pay extra. A few valuable items, such as art, collectibles, and antiques are covered to a specific (low) amount; if you own more, you'll have to itemize them and pay extra.

Your policy will also cover you for some types of personal liability—if the letter carrier trips over your kid's skateboard, your policy will pay for his medical expenses and other losses. In addition, if you injure someone off your property, you will likely be covered if the injury doesn't involve a motor vehicle.

How much insurance do you need? You probably don't need to cover the full value of your property; at least 40% (and often more) of the value is the land itself, which will likely still be there even if your house is destroyed. The coverage most people select is "guaranteed replacement." If the house is insured for 100% of the cost to repair or replace, guaranteed replacement means the insurance company will repair or replace it for the full amount.

Fewer and fewer insurance companies write policies for "100% guaranteed replacement," however, because this policy replaces your house at full value even if the value as stated in the policy is less than the house's actual value, which it is apt to be after a few years. Instead, most policies insure for 125%, twice the amount, or somewhere in between of the dwelling's value stated in the policy. At the same time, your lender cannot require hazard insurance coverage for more than the replacement cost of the house.

If you're in a high-risk fire area, make sure your policy covers foundation replacement. As many fire victims have discovered, repairing the foundation is an expensive proposition. If you conduct business out of your home, you probably need a rider to cover your business equipment—computer, fax machine, cellular phone and the like.

In addition, you may want an earthquake rider on your policy, which costs a few hundred dollars more than the basic policy. Houses near active faults or made of brick may be more expensive to insure. The problem with earthquake insurance is the high deductible—typically 10% to 15% of the policy amount. That means if you have a $200,000 policy, you won't get any benefits unless the damage is more than $20,000 (with a 10% deductible) or $30,000 (with a 15% deductible).

Another rider to consider for those possibly affected is flood coverage. For homes located in flood areas, the extra coverage can cost up to $300 per year and require a $500 deductible. Lenders require flood insurance for property in designated flood hazard areas. (See Chapter 19, Section C, for a discussion of seller disclosures regarding flood and seismic hazards. Also, see Appendix 1 for information on the areas of California susceptible to earthquakes and floods.)

Shop around for insurance. Homeowner's insurance rates can vary up to 30% from company to company. Another way to save money is to opt for a larger than usual deductible. By increasing your deductible to $250 (or more), you may save about 10% on your premiums. Also, ask your insurance agent what discounts are available for new or remodeled houses, houses with a smoke detector or security system or near a fire hydrant.

Price isn't the only factor to consider when choosing insurance. Some companies may have a better reputation than others for processing claims fairly and quickly. If you live near an area where there was a severe fire, earthquake or flood, ask community organizations which insurers were particularly responsive to consumers (and which ones to avoid).

Once your arrange your insurance, have your insurance agent deliver your policy to the escrow holder before closing. Your lender will not approve your loan until your insurance takes effect. Many lenders will want you to prepay the first year of hazard insurance by the closing; ask if you can pay semi-annually, quarterly or monthly, if your budget is tight.

If you are buying a condominium, you usually don't buy your own policy, but get added to the one for your building. Your lender will require that the association's policy adequately covers your unit and the common areas. If it doesn't, you may have to meet with the condo association *before* your deal closes and convince the association to increase its coverage. You'll probably need the seller's help.

If the association's policy covers only the common areas, then you will need your own, separate, policy.

INSURANCE INFORMATION

For general information on homeowner's insurance or to file a complaint about an insurance company, contact the Department of Insurance Consumer Hotline, 3450 Wilshire Blvd., Los Angeles, CA, 90010. (800) 927-4357.

DO YOU NEED LIFE INSURANCE?

Some insurance companies will try to sell you life insurance or credit insurance so your heirs can pay off the mortgage if you die. Unless your survivors could not afford the monthly payments without you, don't bother. Even then, look for a policy which lets your survivors use the money as they wish, not just to pay off the mortgage. For this purpose, a term policy covering the period for which survivors (often small children) are vulnerable to losing the house if you die is far cheaper than a whole life policy, and just as good.

FINDING EARTHQUAKE INSURANCE CAN BE RISKY

Whenever an insurance company issues a homeowner's insurance policy in California, it must offer earthquake insurance. The offered policy must cover loss or damage to the dwelling and its contents and living expenses for the occupants if the house is temporarily uninhabitable. (Insurance Code § 10083). As a result of several earthquakes in California, most notably the Northridge earthquake of 1994, insurance companies have been seeking ways to circumvent their legal requirement to offer earthquake insurance. Many homebuyers have been unable to close escrow because they could not purchase property insurance—not because of the property insurance, but because of the fact that the carrier writing the property insurance would then have to offer earthquake insurance. In early 1996, the Legislature amended the Insurance Code to enable insurers to offer applicants a "mini" earthquake policy on the dwelling structure and personal property. These mini-earthquake policies are generally very expensive, have limited coverage, and contain large deductibles. In many cases, even the mini-policies are difficult to find. The end result is the extraordinary availability of earthquake insurance. To protect yourself when buying a house, we recommend you include a contingency in your offer contract that makes your house purchase dependent upon your securing adequate hazard insurance. (See Chapter 16, Section C10, Other Contingencies.)

---

insurer about a "binder" policy which will give you a refund when you resell.

Financial institutions require title insurance whenever they finance a house sale. If you pay all cash or borrow from Uncle Stanley, or if the seller takes back a second, you (or you and Uncle Stanley or you and the seller) must decide whether to buy title insurance. We recommend it, even if you search the title yourself at the County Recorder's Office and believe title is clear. In the future, you don't want any unpleasant surprises.

Financial institutions require a California Land Title Association (CLTA) policy and an American Land Title Association (ALTA) policy. The CLTA policy covers items in the public record, such as mortgage liens, trust deed liens or judgment liens. The ALTA policy is more extensive, insuring against claims found both in the public record and by physically inspecting the house, such as unrecorded easements, boundary disputes and physical encroachments.

The policies also differ regarding how much they cover and who they benefit. The CLTA policy insures to the amount of the purchase price and benefits you. The ALTA policy insures to the amount of the loan and benefits the lender. If you'll occupy the house, the CLTA policy you receive will include the same extended coverage the lender gets on the ALTA policy. If you won't be occupying the house, you can buy the extended coverage for about 30% above the policy cost.

As soon as you and the seller sign the house purchase contract, you should order a preliminary title report (also called a prelim or pre) on the property. Clause 10 of our offer makes your approval of a preliminary title report a contin-

D. Obtain Title Report and Title Insurance

Title insurance secures both you and your lender against unknown clouds on the legal title to the property. The title insurance company insures against the possibility of undisclosed legal challenges or liens against the property, such as an unrecorded deed, a forged deed or an unrecorded easement—the right of someone else to use your property for a specific purpose (for example, the right the previous owner granted your neighbor to share your extra-wide driveway). If you think you might sell the house within the next two years, ask your title

CALIFORNIA CONDO

gency. (In northern California, the escrow holder—a title insurance company—will often order the policy itself.) This report is a statement summarizing the current condition of the title to the property, including liens, encumbrances, covenants, conditions and restrictions (CC&Rs) and easements. You want the prelim early in escrow so that you, the seller and lender have time to address any problems that turn up.

The most common problems require the seller to pay off liens from the sale proceeds. These problems threaten your deal with the seller only if the seller disputes the lien and refuses to instruct the escrow holder to pay the lienholder. Other problems include a newly discovered easement, lawsuits disputing the boundary line or filed against the seller, an unknown heir (if the previous owner recently died) or an unexpected owner (such as a previous spouse). If any of these situations come up, the seller will likely need the help of a lawyer. (See Chapter 21, Section H.)

If problems arise with the title that the seller cannot quickly resolve, you can:

* refuse to go through with the sale
* give the seller an extension of time (if you think the extra time will help), or
* buy the house with less than perfect title. Deciding whether or not to do this is beyond the scope of this book; consult an experienced real estate lawyer.

If the prelim showed no problems or all problems have been remedied (or you're agreeing to take less than perfect title), when escrow is ready to close the title insurance company checks the public records for any changes since the prelim was issued. If all is the same (as is the usual case), the prelim becomes the final title report. Any changes are reported in a supplemental title report. You and your lender must decide whether to close or call the deal off under the contract provision (Clause 14 in our form) requiring the seller to provide clear title.

E. Conduct Final Physical Inspection of Property

A few days before escrow closes, re-inspect the property to make sure everything is in order. (Clause 15 of our contract gives you the right to inspect the property three days prior to the close of escrow.) You'll want to make sure:

* No damage has occurred to the house since you agreed to buy it.
* The fixtures and personal property the seller agreed to sell you are still in the house.
* All work to be completed is done to your satisfaction (this is especially important with new houses).
* The house is empty—that is, the seller (or tenant) has moved (unless your agreement lets him stay longer).

If you discover a problem during this final inspection, you can:

* Insist that the closing be delayed until the seller fixes the problem.
* Insist that the seller credit you in escrow with a sum of money sufficient so you can remedy the problem—this means you pay that much less for the house.
* Conclude that the problem isn't significant and close anyway.

If you're at a real deadlock, consider mediation, as our contract (Clause 23), and many standard real estate contracts, require.

If you're buying a new house, be sure to re-read Chapter 7, on dealing with final inspections, construction delays and other problems.

WHAT ARE LIENS?

A lien is a claim for money. When properly recorded against the property, the lien makes the property security for payment. Other common liens are for unpaid taxes and debts owed to contractors who worked on the property but were never paid (called a mechanic's lien).

COUNTY PROPERTY TAX EXEMPTION

When real estate is sold in California, the county assesses the value of the property and imposes property taxes accordingly. This will be done shortly after you close on the sale. Be sure to take a careful look at the assessment statement. If you will occupy the property you are buying, in most counties each year you are entitled to a homeowner's property tax exemption of up to $7,000 on the assessed value of the property. If you move in after March 1, you are entitled to 80% of the full amount for the first year. If the assessment statement does not include the exemption, call your county tax assessor's office and find out how to file for it.

<table>
<tr><td>

TIPS ON CHOOSING A CLOSING DATE

Clause 3 of our Contract to Purchase Real Property form (Chapter 16) allows you to specify the date for closing escrow. You won't be able to set a firm closing date until all contingencies are removed, and you'll need to negotiate the date with the seller depending on your individual needs—for example, if you want the closing date to coincide with the end of your lease. If you have a choice, here's some money-saving advice on choosing a closing date:

• The later in the month your closing date, the less prorated interest you'll owe in closing costs. If you close on the second of June, you'll need to prepay interest from June 2nd through the end of the month. If you close on June 28, you'll only need to prepay interest for a few days.

• Don't close escrow on a Monday because you may end up paying extra interest. Lenders must fund a loan, and start charging the buyer interest, the day before escrow closes. Closing on a Monday requires the lender to fund the loan on the previous Friday; this means you end up paying interest over the weekend, before you even own the property.

</td></tr>
</table>

F. Closing Escrow

Until all contingencies in the buyer's offer are removed, no firm closing date can be set. Thus, during the early and middle stages of an escrow, the closing date is projected, not firm.

Escrow cannot close until the escrow holder records a deed naming you the new owner and issues checks to the seller and all others entitled to be paid from the proceeds (such as the seller's lender and any lienholders). If rehabilitation work must be done to repair damage or substandard conditions discovered in an inspection report, money may be held by the escrow holder after the sale closes to pay the contractor.

The paperwork necessary for closing escrow should be completed a minimum of four working days before the expected closing date. You and the seller—not necessarily together—must go to the escrow holder's office to review and

sign the papers. The four day gap allows for delays in the transmittal of the loan documents between the lender(s) and the escrow holder.

The forms you'll be required to sign may include:

• Final escrow instructions. In northern California, the escrow holder prepares two slightly different sets of instructions—one for the seller and one for the buyer —so read them carefully to be sure that you and the seller are in agreement; in southern California, the buyer and seller sign identical escrow instructions.

• Copy of the preliminary title report.

• Deed of trust (and other forms) from the lender.

• Copies of structural pest control and other inspection reports.

• FIRPTA (Foreign Investment in Real Property Tax Act) statement (discussed in Clause 12 of our offer form).

• Fund disbursement (or loan assumption) documents provided by the lender.

• Any rental agreement between you and the seller if the seller will live in the house for a while after the close.

• Settlement statement listing all costs, prepared by the escrow holder.

• Statements authorizing an impound account.

• A perjury statement where you attest to the truth of the information you provided.

• Statement showing your hazard insurance coverage.

After you've completed all your inspections and both you and the seller have signed all the closing papers, you can either bring in your cashier's check or have money wired from your bank for the down payment and closing costs. Don't be in a hurry to deposit your check, or wire your money. Once your money is in escrow, you're no longer earning interest on it. More importantly, if something goes wrong, it will be hard to get your money back.

If you deposit your money by check, it must actually be available by the closing date. Especially if you will use a non-local check, ask the escrow holder to tell you how many days in advance of closing your check must be submitted. Using a cashier's check will be cheaper than arranging in advance to have the money transferred from your bank to the escrow holder's bank by wire on the day of closing. Banks usually charge $5-$10 for a cashier's check and up to $35 to wire money.

Chapter 21 covers what happens if there are delays or problems during escrow.

CLOSING COSTS AND LOAN FEES

Closing costs and loan fees usually add up to 2% to 5% to your mortgage. Some fees are paid when you take out the loan, or at the same time you arrange inspection reports, but most are paid the day you close escrow. Not all lenders and escrow holders require all the fees (some are waived as part of special offers.) When escrow closes, you'll receive a statement with an itemized list of the closing costs.

Typical closing costs and loan fees are:

Appraisal fees

Charged by an appraiser hired by the lender to appraise the property to be sure it's worth what you've agreed to pay. Fees usually run between $275 and $350 for a regular-sized single family home, and somewhat more for a very large, or multiple-unit building. (See Chapter 13 for more on appraisals.)

Application fee

Loan application fees (typically $450-$600) cover the lender's cost of processing your loan.

Assumption fee

Typically 1% of the loan balance to assume the seller's existing ARM; to assume an FHA or VA loan, the fee will range from $50 to $100.

Attorney's fee

Normally lawyers don't participate in the purchase and sale of residential real property in California. If problems develop, however, such as the need to evaluate or clear title, an attorney may be hired.

Credit report

Should cost $45-$50 to check your credit. While standard credit checks cost $8, for home loans the lender checks two credit reporting agencies files and the county records for judgment and tax liens.

Escrow company fees

An escrow company that is not a title insurance company may charge a nominal fee for doing the escrow work.

Garbage fees

Real estate business slang for a number of small fees, including notary, courier and filing fees, which typically run from $150 to $250.

Loan fees

This includes points (one point is 1% of the loan principal) and an additional fee, usually between $100 and $450. Lenders also often charge $150 to $250 to complete the loan paperwork.

Physical inspection reports

May add several hundred dollars or more, depending on how many are requested. If you pay these at the time of the inspection directly to the inspectors, you can save a few dollars. Escrow companies will charge $25-$50 if they pay off your inspectors in escrow.

Prepaid homeowner's insurance

Amount as required by lenders, typically one year; depends on the house's value, level of coverage and location of the house.

Prepaid interest on the loan

You'll be asked to pay per diem interest in advance, from the date your loan is funded to the end of that month. The maximum you'll be charged is 30 days of interest.

Prepaid property taxes

Depends on tax assessment; covers the time period between closing and your first monthly mortgage payment. Some lenders have you prepay one or two months in addition.

Private mortgage insurance

If you make a down payment of less than 20%, most lenders will require private mortgage insurance or PMI. Depending on the policy, you may need to pay as much as 14 months' worth of PMI premiums at the close of escrow. This can easily add up to $1,000 or more. For details on various PMI policies, see Chapter 4, Section C.

Recording and filing fees

The escrow holder will charge about $100 for drawing up, reviewing and recording the deed of trust and other legal documents. The total escrow and title fees can amount to 0.5% of the loan.

Survey fee

May be needed to show plot measurements if house has easements; will run about $150.

Tax service fee

Issued to notify the lender if you default on your property taxes; usually costs about $75 to $80.

Title search and title insurance

Only in northern California does the buyer pay the title costs. Most lenders require title insurance for the face amount of their mortgage or for the value of their loan. Title insurance is a one-time premium which costs about .75% of the cost of your house.

Transfer tax

Tax assessed by the county when the property changes hands. May be split with seller, in which case costs about $.55 per $1,000. Many cities also charge transfer tax; it varies city to city, but usually is not more than 1.5% of the purchase price.

WHERE TO COMPLAIN ABOUT AN ESCROW OR TITLE INSURANCE COMPANY

If you have any problem with your escrow company, contact the Department of Corporations at (800) 347-6995; this state agency regulates independent escrow companies. The Department of Insurance oversees title insurance companies and can be reached at (800) 927-4357.

PUTTING THUMB TO INK WHEN YOU SIGN YOUR DEED

Beginning January 1, 1996, people who buy (or refinance) real estate in California must provide a thumb or fingerprint in addition to a signature. (*Government Code § 8206.*) The law is meant to protect you from becoming the victim of a real estate scam artist.

The only transactions exempt from the law are those involving:

- deeds of reconveyance
- trustee's deeds from a foreclosure sale, and
- deeds involving California property signed outside of the state.

This statewide legislation follows a three-year pilot program in Los Angeles county that virtually eliminated attempts to forge deeds and steal property from those most vulnerable.

CHAPTER

19

Check Out a House's Condition

Before you finalize your house purchase, you'll want to check out its condition. If the house is in good shape, you can proceed knowing that you're getting what you paid for. If inspections discover problems, you can negotiate with the seller to have her pay for necessary repairs, or you can back out of the deal, assuming your contract is properly written to allow you to do so. (See Clause 9 in our offer form, Chapter 16.) In either case, having a house inspected gives you an opportunity to further study whether it will truly make you a good affordable home.

A. Short History of California House Inspections

Before outlining our process for accurately assessing the condition of a house, a few words about current trends in inspecting houses and disclosing defects are in order. Understand at the outset that today's house inspection practices reflect a fear of lawsuits as well as a genuine desire to be sure a house is safe and sound.

Until the mid-1980s, California houses, like houses in most states, were sold with a caveat emptor (buyer beware) approach. As long as the seller didn't fraudulently conceal defects, the buyer was responsible for discovering the physical problems. If the buyer missed a roof full of holes or a foundation full of bugs, too bad. Not surprisingly, with this system, buyers and their lenders were very concerned not to miss major defects in the house. As a result, buyers routinely made all offers to purchase a house contingent upon a structural pest control inspection to determine if there was damage in need of repair.

Unfortunately, this didn't solve the problems, because looking for damage in a house solely through structural pest control inspections conducted just before sale left a great deal to be desired. This should be obvious, because a pest control inspection looks for termites, fungus and wood-destroying beetles, yet not for other types of problems. Many complex systems in a house (electricity, heating, plumbing, insulation) aren't routinely checked in a pest control inspection—nor are structural defects that don't relate to termites and other pests, or to earthquake vulnerabilities.

In some sales, it later became obvious that the seller (and sometimes his agent) knew about a particular undiscovered defect, but never said a word, hoping the buyer's pest control inspector would overlook it. This seemed so unfair that California courts began to question this "find-it-if-you-can" system and it started holding sellers and their agents financially liable for not disclosing known problems with a house. Several state and local laws now require sellers to provide specific information on the condition of the house as well as disclose potential hazards from floods, earthquakes, fire, environmental hazards and other problems.

B. Real Estate Transfer Disclosure Statement

In 1987, the California legislature passed a law requiring sellers to affirmatively disclose considerable information about the condition of the house, on a Real Estate Transfer Disclosure Statement form ("TDS" in real estate shorthand). (Civil Code § 1102.) The TDS includes three types of disclosures:

* items included in the property such as a burglar alarm or trash compactor
* information on defects or malfunctions in the building's structure, such as the roof or windows
* a variety of special issues such as the existence of a homeowner's association (and any covenants, conditions and restrictions or CC&Rs), environmental hazards like asbestos and lead-based paint, whether or not remodeling was done with permits and met local building codes, and neighborhood noise problems or nuisances.

We include a sample Real Estate Transfer Disclosure Statement (TDS) here so you'll have time to familiarize yourself with this form. The TDS you'll be handed as part of your purchase will contain the identical language, as the disclosures are specified by state law. (Civil Code § 1102.1.)

⚠ EXEMPTIONS FROM TRANSFER DISCLOSURE STATEMENT Certain properties, including foreclosures and probate sales and buildings with more than four units, are exempt from state disclosure laws. In these cases, be sure to get a professional home inspection before closing the deal. (See Section I, below.)

1. Examining the Seller's Disclosure Statement

Sellers must provide you a copy of the Transfer Disclosure Statement "as soon as practicable before transfer of title." (Civil Code § 1102.2.) It's to your advantage to get a copy of the TDS as soon as possible; you don't want to invest the time and money in the housebuying process, only to discover problems just before you close escrow.

Often, seller's disclosure forms are only cursorily filled out, and you'll need to ask questions for additional information. If the form you receive is sparse, you're confused about any of the seller's disclosures or you simply want more details, make a written request for more information; send a copy to the seller's agent and keep a copy for yourself. Insist on a written response from the seller.

In your request, ask not only for elaboration on the Real Estate Transfer Disclosure Statement, but also for any other recent inspection reports the seller may have authorized, such as a pest inspection (especially if you're in southern California). By law, all pest control reports commissioned within the last two years are kept on file at the Structural Pest Control Board, 1430 Howe Ave., Suite 3, Sacramento, CA 95825, (916) 263-2544, and are available for a small fee. (See Section I1, below for more on pest control reports.)

SAMPLE LETTER REQUESTING FURTHER SELLER'S DISCLOSURE

February 22, 199X

Dear _____:

I have received your Real Estate Transfer Disclosure Statement, dated _____. In item _____, you indicate that _____ _____.

Please explain this condition more fully. Specifically, I would appreciate your letting me know in writing answers to the following questions:

1.

2.

3.

Also, please send me copies of any inspectors' reports which deal with any aspect of the physical condition of the property. Thank you for your cooperation.

Sincerely,

Also, be sure to carefully read the visual disclosures made by your agent and the seller's agent. The seller may not notice obvious defects she's lived with every day (such as cuts in linoleum) that an agent might see.

2. When to Go Beyond the Real Estate Transfer Disclosure Statement

In addition to considering face value the information disclosed, examine the disclosure statement for clues to other problems and follow-up with a professional inspection. (See Section I.) For example, if the seller says that several windows won't open, they simply may be painted shut. But it's also possible that the house has settled and the window frames are no longer properly aligned. Similarly, cracks in the dining room ceiling may mean no more than that the plaster is old, which would be relatively easy and cheap to repair, or it may be a clue to significant earth movement or to an otherwise unstable foundation. In either case, have the foundation checked extra carefully. The books on home inspections listed below will help you evaluate disclosure statements and inspection reports.

REAL ESTATE AGENTS' DISCLOSURES

California law requires licensed real estate agents (brokers and salespeople) to conduct a "reasonably competent and diligent" visual inspection of property and to disclose to you anything that would affect the value or desirability of the property. (Civil Code §§ 2079, 2079.3.)

This obligation is on both your agent and the agent representing the seller.

Agents do not have to inspect inaccessible areas or review public documents affecting title to or use of the property.

---

3. Handling Problems With the Transfer Disclosure Statement

The law specifically allows buyers, in deciding whether and on what terms to buy the house, to rely on a seller's disclosure statement. Even if your offer was not contingent upon your approving inspection reports, state law allows a person to terminate his or her offer to purchase real property three days after personal delivery of a Real Estate Transfer Disclosure Statement (five days from mailing). (Civil Code § 1102.3.)

REAL ESTATE TRANSFER DISCLOSURE STATEMENT
(California Civil Code § 1102, et seq.)

THIS DISCLOSURE STATEMENT CONCERNS THE REAL PROPERTY SITUATED IN THE CITY OF _____ ,

COUNTY OF _____ **, STATE OF CALIFORNIA, DESCRIBED AS** _____

_____ .

THIS STATEMENT IS A DISCLOSURE OF THE CONDITION OF THE ABOVE DESCRIBED PROPERTY IN COMPLIANCE WITH SECTION 1102 OF THE

CIVIL CODE AS OF _____ **, 19___. IT IS NOT A WARRANTY OF ANY KIND BY THE SELLER(S) OR ANY AGENT(S) REPRE-**

SENTING ANY PRINCIPAL(S) IN THIS TRANSACTION, AND IT IS NOT A SUBSTITUTE FOR ANY INSPECTIONS OR WARRANTIES THE PRINCIPAL(S)

MAY WISH TO OBTAIN.

I
COORDINATION WITH OTHER DISCLOSURE FORMS

This Real Estate Transfer Disclosure Statement is made pursuant to Section 1102 of the Civil Code. Other statutes require disclosures, depending upon the details of the particular real estate transaction (for example: special study zone and purchase-money liens on residential property).

Substituted Disclosures: The following disclosures have or will be made in connection with this real estate transfer, and are intended to satisfy the disclosure obligations on this form, where the subject matter is the same:

☐ Inspection reports completed pursuant to the contract of sale or receipt for deposit.

☐ Additional inspection reports or disclosures: _____

_____

_____

_____

II
SELLER'S INFORMATION

The Seller discloses the following information with the knowledge that even though this is not a warranty, prospective Buyers may rely on this information in deciding whether and on what terms to purchase the subject property. Seller hereby authorizes any agent(s) representing any principal(s) in this transaction to provide a copy of this statement to any person or entity in connection with any actual or anticipated sale of the property.

THE FOLLOWING ARE REPRESENTATIONS MADE BY THE SELLER(S) AND ARE NOT THE REPRESENTATIONS OF THE AGENT(S), IF ANY. THIS

INFORMATION IS A DISCLOSURE AND IT IS NOT INTENDED TO BE PART OF ANY CONTRACT BETWEEN THE BUYER AND SELLER.

Seller   ☐ is   ☐ is not occupying the property.

A. The subject property has the items checked below (read across):

☐ Range	☐ Oven	☐ Microwave	☐ Dishwasher	☐ Trash Compactor
☐ Garbage Disposal	☐ Washer/Dryer Hookups	☐ Window Screens	☐ Rain Gutters	
☐ Burglar Alarms	☐ Smoke Detector(s)	☐ Fire Alarm		
☐ T.V. Antenna	☐ Satellite Dish	☐ Intercom		

☐ Central Heating   ☐ Central Air Conditioning   ☐ Evaporator Cooler(s)   ☐ Wall/Window Air Conditioning

☐ Sprinklers   ☐ Sump Pump   ☐ Water Softener   ☐ Public Sewer System   ☐ Septic Tank

☐ Patio/Decking   ☐ Built-in Barbecue   ☐ Gazebo

☐ Sauna   ☐ Pool   ☐ Spa   ☐ Hot Tub

☐ Security Gate(s)   ☐ Automatic Garage Door Opener(s)*   ☐ Number of Remote Controls _____

☐ Garage: ☐ Attached   ☐ Not Attached   ☐ Carport

☐ Pool/Spa Heater: ☐ Gas   ☐ Solar   ☐ Electric

☐ Water Heater: ☐ Gas   ☐ Solar   ☐ Electric

☐ Water Supply: ☐ City   ☐ Well   ☐ Private Utility   ☐ Other _____

☐ Gas Supply: ☐ Utility   ☐ Bottled

☐ Exhaust Fan(s) in _____   ☐ 220 Volt Wiring in _____

☐ Fireplace(s) in _____   ☐ Gas Starter

Roof(s): Type: _____   Age: (approx.) _____

Other: _____   _____

Other: _____   _____

Are there, to the best of your (Seller's) knowledge, any of the above that are not in operating condition?

☐ Yes ☐ No. If yes, then describe (attach additional sheets if necessary): _____

_____

_____

_____

_____

B. Are you (Seller) aware of any significant defects/malfunctions in any of the following?

☐ Yes ☐ No. If yes, check appropriate space(s) below.

☐ Interior Walls   ☐ Ceilings   ☐ Floors   ☐ Exterior Walls   ☐ Insulation

☐ Roof(s)   ☐ Windows   ☐ Doors   ☐ Foundation   ☐ Slab(s)

☐ Driveways   ☐ Sidewalks   ☐ Walls/Fences   ☐ Electrical Systems   ☐ Plumbing/Sewers/Septics

☐ Other Structural Components (describe): _____

_____

_____

_____

If any of the above is checked, explain (attach additional sheets if necessary): _____

_____

_____

_____

_____

_____

*This garage door opener may not be in compliance with the safety standards relating to automatic reversing devices as set forth in Chapter 12.5 (commencing with Section 19890) of Part 3 of Division 13 of the Health and Safety Code.

C. Are you (Seller) aware of any of the following:

☐ Yes ☐ No   1. Substances, materials, or products which may be an environmental hazard such as, but not limited to, asbestos, formaldehyde, radon gas, lead-based paint, fuel or chemical storage tanks, and contaminated soil or water on the subject property.

☐ Yes ☐ No   2. Features of the property shared in common with adjoining landowners, such as walls, fences and driveways, whose use or responsibility for maintenance may have an effect on the subject property.

☐ Yes ☐ No   3. Any encroachments, easements or similar matters that may affect your interest in the subject property.

☐ Yes ☐ No   4. Room additions, structural modifications, or other alterations or repairs made without necessary permits.

☐ Yes ☐ No   5. Room additions, structural modifications, or other alterations or repairs not in compliance with building codes.

☐ Yes ☐ No   6. Fill (compacted or otherwise) on the property or any portion thereof.

☐ Yes ☐ No   7. Any settling from any cause, or slippage, sliding, or other soil problems.

☐ Yes ☐ No   8. Flooding, drainage, or grading problems.

☐ Yes ☐ No   9. Major damage to the property or any other structures from fire, earthquake, floods, or landslides.

☐ Yes ☐ No   10. Any zoning violations, nonconforming uses, or violations of "setback" requirements.

☐ Yes ☐ No   11. Neighborhood noise problems or other nuisances.

☐ Yes ☐ No   12. CC&Rs or other deed restrictions or obligations.

☐ Yes ☐ No   13. Homeowners' Association which has any authority over the subject property.

☐ Yes ☐ No   14. Any "common area" (facilities such as pools, tennis courts, walkways, or other areas co-owned in undivided interest with others).

☐ Yes ☐ No   15. Any notices of abatement or citations against the property.

☐ Yes ☐ No   16. Any lawsuits against the seller threatening to or affecting this real property, including any lawsuits alleging a defect or deficiency in this real property or "common areas" (facilities such as pools, tennis courts, walkways, or other areas co-owned in undivided interest with others).

☐ Yes ☐ No   17. The property is located within a wildland area which may contain substantial forest fire risks and hazards and is subject to the requirements of Sec. 4291 of the Public Resources Code.

If the answer to any of these is yes, explain (attach additional sheets if necessary): _____

_____

_____

_____

_____

Seller certifies that the information herein is true and correct to the best of the Seller's knowledge as of the date signed by the Seller.

Seller _____   Date _____

Seller _____   Date _____

III

AGENT'S INSPECTION DISCLOSURE (LISTING AGENT)

(To be completed only if the seller is represented by an agent in this transaction.)

THE UNDERSIGNED, BASED ON THE ABOVE INQUIRY OF THE SELLER(S) AS TO THE CONDITION OF THE PROPERTY AND BASED ON REASON-ABLY COMPETENT AND DILIGENT VISUAL INSPECTION OF THE ACCESSIBLE AREAS OF THE PROPERTY IN CONJUNCTION WITH THAT INQUIRY, STATES THE FOLLOWING:

☐ Agent notes no items for disclosure.

☐ Agent notes the following items: _____

_____

_____

_____

_____

Agent (Print Name of Broker Representing Seller) _____

By (Associate Licensee or Broker's Signature) _____

Date _____

IV
AGENT'S INSPECTION DISCLOSURE (SELLING AGENT)

(To be completed only if the agent who has obtained the offer is other than the agent above.)

THE UNDERSIGNED, BASED ON A REASONABLY COMPETENT AND DILIGENT VISUAL INSPECTION OF THE ACCESSIBLE AREAS OF THE

PROPERTY, STATES THE FOLLOWING:

☐ Agent notes no items for disclosure.

☐ Agent notes the following items: _____

_____

Agent (Print Name of Broker Obtaining Offer) _____

By (Associate Licensee or Broker's Signature) _____

Date _____

V

BUYER(S) AND SELLER(S) MAY WISH TO OBTAIN PROFESSIONAL ADVICE AND/OR INSPECTIONS OF THE PROPERTY AND TO PROVIDE FOR

APPROPRIATE PROVISIONS IN A CONTRACT BETWEEN BUYER(S) AND SELLER(S) WITH RESPECT TO ANY ADVICE/INSPECTION/DEFECTS.

I/We Acknowledge Receipt of a Copy of this Statement.

Seller _____   Date _____

Seller _____   Date _____

Buyer _____   Date _____

Buyer _____   Date _____

Agent (Print Name of Broker Representing Seller) _____

By (Associate Licensee or Broker's Signature) _____

Date _____

Agent (Print Name of Broker Obtaining the Offer) _____

By (Associate Licensee or Broker's Signature) _____

Date _____

SECTION 1102.2 OF THE CIVIL CODE PROVIDES A BUYER WITH THE RIGHT TO RESCIND A PURCHASE CONTRACT FOR AT LEAST THREE DAYS

AFTER THE DELIVERY OF THIS DISCLOSURE, IF DELIVERY OCCURS AFTER THE SIGNING OF AN OFFER TO PURCHASE. IF YOU WISH TO

RESCIND THE CONTRACT, YOU MUST ACT WITHIN THE PRESCRIBED PERIOD.

A REAL ESTATE BROKER IS QUALIFIED TO ADVISE ON REAL ESTATE. IF YOU DESIRE LEGAL ADVICE, CONSULT YOUR ATTORNEY.

A buyer may alternatively decide to proceed with the sale and negotiate the cost of making repairs with the seller. (See Chapter 18, Section B.)

The law requires a seller or his agent to disclose only defects within his personal knowledge. Nonetheless, some sellers worry about being sued and not being able to prove that they didn't know about a certain problem. In short, they now have a good reason to discover and disclose defects, just as do buyers.

A wise seller will disclose all possible (and sometimes even imagined) defects to protect against possible future lawsuits, often in a supplement to the TDS. On a form recommended by some San Francisco Realtors, for instance, sellers are asked to answer if they are aware of any problems, such as:

• damages caused by animals

• neighborhood animal problems

• criminal activities on the property, and

• diseased trees on the property.

Not all sellers and agents are savvy enough to provide detailed disclosures. Some still try to cover up serious problems, hoping that you and your inspector won't find them, and, as a result, you'll pay more for the house. The seller may be sued later, but some sellers don't think this far ahead. (For handling these types of legal problems, see Chapter 21, Section E.)

DISCLOSURES REQUIRED WITH FHA LOANS

As of May, 1996, the Department of Housing and Urban Development (HUD) requires new disclosures regarding home inspections for borrowers seeking Federal Housing Administration (FHA) financing. All FHA borrowers must be given a new form, "The Importance of a Home Inspection." This form must be signed and dated by the borrower before the execution of the sales contract. For more information on FHA loans, see Chapter 11, Section B.

C. Flood, Seismic and Fire Hazards Disclosures

The Transfer Disclosure Statement includes information on many hazards affecting the house, some of which require additional disclosures. These disclosures may be on the TDS or on a separate form.

Also, see Appendix 1, Welcome to California, which discusses areas of the state susceptible to various natural disasters.

1. Flood Hazards

Federal law requires that sellers tell you if the property is in a Special Flood Hazard Area designated by the Federal Emergency Management Agency (FEMA), in a Flood Insurance Rate Map (or Flood Hazard Boundary Map (FHBM)). (42 U.S.C. §§ 4104, 4106.) This information is important because lenders may require flood insurance as a condition of granting financing if property in a Special Flood Hazard Area is security for a loan.

2. Seismic Hazards

State law requires sellers to tell you whether or not:

• The property lies within a delineated earthquake fault zone, as identified by the California State Geologist. (Public Resources Code §§ 2621-2625.) The designations are puzzling, at least to a layperson. For example, San Francisco is not within an earthquake fault zone. That's because the fault line isn't in San Francisco proper—it is offshore—although San Francisco certainly has experienced the ravages of earthquakes.

• The property lies within an area designated as a Seismic Hazards Zone. (Public Resources Code §§ 2690-2699.6.)

• In addition, if the property you are buying has had a new or replacement water heater installed since January 1, 1991, it must be braced, anchored or strapped to resist falling or displacement during an earthquake. Anyone selling property with such a water heater must certify to you in writing that the heater complies with the law.

• The property has any known seismic deficiencies, such as whether or not the house is bolted or anchored to the foundation and whether cripple walls, if any, are braced. (Government Code § 8897.) The seller is not required to hire anyone to help her evaluate her house, nor is she required to strengthen any weaknesses that exist. If the house was built in 1960 or later, oral disclosure is enough. If her house was built before 1960, she must disclose in writing and sign the disclosure form, Residential Earthquake Hazards Report, included in a booklet called The Homeowner's Guide to Earthquake Safety. The booklet is available (for a small fee) from the Seismic Safety Commission, 1900 K Street, Suite 100, Sacramento, CA 95814, (916) 322-4917.

3. Fire Hazards

If the property is located in a wildland area where the state is responsible for controlling fires, the seller must disclose that fact to prospective buyers on the Real Estate Transfer Disclosure Statement. (Public Resources Code § 4136.)

California requires all single family dwellings—and each unit of multi-unit dwellings—to have smoke detectors installed in all sleeping rooms before the close of escrow. (Health and Safety Code §§ 13113.7 and 13113.8.)

VICTORIAN

D. Environmental Hazards

Item C.1 on the Transfer Disclosure Statement asks the seller to identify environmental hazards on the property such as radon gas and contaminated soil. In addition, sellers should provide prospective homebuyers a copy of *Environmental Hazards: A Guide for Homeowners and Buyers,* which provides information on different environmental hazards which may be on or near the property, such as asbestos, formaldehyde, lead and hazardous wastes, and lists federal and state agencies for more information. This booklet, published by the California Department of Real Estate and the Department of Health Services, is available from the California Association of Realtors (CAR). For price and order information, call CAR at their Los Angeles office: (213) 739-8200.

Section J5, below, discusses specialized inspections for various environmental hazards.

E. Lead

HUD rules require that applicants for FHA mortgages be given a lead-based paint notice disclosure form before signing the final sales contract. Lead paint in homes financed by the FHA must be removed or repainted.

California law requires that a seller disclose lead-based paint hazards to prospective buyers. (Civil Code § 1102.) Furthermore, sellers of houses built before 1978 must comply with the Residential Lead-Based Paint Hazard Reduction Act of 1992, also known as Title X. Sellers must:

- disclose all known lead-based paint and hazards in the house
- give buyers a pamphlet prepared by the U.S. Environmental Protection Agency (EPA) called *Protect Your Family from Lead in Your Home.*
- include certain warning language in the contract as well as signed statements from all parties verifying that all requirements were completed
- keep signed acknowledgments for three years, as proof of compliance, and
- give buyers a ten-day opportunity to test the housing for lead.

If a seller fails to comply with Title X requirements, you can sue the seller for triple the amount of damages.

For more information, contact the National Lead Information Clearinghouse—by phone at (800) 424-LEAD, by fax at (202) 659-1192, or by Internet E-mail to ehc@cais.com.

F. Disclosure of Deaths and/or AIDS

State law implies that the seller should disclose any death he knows of, within three years, on the property. (Civil Code § 1710.2.) If a death occurred more than three years before, the seller need disclose it only if asked by the buyer. There is no cause of action against an owner or agent who fails to disclose a death on the property more than three years before the sale.(*Reed v. King*, 145 Cal. App. 3d 261 (1983).)

A seller need not disclose that an owner had, or died from, AIDS, but the property owner or his agent should answer honestly any direct questions on this subject.

G. Disclosure of Military Ordnance

Sellers who know of any former federal or state ordnance locations (once used for military training purposes which may contain potentially explosive munitions) within one mile of the property must provide written disclose to the buyer as soon as practicable before transfer of title. (Civil Code § 1102.15.)

H. Local Disclosures

Many cities and counties have local disclosure requirements. To make sure the seller complies, check with the local city or county planning or building department for any local requirements. For example:

- Los Angeles sellers must disclose applicable zoning laws.
- Many municipalities require sellers to upgrade insulation before selling and take specific energy-efficiency measures.
- Many coastal areas restrict owners from making structural modifications to their property without a permit.
- Daly City, Oakland and San Francisco require sellers to buy and disclose Residential Building Records Reports (3-R Reports), which show zoning restrictions and building permits on the property.
- Some communities adjacent to agricultural or timber production zones require sellers to disclose agricultural nuisances such as noise, odors and dust.

- Sellers of property in designated "community facilities") districts must disclose information on special taxes for police or fire departments, libraries, parks and schools. (Civil Code §1102.6b.)
- San Jose has its own geologic disclosure requirements, in addition to state seismic hazards disclosures discussed in Section C2, above.

Sellers in communities with local disclosure requirements passed after July 1990 must use a special form, the Local Option Transfer Disclosure Statement. (Civil Code §1102.6a.)

I. Inspecting the Property Yourself

At some point, you'll want to arrange professional inspections. (See Section J, below.) Before you get this far, you should first conduct your own inspection—ideally, before you make a formal written offer so that you can save yourself the trouble should you find serious problems.

Several inexpensive books provide considerable detail on how to inspect a house (see below). We recommend that you read these carefully and do your own detailed inspection, focusing on items of particular importance to you and your family. For example, if you're a light sleeper and highly sensitive to noise, a clattering central heating system may be a substantial defect. Or, if you're buying a condo, be sure to visit the unit in the evening when neighbors are more likely to be home to observe any loud noises. A unit very quiet mid-day might clearly hear a neighbor's radio or TV in the evening.

To make the most of your inspection, bring along a note pad, tape measure, camera, flashlight and a copy of the House Priorities Worksheet you prepared in Chapter 1.

 BOOKS ON HOUSE INSPECTIONS

The following do-it-yourself house inspection books are particularly good:

Inspecting a Home or Income Property, by Jim Yuen (Ten Speed Press). Yuen is a long time California building inspector, and his book is one of the best available for Californians. Illustrations show how to find dozens of hidden problems. No other book is as detailed on the construction problems a typical California house buyer is likely to encounter.

How to Inspect a House, by George Hoffman (Addison-Wesley), is beautifully written, but general. His forte is showing how to discover major problems, such as a bad foundation, leaky roof or malfunctioning fireplace.

The Termite Report: A Guide for Homeowners and Home Buyers on Structural Pest Control, by Donald Pearman (Pear Publishing), is an excellent guide to discovering many hidden pest problems. It contains a detailed sample structural pest control report with lots of helpful information on how to interpret it.

REQUEST COPIES OF UTILITY AND WATER BILLS

While sellers are not required to tell you how much they pay the gas and electric company every month, ask to see past bills, especially for the winter months, or ask the seller how much she generally pays. Gas and electric bills can vary a lot, depending on a house's location, size and insulation, and the type and age of the furnace and hot water heater. Some local ordinances require sellers to improve substandard insulation, place insulation blankets around water heaters and install low-flow shower heads prior to sale, all of which can lower utility bills.

If utility bills are high, ask the local gas and electric company to conduct an energy check or audit. Many do it at no charge, identifying the problems, recommended solutions and costs. If your utility company won't help, or will take too long, ask for the names of private companies who conduct energy audits.

With water bills, look for any sudden increase in water usage. In older houses especially, this may be a tip-off that main pipes are leaking. Also, it's a good idea to ask the seller what emergency plumbing service she uses. If she responds that she hasn't needed one, fine. But if she gives you a name, insist on a thorough check of buried sewer lines; they may be in the process of failing.

J. Arranging Professional Inspections

In addition to inspecting the house yourself and examining the seller's disclosure and inspection reports, you'll want to hire a general contractor to inspect the property, and a licensed structural pest control inspector to check for pest damage. This should be done after your written purchase offer has been accepted by the seller (which should be contingent upon your

approving the results of one or more inspections; see Clause 9 of our offer form, Chapter 16). Make sure you have the seller's Transfer Disclosure Statement so that the inspectors can follow-up on any problems identified therein. You may also want to arrange more specialized inspections after reviewing disclosure reports.

Chapter 18, Section B, discusses how to remove inspection contingencies and negotiate on the cost of repairs.

Chapter 7, Section I, discusses new home inspections.

1.   Structural Pest Control Inspection

An inspection by a licensed structural pest control inspector, covering infestation by termites and flying beetles, dry rot and other fungal conditions, is almost always required by the lender. If you don't make it a condition of the contract, your lender may, particularly if you put down less than 20% of the purchase price. If the seller has a termite report done before she puts her house up for sale, you should still get your own done.

Some inspectors are less picky than others, and the seller has a motive (he wants the deal to go through) to pick someone who won't be too fussy. Pest control reports are not costly, beginning at about $150 for a typical single-family dwelling. In a condo, you may need an authorization from the homeowner's association for the pest control inspector to look at common areas.

2.   General Contractor's Inspection

A licensed general contractor normally inspects all major house systems, from top to bottom. The inspector will examine the general conditions of the site, such as drainage, retaining walls, fences (some skip the fences—remind them to look) and driveways; the integrity of the structure and the foundation; the condition of the roof, exterior and interior paint, doors and windows, plumbing, electrical and heating systems. A growing number of inspectors test for lead in water or radiation exposure around a built-in microwave. Specialized inspections, such as for seismic safety or asbestos hazards, should be arranged as needed.

MAKE SURE THE UTILITIES ARE WORKING

Before arranging a home inspection, be sure that the water, gas, and electricity will be on, pilot lights lit, and all appliances in working order. If you can, schedule a nice heavy rain so you can check the condition of the roof, gutters, and downspouts.

3.   How to Find a Good Inspector

A reliable personal recommendation is the best way to find a general contractor and structural pest control inspector. Remember, as the buyer, you want someone who will be thorough and tough, not someone who is willing to overlook "small problems." Be careful about asking your real estate agent for a referral. After all, your agent is almost surely extremely anxious that your deal go through and therefore may recommend an inspector not overly persnickety about identifying problems. One good approach is to ask a real estate professional not connected with your sale who she would hire to inspect a house she was buying.

Many people ask if it's better to hire an inspector who doesn't bid on the work (most pest control companies do). Recognizing that there is an inherent conflict of interest, we wish the answer was an unequivocal yes. Unfortunately, there are so many inexperienced people who call themselves house inspectors (there's no special licensing requirement) that this isn't necessarily true. In fact, it's possible that even allowing for the conflict of interest inherent in inspecting and bidding on the same job, a contractor who has been doing hands-on work in houses for years may do the best inspection. Especially with expensive older houses, where undiscovered problems can quickly amount to tens of thousands of dollars, you may want to hire two contractors—one who will bid on the work and one who won't.

Inspectors who are members of the American Society of Housing Inspectors (ASHI) or the California Real Estate Inspection Association (CREIA) cannot do contracting work as a condition of membership. Both professional associations provide local referrals. ASHI may be reached at (800) 743-2744. CREIA's phone number is (800) 388-8443.

Assuming the person making the inspection doesn't do repair work, you'll need to get specific bids from contractors. Get two or three bids from reliable firms. You want the work done well, so you don't necessarily want to accept the cheapest bid. A useful brochure, *What You Should Know Before You Hire a Contractor*, is available free-of-charge from the Contractors State License Board, by calling (800) 321-2752.

Before finally deciding who to hire, get several references and check the status of each individual's license and any outstanding complaints with the Contractors State License Board (phone number above) and the Structural Pest Control Board, at (800) 737-8188.

4.   Inspections and Reports

The general contractor's inspection should take at least two to three hours, while the pest control inspection should take about an hour. Accompany the inspector during their examination. You will learn a lot and better understand the report he'll later write. You can also find out about the maintenance and preservation of the house and ask questions. The inspector should point out any problems and indicate which are truly important and which are minor, and give a rough estimate of the costs involved for repairs. If a friend or relative has experience in any aspect of construction, bring him or her along. Another set of eyes that know what to look for is always a help.

Expect to receive the general contractor's report after a short time (a few days or up to a week, depending on the inspector), and the pest control report within about five days. Both reports should detail the condition of all major components of the house inspected or checked for infestation, and estimated repair costs.

As mentioned earlier, house inspection contractors often worry about their liability should they fail to discover a serious defect. This is good to the extent it encourages thoroughness,

STARTER HOME

but, unfortunately, it can also result in overly defensive inspecting. Here's how to filter out inspector paranoia while reading an inspection report:

- Contractors' reports sometimes include long-winded disclaimers written by lawyers. For example, most state that the inspector takes no responsibility for the condition of the subsoil or the interior of sealed walls. While this boilerplate language may sound scary, it's usually not a tip-off that all sorts of problems are lurking just out of sight. The inspector is simply trying to protect himself against the possibility of future lawsuits.

- Find the paragraphs that talk about the house in question. Pay attention first to statements describing the tests he didn't conduct or areas not inspected. If you have educated yourself by reading good house inspection books, you'll be in a fairly decent position to determine if any areas or systems were left out that shouldn't have been. Next, focus on what the inspector did discover. For example, if he found evidence of insects or poor water pressure, or recommends inspections by a foundation or fireplace expert, check further.

- Get a second opinion if a general contractor or pest control inspector discovers a potentially serious problem. Arrange for the follow-up inspection to be conducted by a specialist.

5. Specialized Inspections Common in California

As discussed above, the seller must disclose environmental and seismic hazards and other problems to the buyer. Some of these may require further follow-up and specialized inspections. For detailed information on asbestos, formaldehyde, lead, radon and hazardous wastes, be sure to see Environmental Hazards: A Guide for Homeowners and Buyers, mentioned in Section D, above.

Asbestos. Exposure to asbestos has been linked to an increased risk of cancer. Normally, a separate asbestos inspection is not necessary unless you suspect problems (generally not the case with homes built since the mid-1970s). A general contractor should tell you if the house contains asbestos insulation around heating systems, in ceilings or other areas. For more information on asbestos inspections, contact an office of the U.S. Consumer Product Safety Commission, State Contractors License Board or American Lung Association. For a specialized inspection, find a licensed asbestos abatement engineer; you can get a list from the California Department of Industrial Relations in Sacramento, at (916) 263-2800.

Electrical. If you or a general contractor suspect problems (more likely if the house was built 25 years ago or more), have an electrician or an electrical engineer do a specialized electrical report. Many general contractors don't have enough knowledge of electrical codes to do an adequate job on a large older house.

Electromagnetic Radiation. If you're considering a home near high-voltage electrical power lines, you may be worried about possible health hazards. Although links between electro-magnetic radiation and diseases such as cancer have not been proven, you may still want to call the local utility company for a test and evaluation of the electromagnetic radiation levels. Some general contractors can test for this as well.

Foundation and Structure. A general contractor can report on these; if he suspects a problem, or you're concerned based upon the seller's disclosures, you'll want an expert to inspect the foundation and structure. All sorts of people, including geotechnical, structural and civil engineers, claim expertise in making inspections for earthquake safety. Too many don't know what they're talking about. Make sure you hire someone with both technical skills and plenty of house inspection experience.

Lead. Exposure to lead-based paint and lead water pipes may lead to serious health problems, especially for children. For information on determining the lead content of paint, contact the California Department of Health Services in Berkeley, at (510) 540-2800. For information on lead in drinking water, contact the EPA Safe Drinking Water Hotline, at (800) 426-2791. See Section E discussion above of state and federal disclosures regarding lead, including how to contact the National Lead Information Clearinghouse.

Hazardous Wastes. Detailed information about known and suspected hazardous waste sites, including landfills, underground storage tanks, and oil spills, within one mile of a house you're considering buying, is available from a private firm, Environmental Risk Information and Imaging Services (ERIIS). A basic report costs $75. For information, contact ERIIS, at 505 Huntmar Park Dr., Herndon, VA 22070, phone: (800) 989-0403. Information on hazardous waste sites is also available from the California Office of Environmental Protection, Office of Hazardous Material Data Management, in Sacramento, phone: (916) 324-2829. This state agency maintains the Hazardous Waste and Substances Sites List (also known as the Cortese list) of hazardous waste problem sites in California.

Plumbing. If the general contractor's report indicates problems, get an in-depth report from a plumber. Your local water department may provide some useful information regarding water pressure and hardness or softness of water. If a house is more than 50 years old, it may be likely that the main sewer line to the street will need replacing before long. General contractors typically do not inspect wells and septic tanks; you'll need to hire a specialist if you want these checked out.

Radon. Radon is a naturally occurring radioactive gas associated with lung cancer. It can enter and contaminate a house built on soil and rock with uranium deposits or through water from some private wells. Radon is not a problem in most of California, but if you're concerned, call the U.S. Environmental Protection Agency Radon Hotline at (800) 767-7236. The California Department of Health Services Radon Program Hotline can also provide information at (800) 745-7236.

Subsoil. If earth movement, especially subsidence or slippage, is a problem or possibility (or if the house is on fill), contact your local building or planning department for any soil reports on file. For information sources on earthquake study zones and hazardous landslide and flood areas in California, see Appendix 1, Welcome to California. In addition, you may want to consult a soils expert who may recommend soil borings.

⚠️ **BE EXTRA CAUTIOUS IF YOU SUSPECT THE HOUSE YOU ARE BUYING IS ON ENVIRONMENTALLY CONTAMINATED PROPERTY THAT HAS BEEN USED FOR TREATING, STORING OR DISPOSING OF HAZARDOUS WASTE**

Under the federal Comprehensive Environmental Response, Compensation and Liability Act of 1990 (CERCLA), known as the "Superfund" Act, the present owner of contaminated property is responsible for the hazard—even if they did not cause, or know of, the contamination. This subject is beyond the scope of this book. For more information on how buyers can limit their liability in this type of situation, contact the nearest office of the U.S. Environmental Protection Agency.

6. Which Inspections Do You Really Need?

As the cost of both buying a house and of making repairs has greatly increased, some very cautious buyers have different specialists check all major areas of the house, such as heating, plumbing, roof and foundation. Involving specialists increases the likelihood that defects will be found and makes excellent sense if the house is old, large, expensive or in obvious poor condition. Before opening your checkbook to every type of inspector known to humankind, however, weigh the expected benefit against the cost involved.

If you're buying a five-year-old house in apparently great shape, you have read up on inspections, and an experienced general contractor and pest control contractor have discovered no problems, spending any money on additional inspections is probably overkill. These guidelines should help you decide how many inspections you need:

• Let your eyes be your first guide; the poorer looking the condition, the more you should use a fine tooth comb. But don't stop there; hidden problems (sometimes covered up by an unscrupulous seller) can cost you many thousands of dollars if not discovered. The house inspection books listed above are excellent guides to discovering many of these problems.

• Age is a factor; houses deteriorate over time, and construction techniques (especially for foundations) weren't always the best years ago. So the older the house, the more it makes sense to examine it closely. Still, many older houses were built well and are in fine shape, so it's by no means the only criterion you should use in deciding how closely to inspect. By contrast, some newer houses wouldn't stand up to one good huff and puff by a self-respecting wolf. (See Chapter 7, Section I, for more on inspecting new houses.)

• The more expensive the house, the more you want to be sure you're getting your money's worth. By contrast, hiring six inspectors to examine a low-cost starter house will rarely be cost-effective. A competent pest control and general contractor inspection should turn up most of the problems.

• In areas where the earth moves often, check the foundation and the subsoil carefully. This is especially true for houses in landslide or earthquake vulnerable areas, and houses built on landfill.

• Look for evidence of seasonal problems. If you are buying a house in the middle of August, the roof won't be leaking or the basement flooding—but it may certainly do so in December. So look carefully at ceilings, attic spaces and basements for stains or water marks. If ceilings have recently been repainted, ask why. If you aren't satisfied with the answer, ask your inspector to check these areas extra carefully and the seller to state in writing that no problems have been covered up.

WHY SOME INSPECTORS ARE PARANOID

In recent years, many buyers, discovering defects after the purchase, have sued the seller and their real estate broker and the property inspector, claiming that the defects should have been discovered and disclosed. As discussed in more detail in Chapter 3, Section D7, the possibility of being sued has made some inspectors ultra-careful (even paranoid) when it comes to emphasizing what's wrong with a house.

If an inspector says apparently sound plumbing and heating systems are old and may fail before long, for example, no one is likely to sue if no problems develop for many years. The inspector may be sued, however, if the same systems cause problems soon after being given a clean bill of health. When a house is inspected a number of times, this overcautious approach can result in an overly negative assessment of a house's condition, as each inspector tends to protect himself by finding more problems than his predecessors.

EXAMPLE: Amy, in the process of making an offer on an older two-story stucco house in the Berkeley Hills, read the book *The Termite Report: A Guide for Homeowners and Home Buyers on Structural Pest Control*, by Donald Pearman (Pear Publishing). She learned that pest control inspectors often fail to probe corners of buildings under inset gutters for hidden rot caused by overflowing, and don't usually get behind the stucco. She also learned that in earthquake zone areas, like Berkeley, this is doubly dangerous, because rotten wood at the corners can make buildings structurally unsafe. Sure enough, when she read the pest control report, no behind-the-stucco probing had been done. She hired another inspector who had a reputation as a real stickler for detail. He probed the corners and discovered serious damage which cost $22,000 to repair. Fortunately, Amy found it in time and got the seller to credit the full amount in escrow.

7. Who Pays for Inspections?

A general contractor's inspection typically costs about $300-$400 for a single family home, and more for a multiple unit dwelling. Structural pest control inspections cost about $150 for an average single family house. Normally, the buyer pays for inspections required as part of his offer to purchase. This is custom, however, not law, and it's possible to negotiate an arrangement where the seller pays, or shares in the cost of inspections.

K. Are the Repairs Really Needed?

As mentioned in Section A, the positive trend towards inspecting California houses thoroughly is likely to turn up previously undiscovered problems. In addition, the concern of inspectors to avoid later lawsuits sometimes results in tagging defects that aren't that serious.

If the house you wish to buy receives reports identifying the need for expensive repair work, here are some questions to ask:

- Have you gotten a second opinion?
- Has one pest control inspector called for very different types of repairs than another? If so, some work probably needs to be done, but you still need to figure out exactly what. For example, what if one inspector recommends chemical treatment of a problem with a fungicide and another recommends replacing wood? Chemical treatments mean introducing highly toxic material into your house, and the treatment is likely to be far less effective than removing the problem wood. Replacing the wood, however, will probably be more expensive.
- Will the inspector who made the report bid on the repair job? As noted earlier, we discourage working with someone who does, if possible. But if you do, be sure to get another report and repair bid.
- Is the problem real (rotten wood) or potential (wood is too near dirt and may rot in the future)? Pest control inspectors must notify the person requesting the report that the information can be divided into two sections: corrective measures for damage from infestations/infections which are evident, and corrective measures for conditions deemed likely to lead to infestation and future problems. For potential problems, ask if the expensive work needs to be done now. Can the situation be monitored? Will less expensive work solve the problem?

- Is the problem getting worse? Or has it been static for years and may not really need to be fixed?
- How did the inspector arrive at the repair cost?
- Can the problem be contained by doing part of the work now and the rest in future years?

Don't simply accept as gospel what the so-called expert tells you. At the very least, get a second opinion from someone committed to helping you arrive at a less expensive solution.

EXAMPLE: Dana's offer for a small, wood frame house on a slope is accepted. When the house is inspected, a pest control inspector finds $15,000 worth of work necessary to cure foundation problems. The seller refuses to pay for the work or lower the price by anything like that amount. Dana can't afford an additional $15,000 to fix the foundation.

Before she panics, Dana asks an architect friend for an opinion. He discovers that most of the damage occurred many years before, and was successfully treated at the time. In his view, the problem had not reoccurred, so there was no need to replace the affected timber. He recommends preventive measures—excavating dirt away from wooden posts and further treating the wood. If the digging is done by high school kids paid at $8 per hour, the total cost should be less than $3,000.

Dana presents the architect's suggestions to the lender and seller. The seller reduces the price by the $3,000 and the lender finances the purchase provided the architect's plan is followed.

QUEEN ANNE

EARTHQUAKE REINFORCEMENTS

Earthquakes in the late 1980s and 1990s have cast much new light on making houses earthquake safe. The time-tested advice to bolt a house to its foundation and install stiff plywood cripple walls in the basement proved to be helpful. These reinforcements typically cost only a few thousand dollars, are exempt from property taxes and are frequently a condition of getting earthquake insurance.

Recent earthquakes have also focused attention on the possibility that vertical earth movements can make houses vulnerable to literally jumping off their foundations. To cope with this danger, it's best to secure the house to the foundation using steel ties, straps and, in some cases, cables. You might also want the cripple walls strengthened with heavy gage metal fasteners and cross bracing. A thorough retrofit of this type typically costs $2,000-$5,000 or more, depending on the size and age of the house, but should be done only after an earthquake expert is consulted.

In addition, it's important to repair termite and other structural damage, or else earthquake retrofit work can actually make a house more susceptible to earthquake damage. Earthquake retrofit services are advertised heavily; many people sound convincing, but actually know so little that they are apt to make the problem worse. For more information on earthquake-proofing your house, see Appendix 1, Welcome to California.

L.   Who Pays for Defects?

If inspections turn up a laundry list of expensive defects, you and the seller will have to negotiate as to who pays what. Because your offer to purchase should have been made contingent upon your approving inspection reports, you have no obligation to proceed with the purchase until you approve of the plan to remedy the defects.

Asking the seller to pay repair costs is appropriate if an inspection turns up a serious problem that requires an expert's follow-up. But if the house is particularly desirable and you have negotiated an excellent price, you may need to pay part of these costs to make sure the deal goes through. (For more on paying for repairs, see Chapter 18, Section B.)

M. Ask for a Home Warranty

Several companies sell home repair warranty contracts to protect purchasers of houses from repair and replacement costs of major appliances and working systems. Typically, these policies cover the heating, air conditioning, plumbing and electrical systems, as well as the water heater and built-in kitchen and laundry appliances. For an extra charge, the policy can also cover pools, spas and even roofs. Under standard home warranties, if one of these systems fails during the coverage period (usually one year), you simply call the warranty company, which sends out a repair person. All you'll have to pay is a deductible of $25 to $50 per visit, depending upon the particular policy.

A growing number of sellers voluntarily include a year service contract as part of the price of the house, particularly with new houses. If the seller doesn't offer you one, it doesn't hurt to ask. Depending on the size and age of the house, a service contract might cost $250-$500. A seller may see this as a bargain if it clinches the sale. Sometimes a buyer's real estate agent will provide a buyer with a home warranty—again, as incentive for the deal to close. A little more than half of the houses sold in California now come with a home warranty.

If no one offers you a policy, you can buy one yourself. Although these policies can be renewed indefinitely, having the coverage makes the most sense during the first year of ownership, when systems and appliances likely to give you trouble will probably do so. Coverage usually begins at the close of escrow.

Several companies offer home warranties. Here are some keys to finding good coverage:

- Be sure the contract covers preexisting conditions that were not known to the seller or discovered in an inspection. This means that if you want a home warranty, you'll need to request one before any inspections take place. Avoid any contract that excludes all preexisting conditions, even if unknown before the coverage begins.
- Be sure you're aware of all restrictions and dollar limits of coverage. For example, while a home warranty might cover the cost of repairing a burst pipe, secondary damage to furniture or carpeting typically won't be covered.
- Find out how disputes are handled and if the warranty requires mediation or arbitration.
- Don't duplicate coverage. If an appliance or system is still covered by its own warranty, don't bother including it in the home warranty unless the warranty that came with the appliance or system will expire shortly. If you choose not to cover a certain item in the home warranty, be sure to ask the insurance company for a fee reduction.

RESOURCES ON HOME WARRANTIES

For more information on home warranties, send a self-addressed stamped business-size envelope to the Home Warranty Association of California, P.O. Box 12038, Marina Del Rey, CA 90295. Ask for a copy of their free brochure, "A Guide to Home Warranties."

The California Department of Insurance licenses home warranty firms and can provide information on the current status of a particular company's license. Call them at (800) 927-4357.

For a discussion of developer's warranties on new homes, see Chapter 7, Section J.

Legal Ownership: How to Take Title

Before escrow closes on your new house, you'll need to choose how to take "title" (documented legal ownership). Title is evidenced by a deed recorded at the County Recorder's Office. The deed contains a description of the property and includes the name(s) of the seller(s) and buyer(s).

➡️ If you've owned a house before, you may be familiar with your options and already know how you want to take title. If so, you can skip this chapter. If you're a first-time homeowner or new to the California community property ownership system, however, read on carefully.

The most important rule to remember about taking title to real property is that there's no best way. As we will explain below, it depends on both your relationship status (married, single, or living (and purchasing) together) and your personal needs and goals.

The rest of this chapter discusses the title options for single people, couples, groups and business partners.

A. One Unmarried Person

If you're in this category, you simply take title in your own name. Many title companies may add "an unmarried man" or "an unmarried woman" to the deed, but it isn't legally required.

For some people, taking title in their own name isn't as easy as it sounds, especially if you have given up your birth name and used several others. The name to put on the deed is the one that appears on your checks, driver's license, passport and other similar documents. This need not be your birth name. If you use more than one name, list the name you most commonly use for business purposes first, followed by A.K.A. ("also known as") and the other name. For example, Robin Smith, who also frequently uses her former married name Robin Jones, could identify herself as Robin Smith A.K.A. Robin Jones.

B. Two or More Unmarried People

Unmarried people who purchase a house together may take title in one of three ways:

- joint tenancy
- tenancy in common, or
- partnership.

The overwhelming majority of unmarried couples or groups own property in joint tenancy or tenancy in common. Partnership is typically appropriate only if you already own a business together and purchase the house as a business asset, or if you buy the house as a business investment to fix it up for resale. (Partnership ownership is discussed in Section E, below.)

1. Joint Tenancy

If you take title to real property as joint tenants, all buyers will share property ownership equally and have the right to use the entire property. The key feature of joint tenancy is "the right of survivorship." When one joint tenant dies, her share automatically goes to the survivor(s), even if she attempted to leave her portion of the house to someone else by will or living trust.

The right of survivorship lets the survivor take the property right after the other's death, without the expense and trouble of probate. Property left in a will must go through formal probate court before being transferred to the new owner (although there is a simplified procedure for property left to a spouse).

While the joint tenants are alive, any owner can end the joint tenancy by deeding his share of the property from himself in joint tenancy to himself in tenancy in common. (Civil Code § 683.2.) This ends the joint tenancy and with it the automatic right of survivorship.

Joint tenancy isn't a good choice for all unmarried couples or groups. First, it necessitates equal ownership shares, so if people want to own the house in unequal shares, joint tenancy won't work. It's most appropriate for people in intimate, long-term relationships, who wish to provide for each other after one dies.

2. Tenancy in Common

Tenancy in common is the appropriate way for many unmarried co-owners to take title to property, except those living together in close, long-term relationships. For property taken in tenancy in common, the co-owners need not own equal shares. Tenancy in common has no right of survivorship—when a tenant in common dies, his share passes to the person named in his will or living trust, or by intestate succession (the laws that govern who gets your property if you fail to specify who you want to receive it). Unless there is some compelling reason against it, owners must typically hold title in an equity-sharing situation as tenants in common (abbreviated "TIC"; see Chapter 3 for details).

If you wish to provide for the survivor when the first partner dies, you can hold property as tenants in common and each put your share into a revocable living trust (discussed in Section F), naming each other as beneficiary, to receive the owner's share on his or her death. If you change your mind and decide not to leave your mate your share, simply change the trust beneficiary of the living trust.

C. Married Couple Owning Together

Married persons may take title to real property as joint tenants or tenants in common (discussed in general above, and specifically for married couples, below). In addition, they have a choice unmarried owners don't have—to take title as community property. This is the choice we recommend for most married couples.

1. Community Property

Community property ownership offers two advantages:
* avoiding formal probate when a spouse dies, and
* easy qualification for a federal income tax break.

a. Probate Avoidance

When one spouse dies, property held as community property goes directly to the surviving spouse without formal probate, unless the deceased left her one-half to someone other than her spouse. A surviving spouse who inherits needs only file a simple affidavit (available from a title insurance company) with the probate court. This can be done without a lawyer; the survivor avoids not only lengthy delays in transferring the property (and title), but also costly probate fees.

The petition and instructions for completing and filing an affidavit with the probate court are included in How to Probate an Estate, by Julia Nissley (Nolo Press).

b. Tax Planning

When title is held in community property, a surviving spouse who inherits the property automatically qualifies for a tax advantage that may be more difficult to achieve if the same property is held in tenancy in common or joint tenancy. The advantage lets the survivor recalculate the entire value of the house to its current market value which can greatly reduce taxable profit when the house is later sold.

Absent a death, as we explained in Chapter 14, if you sell your house and don't buy another, your profits are determined by adding the price you originally paid for your house to the cost of capital improvements, and then subtracting this total from the amount the house sells for less the costs of sale. If you haven't yet read Chapter 14, Section C, we highly encourage you to do so now. It discusses the tax considerations when selling one house and buying another.

JOINT TENANTS SHOULD SEE A TAX ACCOUNTANT FOR MORE INFORMATION

A 1988 IRS ruling suggests that the tax break, called a "stepped-up basis" (described below), may apply when spouses take title as joint tenants because state law construes joint tenancy as a form of community property for married couples.

TAKING TITLE AS JOINT TENANTS

If you want to take title as joint tenants, the deed should specify that you hold title as joint tenants with right of survivorship. For example, the deed may say "Fred Parks and Pat Parks, tenants in common, hereby grant to Denise Baker and Robert Barnes, as joint tenants with right of survivorship, [the legal description of the property]." You need not use a form with "Joint Tenancy Deed" printed on it, though it's fine if you do. A "Grant Deed" or a "Quit Claim Deed" will also form a legal joint tenancy as long as the proper legal language is used.

TAKING TITLE AS TENANTS IN COMMON

In California, a transfer of real property to two or more persons automatically creates a tenancy in common unless the deed says otherwise. No special words are necessary. Either of the following would create a tenancy in common: "Fred Parks hereby grants to Darrell Buckner, Len Ryan, and Roberta Fernandez, as tenants in common, [the legal description of the property]" or "Fred Parks hereby grants to Nolan Gooden and Dwight Wilson [the legal description of the property]."

If ownership is to be unequal, it's best to write a separate contract specifying each person's ownership percentage and what happens if one person wants to sell or dies. Two Nolo's books—*The Living Together Kit,* by Warner & Ihara, and *A Legal Guide for Lesbian and Gay Couples,* by Curry, Clifford & Leonard—contain tenancy in common (and joint tenancy) contracts. Regardless of the percentages, however, each person owns an undivided portion of the entire house, not a particular part of it.

TAKING TITLE AS COMMUNITY PROPERTY

For a married couple to own their house as community property, the deed need simply say "Fred Parks hereby grants to Mabel Rivera and Albert Rivera, as community property, [the legal description of the property]."

LEAVING YOUR HALF TO SOMEONE OTHER THAN YOUR SPOUSE

If you and your spouse own a house as community property, you can leave your half, through a will or living trust, to anyone you choose. When you die, your spouse's half remains his. Your half goes to whomever you named. If you name no one, it goes to your surviving spouse.

EXAMPLE: Carmen and Al buy a house in 1971 for $60,000. Over the years, they make $40,000 in capital improvements. They sell their house in 1994 for $350,000 (after costs of sale are subtracted) and must declare $250,000 of taxable profit.

In tax lingo, what Carmen and Al originally paid for the house ($60,000) plus the cost of improvements ($40,000) is their "adjusted cost basis" in the property ($100,000). Their taxable profit is the selling price ($350,000) less the cost basis. Thus the higher the cost basis, the lower the taxable profit.

As just mentioned, when a property owner dies, the tax rules change. The cost basis of the portion owned by the deceased person increases ("steps up") to the property's value at his death. If the property isn't community property, the basis of the survivor's share stays the same. Only the half inherited from the deceased spouse gets a stepped-up basis. Thus, the survivor's new cost basis on the entire property is the stepped up basis of the part from the deceased spouse plus the basis of the survivor's share.

To make this clear, let's return to Carmen and Al. Assume that they owned their house as tenants in common (not as community property) and that Carmen has died and left her half to Al. The cost basis on Carmen's half of the property now increases from $50,000 (half of the $60,000 purchase price plus $40,000 improvements) to $175,000 (half of the $350,000 value at the time of her death). Al's half remains $50,000; as owner of the entire property, his total cost basis becomes $225,000 ($175,000 plus $50,000). If Al sells the house for $350,000, his taxable profit would be $125,000. As you can see, the stepped-up basis on half of the property greatly reduces the amount of taxable profit.

If Carmen and Al had taken title to the property as community property, the survivor would qualify for a 100% stepped-up federal cost basis, not just on the half of the house belonging to the spouse who died. When Carmen dies, the cost basis of the house steps up from $100,000 ($60,000 purchase price plus $40,000 improvements) to $350,000 (value at the time of Carmen's death). Now, if Al sold the property for that amount, he'd have no taxable profit from the sale.

It's possible to argue, even if you didn't hold title as community property, that the property was in fact community property, held in joint tenancy or tenancy in common "for

FORMS OF REAL PROPERTY CO-OWNERSHIP

	Tenancy in Common	Joint Tenancy	Partnership	Community Property
Creation	Deed must transfer property to two or more persons "as tenants in common" or without specifying how title is to be held.	Deed must transfer property to two or more persons "as joint tenants" or "with right of survivorship."	Deed must transfer property to the name of the partnership, or partnership funds must be used to buy it.	Deed must transfer property to a married couple "as community property" or "as husband and wife."
Shares of co-owners	May be unequal. (This is specified on the deed.)	All joint tenants must own equal shares.	Determined by partnership agreement or Uniform Partnership Act.	Each spouse owns half.
Survivorship	On co-owner's death, interest passes to heirs under intestate sucession law or beneficiaries under will or living trust.	Deceased joint tenant's share goes to surviving joint tenants, even if will is to the contrary.	Interests usually go to partner's heir or beneficiaries, but partnership agreement may limit this.	Spouse can leave his or her half to anyone; if nothing to the contrary, goes to surviving spouse.
Probate	Interest left by will is subject to probate. Simplified procedure available if left to spouse.	No probate necessary to transfer title to surviving joint tenants.	Interest left by will is subject to probate.	Simplified probate procedure available to transfer title to surviving spouse.
Termination	Any co-owner may transfer his or her interest or get partition order from court. Co-owners can create joint tenancy (or community property ownership, if they're married) by signing a new deed.	Joint tenant may end joint tenancy by transferring interest to himself or another as tenants in common, or may get partition order from court.	Governed by partnership agreement or Uniform Partnership Act.	Both spouses must agree to transfers of community real estate.

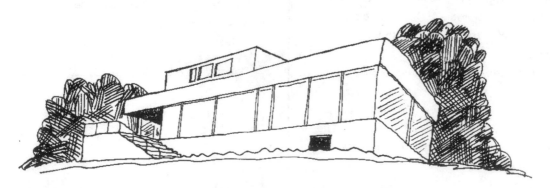

INTERNATIONAL STYLE

convenience." But there are no drawbacks to holding title as community property, and you can save yourselves an argument with the IRS.

2. Joint Tenancy

What about holding co-owned property in joint tenancy which, remember, comes with an automatic right of survivorship? Some spouses like this because the right of survivorship makes it harder for a spouse to leave his half of the property to someone other than his spouse. But, as we explained in Section B1, this isn't a significant advantage because either spouse (without the other's knowledge) may end the joint tenancy at any time by preparing a new deed, thus ending the right of survivorship. Once this is done, either spouse can leave his share of the property to anyone.

But what about qualifying for a stepped-up tax basis? Do you lose this big advantage if you hold title in joint tenancy? Not necessarily. If you want to put your co-owned property in joint tenancy and qualify for a stepped-up cost basis too, you simply need to be able to convincingly document to the IRS that the property is community property. Some experts recommend that you place the words "community property held in joint tenancy" on the deed. Before taking property in joint tenancy, read Section B1, which discusses joint tenancy's features.

Separate and Community Property Explained

Separate property is property acquired by one spouse prior to marriage, after permanent separation or during marriage by gift or inheritance. If separate property is sold, and other property is bought with the proceeds, it too is separate property.

Community property is all money earned or otherwise acquired by either spouse during the marriage (except for rents, dividends, interest and the like earned on separate property). In addition, a spouse can turn his or her separate property into community property by stating that intention in writing.

Marital Property Agreement #1

Diane Holst and James Kelvin, husband and wife, agree as follows:

1. We purchased the house at 9347 24th Street, Anaheim, California, using as a down payment Diane's separate property plus a small amount of community property.

2. We hold title to the house as tenants in common.

3. Diane agrees to pay mortgage payments and taxes from her separate property, with only a small amount of community property being used for improvements.

4. As a result, Diane owns 80% of the equity in the house, and James owns 20%.

5. We intend this document to rebut the presumption of Civil Code § 4800.2 that, at dissolution, property held in joint title is community property. We do not wish the property to be treated as community property if we dissolve our marriage.

3/24/9X	*Diane Holst*
Date	Diane Holst
3/24/9X	*James Kelvin*
Date	James Kelvin

State of California
County of *Alameda* }

On _____ *March 24* _____ ,19 *9X*
before me, *Nora Publik, Notary Public* ,
personally appeared _____ *Diane Holst* _____
and _____ *James Kelvin* _____ ,
personally known to me (or proved to me on the basis of satisfactory evidence) to be the persons whose names are subscribed to the within instrument and acknowledged to me that they executed the same in their authorized capacities, and that by their signatures on the instrument the persons, or the entity upon behalf of which the persons acted, executed the instrument.
WITNESS my hand and official seal.

Signature _____ *Nora Publik* _____

[SEAL]

3. Tenants in Common

While married couples rarely hold property as tenants in common, it is occasionally done. If, for example, the house was bought with the separate property of the husband and the separate property of the wife, and they want to keep it in separate shares, tenancy in common makes sense.

Tenancy in common lets spouses own the property in unequal shares. The specific shares, however, must be identified in writing, and the document should be recorded with the County Recorder. Otherwise, property held in tenancy in common is presumed to be community property if you die or divorce. Marital Property Agreement #1, above, is a sample agreement for spouses who hold unequal shares of their house as tenants in common. This is a tricky area of law; have a real estate lawyer look at any agreement you draft.

D. Married Person Owning Alone

If a married person owns property separately, title should be in his name alone, and the couple should sign and record (with the deed) an agreement declaring their intention that one spouse owns the property as his separate property. Otherwise, if the couple divorces and disagrees about ownership, a court will characterize the property as community or separate depending on what funds (community or separate) paid for it, not whose name is on the deed. Because most couples mix and spend separate and community funds without regard to type, what property was used to pay the mortgage, insurance, improvements and taxes won't always be clear.

⚠️ A house that starts out as separate property may easily become a mix of separate and community. For example, if Jeff and Maida, a married couple, buy a house using Jeff's pre-marital earnings for the down payment and then use income earned during marriage for the insurance, taxes, mortgage payments and improvements, everything but the down payment is community property, no matter what the deed says. Jeff and Maida can change this only by signing a written agreement.

To put your understanding in writing, use Marital Property Agreement #2, below.

MARITAL PROPERTY AGREEMENT #2

We, Brian Morgan and Laura Stein, husband and wife, hereby agree that:

1. Brian Morgan holds title to a vacation cabin at Lake Tahoe, the address of which is 43566 Lake Tahoe Drive, Lake Tahoe, California, which he owned prior to our marriage as separate property.

2. Although the mortgage, maintenance and improvements on the cabin have been, and will be, paid during our marriage with savings that are partially community property, we intend that Brian Morgan own the cabin as his separate property.

3. We make this agreement in light of the fact that Brian's earnings constitute a greater portion of our community savings, and that upon Brian's death, we both want the cabin to be inherited by Scott Morgan, Brian's son.

9/30/9X	*Brian Morgan*
Date	Brian Morgan
9/30/9X	*Laura Stein*
Date	Laura Stein

State of California

County of ___*Alameda*___ }

On _____ *September 30*___, 19 *9X*
before me, __*Jon Dough, Notary Public*__,
personally appeared __*Brian Morgan*__
and __*Laura Stein*__,
personally known to me (or proved to me on the basis of satisfactory evidence) to be the persons whose names are subscribed to the within instrument and acknowledged to me that they executed the same in their authorized capacities, and that by their signatures on the instrument the persons, or the entity upon behalf of which the persons acted, executed the instrument.

WITNESS my hand and official seal.

Signature __*Jon Dough*__

[SEAL]

E. Partnership

Partnership may be appropriate for people already in a business together who purchase a house as a business asset, or people buying a house purely as an investment to fix up and resell.

Property acquired with partnership funds is presumed to belong to the partnership, absent an agreement to the contrary. What the partners can do with the property once it's transferred to the partnership is governed either by their partnership agreement or, if they have no agreement, the Uniform Partnership Act. (Corp. Code §§ 15001 and following.)

Homebuyers don't usually form a partnership to purchase a house, so we do not discuss partnership rules in detail here. For more information on partnership law and written partnership agreements, see *The Partnership Book,* by Clifford & Warner (Nolo Press) and *Nolo's Partnership Maker* software to create a partnership agreement.

F. Placing the Property in a Living Trust

Unless you take title to your house as joint tenants or community property, you should think about keeping the house from going through probate at your death. Probate is a long and expensive court process where assets are distributed by the terms of a will, or if there is no will, by the laws of the state.

Fortunately, avoiding probate is relatively easy. You set up a revocable living trust, name yourself as the trustee (which means you keep control over the property), and name a beneficiary to receive the property when you die. The beneficiary can be anyone—a spouse, lover, child, a charity or whomever. You prepare, sign and record a deed transferring ownership from yourself to the living trust. When you die, the beneficiary takes title usually in a few weeks without probate.

Because you name yourself as trustee of your own living trust, you keep control over the property while you're alive. You can easily change the title to the house, sell the house or change the trust beneficiary.

To create a living trust, you must prepare and sign the trust document papers. They appoint you as trustee and set out the terms of the trust, including how you are to manage the property, that the trust is revocable and when ownership should be transferred to the beneficiary. We recommend *Nolo's Living Trust* (computer software) or *Plan Your Estate,* by Clifford & Jordan (Nolo Press), which contains a tear-out, fill-in living trust form with step-by-step instructions. Before putting your house into a trust, however, check with the lender to see if changing title triggers any due-on-sale provision (requiring full payment when ownership changes) of your mortgage.

If you decide to create a living trust but don't have it ready when you buy your house, take title in your name or, if you own the house with someone else, in your name and the other person's name. After you create the trust, transfer title to the house (if you're the sole owner) or your share of the house, to the trust. If you are married, you'll need your spouse's consent to transfer your share of community property. This is simple to do; see *The Deeds Book,* by Mary Randolph (Nolo Press).

TAKING TITLE AS A PARTNERSHIP

When a partnership buys a house, the deed states the business name used by the partnership, or the partners' names themselves, such as, "Fred Parks hereby grants to the Stobert Partners, [the legal description of the property]" or "Fred Parks hereby grants to Linda Stone and Blake Herbert, a partnership, [the legal description of the property]."

If Something Goes Wrong During Escrow

The likelihood of a major disaster—such as the seller dying or an earthquake destroying the house—befalling your purchase is slim. But it's possible during escrow that something will go wrong. A missing or incorrect loan document or last-minute title problems may simply delay closing a bit. While inconvenient, you'll still end up with the house. More serious problems may jeopardize the whole deal. This chapter presents a brief overview of what may happen if your deal threatens to unravel. If you and the seller both agree to rescind the contract, there's no problem. Simply complete the Release of Real Estate Purchase Contract form in Chapter 18. If either of you wants to close the deal, however, you'll need the expeditious help of an experienced real estate lawyer.

Difficulties in removing contingencies are not covered by this chapter. We don't discuss the process of inspecting a house and removing these and other contingencies here. In Chapter 18, Section B, we deal with what to do if the need for expensive repairs is discovered or you or the seller can't fulfill some other contingency, such as your getting financing or needing to sell your existing house.

A. The Seller Backs Out

Backing out of the deal, or breaching the contract, technically means failing to perform without a legal excuse. What a court might consider a "legal excuse," and therefore allow the termination of the contract, depends on the application of contract law principles to the circumstances of the transaction. The many twists and turns of that subject are well beyond the scope of this book.

But suppose a seller backs out of the deal after you have met or waived all contingencies simply because he doesn't want to sell the house, gets another offer that he likes better, or his other house deal fell through. Isn't that a clear breach of contract? Yes, and your remedy is normally to mediate or arbitrate (an option in many standard real estate contracts, including Clauses 23 and 24 of our form), or sue, requesting that the seller sell you the house and pay you damages based on your out-of-pocket costs.

EXAMPLE: Alex and Mack signed a contract for Alex to sell his home to Mack for $250,000. Alex wasn't completely happy with the price and Mack knew he'd gotten a good deal. Mack quickly removed the contingencies and was ready to close the deal. But Alex received an offer for $270,000, which he wanted to accept. He tried to cancel the deal with Mack, offering to return his deposit. Mack refused and pointed out that if Alex didn't complete the deal, he'd be in breach of the contract.

Alex's lawyer advised him that if he accepted the other offer, Mack would probably pursue arbitration (they had checked it off on their contract) and win, and the arbitrators would order Alex to sell the house to Mack and pay Mack's court costs, attorneys' fees, costs of storing furniture and costs of living elsewhere. Nevertheless unhappy, Alex honored his contract with Mack.

B. The Seller Refuses to Move Out

In rare circumstances, the seller may refuse to move out even though the house is legally yours. If it's a matter of a few days, and it's not too inconvenient, you may let the seller stay and pay rent. Prepare a short-term rental agreement. The seller's real estate agent or your agent are in the best position to draft such an agreement. You don't have to amend your contract as long as you and the seller sign the agreement. Be sure to set a strict deadline with a high penalty for every day the seller remains after the deadline.

But you may face a bigger problem if the seller or a tenant currently living on the property has no intention of leaving. To force a "holdover" seller from your property, you must follow the same procedure as a landlord uses to evict a tenant—and file an unlawful detainer lawsuit in municipal court. You can do this even if your purchase contract includes a mediation or arbitration clause, providing unlawful detainers are listed as an exception to the dispute clause (as is the case with Clause 24 in our offer form). See *The Landlord's Law Book, Volume 2: Evictions*, by David Brown (Nolo Press) for step-by-step instructions and forms needed to file an eviction lawsuit in California.

C. You Back Out

If you refuse to go through with the deal without a good reason, the seller can pursue mediation, arbitration or a lawsuit, requesting you pay her damages. Damages aren't always easy to determine, however, because the seller has a duty to try to limit (mitigate, in legalese) her losses by selling the house to someone else. To avoid arguing over the amount of the loss, most house purchase contracts provide a specific figure (liquidated damages) for the seller's maximum damages if you breach the contract. (See our contract in Chapter 16, Clause 22.)

A liquidated damages clause means that the maximum amount the seller is entitled to is the stated amount. Disputes are often settled by the buyer and seller agreeing to allow the seller to keep part, but not all, of the deposit. Canny buyers know that sellers who are under pressure to find another buyer and transfer clear title want to get a deal-gone-bad behind them and are therefore often willing to compromise on the amount of the deposit they get to keep.

D. The Seller Dies

Technically, a contract to buy a house is enforceable even if the seller dies because a deceased person's estate is responsible for fulfilling that person's lawful obligations. Just the same, you can safely bet your grandfather's Indian head nickel that the title insurance and/or escrow company will put on the brakes and call in their attorneys if the seller dies.

The executor of the seller's estate, and possibly the seller's inheritors, may want to get out of the deal. This could be a blessing in disguise, because after a seller dies, completing a house purchase transaction often becomes more complicated and time-consuming than when the seller was alive, especially if the house is part of an estate that must be probated. If the seller's inheritors do want out, insist that they reimburse you for any expenses you've thus far incurred.

If you and the inheritors want to proceed, be patient and sensitive. Try to determine whether the sale is likely to go through without difficulty. (Talking to an estate planning

GREEK REVIVAL

lawyer should help.) If settling the estate will be simple (for example, a child inherits all the property under the terms of a living trust, which is not subject to probate), the delay with the sale will probably be short. If settling the estate will be more complicated (for instance, the estate must be probated and 17 people claim the seller owed them money), consider discussing with the lawyer the best way to get out of the deal and look for another house.

E. You Discover a Defect in the Property

If you feel that a seller knew about a defect—such as a basement that floods in a heavy rain—before the sale and failed to disclose it, contact the seller and his broker and ask for money to correct the problem. If they turn down your request, and you can document that the defect was longstanding and should have been known to the seller, you have a good chance of going to court and recovering damages. You may sue both the seller and his broker in small claims court (up to $5,000). The California edition of *Everybody's Guide to Small Claims Court*, by Ralph Warner (Nolo Press) shows how. If more than $5,000 is involved, consider filing suit in municipal court (up to $25,000). *Everybody's Guide to Municipal Court*, by Roderic Duncan (Nolo Press) covers municipal court cases. If more money is involved or the situation is complicated, you'll need to obtain legal advice. (See Section H, below.)

As long as the defect is disclosed, however, there is usually no legal liability. If the disclosure doesn't happen until late in escrow, however, you (the buyer) may have the right to get out of the deal or to be compensated. Again, you'll need legal advice for this type of situation. Your lawyer will want to consult *Jue v. Smiser* (28 Cal. Rptr. 2d 242), a case covering disclosure late in escrow.

F. The House Is Destroyed by Natural Disaster (Fire, Earthquake, Flood)

As explained in Chapter 16, Putting Your Offer in Writing (Clause 21), destruction of the house is handled as follows: If you have either physical possession of, or legal title to, the property, you are responsible for its physical condition and insurance. Otherwise, the seller is responsible. Thus the seller should make sure her homeowner's policy is in force until the close of escrow, at which moment, your policy goes into effect.

If the house is flooded three days before escrow closes, the seller can pay for the repairs and deliver the property in the condition it was in before the flood. If you want out of the deal, however, simply refuse to grant an extension to the seller to make the repairs.

G. House-Hungry Martians Take Possession of the House

While we don't expect your deal to be threatened by extraterrestrials, we include this heading to remind you that in this weird and wacky world of ours, all sorts of unexpected events can frustrate even the best plans. If you suddenly find your house purchase threatened from a totally unexpected angle (for example, the state announces that construction of a new freeway running through the house's kitchen will begin in a month), see an experienced real estate lawyer pronto.

H. Finding a Lawyer

This chapter points out a few instances when an attorney's advice or services may be useful. Finding a good, reasonably priced lawyer is not always an easy task. If you just pick a name out of the phone book, you may get a lawyer who's not qualified to deal with your particular problem, one who will charge too much, or both. If you use the attorney who drew up your family will, you may end up with someone who knows nothing about real estate law.

As a general rule, experience is most important. The best way to find a lawyer who specializes in real estate law is through a trusted person who has had a satisfactory experience with one. Your agent may have some suggestions (unless, of course, your legal problem involves your agent).

The worst referral sources are:

- heavily advertised legal clinics, which are less likely to offer competitive rates for competent representation in this specialized area, and
- referral panels set up by local bar associations, which sometimes refer people to inexperienced practitioners who don't have enough clients and use the panel as a way of generating needed business.

Once you get a good referral, call the law offices that have been recommended and state your problem. Find out the hourly fee and cost of an initial visit. Most lawyers charge $100 to $200 an hour. If you feel the lawyer is qualified to handle your problem, make an appointment to discuss your situation.

Beware of lawyers who offer "free consultations." Lawyers who will see you for nothing have every motive to think up some sort of legal action that requires their services. If you insist on paying fairly for an attorney's time, you are far more likely to be advised that no expensive legal action is necessary.

Here are some things to look for in your first meeting:

- Will the lawyer answer all your questions about fees, her experience in real estate matters, and your particular legal problem? Stay away from lawyers who make you feel uncomfortable asking questions.
- Is the lawyer willing to answer your specific questions over the phone and charge you only for the brief amount of time the conversation lasted? Or does she insist on a more time-consuming (and profitable) office appointment? If the lawyer won't give you any advice over the phone despite your invitation to bill you for it, find someone else.
- Does the lawyer represent sellers, too? Chances are that a lawyer who represents both buyers and sellers can advise you well on how to avoid many legal pitfalls of buying a house.

⚠ If your contract has an attorney fees provision (see Clause 25 of our form), you are entitled to recover your attorney fees if you win a lawsuit based on the terms of that agreement. There's no guarantee, however, that a judge will award attorney fees equal to your attorney's actual bill, or that you will ultimately be able to collect the money from the seller.

GETTING YOUR DEPOSIT BACK

As mentioned in Chapter 18, Section B6, if the deal falls through, you and the seller should sign a Release of Real Estate Purchase Contract form. If one of you refuses to sign within 30 days following a written demand to do so from the other, the person who refuses to sign may be liable to the other for attorney fees and damages of three times the amount deposited in escrow—no more than $1,000 and no less than $100. (Civil Code § 1057.3.)

FELICITY AND MELINDA: EARTHQUAKE JITTERS

Everything was progressing smoothly. We had contracts to buy one house and sell our existing one. The buyers of the house we were selling had the house inspected and signed off. Then a big earthquake hit. Our house suffered no damage, but the buyers wanted to pay less. They claimed that the earthquake had generally lowered real estate values. After much haggling, we agreed to a small reduction in price, provided they increase their deposit to $4,000 and sign that it was non-refundable. We didn't have to lower the price, but we wanted to close on our new house and needed to get our money out of the old one.

Three weeks later, on the day the buyers got notice of their loan approval, they backed out. The earthquake had scared them and they changed their mind about living in California. Then they demanded that half of their non-refundable deposit be refunded! We were furious. A lawyer told us that going to binding arbitration or suing would be costly, would risk clouding the title of the house and could prevent an easy sale to someone else. Nevertheless, we asked the lawyer to write a stiff letter demanding the full amount. As a result, the chicken-hearted former buyers agreed to let us keep $3,000, which meant we ended up with $2,700 after our lawyer got his fee.

■

Appendix 1

Welcome to California*

*Substantial research and writing for this Appendix was contributed by Tim Devaney, a writer and geographer who lives in Oakland.

This Appendix is intended primarily for house purchasers who are:

- new to California
- moving from one part of the state to another, or
- first-time purchasers.

Long time residents of California who are selling one house to buy another in the same area will likely already have considered most of the issues discussed here, but still may want to review this material to be sure they haven't overlooked something important.

Buying a house in California involves many of the same choices and decisions purchasers face buying a house anywhere else. So if you're new to the state but are experienced in the house purchase game, most of what you have learned will be relevant here. There are a number of things, however, unique to life on the Pacific coast—and to California in particular—that people who come here from other states or countries should be aware of.

A. Climate and Geography

Most people who move to California come here under the influence—the influence of the media. Impressions of the state are created by movie and television depictions of California's endless summer. And why not? On New Year's day, while you're snow-bound in the East or Midwest, the Rose Bowl is being broadcast from Pasadena, where the temperature is invariably 80 degrees. You're forgiven for your initial view of California.

Yet reality, even reality California-style, tends to come without a suntan in January. If you doubt this, trade your sunglasses for reading glasses and look at a map of the United States. Notice how far California stretches from top to bottom—a state of such varied latitude just can't be uniformly warm and sunny year round. Sure, you might tan in January in San Diego on a particularly nice day, where you'd be on the same latitude as Cairo. But tanning is the last thing you'd do in Crescent City, near the Oregon border, which is as far north as Boston, and gets significantly more wintertime precipitation.

The key to understanding California climate is in the word "variety." If you doubt this, consider that the state holds the U.S. records for highest and lowest summer temperatures and for greatest annual snowfall. Much of the San Francisco Bay Area (called "northern" California, but really part of the middle coast) has a Mediterranean climate—temperate, dry summers and relatively mild, wet winters. Summers along the coast are kept cool by the high fog which rolls in at night—thus the remark attributed to Mark Twain, "The coldest winter I ever spent was a summer in San Francisco." Twain could have found all the summer he ever wanted just a few miles inland, though, where 100 degree temperatures abound.

To the far north, the coast is practically a rain forest, where California's famous redwoods thrive and rainfall can exceed 100 inches a year. Inland, in the far north of the state, snow-capped Mount Shasta is often viewed as a symbol for the mountain regions of the state.

Most 14,000-foot peaks are in the Sierra Nevada mountain range, far to the south, and along the eastern side of the state. The Sierra is not only the source of much of the state's water, but provides relatively abundant low-cost power and, happily for all who love its spectacular natural beauty, is within a reasonable drive of many of the state's population centers.

In southern California, the climate is semi-arid; Los Angeles has dry, pleasant winters and warm summers which attract flocks of people. Southeastern California is a desert (the best known city is Palm Springs), inhabited by cacti and retired actors and within a few hours' drive of most of the southern part of the state.

B. Microclimates

In much of the state, especially in the San Francisco and Los Angeles areas, the local weatherperson's favorite word is "variable." The typical weather pattern, influenced by the topography near the coast, can change radically within just a few miles. Close to Los Angeles, in beach-front Santa Monica, the July high averages 75 degrees, but heats up to 95 degrees in Canoga Park, just 15 miles north in the San Fernando Valley. Near San Francisco, Half Moon Bay on the coast averages a July high of 64 degrees, while 25 miles inland, in Walnut Creek, the average climbs to 87.

More locally still, the weather within one city's limits can change considerably from neighborhood to neighborhood: Summer in San Francisco's Sunset District, for instance, is far cooler and foggier than in the warmest neighborhood, the Mission, just a few miles to the east. Many people new to California find it hard to accept how radical local climatic variations can be. After all, in most places the weather is much the same on both sides of a city, county or even state.

How close your house is to the coast is a big factor in determining the weather you'll be enjoying—or complaining about. Hills and valleys are also important: West-facing slopes generally get more rain and lower temperatures than east-facing ones. So, however sunny a weather picture a real estate broker paints for you, listen with a drop of skepticism. If you can, ask a local resident what the weather is like.

AVERAGE PRECIPITATION AND TEMPERATURES THROUGHOUT THE STATE

Location	Annual Precipitation (in.)	Temperatures (Fahrenheit)			
		January		July	
		Max.	Min.	Max.	Min.
Alturas	12.01	42.2°	15.6°	87.6°	43.2°
Bakersfield	5.72	56.9°	38.6°	98.5°	69.6°
Bishop	5.37	53.5°	22.0°	97.2°	56.1°
Eureka	37.53	54.4°	41.5°	61.8°	52.3°
Fresno	10.60	54.1°	37.4°	98.6°	65.1°
Imperial	2.75	69.3°	42.0°	106.0°	77.6°
Los Angeles	14.77	67.7°	48.9°	84.0°	64.5°
Paso Robles	13.95	61.2°	31.6°	92.8°	50.4°
Redding	33.30	55.3°	35.7°	98.3°	64.7°
Sacramento	17.52	52.7°	37.7°	93.2°	58.1°
San Diego	9.90	65.9°	48.9°	76.2°	65.7°
San Francisco	19.71	56.3°	45.8°	64.6°	53.5°
Susanville	14.30	40.3°	19.6°	89.3°	49.9°

Source: *California Statistical Abstract 1995* published by the Department of Finance. Averages are for the 30-year period from 1961-90.

RESOURCES: WEATHER
The University of California Press publishes two good paperbacks on the variable weather of the San Francisco and Los Angeles areas—*Weather of the San Francisco Bay Region*, by Gilliam, and *Weather of Southern California*, by Baily. Both are available from California-Princeton Fulfillment Services, 1445 Lower Ferry Road, Ewing, NJ 08618, (800) 822-6657. If you're told that a book is out of stock, let the clerk know that the Richmond, California warehouse has plenty of books in stock even if the New Jersey warehouse does not. (California-Princeton Fulfillment Services is the exclusive distributor of these books; you can't call the Richmond warehouse and order them yourself.) Local bookstores may also carry these books.

C. Natural Hazards

The midwest has floods and tornadoes, the southeast gets hurricanes, the north is crippled by snowstorms—but California still seems to be getting more than its share of natural disasters. The four major natural hazards you'll find in California are earthquakes, fires, floods and droughts.

1. Earthquake

When visitors ask, "How can you live here knowing the 'Big One' is coming?," Californians can't resist a show of jaded bravado: "There's nothing I can do about it, so why should I worry?" A cavalier response, but when weighed against the other benefits of living in California, we stay.

In truth, there have been, and likely will continue to be, devastating earthquakes and many smaller ones in the next 50 years. And in a state where faults underlie the land like a capillary system and the most populated cities are on the coast, the area of highest fault activity, there are no areas where you are completely safe from earthquakes. (Take a look at the fault map on the following page.) While the odds of a quake damaging your home or the home of someone you know is unfortunately significant, you can, fortunately, take steps to minimize the risk of severe damage.

a. How Safe Is the Site?

Surprisingly, proximity to a major fault is not the primary factor that affects how well a house will hold up during an earthquake, according to seismic experts. Instead, they point out, other geologic and geographic factors should be examined, as should the structure of the house itself:

- To begin, an unstable hillside is not a good place to be if an earthquake hits because of the potential for landslides. In the San Francisco Bay Area, for example, Dr. Robert Uhrhammer of the University of California, Berkeley, Seismology Center, predicts that a sizable quake on the Hayward fault (one of the state's most dangerous), which runs through the Oakland and Berkeley hills on the east side of San Francisco Bay, will result in more homes being damaged from landslides than from shaking. The danger of a slide depends on the soil condition—rock is preferable to unconsolidated dirt. Flat, solid ground is even better.

- The worst place for a house to be built is on fill. (Artificial fill is common along many California bays and rivers, including, most notably, the San Francisco Bay; the houses destroyed in San Francisco's Marina District in the Loma Prieta earthquake of October 1989 were all on artificial fill.) Some newer types of fill are sturdier than older ones, and in a strong quake with a lot of vigorous shaking, older fill and bay mud may have a tendency to lose cohesiveness and liquefy. A house built on fill won't necessarily sink, but it could tilt. A recent earthquake in Japan left an apartment building built on landfill leaning at almost a 45 degree angle.

- Another warning: Don't buy a house downstream from a dam. Some dams in California will fail (leak or even break) in a really strong earthquake.

A geologist or soils engineer can evaluate the site and give you an opinion on its safety. Seismic maps may also help you evaluate the earthquake hazards of a particular area. (See Resources: Earthquakes, below.)

b.   How Safe Is the Structure?

Even more important than where a house is built is what it's made of. "Most wood frame houses won't suffer significant structural damage, even in a large earthquake with a lot of ground shaking," says Dr. Uhrhammer. Wood frame houses are quite flexible and, if properly secured to their foundations, will shake but not break. In the 1906 quake, a large number of houses in the San Francisco hills survived with only cosmetic damage. Dr. Uhrhammer says that masonry houses are significantly less earthquake resistant than wood frame houses and he describes an unreinforced brick house a few stories tall as "extremely dangerous."

RESOURCES: EARTHQUAKES

California Seismic Safety Commission publishes *The Homeowner's Guide to Earthquake Safety* which includes the seismic disclosure form discussed in Chapter 19 of this book. The Commission's Sacramento office is (916) 322-4917.

California Department of Conservation, Division of Mines and Geology publishes seismic hazard data and fault zone maps. Their Sacramento number is (916)-445-5716. Similar information may be available from your city or county planning department.

State Office of Emergency Services (OES) provides local and regional earthquake maps and a wide variety of material on earthquake preparedness, including a do-it-yourself video on retrofitting wood frame houses and earthquake safety guides for businesses and schools. Contact a regional Earthquake Preparedness Project: Oakland, (510) 540-2713; Pasadena, (818) 304-8383; Santa Barbara, (805) 568-1207; San Diego, (619) 525-4287.

Peace of Mind in Earthquake Country, by Peter Yanev (Chronicle Books) is the best book around on earthquake preparedness. This fascinating and well-written book tackles potentially life-and-death questions, such as: How safe is the house you live in or are considering buying? What do you need to know about geologic factors such as type of soil and proximity to active faults? What can you do to retrofit your house and minimize interior damage from earthquakes? Where is the next major earthquake most likely to hit in California? Should you buy earthquake insurance?

Building Education Center, is a nonprofit organization that offers all-day seminars and publications on earthquake retrofitting. 812 Page St., Berkeley, CA, 94710, (510) 525-7610.

Earthquake Outlet is a retail outlet and mail order business that sells a wide variety of ingenious earthquake-safety products, including pre-assembled emergency kits and survival equipment. 981 San Pablo Ave., Albany, CA, 94706, (510) 526-3587; 2225 Broadway, Redwood City, CA, 94063, (415) 368-8800.

Safe Homes, Safe Neighborhoods: Stopping Crime Where You Live by Stephanie Mann with M.C. Blakeman (Nolo Press). Although its main focus is how to bring neighbors together for crime prevention, this book includes an appendix on preparing the neighborhood to deal with disaster.

2.   Fire

In the late 1980s and early 1990s, California's forest fires, particularly in Southern California and the Oakland hills, made national headlines. The fires that pose the greatest threat to houses are grass and brush fires, most common in dry southern California, where large areas of parched brush and chaparral spark easily to flame. But, as the Oakland fire aptly demonstrated, these fires aren't limited to southern California, as fires begin in dry canyons all over the state. And once started, they can spread incredibly quickly, destroying thousands of homes, especially when fanned by hot winds that blow from the interior valleys toward the coast.

CALIFORNIA FAULT MAP

If you are considering buying a house near a wild canyon or hill area, look at whether you can reduce the risk of fire by clearing a wide area around it. Pay attention to what the house is made of; shake roofs and wood shingles are far more dangerous than tile roofs and stucco. Some cities have outlawed wood shingles for new construction.

RESOURCES: WILDFIRES

For fire safety information, call your city's fire department or the county Office of Emergency Services. Many cities and counties in high risk-areas have implemented special programs to reduce fire danger and improve fire department response to wildfires.

3. Flood

It hardly seems fair, but the same hills and canyons that make fires so hard to control in the summer are prone to dangerous floods and mudslides in the winter. The steep canyons in the San Gabriel mountains above Los Angeles are notorious for the torrents of water, mud and boulders that have demolished many expensive homes over the years.

Houses by the ocean are also vulnerable to flood damage. Every year, Pacific storms combine with normal high tides to produce huge waves which roll over the beaches. The Russian and Sacramento rivers in northern California have flooded so often that locals know where the danger spots are. So, if you're considering buying a house close to a stream or river, ask someone who has lived nearby for many years about floods. If you're told that the area flooded 40 years back or just last year, consider buying a bit higher up because floods can recur at any time.

RESOURCES: FLOODS AND LANDSLIDES

National Flood Insurance Program (NFIP), in Baltimore, (800) 358-9616, publishes hundreds of flood zone maps for California. For information on NFIP flood insurance policies, call (800) 638-6620.

U.S. Geological Survey, Earth Sciences Information Center in Menlo Park, (415) 329-4390, can supply information about landslide susceptibility in California.

4. Drought

In the late 1980s, California, like much of the U.S., suffered the effects of a drought, and many counties were on rationing. Rationing programs vary according to the severity of the drought. But they also vary depending on where you live—some water districts are harder hit than others.

For instance, in the summer of 1988, the neighboring towns of San Ramon and Dublin, east of San Francisco, were affected very differently by the drought. San Ramon is part of the East Bay Municipal Utilities District (EBMUD), while Dublin, right next door, is not. Most of the time, you would prefer to be living in EBMUD territory, because the mountain water distributed by the district is of very high quality. (See Section D1, below.) But there's less of it, so it's rationed during a drought. Dublin's water comes from the Sacramento River, which is of low quality, but plentiful. Thus, San Ramon residents were limited to 400 gallons of great-tasting water per day per household, took short showers and watched their lawns dry up. Across the street, Dublin residents had as much mediocre water as they wanted, sang in their showers and watered away in their gardens.

Droughts aren't limited to San Ramon and Dublin; they take place all over California. Which town you live in can be very important in terms of water quality and availability. Historically, however, droughts have come only at widely spaced intervals. Thus, it's probably better to seek high quality water, landscape with drought-tolerant plants and console yourself during dry times with a fresh glass from the tap.

D. Pollution

Like any other state, California has its environmental problems. Some make a place unpleasant; others make it unhealthy, especially if you're particularly sensitive to environmental contaminants.

1. Water Pollution

Many towns and cities in California, including San Francisco, get drinking water good enough to bottle and sell. That's because it comes from mountain river reservoirs. Other parts of the state are not so lucky. Southern California, Los Angeles included, must import most of its water, often from as far away as the Colorado River. The water is not as pure as mountain water, and tastes bad too.

"Where does it come from?" is the most important question to ask in determining the quality of a water supply. In general, water from above-ground sources is good water. Water pumped from ground aquifers can be just as good, but can also be polluted with health-threatening substances, such as toxic waste from industrial sources, or agricultural chemicals. In a number of California areas, water quality isn't too different from that in developing countries. People who can afford to do so drink bottled water.

The key to determining water quality is to find out the source for a particular town. Often, one part of a county—Santa Clara, for example—will have excellent water piped in from the mountains, while a few miles away the water will be wretched.

 RESOURCES: WATER QUALITY AND WATER POLLUTION

Ask the local water district where the water comes from. If it's pumped from the ground or comes from a river, demand information on recent water quality tests.

The best source for candid information on all pollution are private environmental groups, such as Citizens for a Better Environment (CBE). They do their own studies and can tell you if a known pollution problem exists in your neighborhood. CBE has offices in San Francisco ((415) 243-8373), and Los Angeles ((213) 486-5114).

Ask the State Water Resources Control Board, Division of Water Quality in Sacramento ((916) 657-0687), about pollution. Another possible source is a regional water quality control board (see the government pages of the phone book for the number). These agencies, however, have limited information—they generally report only complaints received, unless a particular area has been tested recently. If so, ask for the results.

2. Toxic Waste

No one in his or her right mind would knowingly buy a house next door to a toxic waste dump. Unfortunately, the presence of toxic waste may not be obvious. Many toxic dumps are buried; other locations have yet to be disclosed. And some dumps may pose broader health threats if their contaminants leak into groundwater supplies.

A 1986 report by the California Legislature stated that all nine major toxic waste landfills in California leak, and that not one met state requirements to prevent leakage. Thousands of smaller waste landfills and underground storage tanks leak into the soil and water, resulting in almost 20 percent of California's major drinking water wells having been chemically polluted. Aquifers, which store water, are not naturally flushed. Once one becomes polluted, it stays that way. The situation is so bad that several communities in California whose aquifers became contaminated have been rendered uninhabitable.

Groundwater contamination is a problem in much of the area south and east of San Francisco, especially where industry is concentrated. For San Francisco itself, and for many localities in the East Bay, the problem is ignored by most because these places get drinking water from the mountains. But to the south, in the Silicon Valley towns of San Jose, Mountain View and others, leaking toxic dumps have been traced to the "clean" semi-conductor industry. Parts of Contra Costa County (north and east of San Francisco), where industry is concentrated, have had toxic contamination problems. Parts of central California and Los Angeles County have hazardous groundwater supplies due to agricultural chemicals polluting aquifers.

 RESOURCES: TOXIC WASTE

Citizens for a Better Environment (contact information is in Section D1).

California Office of Environmental Protection, Office of Hazardous Material Data Management, Sacramento, (916) 327-1848. This state agency maintains the Hazardous Waste and Substances Sites List. (For more information on hazardous waste inspections and sites, see Chapter 19 of this book.)

The California Environmental Directory: A Guide to Organizations Concerned with Hazardous Materials in California should be in most libraries. If you can't find it contact the publisher, the California Institute for Public Affairs in Sacramento at (916) 442-2472.

3. Air Pollution

The air quality in California varies about as much as the weather, as the two are closely related. Residents breathe easier near the coast, where the air circulates regularly, keeping the smog from ever getting really thick. For example, the city of San Francisco and communities on the coast just to the north and south of San Francisco have some of the cleanest air in the state, especially during the summer. This is because the fog and wind blow the air to the east (inland), making room for the cool, clean ocean air to fill its place.

Unfortunately, if you enjoy hot weather, learn to like polluted air. Anywhere the air sits still long enough to really warm up, pollution collects, particularly in the summer. Areas of the state east of the coastal range are blocked from the cleansing incursions of sea air. The Central Valley is often thick with smog, as are the San Gabriel and San Fernando valleys in southern California. Ditto the Livermore Valley, east of San Francisco, where a few years ago the development of a new town was blocked, in part because air pollution was already dangerous.

Los Angeles has some of the most polluted air in the U.S. Despite efforts to convert to cleaner fuels, the situation is expected to worsen in the '90s as more cars and industry fill the area. The Pacific winds blow much of L.A.'s smog inland to the rapidly developing Riverside and San Bernadino counties, where most new affordable houses are being built. L.A.'s coastal communities—Pacific Palisades, Santa Monica, Venice, Palos Verdes—have relatively clean air, and the most expensive houses in the L.A. metropolitan area.

Many people consider air pollution more of a nuisance than a hazard, but recent studies show that air-borne toxins pose a threat to anyone living near industry, including the "clean" computer industry. One survey linked exposure to air toxins with high cancer rates near Contra Costa County's petrochemical plants. If you're sensitive to air pollution, you'll want to move close to the coast or the Sierra foothills and avoid most areas in between, although there are still many rural parts of northern and central California where the air is relatively clean.

 RESOURCES: AIR POLLUTION

Citizens for a Better Environment (contact information is in Section D1).

A local or regional air quality district such as Bay Area Air Quality Management District, (415) 749-4900; South Coast Air Quality Management District, (909) 396-2000; or San Joaquim Valley Unified Air District, (209) 497-1000. A city manager's or mayor's office should be able to refer you to a specific air quality district.

E. Nuclear Plants

Atomically speaking, California is in better health than many other states. While four commercial nuclear power plants were built, only two are operational—the Diablo Canyon plant in San Luis Obispo, 200 miles north of Los Angeles, and the San Onofre Nuclear Generating Station between Los Angeles and San Diego. Safety fears led to the close of the other two—the Humboldt Bay nuclear plant in Eureka and Rancho Seco near Sacramento. Many people believe it makes sense to avoid buying a house near any of the power plants, as serious safety questions have been raised about all four. These questions often center on whether the plants will withstand a strong earthquake, although operations problems (at the two up and working) also arise.

Many experts argue that the Diablo Canyon plant should never have been built. Diablo Canyon was licensed in 1966, when the closest earthquake fault was thought to be 20 miles away. Then in 1971 a major fault was discovered just three miles away. Scientists debated the size and likelihood of an earthquake on the newly-discovered fault, and concluded that an 8.0 quake was possible, causing groundshaking three times stronger than the reactors could withstand. In 1976, the Nuclear Regulatory Commission decided that the fault was not capable of such a large quake, and Diablo Canyon went online.

To make matters worse, Diablo Canyon's support cooling pipes (built to work during earthquakes) were originally put in backwards. The support structures have since been corrected, but this is the sort of horror story that has led some people to conclude that it doesn't make sense to live anywhere near a nuclear power plant.

At the San Onofre Nuclear Generating Station, the builders repeated the Diablo Canyon mistake—cooling pipe supports were installed backwards and had to be rebuilt. San Onofre's reactors need supports because the plant is next door to the Newport-Inglewood Fault, a fault on which an estimated 7.5 quake could happen. San Onofre was built to withstand a quake of only 6.5 magnitude.

Even when a reactor is shut down, a hazard remains. At all of California's commercial nuclear power plants, spent fuel is stored in open containment ponds, awaiting the construction of a high-level waste repository, tentatively scheduled for completion in the year 2003. Should an earthquake occur before 2003 and a containment pond crack and lose its water, the spent fuel could melt down and release radioactivity.

If you decide to live near a nuclear plant, a house to the north or west will be safer from possible releases of radioactivity than a house to the south or east, as winds in California blow toward the south and southeast 80 percent of the time.

One of the safest urban areas, from a nuclear standpoint, is the San Francisco Bay Area, as there are no large commercial nuclear facilities nearby. Still, research and military reactors operate in the north San Francisco Bay Area, as they do throughout the state.

RESOURCES: NUCLEAR PLANTS

The Abalone Alliance informs people of the threats posed by nuclear power in California. They are located at 2940 16th Street, Suite 310, San Francisco, CA 94103, (415) 861-0592.

In Southern California, contact the Alliance for Survival, 200 North Main Street, Suite M-2, Santa Ana, CA 92701, (714) 547-6282.

F. Schools

The 1996-97 California budget provided nearly $32 billion for elementary and high school education. Sounds like a lot of money. It's not. California spends less annually per student than most industrial states—about $4,000 per student less than New York. And California has among the largest number of pupils enrolled per teacher in the country—over 24 (compared to the national average of 17). This said, California has many excellent public schools—the problem is finding them. The solution is to look yourself, not to simply ask your real estate agent "How are the schools around here?" Real estate agents will too often tell you what they think you want to hear.

Since California's Proposition 13 cut taxes, schools have had less money. Some schools are in worse shape than others, but all have had to cut back programs, usually in sports, art, music and drama. At some schools, where parent interest is high and financial resources available, parents pay to keep "non-essential" programs going.

Many people assume that the best schools are in the rich communities. This isn't always true. Money, by itself, doesn't guarantee good schools, although parents in prosperous areas (who themselves tend to have a relatively high level of education) usually take considerable interest in educating their children. But you don't need to live in Encino to find good public schools. Many middle-class cities have excellent public schools because parents get involved.

To learn about average class size, course offerings, instructional practices and available services, start by calling and visiting local schools and school districts. Ask for the *School Accountability Report Card*, which each school must prepare annually. This report covers a range of important topics, including expenditures per student and types of services funded; class sizes and teaching loads; student achievement and progress toward meeting academic goals; assignment of teachers outside of their subject areas of competence; quality and currency of textbooks and instructional materials; availability of qualified personnel to provide counseling and other student support services; dropout rates; safety, cleanliness and adequacy of school facilities; classroom discipline and climate for learning; teacher and staff training; quality of school instruction and leadership.

Arrange to visit schools you're considering. Observe the atmosphere by sitting in on classes, and talking to some parents or teachers. And look for locally produced publications such as a school newsletter or parent handbook.

The State Department of Education in Sacramento can also provide useful information. The Department's California Assessment Office can provide five-year rating summaries of test scores for either individual schools or districts. They measure academic quality and performance solely by their standardized CAP test, administered to 3rd, 6th, 8th and 12th grade students annually. To request CAP summaries, call (916) 657-3011. The Educational Demographics Unit provides much data for schools and districts, including enrollment figures, racial and ethnic information, language census data and even dropout rates. Call them in Sacramento at (916) 657-2676.

Check out local resources at public libraries. Look under "Schools" in the index of local newspapers at a public library for articles on how active the district PTA is and how well-attended parent open houses are. Local civic groups, such as the League of Women Voters or PTA, often publish ratings of local schools. Ask a reference librarian for help finding these. If you're interested in private schools, ask for information on local guides, such as *McCormack's Guides*, discussed in Section I, below.

Contact EdSource, a nonprofit resource center that distributes impartial statewide information about Kindergarten through 12th grade education. EdSource publishes numerous pamphlets discussing school budgets and finances, the ramifications of state education legislation, demographics and bilingual education.

If EdSource doesn't have what you need, they can help you find it. Contact them at 4151 Middlefield Road, Suite 100, Palo Alto, CA 94303, (415) 857-9604.

DESEGREGATION AND CALIFORNIA SCHOOLS

Desegregation in California often means busing. In big cities like Los Angeles, the bus ride can be over an hour. In many urban school districts, parents can't choose what school their kids will attend. Even the concept of the neighborhood school for young kids is long gone.

Some parents don't like the effect of this public policy, and for this and other reasons (class size, test scores, parent participation) enroll their children in private schools. Other parents see great value in sending their kids to public schools with children from a diverse mix of ethnic backgrounds. To find out more about busing, desegregation and racial make-up, call the local school district.

G. Traffic

In California cities, traffic has replaced weather as the favorite topic of conversation; as more people move here, traffic gets worse. People from outside California who experience heavy commute traffic tend to think that their situation is the same as the average Californian's. It isn't.

"Gridlock" is a word that strikes fear into the heart of every commuter. But for a long time, for many Californians, it has been more an ominous idea than a reality—kind of like the Greenhouse Effect. Not any more: on many of the state's highways, gridlock is here, and not only during traditional commute hours.

In the San Francisco Bay Area, people in the North Bay and East Bay commonly arise before dawn, and drive hours to reach major urban centers. Some transportation experts predict that by the year 2020 it may take *four hours* to cross the Bay Bridge into San Francisco in the morning.

In the state's fastest growing urban areas, such as San Diego and Sacramento, once rare traffic jams are a part of the daily routine.

In Los Angeles, of course, traffic is worse than anywhere in the country. Los Angeles has four of North America's five busiest freeways. Traffic typically crawls from morning to midnight. Even on L.A.'s less crowded freeways, rush "hour" lasts from 7 a.m. to 10 a.m. and from 3 p.m. to 7 p.m.

Before you buy a house in California, figure out how you are going to get to work. Is driving reasonable? Will it be in ten years? Don't assume you can jump in the car and turn the key. Sometimes in California, you *can't* always get there from here (at least not before 9 a.m.).

Consider the availability of public transportation. As traffic continues to worsen, rapid transit may be the only alternative. Several areas, including the San Francisco Bay Area, have commuter trains. Even good bus systems save a great deal of time (not to mention stress), as freeway planners emphasize express lanes.

In places without rapid transit systems, many people are moving into the city. Paradoxically, this is happening just as many employers are moving their operations out of expensive downtown office space into the less expensive suburbs. The result is that many employees make an easier "reverse commute" to work. (But as the suburbs continue to grow in some parts of the state, the commute and the reverse commute are beginning to look frighteningly similar.) And of course, if you live near your job, you can avoid a commute altogether. If you work in the city, a house there may cost more, but this extra cost is increasingly likely to balance against your commuting (and sometimes parking) costs. This is a popular approach in L.A., when people are "rediscovering" downtown and the advantages of living close to work.

RESOURCES: TRANSPORTATION
Check the nearest office California Department of Transportation (CalTrans) for information on ride-sharing and transportation planning, or call the state office in Sacramento at (916) 445-7665. Also city traffic departments may be of some help.

H. Crime

Crime always ranks high when people are asked about the social problems that most concern them. Indeed, in many areas neighbors are so concerned they have banded together to form crime prevention groups.

Picking an area that is reasonably safe is a major concern when purchasing a house, especially if you have children. But always bear in mind that no neighborhood, no matter how affluent or well policed, is immune from crime. Also understand that a substantial percentage of the crime that occurs in any neighborhood is committed by people who live there— often teenagers and others who feel alienated, bored or angry. There is no way to escape this type of crime except by taking home security precautions and working with others as part of neighborhood groups designed to help local teenagers channel energy into healthier activities.

But what about criminals who enter a neighborhood from the outside, specifically to steal, sell drugs or otherwise cause serious mischief? While this type of crime does occur, the media has exaggerated the danger most of us face in most neighborhoods. Still, it's sensible to be aware of a neighborhood's crime level when buying a house. Here are a few suggestions:

- Some cities have far less crime than others. The California Attorney General's Office publishes statewide statistics adjusted by population in *Crime and Delinquency in California*. It's available from the Law Enforcement Information Center in Sacramento at (916) 227-3509.
- You can check on crime types and frequency with the local police department. Although they may not keep statistics on a block-by-block basis, you may be able to get numbers for the general neighborhood you are considering.
- *Safe Homes, Safe Neighborhoods*, by Stephanie Mann with M.C. Blakeman (Nolo Press) includes a section on researching neighborhood crime problems and covers all aspects of neighborhood crime prevention from home security to child safety.
- Neighborhoods with active, effective neighborhood watch groups, where residents understand the importance of keeping their eyes on the street and maintaining good communication among neighbors, are usually much safer than those which remain unorganized.
- Those who are seriously worried about crime may want to live in a community secured with walls and guards. But check with residents before you assume security is tight— some of these communities have become targets for burglars who easily evade lax security systems.
- Upscale suburban areas next to very poor ones are almost always targets for robbery and burglary. So before you buy, drive twenty blocks in every direction. Look for graffiti, broken windows, bars on doors or boarded up buildings. If you find yourself rolling up your window in your car, you'll likely need a burglar alarm and maybe bars on the windows at home.
- In California cities, neighborhood safety changes block to block, driven by many factors, most of which are invisible to newcomers. Ask long-time city residents in what areas they would feel safe walking the dog at 10 p.m. Then confirm what you hear by talking to patrol cops; take any advice from a real estate agent with a grain of salt—they earn a commission regardless of how safe the neighborhood is.

I. Additional Information on California

For separate guides to many California counties, see *McCormack's Guides*, annual publications providing a range of local information on schools (public and private), demographics, crime, weather, home prices, jobs, recreation, child and health care and other topics of interest to newcomers, including profiles of individual cities. *McCormack's Guides* are available at many bookstores or by calling (800) 222-3602.

For an overview of a myriad of California topics see *The California Handbook*, available from the California Institute of Public Affairs in Sacramento, (916) 442-2472. This comprehensive guide describes thousands of organizations and publications concerned with all aspects of California, from the environment and social issues to the state's economy, education and history.

CALIFORNIA COUNTY POPULATION DENSITY

In Alphabetic Order			In Order of Density		
County	Population	Population Per Sq. Mile	County	Population	Population Per Sq. Mile
Alameda	1,337,100	1,619.9	San Francisco	752,000	8,254.7
Alpine	1,200	1.7	Orange	2,557,300	3,257.3
Amador	32,700	54.4	Los Angeles	9,158,400	2,245.1
Butte	197,100	118.4	Alameda	1,337,100	1,619.9
Calaveras	36,700	35.4	San Mateo	680,900	1,282.8
Colusa	17,300	15.0	Santa Clara	1,563,800	1,188.4
Contra Costa	855,100	1,071.7	Sacramento	1,121,200	1,104.3
Del Norte	27,900	27.8	Contra Costa	855,100	1,071.7
El Dorado	140,900	78.1	San Diego	2,648,600	618.7
Fresno	733,300	122.3	Santa Cruz	236,900	538.9
Glenn	26,300	19.9	Solano	369,500	423.6
Humboldt	126,500	35.1	Marin	241,300	410.4
Imperial	131,000	28.5	Ventura	700,100	375.7
Inyo	18,800	1.9	San Joaquin	514,500	358.2
Kern	603,000	73.8	Stanislaus	405,600	266.6
Kings	111,200	77.5	Sonoma	416,300	260.6
Lake	55,700	42.0	Riverside	1,328,300	183.4
Lassen	28,900	6.2	Napa	116,900	146.7
Los Angeles	9,158,400	2,245.1	Yolo	148,800	143.9
Madera	102,900	47.9	Santa Barbara	389,200	141.8
Marin	241,300	410.4	Placer	194,100	128.8
Mariposa	15,800	10.8	Fresno	733,300	122.3
Mendocino	83,600	23.8	Butte	197,100	118.4
Merced	193,400	96.3	Sutter	71,100	117.1
Modoc	10,300	2.4	Monterey	375,600	113.0
Mono	10,400	3.4	Yuba	62,600	98.0
Monterey	375,600	113.0	Merced	193,400	96.3
Napa	116,900	146.7	Nevada	85,500	86.2
Nevada	85,500	86.2	El Dorado	140,900	78.1
Orange	2,557,300	3,257.3	Kings	111,200	77.5
Placer	194,100	128.8	San Bernardino	1,556,300	77.2
Plumas	20,900	8.0	Kern	603,000	73.8
Riverside	1,328,300	183.4	Tulare	340,400	70.3
Sacramento	1,121,200	1,104.3	San Luis Obispo	228,400	68.7
San Benito	40,100	28.7	Amador	32,700	54.4
San Bernardino	1,556,300	77.2	Madera	102,900	47.9
San Diego	2,648,600	618.7	Lake	55,700	42.0
San Francisco	752,000	8,254.7	Shasta	161,000	41.8
San Joaquin	514,500	358.2	Calaveras	36,700	35.4
San Luis Obispo	228,400	68.7	Humboldt	126,500	35.1
San Mateo	680,900	1,282.8	San Benito	40,100	28.7
Santa Barbara	389,200	141.8	Imperial	131,000	28.5
Santa Clara	1,563,800	1,188.4	Del Norte	27,900	27.8
Santa Cruz	236,900	538.9	Mendocino	83,600	23.8
Shasta	161,000	41.8	Tuolumne	52,600	22.9
Sierra	3,400	3.5	Glenn	26,300	19.9
Siskiyou	45,200	7.2	Tehama	54,000	18.1
Solano	369,500	423.6	Colusa	17,300	15.0
Sonoma	416,300	260.6	Mariposa	15,800	10.8
Stanislaus	405,600	266.6	Plumas	20,900	8.0
Sutter	71,100	117.1	Siskiyou	45,200	7.2
Tehama	54,000	18.1	Lassen	28,900	6.2
Trinity	13,500	4.2	Trinity	13,500	4.2
Tulare	340,400	70.3	Sierra	3,400	3.5
Tuolumne	52,600	22.9	Mono	10,400	3.4
Ventura	700,100	375.7	Modoc	10,300	2.4
Yolo	148,800	143.9	Inyo	18,800	1.9
Yuba	62,600	98.0	Alpine	1,200	1.7
Statewide	31,551,400.0	198.8	Statewide	31,551,400.0	198.8

CALIFORNIA COUNTY MAP

Appendix 2

REGIONAL MEDIAN HOUSE PRICE LIST

This table gives the median house prices (provided by the California Association of Realtors) for single-family detached houses as of May 1996 for 16 California regions.

Region	May 1996 Median Price
Los Angeles	$170,530
San Francisco (including Santa Clara)	272,570
Santa Clara	275,810
San Diego	172,050
Orange County	216,550
Central Valley (including Sacramento)	108,700
Sacramento	118,000
Palm Springs/Lower Desert	110,200
Monterey	234,410
Northern Wine Country	184,040
Northern California	134,050
Riverside/San Bernardino	115,020
Ventura Area	212,200
Santa Barbara Area	237,120
High Desert	108,470
San Luis Obispo	168,230
State	179,095
United States	117,400

Appendix 3

Planning Your Move

The following will help you plan your move.

A. Tax Deductible Moving Expenses

You may deduct job-related moving expenses from your gross income on your federal tax return if:

- the distance from your old home to your new job is at least 50 miles more than the distance from your old home to your old job
- the distance from your new home to your new job is less than the distance from your old home to your new job; this test need not be met if your employer said you'd lose your job if you didn't move, and
- you work full-time.

    If you pass the three tests, list your deductible moving expenses in items 1-3 below.

RESOURCES ON PLANNING YOUR MOVE

For a booklet on tax deductible moving costs, contact the California Association of Realtors, 525 South Virgil Avenue, Los Angeles, CA 90020, (213) 739-8200.

For more information on tax deductible moving expenses, see IRS Publications 521 and 523.

Contact the state Public Utilities Commission ((800) 848-5580) for a consumer guide to choosing a moving company.

1. Direct Moving Expenses

Airline/train/boat/bus tickets	$ _____
Car use (9¢ per mile)	$ _____
Gas and oil for car	$ _____
Truck or car rental	$ _____
Gas & oil for truck	$ _____
Professional mover's fee	$ _____
Lodging during trip	$ _____
Food during trip	$ _____
Long-distance phone calls to arrange move	$ _____
Storing possessions before moving into new home	$ _____

2. Lease Termination Expenses

To end lease	$ _____
To find new tenant	$ _____

3. **Costs of Selling and/or Buying Home(s)**

Real estate commission or
hourly fees (selling) $ _____

State transfer tax (selling) $ _____

Hourly fees paid to buyer's
broker (buying) $ _____

Appraisal fees (buying) $ _____

Attorney and/or
accountant fees (either) $ _____

Escrow fees (either) $ _____

Title fees (either) $ _____

Points and other loan
fees (either) $ _____

Prepaid interest on your
loan (buying) $ _____

B. **Two Weeks Before Moving**

☐ Transfer school records & transcripts

☐ Close bank & safe deposit box accounts

☐ Purchase traveler's checks

☐ Cancel deliveries (oil, newspaper, diapers, laundry)

☐ Cancel utilities (gas, electric, cable, phone, water, garbage); transfer services (if possible) or arrange new services; request deposit refunds

☐ Get recommendations for (or secure, if a medical condition needs regular attention) new doctors, dentist and veterinarian; if possible, photocopy medical records to have with you

☐ Get reference letters, if you'll need to find a job

☐ Cancel membership (and transfer membership, if relevant) in religious, civic and athletic organizations

☐ Have car serviced for travel

☐ Buy travel insurance

☐ Get maps

☐ Line up storage facility

☐ Arrange moving pets

☐ Finalize arrangements with moving company

☐ Tell close friends and relatives your schedule

C. **Things to Remember While Packing**

☐ Label boxes on top and side (your name, new city, room of house, contents)

☐ Pack old phone books

☐ Assemble moving kit (hammer, screwdriver, pliers, tape, nails, tape measure, scissors, flashlight, cleansers, cleaning cloths, rubber gloves, garbage bags, light bulbs, extension cords, step stool, mop, broom, pail, vacuum cleaner)

☐ Keep the basics handy (comfortable clothes, toiletries, towels, alarm clock, disposable plates, cups and utensils, can opener, one pot, one pan, sponge, paper towels, toilet paper, plastic containers, toys for kids)

☐ Carry jewelry, extremely fragile items, currency & important documents

☐ Make other arrangements if moving company won't move antiques, art collections, crystal, other valuables or plants

D. Whom to Send Change of Addresses

☐ Subscriptions

☐ Government agencies you regularly deal with (VA, Social Security Administration, etc.)

☐ Charge & credit accounts

☐ Installment debt (such as student loan or car loan)

☐ Frequent flyer programs

☐ Brokerage account houses

☐ Insurance agent/companies

☐ Medical providers (if you'll be able to use them after moving)

☐ Catalogues you want to keep receiving

☐ Charities you wish to continue donating to

☐ Post office. (If you're trying to get off of catalogue and other direct mailing lists, don't send a change of address to the post office. Instead, notify all those marketers on whose lists you want to remain and tell them not to trade or sell your name. Otherwise, you'll be inundated because many direct marketers get the post office address changes.)

E. Things to Do After Moving In

☐ Open bank accounts

☐ Open safe deposit box account

☐ Begin deliveries (oil, newspaper, diapers, laundry)

☐ Register to vote

☐ Change (or get new) driver's license

☐ Change auto registration

☐ Install new batteries in existing smoke detectors (and install any additionally needed smoke detectors); buy fire extinguisher

☐ Hold party for your house scouts and moving helpers and take yourself out for a congratulatory dinner!

■

Forms

Instructions for the forms in this appendix can be found in the following chapters:

HOUSE PRIORITIES WORKSHEET

Address : _____   **Price: $** _____

_____   **Contact:** _____

Date: _____   **Phone Number:** _____

Mandatory Priorities:

☐ _____

☐ _____

☐ _____

☐ _____

☐ _____

☐ _____

☐ _____

☐ _____

Secondary Priorities:

☐ _____

☐ _____

☐ _____

☐ _____

☐ _____

☐ _____

☐ _____

☐ _____

Absolute No Ways:

☐ _____

☐ _____

☐ _____

☐ _____

☐ _____

☐ _____

☐ _____

Comments About the Particular House:

_____

_____

_____

FAMILY FINANCIAL STATEMENT

	Borrower	Co-Borrower
Name	_____	_____
Address	_____	_____
	_____	_____
Home phone number	_____	_____
Employer's name and address	_____	_____
	_____	_____
Work phone number	_____	_____

WORKSHEET 1: INCOME AND EXPENSES

I. INCOME	Borrower ($)	Co-Borrower ($)	Total ($)
A. Monthly gross income			
1. Employment	_____	_____	_____
2. Public benefits	_____	_____	_____
3. Dividends	_____	_____	_____
4. Royalties	_____	_____	_____
5. Interest & other investment income	_____	_____	_____
6. Other (specify):	_____	_____	_____
B. Total monthly gross income	_____	_____	_____

II. MONTHLY EXPENSES	Borrower ($)	Co-Borrower ($)	Total ($)
A. Non-housing			
1. Child care	_____	_____	_____
2. Clothing	_____	_____	_____
3. Food	_____	_____	_____
4. Insurance	_____	_____	_____
a. auto	_____	_____	_____
b. life	_____	_____	_____
c. medical & dental	_____	_____	_____
5. Medical & dental care (not insurance)	_____	_____	_____
6. Personal	_____	_____	_____
7. Education	_____	_____	_____
8. Taxes (non-housing)	_____	_____	_____
9. Transportation	_____	_____	_____
10. Other (specify):	_____	_____	_____
B. Current housing			
1. Mortgage payment	_____	_____	_____
2. Taxes	_____	_____	_____
3. Insurance	_____	_____	_____
4. Utilities	_____	_____	_____
5. Rent	_____	_____	_____
C. Total monthly expenses	_____	_____	_____

WORKSHEET 2: ASSETS AND LIABILITIES

I. ASSETS (Cash or Market Value)	Borrower ($)	Co-Borrower ($)	Total ($)
A. Cash and cash equivalents			
1. Cash	_____	_____	_____
2. Deposits (list):	_____	_____	_____
_____	_____	_____	_____
_____	_____	_____	_____
_____	_____	_____	_____
B. Marketable securities			
1. Stocks & bonds (bid price)	_____	_____	_____
2. Other securities	_____	_____	_____
3. Mutual funds	_____	_____	_____
4. Life insurance	_____	_____	_____
5. Other (specify):	_____	_____	_____
_____	_____	_____	_____
_____	_____	_____	_____
C. Total cash & marketable securities	_____	_____	_____
D. Non-liquid assets			
1. Real estate	_____	_____	_____
2. Retirement funds	_____	_____	_____
3. Business	_____	_____	_____
4. Motor vehicles	_____	_____	_____
5. Other (specify):	_____	_____	_____
_____	_____	_____	_____
_____	_____	_____	_____
_____	_____	_____	_____
E. Total non-liquid assets	_____	_____	_____
F. Total all assets	_____	_____	_____

II. LIABILITIES	Outstanding Balance ($)	Monthly Payment ($)	Months Remaining
A. Debts			
1. Real estate loans	B C _____	_____	_____
2. Student loans	B C _____	_____	_____
3. Motor vehicle loans	B C _____	_____	_____
4. Child or spousal support	B C _____	_____	_____
5. Personal loans	B C _____	_____	_____
6. Credit cards (specify):	B C _____	_____	_____
_____	B C _____	_____	_____
_____	B C _____	_____	_____
_____	B C _____	_____	_____
7. Other (specify):	B C _____	_____	_____
_____	B C _____	_____	_____
_____	B C _____	_____	_____
B. Total Liabilities	_____		

III. NET WORTH (Total assets minus total liabilities)   _____

MONTHLY CARRYING COSTS WORKSHEET

1. Estimated Purchase Price $ _____

2. Down Payment $ _____

3. Loan Amount (line 1 minus line 2) $ _____

4. Interest Rate   _____ %

5. Mortgage Payment Factor   _____

6. Monthly Mortgage Payment (multiply line 3 by line 5) $ _____

7. Homeowner's Insurance (monthly) $ _____

8. Property Taxes (monthly) $ _____

9. Total Monthly Carrying Costs (add lines 6-8) $ _____

10. Long-Term Debts (monthly payments)

      _____ $ _____

      _____ $ _____

      _____ $ _____

      _____ $ _____

      Total Long-Term Debts (monthly payments) $ _____

11. Private Mortgage Insurance $ _____

12. Homeowners' Association Fee $ _____

13. Total Monthly Carrying Costs and Long-Term Debts (add lines 9-12) $ _____

14. Lender Qualification (between .28 and .38)   _____ %

15. Monthly Income to Qualify (divide line 13 by line 14) $ _____

16. Yearly Income to Qualify (mutiply line 15 by 12) $ _____

MORTGAGE RATES AND TERMS TABLE

Lender _____   _____   _____

Loan agent _____   _____   _____

Phone number _____   _____   _____

Date _____   _____   _____

1. General Information

	Column 1	Column 2	Column 3
Fixed or adjustable	☐ F ☐ A	☐ F ☐ A	☐ F ☐ A
Fixed rate mortgage interest rate	_____ %	_____ %	_____ %
Government financing	☐ Y ☐ N	☐ Y ☐ N	☐ Y ☐ N
Minimum down payment	_____ %	_____ %	_____ %
PMI required	☐ Y ☐ N	☐ Y ☐ N	☐ Y ☐ N
Impound account	☐ Y ☐ N	☐ Y ☐ N	☐ Y ☐ N
Term	_____ Years	_____ Years	_____ Years
Assumable	☐ Y ☐ N	☐ Y ☐ N	☐ Y ☐ N
Prepayment penalty	☐ Y ☐ N	☐ Y ☐ N	☐ Y ☐ N
Negative amortization (adjustables only)	☐ Y ☐ N	☐ Y ☐ N	☐ Y ☐ N
Rate lock-in available	☐ Y ☐ N	☐ Y ☐ N	☐ Y ☐ N
Cost to lock-in	21 Days $_____	21 Days $_____	21 Days $_____
	30 Days $_____	30 Days $_____	30 Days $_____
	45 Days $_____	45 Days $_____	45 Days $_____

2. Debt-to-Income Ratios Information

Allowable monthly carrying costs as % of income	_____ %	_____ %	_____ %
Allowable monthly carrying costs plus long-term debts as % of monthly income	_____ %	_____ %	_____ %
Maximum loan you qualify for based on debt-to-income ratios	$_____	$_____	$_____

3. Loan Costs

	Column 1	Column 2	Column 3
Number of Points	_____	_____	_____
Cost of Points	$_____	$_____	$_____
PMI	$_____	$_____	$_____
Additional loan fee	$_____	$_____	$_____
Credit report	$_____	$_____	$_____
Application fee	$_____	$_____	$_____
Appraisal fee	$_____	$_____	$_____
Miscellaneous fees	$_____	$_____	$_____
Estimated total loan costs	$_____	$_____	$_____

4. Time Limits

	Column 1	Column 2	Column 3
Credit/employment check	_____ Days	_____ Days	_____ Days
Lender appraisal	_____ Days	_____ Days	_____ Days
Loan approval	_____ Days	_____ Days	_____ Days
Loan funding	_____ Days	_____ Days	_____ Days
Loan due date each month	_____	_____	_____
Grace period	_____ Days	_____ Days	_____ Days
Late fee	_____ % Pmt	_____ % Pmt	_____ % Pmt

5. Other Features [such as a discount if you have an account with a certain bank, or a lender buydown (discount) of interest rate on initial payments]

Column 1	Column 2	Column 3
_____	_____	_____
_____	_____	_____

_____   _____   _____   _____

_____   _____   _____   _____

6. Fixed Rate Two-Step Loans

Initial annual interest rate	_____%	_____%	_____%
Over how many years	(_____ Years	_____ Years	_____ Years

7. Fixed Rate Balloon Payment Loans

Interest rate	_____%	_____%	_____%
Monthly payment	$_____	$_____	$_____
Term of loan	_____ Years	_____ Years	_____ Years
Amount of balloon payment	$_____	$_____	$_____

8. Convertible Loans

Earliest conversion period	_____ Months	_____ Months	_____ Months
Conversion window	_____ Weeks	_____ Weeks	_____ Weeks
Index: 11th District COFI	☐ _____%	☐ _____%	☐ _____%
6 Mo. T-Bills	☐ _____%	☐ _____%	☐ _____%
1 Yr. T-Bills	☐ _____%	☐ _____%	☐ _____%
6 Mo. LIBOR	☐ _____%	☐ _____%	☐ _____%
Other _____	☐ _____%	☐ _____%	☐ _____%
Margin	_____%	_____%	_____%
Conversion fee	$_____	$_____	$_____

9. Adjustable Rate Mortgages (ARMs)

Index: 11th District COFI	☐ _____%	☐ _____%	☐ _____%
6 Mo. T-Bills	☐ _____%	☐ _____%	☐ _____%
1 Yr. T-Bills	☐ _____%	☐ _____%	☐ _____%
6 Mo. LIBOR	☐ _____%	☐ _____%	☐ _____%
Other _____	☐ _____%	☐ _____%	☐ _____%
Margin	_____%	_____%	_____%
Convertible	☐ Y ☐ N	☐ Y ☐ N	☐ Y ☐ N
When	_____ Year	_____ Year	_____ Year
Initial interest rate	_____%	_____%	_____%
How long	____ Mos. ____Yrs.	____ Mos. ____Yrs.	____ Mos. ____Yrs..
Interest rate cap (with negative amortization) or	_____%	_____%	_____%
Interest rate cap (without negative amortization)	_____%	_____%	_____%
Adjustment period	_____ Months	_____ Months	_____ Months
Life-of-loan (overall) cap	_____%	_____%	_____%
Initial payment	_____ Months	_____ Months	_____ Months
Payment cap	_____%	_____%	_____%
Payment cap period	_____ Months	_____ Months	_____ Months
Highest payment or interest rate in: 6 months	____% $_____	____% $_____	____% $_____
12 months	____% $_____	____% $_____	____% $_____
18 months	____% $_____	____% $_____	____% $_____
24 months	____% $_____	____% $_____	____% $_____
30 months	____% $_____	____% $_____	____% $_____
36 months	____% $_____	____% $_____	____% $_____

10. Hybrid Loans

Initial interest rate	_____%	_____%	_____%
Term as a fixed rate loan	_____ Years	_____ Years	_____ Years
Interest rate at first adjustment period	_____%	_____%	_____%

CONTRACT TO PURCHASE REAL PROPERTY

Property address, including county: _____

_____ .

Date: _____, 19_____

(Buyer) _____ ,

makes this offer to purchase the property described above, for the sum of _____

_____ dollars ($_____). Buyer includes a deposit, in the amount of

_____ dollars

($_____), evidenced by ☐ cash ☐ cashier's check ☐ personal check ☐ promissory note ☐ other.

1. Financial Terms

This offer is contingent upon Buyer securing financing as specified in Items D, E, F & G below within _____ days from acceptance of this offer.

$ _____ **A. DEPOSIT TO BE APPLIED TOWARD THE DOWN PAYMENT**, payable to (Payee) _____ ,

_____ , to be held uncashed until

the acceptance of this offer. If this offer is accepted, the deposit shall be delivered to Payee and applied toward the down payment.

$ _____ **B. DOWN PAYMENT INCREASE**, to be paid into escrow ☐ within _____ calendar days of acceptance, or

☐ on or before _____ .

$ _____ **C. DOWN PAYMENT BALANCE**, to be paid into escrow on or before the close of escrow.   .

$ _____ **D. FIRST LOAN—NEW LOAN.** Buyer shall obtain a new loan, amortized over not fewer than ____ years. Buyer's financing shall be:

☐ Conventional (name of lender, if known) _____

☐ Private (name of lender, if known) _____

☐ Government (specify): ☐ VA ☐ FHA ☐ Cal-Vet ☐ CHFA

☐ Other: _____

Buyer's mortgage shall be

☐ at a maximum fixed rate of _____%

☐ an adjustable rate loan with a maximum beginning rate of _____%, or

☐ (fill in any other requirements here) _____

_____ .

$ _____ **E. FIRST LOAN—EXISTING LOAN.** Buyer shall ☐ assume ☐ buy

subject to an existing loan under the same terms and conditions that Seller has with _____

_____ , the present lender.

The approximate remaining balance is $ _____ , at the current rate of interest of _____ % on a

☐ fixed ☐ adjustable rate loan, for a remaining term of approximately _____ years, secured by a First Deed of Trust.

$ _____ **F. SECOND LOAN—NEW LOAN.** Buyer shall obtain a new loan, amortized over not fewer than _____ years. Buyer's

financing shall be:

☐ Conventional (name of lender, if known) _____

☐ Private (name of lender, if known) _____

☐ Government (specify): ☐ VA ☐ FHA ☐ Cal-Vet ☐ CHFA

☐ Other: _____

Buyer's mortgage shall be ☐ at a maximum fixed rate of _____ %, ☐ an adjustable rate loan with a maximum

beginning rate of _____%, or ☐ (fill in any other requirements here) _____

_____

$ _____ **G. SECOND LOAN—EXISTING LOAN.** Buyer shall ☐ assume ☐ buy subject to an existing loan under the same terms and conditions that Seller has with , the present lender. The approximate remaining balance is $ _____ , at the current rate of interest of _____ % on a ☐ fixed ☐ adjustable rate loan, for a remaining term of approximately _____ years, secured by a Second Deed of Trust.

$ _____ **H. TOTAL PURCHASE PRICE, EXCLUDING EXPENSES OF SALE AND CLOSING COSTS.**

$ _____ **I. OTHER. (See Paragraph _____ of this contract for additional terms and conditions.)**

LOAN APPLICATION. Buyer shall submit complete loan application and financial statement to lender(s) within 5 days after acceptance. If Buyer, after making a good-faith effort, does not secure financing by the time specified, this contract shall become void, and all deposits shall be returned to Buyer.

GOVERNMENT FINANCING. In the event of FHA or VA financing, Buyer shall not be obligated to complete the purchase, nor shall Buyer forfeit the deposit, if the offer price exceeds the property's FHA or VA appraised value. Buyer shall, however, have the option of proceeding with the purchase from any above-named lender or a different lender without regard to the appraised value.

EXISTING LOAN. If Buyer is assuming any loans or purchasing the property subject to any loans, Seller shall, within 7 days after acceptance, deliver to Buyer copies of all applicable notes and deeds of trust, loan balances and current interest rates. Buyer's obligation under this contract is conditioned upon Buyer's written approval of the documents within 7 days after receipt. If Buyer does not accept the documents, either party may terminate this contract.

SELLER FINANCING. The following terms apply only to financing extended by Seller.

1. The rate specified as the maximum interest rate in D or F, above, shall be the actual fixed interest rate for seller financing.
2. The loan documents shall be prepared in the form customarily used by Escrow Agent, identified in Clause 3.
3. The promissory note and deed of trust shall include the following:
   a. Request for Notice of Default on senior loans.
   b. Seller's right to have Buyer execute and pay for a Request for Notice of Delinquency.
   c. Acceleration clause making the loan due, at Seller's option, upon the sale or transfer of the property.
   d. Title insurance coverage insuring Seller's deed of trust interest in the property.
   e. Late charge of 6% of the amount of any installment received more than 10 pays after the date it is due.
   f. Obligation of Buyer to maintain fire and extended insurance with Seller named as loss payee at least to cover lesser of replacement of improvements or the liens on the property.
4. Seller shall obtain at Buyer's expense a tax service to notify Seller in the event of a property tax delinquency by Buyer.
5. If the property contains 1-4 dwelling units, Buyer and Seller shall execute a Seller Financing Disclosure Statement as provided by the arranger of credit as soon as is practicable prior to the statements reflecting Buyer's financial condition in such detail as is customarily required by institutional lenders. Seller shall keep these documents confidential and use them only to approve Buyer's creditworthiness. Seller shall notify Buyer in writing within 7 days after receipt of Seller's approval or disapproval of Buyer's credit.
6. Buyer shall notify Seller in writing within 7 days after receipt of the Seller Financing Disclosure Statement of Buyer's approval or disapproval of the financing terms offered by Seller.

2. Occupancy

Buyer ☐ does ☐ does not intend to occupy the property as Buyer's primary residence.

3. Escrow

Buyer and Seller shall deliver signed escrow instructions to _____

_____ , escrow agent

located at _____

_____ , within

a reasonable time before the close of this sale. Escrow shall close within _____ days of acceptance of this offer. The escrow fee shall be paid by Buyer.

4. Prepayment Penalty and Assumption Fee

Seller shall pay any prepayment penalty or other fees imposed by any existing lender who is paid off during escrow. Buyer shall pay any prepayment penalty, assumption fee or other fee which becomes due after the close of escrow on any loans assumed from Seller.

5. Expenses of Sale

Expenses of sale, settlement costs and closing costs shall be paid for as follows:

	Buyer	Seller	Shared Equally	
A.	☐	☐	☐	Escrow fees
B.	☐	☐	☐	Title search
C.	☐	☐	☐	Title insurance for buyer/owner
D.	☐	☐	☐	Title insurance for buyer's lender
E.	☐	☐	☐	Deed preparation fee
F.	☐	☐	☐	Notary fee
G.	☐	☐	☐	Recording fee
H.	☐	☐	☐	Attorney's fee (if attorney hired to clarify title)
I.	☐	☐	☐	Documentary transfer tax
J.	☐	☐	☐	Pest control inspection report
K.	☐	☐	☐	General contractor report
L.	☐	☐	☐	Roof inspection report
M.				Other inspections (specify):
1.	☐	☐	☐	_____
2.	☐	☐	☐	_____
3.	☐	☐	☐	_____
4.	☐	☐	☐	_____
N.	☐	☐	☐	One-year home warranty (specify covered items): _____
				_____
				_____
O.				Other (specify):
1.	☐	☐	☐	_____
2.	☐	☐	☐	_____
3.	☐	☐	☐	_____
4.	☐	☐	☐	_____

6. Property Tax and Insurance Prorations; Non-Callable Bonds

Seller shall be responsible for payment of Seller's prorated share of real estate taxes and assessments accrued until the deed transferring title to Buyer is recorded. Buyer understands that the property shall be reassessed upon change of ownership and that Buyer shall be sent a supplemental tax bill which may reflect an increase in taxes based on property value.

Any premiums on insurance carried over from Seller to Buyer and any homeowners' association dues and regular assessments, interests, rents shall be prorated, that is, Seller shall pay the portion of the premiums and fees while title is in Seller's name and Buyer shall pay the portion of the premiums and fees while title is in Buyer's name.

Homeowners' association special assessments shall be ☐ paid current by Seller (payments not yet due shall be assumed by Buyer without credit toward the purchase price) or ☐ _____
_____

Buyer agrees to assume non-callable assessment bond liens (those which cannot be paid off by Seller) as follows: _____
_____
_____

7. Fixtures

All fixtures and fittings that are permanently attached to the property or for which special openings have been made, are included, free of liens, in the purchase price, including built-in appliances, electrical, plumbing, light and heating fixtures, garage door openers/remote controls, attached carpets and other floor coverings, screens, awnings, shutters, window shades, blinds, television antennas/satellite dishes and related equipment, private integrated phone systems, air coolers/conditioners, pool/spa equipment, water softeners (if owned by Seller), security systems/alarms (if owned by Seller), attached fireplace equipment, mailbox, in-ground landscaping including trees/shrubs, EXCEPT: _____

_____

_____

8. Personal Property

The following items of personal property, free of liens and without warranty of condition (unless otherwise provided), are INCLUDED in the sale:

☐ Stove ☐ Oven ☐ Refrigerator ☐ Washer ☐ Dryer ☐ Freezer ☐ Trash Compactor ☐ Dishwasher

_____

_____

_____

9. Inspection Contingencies

This offer is conditioned upon Buyer's written approval of the following inspection reports. All inspections shall be carried out within _____ days of acceptance of the offer. Buyer shall deliver written approval or disapproval to Seller within 3 days of receiving each report. If Buyer does not deliver a written disapproval within the time allowed, Buyer shall be deemed to approve of the report.

Seller is to provide reasonable access to the property to Buyer, his/her agent, all inspectors and representatives of lending institutions to conduct appraisals.

☐ A. Pest control report, covering the main building and ☐ detached garage(s) or carport(s); ☐ the following other structures on the property:

_____

_____ . Buyer may elect to pay for all, a portion or none of the cost of the work recommended by the report.

☐ B. General contractor report as to the general physical condition of the property including, but not limited to, heating and plumbing, electrical systems, solar energy systems, roof, appliances, structural, soil, foundation, retaining walls, possible environmental hazards, location of property lines, size/square footage of the property and water/utility restrictions.

☐ C. Plumbing contractor report.

☐ D. Soils engineer report.

☐ E. Energy conservation inspection report in accordance with local ordinances.

☐ F. Seismic safety report.

☐ G. Environmental hazards inspection reports including, but not limited to, asbestos, radon gas, lead-based paint and hazardous wastes.

☐ H. City or county inspection report.

☐ I. Roof inspection report.

☐ J. General contractor report at the following phases of construction (specify) _____

_____

_____

☐ K. Other (specify) _____

_____ .

If Buyer and Seller, after making a good-faith effort, cannot remove in writing the above contingencies by the time specified, this contract shall become void, and all deposits shall be returned to Buyer.

10. Other Contingencies

This offer is contingent upon the following:

☐ A. Buyer receiving and approving preliminary title report within _____ days of acceptance of this offer.

☐ B. Seller furnishing declaration of restrictions, CC&Rs, bylaws, articles of incorporation, rules and regulations currently in force, other governing documents, one year's homeowners' association minutes, financial statements of the owners' association for the past three years, a statement of reserves, assignment of parking spaces within _____ days of acceptance.

☐ C. Sale of Buyer's current residence, the address of which is _____
_____ , by_____,19____

☐ D. Seller furnishing rental agreements within _____ days of acceptance

☐ E. Seller providing Buyer with a home warranty to cover the following: _____
_____
_____

☐ F. Other: _____
_____
_____
_____
_____
_____
_____

Buyer shall deliver written approval or disapproval to Seller within 3 days of receiving each report, statement or warranty. If Buyer does not deliver a written disapproval within the time allowed, Buyer shall be deemed to approve of the report, statement or warranty. If Buyer and Seller, after making a good-faith effort, cannot remove in writing the above contingencies, this offer shall become void, and all deposits shall be returned to Buyer.

11. Condition of Property

Seller represents that the roof, heating, plumbing, air conditioning, electrical, septic, drainage, sewers, gutters and downspouts, sprinklers, as well as built-in appliances and other equipment and fixtures, are in working order. Seller agrees to maintain them in that condition, and to maintain all landscaping, grounds and pools, until possession of the property is delivered to Buyer. Seller shall, by the date of possession, replace any cracked or broken glass.

12. Foreign Investors

If Seller is a foreign person as defined in the Foreign Investment in Real Property Tax Act, Buyer shall, absent a specific exemption, have withheld in escrow ten percent (10%) of the gross sale price of the property. Buyer and Seller shall provide the escrow holder specified in Clause 3 above with all signed documentation required by the Act.

If Seller has a last known address outside of California or if Seller's proceeds will be paid to a financial intermediary of Seller, under California Revenue and Tax Code, Buyer, unless an exemption applies, must deduct and withhold 3-1/3% of the gross sales price from Seller's proceeds and send it to the Franchise Tax Board.

13. Rent Control

The property ☐ is ☐ is not located in a city or county subject to local rent control. A rent control ordinance may restrict the rent that can be charged for this property, limit the right of the owner to evict the occupant for other than "just cause" and control the owner's rights and responsibilities.

14. Title

At close of escrow, title to the property is to be clear of all liens and encumbrances of record except those listed in the preliminary title report and agreed to be assumed by Buyer. Any such liens or encumbrances assumed by Buyer shall be credited toward the purchase price. If Seller cannot remove liens or encumbrances not assumed by Buyer, Buyer shall have the right to cancel this contract and be refunded his/her deposit and costs of inspection reports.

15. Possession

Buyer reserves the right to inspect the property three days before the close of escrow. Seller shall deliver physical possession of property, along with alarms, alarm codes, keys, garage door openers and all other means to operate all property locks, to Buyer: ☐ at close of escrow ☐ no later than _____ days after the close of escrow.

If Buyer agrees to let Seller continue to occupy the property after close of escrow, Seller shall deposit into escrow for Buyer a prorated share of Buyer's monthly carrying costs (principal, interest, property taxes and insurance), for each such day, subject to the terms of a written agreement, specifying rent or security deposit, authorizing a final inspection before Seller vacates and indicating the length of tenancy, signed by both parties.

16. Agency Confirmation and Commission to Brokers

The following agency relationship(s) are confirmed for this transaction:

Listing agent: _____ is the agent of:

☐ Seller exclusively   ☐ Buyer and Seller

Selling agent: _____ is the agent of:

☐ Buyer exclusively   ☐ Seller exclusively   ☐ Buyer and Seller

Notice: The amount or rate of real estate commissions is not fixed by law. They are set by each Broker individually and may be negotiable between the Seller and Broker.

Buyer and Seller shall each pay only those broker's commissions for which Buyer and Seller have separately contracted in writing with a broker licensed by the California Commissioner of Real Estate.

$_____ or _____% of selling price to be paid to _____

by ☐ Seller ☐ Buyer.

$_____ or _____% of selling price to be paid to _____ by

☐ Seller ☐ Buyer.

17. Advice

If Buyer or Seller wishes advice concerning the legal or tax aspects of this transaction, Buyer or Seller shall separately contract and pay for it.

18. Backup Offer

☐ This offer is being made as a backup offer. Should Seller accept this offer as a backup offer, the following terms and conditions apply:

If Seller accepts this offer as a primary offer, he/she must do so in writing. Until that time, Buyer's deposit check shall be held uncashed.

Buyer has 24 hours from receipt of Seller's written acceptance to ratify it in writing. If Buyer fails to do so, Buyer's offer shall be deemed withdrawn and any contractual relationship between Buyer and Seller terminated.

19. Duration of Offer

This offer is submitted to Seller by Buyer on _____, 19_____, at _____ ☐ a.m. ☐ p.m. , Pacific Time, and will be considered revoked unless a copy of this contract with Seller's signature accepting it is delivered in person, by mail or fax and personally received by Buyer or Buyer's real estate agent not later than _____ ☐ a.m. ☐ p.m. on _____, 19_____, or, if prior to Seller's acceptance of this offer, Buyer revokes this offer in writing.

20. Other Terms and Conditions

_____

_____

_____

21. Risk of Damage to Property

All risk of loss to the property which occurs after this offer is accepted shall be borne by Seller until title has been conveyed to Buyer. Any damage totaling _____% or less of the purchase price shall be repaired by Seller prior to the transfer of title. If the land or improvements are destroyed or material damaged in an amount exceeding _____% of the purchase price, Buyer shall have the option of either terminating this agreement and recovering all deposits made or purchasing the property in its then condition.

22. Liquidated Damages

If Seller accepts this offer, and Buyer later defaults on the contract, Seller shall be released from Seller's obligations under this contract. By signing their initials here, Buyer (_____) and Seller (_____) agree that if Buyer defaults, Seller shall keep no more than three percent (3%) of the purchase price stated above if the property is a dwelling with no more than four units, one of which Buyer intends to occupy as Buyer's residence.

Seller shall retain the right to proceed against Buyer for any other claim or remedy Seller may have, other than for breach of contract. In the event of a dispute, funds deposited into escrow are not released automatically and require mutual, signed release instructions from Buyer and Seller, a judicial decision or an arbitration award.

23. Mediation of Disputes

If a dispute arises out of, or relates to, this agreement, Buyer and Seller ☐ agree ☐ do not agree to first try in good faith to settle the dispute by non-binding mediation before resorting to court action or binding arbitration. Mediation is a process in which parties attempt to resolve a dispute by submitting it to an impartial, neutral mediator who is authorized to facilitate the resolution of the dispute but who is not empowered to impose a settlement on the Buyer and Seller.

To invoke mediation, one party shall notify the other of his/her intention to proceed with mediation and shall provide the name of a chosen mediator. The other party shall have seven days to respond. If he/she disagrees with the first person's chosen mediator, the parties shall ask the escrow holder to choose the mediator or to recommend someone to choose the mediator. The mediator shall conduct the mediation session or sessions within the next three weeks. Before the mediation begins, Buyer and Seller agree to sign a document limiting the admissibility in arbitration or a lawsuit of anything said or admitted, or any documents prepared, in the course of the mediation.

Costs of mediation shall be divided equally between Buyer and Seller.

_____ Buyer	_____ Seller
_____ Buyer	_____ Seller

24. Arbitration of Disputes

Any dispute or claim in law or equity between Buyer and Seller arising out of this contract or any resulting transaction which is not settled by mediation shall be decided by neutral, binding arbitration and not by court action except as provided by California law for judicial review of arbitration proceedings.

The arbitration shall be conducted in accordance with the rules of either the American Arbitration Association (AAA) or Judicial Arbitration and Mediation Services, Inc. (JAMS). The selection between AAA and JAMS rules shall be made by the claimant first filing for the arbitration. The parties to an arbitration may agree in writing to use different rules and/or arbitrator(s). In all other respects, the arbitration shall be conducted in accordance with Part III, Title 9 of the California Code of Civil Procedure.

Judgment upon the award rendered by the arbitrator(s) may be entered in any court having jurisdiction thereof. The parties shall have the right to discovery in accordance with Code of Civil Procedure § 1283.05. The following matters are excluded from arbitration hereunder: (a) a judicial or non-judicial foreclosure or other action or proceeding to enforce a deed of trust, mortgage, or installment land sales contract as defined in Civil Code § 2985, (b) an unlawful detainer action, (c) the filing or enforcement of a mechanic's lien, (d) any matter which is within the jurisdiction of a probate or small claims court, and (e) an action for bodily injury or wrongful death, or for latent or patent defects, to which Code of Civil Procedure § 337.1 or § 337.15 applies. The filing of a judicial action to enable the recording of a notice of pending action, for order of attachment, receivership, injunction, or other provisional remedies, shall not constitute a waiver of the right to arbitrate under this provision.

Any dispute or claim by or against broker(s) and/or associate licensee(s) participating in this transaction shall be submitted to arbitration consistent with the provision above only if the broker(s) and/or associate licensee(s) making the claim or against whom the claim is made shall have agreed to submit it to arbitration consistent with this provision.

"NOTICE: BY INITIALING IN THE SPACE BELOW YOU ARE AGREEING TO HAVE ANY DISPUTE ARISING OUT OF THE MATTERS INCLUDED IN THE 'ARBITRATION OF DISPUTES' PROVISION DECIDED BY NEUTRAL ARBITRATION AS PROVIDED BY CALIFORNIA LAW AND YOU ARE GIVING UP ANY RIGHTS YOU MIGHT POSSESS TO HAVE THE DISPUTE LITIGATED IN A COURT OR JURY TRIAL. BY INITIALING IN THE SPACE BELOW YOU ARE GIVING UP YOUR JUDICIAL RIGHTS TO DISCOVERY AND APPEAL, UNLESS THOSE RIGHTS ARE SPECIFICALLY INCLUDED IN THE 'ARBITRATION OF DISPUTES' PROVISION. IF YOU REFUSE TO SUBMIT TO ARBITRATION AFTER AGREEING TO THIS PROVISION, YOU MAY BE COMPELLED TO ARBITRATE UNDER THE AUTHORITY OF THE CALIFORNIA CODE OF CIVIL PROCEDURE. YOUR AGREEMENT TO THIS ARBITRATION PROVISION IS VOLUNTARY."

"WE HAVE READ AND UNDERSTAND THE FOREGOING AND AGREE TO SUBMIT DISPUTES ARISING OUT OF THE MATTERS INCLUDED IN THE 'ARBITRATION OF DISPUTES' PROVISION TO NEUTRAL ARBITRATION."

Buyer's(s') Initials _____/_____   Seller's(s') Initials _____/_____

25. Attorneys' Fees

If litigation or arbitration arises from this contract, the prevailing party shall be reimbursed by the other party for reasonable attorneys' fees and court or arbitration costs.

26. Entire Agreement

This document represents the entire agreement between Buyer and Seller. Any modifications or amendments to this contract shall be made in writing, signed and dated by both parties.

27. Time Is of the Essence

Time is of the essence in this transaction.

28. Disclosures

_____ By initialing here, Buyer requests a copy of the Real Estate Transfer Disclosure Statement.

_____ By initialing here, Buyer requests copies of geologic, seismic and flood hazard disclosures.

_____ By initialing here, Buyer requests a copy of *The Homeowner's Guide to Earthquake Safety.*

_____ By initialing here, Buyer requests a copy of *Environmental Hazards: A Guide for Homeowners and Buyers.*

_____ By initialing here, Buyer requests a lead-warning statement.

_____ By initialing here, Buyer requests a copy of the following disclosures: (specify) _____

_____

29. Buyer's Signature

This constitutes an offer to purchase the above listed property.

Selling Broker _____   Buyer _____

By Selling Agent _____   Buyer _____

Broker's Address _____   Broker's Telephone _____

_____   Broker's Fax _____

_____

Date: _____ , 19____

30. Seller's Acceptance

The undersigned Seller ☐ accepts ☐ accepts subject to the attached counteroffer the foregoing offer and agrees to sell the property on the terms and conditions stated above.

Seller agrees to pay compensation for services as follows:

☐ _____ % of the sales price or ☐ $_____ to (Listing Broker) _____

_____

☐ _____ % of the sales price or ☐ $_____ to (Selling Broker) _____

_____

payable on recordation of the deed or other evidence of title. If the sale is prevented due to the default of Seller, the commission shall be paid at default. If the sale is prevented due to the default of Buyer, the commission shall be paid only if and when Seller collects damages from Buyer.

Listing Broker _____   Seller _____

By Listing Agent _____   Seller _____

Broker's Address _____   Broker's Telephone _____

_____   Broker's Fax _____

_____

Date: _____ , 19____

EXTENSION OF OFFER TO PURCHASE REAL PROPERTY

(Buyer) _____

extends the offer made to purchase the real property at (address) _____

_____ ,

_____

made on (date) _____ , until (time) _____ ☐ a.m. ☐ p.m. on (date) _____ .

_____   _____
Offerer/Buyer   Date

_____   _____
Offerer/Buyer   Date

COUNTEROFFER [COUNTER COUNTEROFFER]

Date:_____

Time: _____ ☐ a.m. ☐ p.m.

In response to the offer [counteroffer] to purchase real property at (address) _____

_____ ,

dated _____ , 19____ , _____

_____ , Buyer [Seller] submits the following counteroffer [counter counteroffer]:

_____

_____

_____

_____

All other terms of the offer [counteroffer] remain the same. This counteroffer [counter counteroffer] expires on _____ , 19 ___

at (time) _____ ☐ a.m. ☐ p.m. unless Buyer [Seller] delivers a written acceptance to Seller [Buyer] or his/her agent before then.

_____   Date

Signature

_____   Date

Signature

ACCEPTANCE

The undersigned Buyer [Seller]   ☐ accepts   ☐ accepts subject to the attached counteroffer

the foregoing offer and agrees to sell the property on the terms and conditions stated above.

Seller agrees to pay compensation for services as follows:

☐ _____ % of the sales price or ☐ $ _____ to (Listing Broker) _____

_____

☐ _____ % of the sales price or ☐ $ _____ to (Selling Broker) _____

_____

payable on recordation of the deed or other evidence of title. If the sale is prevented due to the default of Seller, the commission shall be paid at default. If the sale

is prevented due to the default of Buyer, the commission shall be paid only if and when Seller collects damages from Buyer.

Buying [Listing] Broker _____

By Buying [Listing] Agent _____

Buyer [Seller] _____

Buyer [Seller] _____

Broker's Address _____

_____

Broker's Telephone _____ Broker's Fax _____

Date: _____ , 19_____

REVOCATION OF OFFER TO PURCHASE REAL PROPERTY

(Buyer) _____

hereby revokes the offer made to purchase the real property at (address) _____

_____ ,

_____

made on (date) _____

_____   _____
Offerer/Buyer   Date

_____   _____
Offerer/Buyer   Date

EXTENDING TIME TO MEET CONTINGENCIES

The material set out below is hereby made a part of the contract dated _____,19 _____ between (Buyer) _____

_____

and (Seller) _____

to purchase real property located at _____

_____ .

The final date for Buyer's removal of all contingencies set out in Clause _____ of the contract, is hereby extended until (month and day) _____

19_____ at (time) _____ ☐ a.m. ☐ p.m.

Signature of Buyer _____ Date _____

Signature of Buyer _____ Date _____

Signature of Seller _____ Date _____

Signature of Seller _____ Date _____

CONTINGENCY RELEASE

(Buyer) _____

of the property at (address) _____

_____ ,

hereby removes the following contingency(ies) from the purchase contract dated _____, 19_____:

_____

_____

_____

_____

_____

If this release is based on accepting any inspection report, a copy of the report, signed by Buyer, is attached, and Buyer releases Seller from liability for any physical defects disclosed by the attached report.

Signature of Buyer _____ Date _____

Signature of Buyer _____ Date _____

Signature of Seller _____ Date _____

Signature of Seller _____ Date _____

RELEASE OF REAL ESTATE PURCHASE CONTRACT

(Buyer) _____

and (Seller) _____

hereby mutually release each other from any and all claims with respect to the real estate purchase contract dated _____, 19 _____

for the property located at: _____

_____

_____

It is the intent of this release to declare all rights and obligations arising out of the real estate purchase contract null and void.

☐ Buyer has received his/her deposit.

☐ Seller has directed the escrow holder to return Buyer's deposit.

Signature of Buyer _____ Date _____

Signature of Buyer _____ Date _____

Signature of Seller _____ Date _____

Signature of Seller _____ Date _____

Index

CATALOG

...more from Nolo Press

☐ Book with disk

CALL 800-992-6656 OR USE THE ORDER FORM IN THE BACK OF THE BOOK

	EDITION	PRICE	CODE
How to Mediate Your Dispute	1st	$18.95	MEDI
How to Write a Business Plan	4th	$21.95	SBS
The Independent Paralegal's Handbook	4th	$29.95	PARA
The Legal Guide for Starting & Running a Small Business	2nd	$24.95	RUNS
Make Up Your Mind: Entrepreneurs Talk About Decision Making	1st	$19.95	MIND
Managing Generation X: How to Bring Out the Best in Young Talent	1st	$19.95	MANX
Marketing Without Advertising	1st	$14.00	MWAD
Mastering Diversity: Managing for Success Under ADA and Other Anti-Discrimination Laws	1st	$29.95	MAST
▣ OSHA in the Real World: (Book w/Disk—PC)	1st	$29.95	OSHA
Pay For Results	1st	$29.95	PAY
The Partnership Book: How to Write a Partnership Agreement	4th	$24.95	PART
Rightful Termination	1st	$29.95	RITE
Sexual Harassment on the Job	2nd	$18.95	HARS
▣ Taking Care of Your Corporation, Vol. 1, (Book w/Disk—PC)	1st	$26.95	CORK
▣ Taking Care of Your Corporation, Vol. 2, (Book w/Disk—PC)	1st	$39.95	CORK2
Tax Savvy for Small Business	1st	$26.95	SAVVY
Trademark: How to Name Your Business & Product	2nd	$29.95	TRD
Workers' Comp for Employers	2nd	$29.95	CNTRL
Your Rights in the Workplace	3rd	$18.95	YRW

CONSUMER

	EDITION	PRICE	CODE
Fed Up With the Legal System: What's Wrong & How to Fix It	2nd	$9.95	LEG
Glossary of Insurance Terms	5th	$14.95	GLINT
How to Insure Your Car	1st	$12.95	INCAR
How to Win Your Personal Injury Claim	2nd	$24.95	PICL
Nolo's Pocket Guide to California Law	4th	$10.95	CLAW

▣ Book with disk

	EDITION	PRICE	CODE
Nolo's Pocket Guide to Consumer Rights 2nd		$12.95	CAG
The Over 50 Insurance Survival Guide 1st		$16.95	OVER50
Trouble-Free Travel...And What to Do When Things Go Wrong 1st		$14.95	TRAV
True Odds: How Risk Affects Your Everyday Life 1st		$19.95	TROD
What Do You Mean It's Not Covered? 1st		$19.95	COVER

ESTATE PLANNING & PROBATE

	EDITION	PRICE	CODE
How to Probate an Estate (California Edition) 8th		$34.95	PAE
Make Your Own Living Trust 2nd		$21.95	LITR
Nolo's Simple Will Book 2nd		$17.95	SWIL
Plan Your Estate 3rd		$24.95	NEST
The Quick and Legal Will Book 1st		$15.95	QUIC
Nolo's Law Form Kit: Wills 1st		$14.95	KWL

FAMILY MATTERS

	EDITION	PRICE	CODE
A Legal Guide for Lesbian and Gay Couples 9th		$24.95	LG
California Marriage Law 12th		$19.95	MARR
Child Custody: Building Agreements That Work 2nd		$24.95	CUST
Divorce & Money: How to Make the Best Financial Decisions During Divorce 3rd		$24.95	DIMO
Get A Life: You Don't Need a Million to Retire 1st		$18.95	LIFE
The Guardianship Book (California Edition) 2nd		$24.95	GB
How to Adopt Your Stepchild in California 4th		$22.95	ADOP
How to Do Your Own Divorce in California 21st		$24.95	CDIV
How to Do Your Own Divorce in Texas 6th		$19.95	TDIV
How to Raise or Lower Child Support in California 3rd		$18.95	CHLD
The Living Together Kit 7th		$24.95	LTK
Nolo's Pocket Guide to Family Law 4th		$14.95	FLD
Practical Divorce Solutions 1st		$14.95	PDS

▣ Book with disk

	EDITION	PRICE	CODE

GOING TO COURT

Collect Your Court Judgment (California Edition 2nd	$19.95	JUDG
The Criminal Records Book (California Edition) 5th	$21.95	CRIM
How to Sue For Up to 25,000...and Win! 2nd	$29.95	MUNI
Everybody's Guide to Small Claims Court (California Edition) 12th	$18.95	CSCC
Everybody's Guide to Small Claims Court (National Edition) 6th	$18.95	NSCC
Fight Your Ticket ... and Win! (California Edition) 6th	$19.95	FYT
How to Change Your Name (California Edition) 6th	$24.95	NAME
Mad at Your Lawyer 1st	$21.95	MAD
Represent Yourself in Court: How to Prepare & Try a Winning Case 1st	$29.95	RYC
Taming the Lawyers 1st	$19.95	TAME

HOMEOWNERS, LANDLORDS & TENANTS

The Deeds Book (California Edition) 3rd	$16.95	DEED
Dog Law 2nd	$12.95	DOG
▣ Every Landlord's Legal Guide (National Edition) 1st	$29.95	ELLI
For Sale by Owner (California Edition) 2nd	$24.95	FSBO
Homestead Your House (California Edition) 8th	$9.95	HOME
How to Buy a House in California 4th	$24.95	BHCA
The Landlord's Law Book, Vol. 1: Rights & Responsibilities (California Edition) 5th	$34.95	LBRT
The Landlord's Law Book, Vol. 2: Evictions (California Edition) 5th	$34.95	LBEV
Neighbor Law: Fences, Trees, Boundaries & Noise 2nd	$16.95	NEI
Safe Homes, Safe Neighborhoods: Stopping Crime Where You Live 1st	$14.95	SAFE
Tenants' Rights (California Edition) 12th	$18.95	CTEN

HUMOR

29 Reasons Not to Go to Law School 1st	$9.95	29R
Poetic Justice 1st	$9.95	PJ

▣ Book with disk

	EDITION	PRICE	CODE

IMMIGRATION

	EDITION	PRICE	CODE
How to Become a United States Citizen	5th	$14.95	CIT
How to Get a Green Card: Legal Ways to Stay in the U.S.A.	2nd	$24.95	GRN
U.S. Immigration Made Easy	5th	$39.95	IMEZ

MONEY MATTERS

	EDITION	PRICE	CODE
Building Your Nest Egg With Your 401(k)	1st	$16.95	EGG
Chapter 13 Bankruptcy: Repay Your Debts	2nd	$29.95	CH13
How to File for Bankruptcy	6th	$26.95	HFB
Money Troubles: Legal Strategies to Cope With Your Debts	4th	$19.95	MT
Nolo's Law Form Kit: Personal Bankruptcy	1st	$14.95	KBNK
Nolo's Law Form Kit: Rebuild Your Credit	1st	$14.95	KCRD
Simple Contracts for Personal Use	2nd	$16.95	CONT
Smart Ways to Save Money During and After Divorce	1st	$14.95	SAVMO
Stand Up to the IRS	3rd	$24.95	SIRS
The Under 40 Financial Planning Guide	1st	$19.95	UN40

PATENTS AND COPYRIGHTS

	EDITION	PRICE	CODE
The Copyright Handbook: How to Protect and Use Written Works	3rd	$24.95	COHA
Copyright Your Software	1st	$39.95	CYS
Patent, Copyright & Trademark: A Desk Reference to Intellectual Property Law	1st	$24.95	PCTM
Patent It Yourself	5th	$44.95	PAT
▣ Software Development: A Legal Guide (Book with disk—PC)	1st	$44.95	SFT
The Inventor's Notebook	1st	$19.95	INOT

RESEARCH & REFERENCE

	EDITION	PRICE	CODE
Law on the Net	1st	$39.95	LAWN
Legal Research: How to Find & Understand the Law	4th	$19.95	LRES
Legal Research Made Easy (Video)	1st	$89.95	LRME

▣ Book with disk

	EDITION	PRICE	CODE

SENIORS

Beat the Nursing Home Trap: A Consumer's Guide	2nd	$18.95	ELD
Social Security, Medicare & Pensions	6th	$19.95	SOA
The Conservatorship Book (California Edition)	2nd	$29.95	CNSV

SOFTWARE

California Incorporator 2.0—DOS	2.0	$47.97	INCI2
Living Trust Maker 2.0—Macintosh	2.0	$47.97	LTM2
Living Trust Maker 2.0—Windows	2.0	$47.97	LTWI2
Small Business Legal Pro—Macintosh	2.0	$25.97	SBM2
Small Business Legal Pro—Windows	2.0	$25.97	SBW2
Small Business Legal Pro Deluxe CD—Windows/Macintosh CD-ROM	2.0	$35.97	SBCD
Nolo's Partnership Maker 1.0—DOS	1.0	$47.97	PAGII
Personal RecordKeeper 4.0—Macintosh	4.0	$29.97	RKM4
Personal RecordKeeper 4.0—Windows	4.0	$29.97	RKP4
Patent It Yourself 1.0—Windows	1.0	$149.97	PYWI
WillMaker 6.0—Macintosh	6.0	$41.97	WM6
WillMaker 6.0—Windows	6.0	$41.97	WIW6

⌑ Book with disk

CALL 800-992-6656 OR USE THE ORDER FORM IN THE BACK OF THE BOOK

ORDER FORM

Code	Quantity	Title	Unit price	Total
		Subtotal		
		California residents add Sales Tax		
		Basic Shipping ($5.50 for 1 item; $6.50 for 2-3 items, $7.50 for 4 or more)		
		UPS RUSH delivery $7.50–any size order*		
		TOTAL		

Name

Address

(UPS to street address, Priority Mail to P.O. boxes)

* Delivered in 3 business days from receipt of order.
S.F. Bay Area use regular shipping.

FOR FASTER SERVICE, USE YOUR CREDIT CARD AND OUR TOLL-FREE NUMBERS

Order 24 hours a day	1-800-992-6656
Fax your order	1-800-645-0895
e-mail	cs@nolo.com
General Information	1-510-549-1976
Customer Service	1-800-728-3555, Mon.-Fri. 9am-5pm, PST

METHOD OF PAYMENT

☐ Check enclosed

☐ VISA ☐ MasterCard ☐ Discover Card ☐ American Express

Account #   Expiration Date

Authorizing Signature

Daytime Phone

PRICES SUBJECT TO CHANGE.

VISIT OUR OUTLET STORES!

You'll find our complete line of books and software, all at a discount.

BERKELEY
950 Parker Street
Berkeley, CA 94720

SAN JOSE
111 N. Market Street, #115
San Jose, CA 95113

VISIT US ONLINE!

on **AOL** — keyword: NOLO   on the **INTERNET** — www.nolo.com

NOLO PRESS 950 PARKER ST., BERKELEY, CA 94710

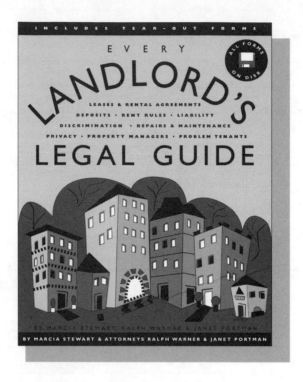

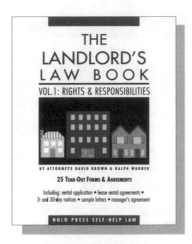
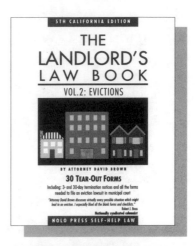

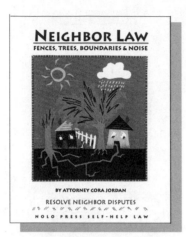

Take 2 minutes & Get a 2-year **NOLO** *News* subscription free!*

NOLO *News* SPRING 1994
Legal & Consumer Information for Everyone

Work-place Rights

INSIDE
10 THINGS BILL COLLECTORS DON'T WANT YOU TO KNOW
KEEPING LEGAL FEES DOWN DURING DIVORCE
WHERE TO FIND NOLO ONLINE
NEW BOOKS FROM NOLO
SMART WAYS TO SAVE MONEY DURING AND AFTER DIVORCE
TAKING CARE OF YOUR CORPORATION VOLUME 1: DIRECTOR & SHAREHOLDER MEETINGS MADE EASY (WITH FORMS ON DISK)
CATALOG INSIDE!

NOLO PRESS

With our quarterly magazine, the **NOLO** *News*, you'll

- **Learn** about important legal changes that affect you
- **Find out first** about new Nolo products
- **Keep current** with practical articles on everyday law
- **Get answers** to your legal questions in *Ask Auntie Nolo's* advice column

- **Save money** with special Subscriber Only discounts
- **Tickle your funny bone** with our famous *Lawyer Joke* column.

It only takes 2 minutes to reserve your free 2-year subscription or to extend your **NOLO** *News* subscription.

CALL
1-800-992-6656

FAX
1-800-645-0895

E-MAIL
NOLOSUB@NOLOPRESS.com

OR MAIL US THIS POSTAGE-PAID REGISTRATION CARD

R E G I S T R A T I O N   C A R D

NAME _____ DATE _____

ADDRESS _____

_____ PHONE NUMBER _____

CITY _____ STATE _____ ZIP _____

WHERE DID YOU HEAR ABOUT THIS BOOK? _____

WHERE DID YOU PURCHASE THIS PRODUCT? _____

DID YOU CONSULT A LAWYER? (PLEASE CIRCLE ONE)   YES   NO   NOT APPLICABLE

DID YOU FIND THIS BOOK HELPFUL?   (VERY)   5   4   3   2   1   (NOT AT ALL)

SUGGESTIONS FOR IMPROVING THIS PRODUCT _____

WAS IT EASY TO USE?   (VERY EASY)   5   4   3   2   1   (VERY DIFFICULT)

DO YOU OWN A COMPUTER? IF SO, WHICH FORMAT? (PLEASE CIRCLE ONE)   WINDOWS   DOS   MAC

BHCA 4.0

"Nolo helps lay people perform legal tasks without the aid—or fees—of lawyers."

—USA TODAY

[Nolo books are ...]"written in plain language, free of legal mumbo jumbo, and spiced with witty personal observations."

—ASSOCIATED PRESS

"...Nolo publications...guide people simply through the how, when, where and why of law."

—WASHINGTON POST

"Increasingly, people who are not lawyers are performing tasks usually regarded as legal work... And consumers, using books like Nolo's, do routine legal work themselves."

—NEW YORK TIMES

"...All of [Nolo's] books are easy-to-understand, are updated regularly, provide pull-out forms...and are often quite moving in their sense of compassion for the struggles of the lay reader."

—SAN FRANCISCO CHRONICLE

NO POSTAGE
NECESSARY
IF MAILED
IN THE
UNITED STATES

BUSINESS REPLY MAIL
FIRST-CLASS MAIL PERMIT NO 3283 BERKELEY CA

POSTAGE WILL BE PAID BY ADDRESSEE

NOLO PRESS
950 Parker Street
Berkeley, CA 94710-9867